GATHERING PACE

The Evolution of Western Society

GENERAL EDITOR

PETER BROOKS, Ph.D.

Lecturer in History, University of Kent at Canterbury

GATHERING PACE

Continental Europe 1870–1945

MAURICE LARKIN

M.A., Ph.D.

Senior Lecturer in History
University of Kent at Canterbury

MACMILLAN

© Maurice Larkin 1969

First published 1969 by
MACMILLAN AND CO LTD
Little Essex Street London WC2
and also at Bombay Calcutta and Madras
Macmillan South Africa (Publishers) Pty Ltd Johannesburg
The Macmillan Company of Australia Pty Ltd Melbourne
The Macmillan Company of Canada Ltd Toronto
Gill and Macmillan Ltd Dublin

Printed in Great Britain by
RICHARD CLAY (THE CHAUCER PRESS) LTD
Bungay, Suffolk

Contents

Technological change and industry
Motive power
Business organisation
Production and international trade

Trade unionism
Socialism
Socialist doctrine
Government

Collective action
The Regime
Bismarck at the helm
No one at the helm

The peasantry
The industrial workers
The landlords
Ethnic minorities

List of Plates

List of Maps

Reproduced by kind permission of Weidenfeld
& Nicolson, from Gilbert, *Recent History Atlas*

Acknowledgements

I should like to thank my colleagues in the Universities of Glasgow and Kent for the benefit of their knowledge and suggestions. When they see the use to which they have been put, they will doubtless be relieved that I have not mentioned them by name. Two who cannot escape, however, are Dr Peter Brooks, the General Editor of the series, and Mr Richard Langhorne. Dr Brooks's vigilance and patience have made this book less unreadable than it would have been, while Mr Langhorne has been a constant source of information and encouragement. I must likewise thank the library and secretarial staff of the University of Kent, especially Mrs Waring and her intrepid team of typists.

From first to last, however, my greatest debt is to my wife, who, like Edna Purviance, has played many roles, notably those of critic, scribe and sustainer of my illusions.

General Editor's Introduction

FOR some time students have found difficulty in getting to grips with more advanced historical study because many textbooks have proved daunting in size and style. Faced with so much factual content and detailed narrative readers have often been denied the balanced yet scholarly judgements that both enliven the past and communicate its significance.

In an attempt to combat this trend, *The Evolution of Western Society* consists of a series of volumes specifically designed for those seeking an introduction to relatively advanced work. Written in readable prose, while avoiding gimmicks, these lively studies present a more topical approach to history by expounding a given period in terms of main-point analysis. In a dozen volumes, a team of university lecturers and school-masters, who are both authorities in their specialist fields and experienced teachers, will give their readers a wide coverage of British and European history from the decline of the Roman Empire to the conflicts of the contemporary world. Each book contains adequate narrative for those obliged to satisfy the demands of public examinations, but every effort has been made to focus interest upon analysis rather than description, and to convey the spirit of each period by means of selected source quotation and visual material. Full bibliographies are included to guide further reading, and, in addition to charts, diagrams and maps, all volumes contain a section devoted to brief lives of important figures, whether artists or churchmen, statesmen or military leaders, scientists or philosophers. Above all, each book is an exercise in three-dimensional history, and presents the reader with the findings of modern scholarship in a com-prehensive, comprehensible and stimulating form.

The author of *Gathering Pace*, Dr Larkin, is well-equipped to contribute a history of Europe from 1870 to 1945. As a pupil of Professor Sir Denis Brogan, Maurice Larkin centred his research on Church–State relations in France during the aftermath of the Dreyfus crisis, working in Cambridge, London and Paris. A Lecturer in the University of Glasgow before coming to Canterbury to take up a new appointment in the Humanities Faculty of the University of Kent, the author is an experienced teacher of Modern European history well able to provide the kind of imaginative yet scholarly treatment that will give students a clear picture of Europe at a decisive stage in its history. This is an entertaining and informative book that can be confidently recommended to sixth-formers, students in colleges and universities, and all general readers interested in the period.

Keynes College   PETER BROOKS
University of Kent at Canterbury
August 1969

INTRODUCTION

Gathering Pace – and Growing Uniformity

'Sewers and birth-rates – it's all so sordid!' is an understandable reaction to the interests of modern historians. But if statistics of social conditions make uninspiring reading, they have perhaps a more pressing claim to the historian's attention than 'the lives of great men', which Carlyle and many of his contemporaries saw as the very essence of history. Everything past is the historian's province; but since he and his reader are only human, he has to be selective. He therefore tends on the whole to adopt a Benthamite approach, giving priority to developments that might be said to have had 'the greatest influence on the greatest number' of people. On this basis the activities of rulers and statesmen demand particular attention only in so far as they affect the lives, thoughts and sensations of a considerable number of other people; and they become historically 'significant' only in terms of this effect. This is not to deny the enormous debt that humanity owes to its outstanding individuals, for it would be a sad day if the historic 'great' of France, for instance, became no more than street-names, associated for ever in the Frenchman's mind with an awkward left turn – or, more compellingly, with one of those cryptic warnings in the Métro: 'Because of repair work, there is danger of death between Edgar Quinet and Raspail.' And could the English 'great' claim even this?

Consequently the method used in this book is to introduce each subject in terms of its social outcome, and then to examine the economic and political factors that made the social outcome what it was.

The accompanying diagram gives a rough indication of the pattern underlying most chapters, the arrow crudely representing the order of historical progression, the Roman numerals the order of presentation.

THE SOCIAL OUTCOME (the cake in slices) I
↑
COLLECTIVE ACTION AND POLITICAL FACTORS (cutting the cake) III
|
THE ECONOMIC FACTORS (making the cake) II

Obviously the truth is much more complex than this. There is a great deal of interaction between all three terms of the 'proposition', while many forms of human pressure by one group on another straddle both the political and economic spheres. Similarly the basic ingredients of the cake will include the multifarious demands of man's mind and emotions, made yet more complex in the mixing and baking. It is true, moreover, that as far as the presentation is concerned, the method used here partly reverses the order of cause and effect, and may at first occasion some confusion for the reader who loves his chronology. Nevertheless this rather eccentric procedure should at least reassure him in advance that what he is reading is relevant to the human condition, and therefore worth his particular attention. Otherwise history may be in danger of seeming to be little more than a sequence of events, to be looked at in the spirit of an antiquary rather than an historian. Too often, history is retailed as a semi-hallowed corpus of 'knowledge', from which the reader is invited to draw what benefit he can.[1]

The main problem in a book of this length is to know what to include and what to leave out. On the whole the Benthamite approach has been attempted. But at the same time there is the

___

[1] There may, however, be readers who feel happier when leaning on the reassuring handrail of a firm chronology. For them the most comforting procedure may be to read the three main sections of the various 'national' chapters in reverse order, beginning with 'The Political Factors'. Like reversible macintoshes, these chapters do bear such treatment – though some of the seams and buttons may chafe a little on first encounter.

problem of overall presentation. In his admirable synthesis, *Europe since Napoleon*, Dr David Thomson commented that

> Europe is something other than just 'one damn country after another'. Of the numerous histories of Europe which fill library shelves, a depressingly large proportion treat their subject as a mere collation of the separate histories of each European nation or state.

Europe is clearly something much more than this. But the current trend of treating European development as 'one coherent story' has perhaps even greater dangers than the old system, even if it makes for livelier reading. All historians, whatever their system, are agreed that life in Europe is the product of the interaction of social, economic and political factors. But since these factors, especially the political factors, vary so markedly from nation to nation, this interaction can ultimately be understood only in terms of individual states – or at least the major ones. Yet there undoubtedly is a great deal of common ground between these states. Therefore there seems to be a strong case for adopting in accentuated form the method used in several volumes of *The New Cambridge Modern History* where the common ground is dealt with in a series of chapters on factors of general concern, while the rest of the book is devoted to chapters on the history of the more important nations. In broad terms, this is the method adopted here, although an attempt has also been made to afford some assessment of the smaller nations – if only in appendices.

When writing a general history, it is always hard to find a succinct title that does not immediately offer a handle to critics. Unquestionably the most important development in the last hundred years has been the material improvement in the lives of the mass of the population; this accordingly occupies the central place in this book. Even so, this improvement is not what has given the period its distinctive flavour as compared with earlier ones. Material improvement has been uneven, both geographically and in time. The east, for example, has been slow to follow the west; and every region has experienced years of recession. Apart from two disastrous wars, the west suffered the Depression of the 1930s, while in the east the people of Soviet

Russia underwent successive crises of great material hardship. Nevertheless, year by year and in every country, men have been increasingly aware of the mounting tempo of life. Only a hermit or a Home Counties commuter could doubt that the last hundred years have witnessed a vast acceleration in the overall pace of human existence. Even the unemployed, standing outside silent, motionless factories, were vaguely conscious that the sports results came through sooner; and they certainly knew that the police could be on the scene much more quickly than before. This growing speed was felt by all classes, including the rich who saw their income cut by mounting taxation and who were therefore less ready to applaud the material improvement of the masses.

In short, acceleration gives this period its character. In the 1870s the telegraph was linking governments with their most distant overseas representatives,[1] while from 1879 the telephone afforded ready contact for increasing numbers of manufacturers, merchants and customers – as well as ministers, civil servants and police. Even Britain's Poet Laureate, Alfred Austin, thought fit to commemorate the illness of the Prince of Wales with the lines:

> Across the wires the electric message came:
> 'He is no better, he is much the same.'[2]

Information that had hitherto taken weeks to collect could be gathered in less than a day, with the result that ministers, businessmen and executives of all kinds were now making more decisions an hour than their predecessors had made in a day. And the results of their decisions were being felt with equal speed. The continuing spread of railways enabled goods to be carried across the Continent at speeds of thirty miles an hour and passengers at sixty, while the improvement of the motor-lorry in the inter-war years brought even the most remote village within the orbit of rapid supply or suppression. Furthermore, from 1919, air services began to link the main European capitals, followed by regular air links spanning the Pacific and

---

[1] The first effective transatlantic cable was completed in 1866.
[2] Gallant attempts have been made to acquit Austin of the paternity of this verse.

the Atlantic by the mid-thirties. Indeed, with the twentieth century, the world became a macrocosm of that splendid institution, the Edwardian department-store, with its criss-crossing of horizontal wires and writhing of vertical tubes, along which money and receipts were jerked or puffed with increasing velocity.

Greater speed helped both to increase profits and to hasten technological improvement and the spread of ideas – though speed, of course, was only one of several factors. Each decade brought a greater measure of change, only the gigantic economic set-back of two world wars preventing the later period fulfilling the promise of earlier decades. Yet even war, by its very insistence on quick solutions, brought rapid advances in technology and scientific discovery, especially in aircraft, medicine and motive-power. It likewise brought far-reaching changes in social thinking. The net result was a remarkable if uneven improvement in material standards of living, despite the economic repercussions of war. For everyone, it was the age of gathering pace.

As the pace grew, however, so did uniformity. Faster and easier contact between east and west encouraged a desire in all countries for 'the best available', irrespective of its roots or nationality. In architecture, clothes and general ways of tackling life's various problems, fashions became increasingly cosmopolitan. National styles slowly faded, except where they were consciously prolonged; and even in the 1930s it was already apparent that a time was approaching when it would be impossible to tell one country's towns from another's, except by the names over shop windows.

Earlier periods, notably the eighteenth century, had seen a cosmopolitan similarity in the clothes, houses and ways of life of the European aristocracy. But this had not been true of the other classes. Indeed the growing influence of the middle classes in the early nineteenth century had tended to prolong and even increase national distinctiveness – though clearly other factors of perhaps greater importance were also involved. By the inter-war years, however, the tastes and preoccupations of the middle classes of east and west had grown much closer together. Whereas even as late as 1905 the merchant of Nijni-Novgorod (see Plate 10a) seemed to belong to an utterly different world from that of his western counterpart, this was no longer true in the 1920s, despite the official barrier of ideology.

It was mainly the working classes, especially the peasantry, who preserved what remained of national distinctiveness in the inter-war years. At first the working classes were open to cosmopolitan influence only indirectly, through the example of the middle classes. Indeed the growing similarity between classes within each country was itself a strong force tending to uniformity. The rising standard of living of the working classes gradually encouraged the more ambitious to adopt middle-class styles and attitudes, and in this way they were slowly absorbing the growing cosmopolitan character of European bourgeois life. Parallel with this development, however, ran the gradual arrival of a transatlantic popular culture, which was itself to become a significant element in the cosmopolitan working-class culture that was to emerge after the Second World War. This infiltration came through dance-music, the cinema and, eventually, the wireless with its relaying of popular song successes. Indeed the converging of popular song traditions was perhaps the most revealing example of the sort of uniformity that lay ahead. Similarly, cheap recreational literature was drawing more and more of its inspiration from America.

These are familiar developments which it would be tedious to elaborate further. Yet they give coherence to a period that often seems to be marked by striking contrasts. It is these contrasts that often attract most attention in the written histories – perhaps inevitably so, as the very act of description tends to lay emphasis on distinctiveness. This tendency has been partly offset in this book by the broadly uniform method of treatment used in most chapters, an approach which is more likely to reveal similarities than the narrative-type history. Although uniformity of treatment has its own dangers, it should perhaps be borne in mind that this book is intended as a practical guide, rather than a continuous narration to be con-

sumed like a novel. Clarity of exposition and variety of treatment often make conflicting demands, the only practical outcome being a compromise that of its nature is bound to leave
something to be desired.

CHAPTER ONE

Europe in 1870: A Balloonist's View

Where people lived

'So, riding on windbags, will men scale the Empyrean.' Even Carlyle must have been surprised at the number who did so in the autumn of 1870; for balloons were the only effective means of escape from a Paris besieged by Prussians. He might have been even more surprised at the Comte Henry de La Vaulx, who thirty years later floated non-stop in a balloon from Paris to Korosticheff in Russia – 1240 miles in thirty-six hours. Men were becoming acquainted with what Europe looked like from the air. And had these intrepid balloonists counted longevity among their many remarkable qualities, they might now be recalling that the distribution of people over the face of Europe in 1870 presented a pattern that in its outline looks familiar enough today.

Concentration was thickest around the southern half of the North Sea. Taken together, Belgium and Holland had an average of 367 people per square mile; but by contrast the countries north of the Baltic had only 17. Elsewhere the extremes were scattered, varying between 35 per square mile in European Russia to 439 in prosperous Saxony. Today the proportions remain much the same, but the overall numbers have doubled. The 261 millions of 1870 have become the 574 of 1965,[1] while the average density per square mile has now

[1] The figures for 1870 can only be approximate, as authorities differ widely in their estimates for eastern Europe. Throughout this book the Urals have been taken as the eastern limit of Europe, despite the difficulties that emerge when incorporating Soviet statistics that do not recognise this dividing-line. The British Isles are likewise excluded.

reached 940 in Holland. Moreover even the most blasé of the balloonists of 1870 would be amazed at the growth of Europe's towns. Whereas well over 40 per cent of Europeans now live in towns of over 20,000 people, this was true of only about 15 per cent in 1870. Indeed less than 40 per cent now live by agriculture, whereas in 1870 it was over 60 per cent. All of which reflects the growth of industry and commerce.

TABLE I

Percentage occupations in the 1870s (Mulhall)

(These are the conclusions of a contemporary, and need to be treated with some caution.)*

	Agriculture	Manufacture	Various
France	51	24	25
Germany	43	34	23
Russia	81	5	14
Austria	55	13	32
Italy	70	7	23
Belgium	40	38	22
Holland	58	12	30
Scandinavia	61	9	30

* Most of the statistics used in the subsequent chapters on individual countries are based on various later authorities, and in some cases differ considerably from those used by Mulhall in this and the other three tables reproduced in this chapter. Since each of the later authors has his own system of calculation, Mulhall's relatively uniform series still has its uses for comparative purposes.

The most thickly populated countries were those where industry was most widespread, for the co-operative effort of modern industry and commerce demanded the concentration of large numbers of men within closely organised communities. People had to live within reach of their work, which meant that the personal domestic needs of the workers and middle class had also to be met within the same district, thus making for further expansion, as shops and houses grew in number. A large population with a rising standard of living generated its own needs, attracting more industry. Indeed in many cases the new economic attractions of the town transcended the original reasons why an industrial town had grown there. But a fertile soil could also encourage density of population, though of a much less impressive order. Very often, however, even areas of low soil fertility were inhabited by unexpected numbers, since a warm climate could permit the survival of extremes of poverty which a colder climate would kill off. A Sicilian needs much less food and fuel to survive than does a Laplander. If moreover, the population was ignorant and improvident, making little attempt to control its numbers, it would achieve a density in excess of what the land would comfortably support, as was true of many of the drier regions of the Latin and Balkan countries. But nowhere was density so great as where industry was thriving.

People and the land

An unusually cosmopolitan balloonist might have noticed that the 1860s had lessened some of the contrasts in Europe's agricultural pattern. 1861–4 saw the abolition of serfdom in Russia, so starting the slow process of turning Russia's agricultural economy from one of vast estates into a mixed one of large estates and innumerable smallholdings. Serfdom now no longer existed in Europe; and from Portugal to the Urals the peasantry who had land either owned it or rented it for cash or kind.

But this did not mean uniformity. Apart from the varieties of land-holding, there was always the mass of landless farm-labourers. Among the land-holders also, there were great economic differences. There was first the more fortunate type of peasant, the peasant farmer who could keep his family in reasonable comfort from the produce of the land that he owned or rented. Since he was a phenomenon that belonged mainly to western and central Europe, his complaints were largely directed against what he saw as neglect rather than oppression: such things as the slowness of the government in putting up tariff-barriers against foreign food imports, or the failure of the government to keep taxation low. Otherwise his main enemies were bad weather, crop pests and diseases – and his richer neighbours with bigger farms, who could cut their production costs and undersell him by using modern labour-saving machinery and methods. In eastern and southern Europe, however, peasant conditions were very different. The Russian peasant was still subject to restrictive state legislation which substituted the local commune for the old landlord as the arbiter of his freedom. The emancipated serfs were likewise crippled with compensation debts (see pp. 153–5), which many could only meet by selling part of their land. On the other hand in Spain, Portugal, southern Italy and the Balkans, it was primarily the infertility of the soil, rather than legal oppression, which made peasant conditions so wretched. Shortage of water made them particularly dependent on the goodwill of the local magnate, who generally controlled the water supply, and who was usually the decisive figure in local politics. At the same time in many countries the inheritance laws insisted on the division of property between heirs, this itself being a major factor in making holdings too small to support a family. But whether the origins of the peasant's discontents were economic, social or political, they all had the effect of driving an increasing number of peasant proprietors into the towns or into becoming landless farm-labourers.

TABLE 2
Agricultural wages in 1880 (Mulhall)

(See note to Table 1)

England	2s 6d daily
Ireland	1s 6d
France	2s 1d
Germany	1s 6d
Russia	1s
Austria	1s 8d
Italy	10d
Holland	1s 8d
Belgium	1s 8d
Scandinavia	1s 2d

It is difficult to compare the standard of living of the peasant of 1870 with that of his counterpart today. Unlike the industrial worker, even the landless labourer's income cannot be adequately measured in terms of the buying-power of his wages.

He sometimes had a small plot or some animals of his own, often enjoying benefits in kind which were not reflected in his monetary wages. Even more difficult to assess is the income of the land-holding peasant who lived by the sale of his produce.

The figures for farm-labourers' wages in Table 2 need to be multiplied by over four to bring them into line with the present value of the £ – while it is worth noticing, for the purposes of comparison, that the average agricultural daily wage in Britain in the mid-1960s was slightly over £2. Both the landed and landless peasantry of 1870 were, of course, without the modern benefits of social insurance and social welfare – to say nothing of the various direct and indirect subsidies to agriculture that have played an increasing role in the economy of the landed peasant in some countries.

People and industry

The workers' purchasing power in the industrialised countries of 1870 was only a third of what it is today, and if are included the various social benefits that a country like France now gives its workers and their families, ranging from sick-pay to free secondary education, the workers' standard of living in the 1960s is perhaps four to five times higher than it was in 1870. Table 3 shows how low wages were, even among the skilled

TABLE 3

Artisans' wages in 1880 (Mulhall)

(See note to Table 1)

(shillings per week)

	Carpenter	Blacksmith	Tailor	Baker	Miner	Plumber
Britain	33	31	25	27	24	33
France	23	23	21	23	15	23
Belgium	23	18	17	18	14	25
Germany	16	15	15	15	16	15
Italy	17	16	18	16		16
Russia	12	13				

artisans whose rates of pay were a third higher or more than those of the unskilled worker. Even when multiplied by four to bring them to current price levels, the highest of them were still only a third of the average weekly wage of a British worker in 1965 (£16), while the lowest, in Russia, was only a sixth of this.

Not only was the worker of 1870 paid much less than now, but he worked harder for it. The average working day in the west was eleven or twelve hours, while in Russia it was thirteen. Moreover the surroundings in which the worker lived were often repellent and unhealthy by modern standards. It is true that he was much less conscious of this squalor than would be someone used to better conditions, but the death and sickness rates showed how vulnerable he was physically to these surroundings while the prevalence of heavy drinking gave some indication of how they affected his mind. In so many cases excessive drinking was an attempt to forget his worries or deaden his sensibility to the wretched conditions in which he lived. As he became addicted, he found that he required a greater quantity of drink to obtain the same result. In western Europe, official deaths from drink in the 1870s were less than a quarter per cent; but it needs to be remembered that this figure did not include the vast majority of alcoholics, who generally died of some other illness because drink had rendered them less resilient. Similarly, convictions for drunkenness were no real measure of alcoholism. The real alcoholic was not the trouble-maker of the streets; he was the man behind the café table, looking vacantly in front of him.

Women's wages were considerably lower than those of men, averaging in most trades only half of a male wage in equivalent work. Of course many working women were married, their wages being only supplements to their husbands' income. For the unmarried woman, however, life was very hard. It is no exaggeration to say that a large proportion of girls were driven into early marriages or concubinage by the sheer necessity of having to find enough money to live on. Those who did not find a partner had to supplement their wages in other ways – often by prostitution.

It would be only too easy to give a picture of unmitigated gloom in describing the living conditions of the working classes in 1870. If living standards were only a fifth to a third of what they are now, this did not necessarily mean that the sum total of that elusive commodity, human happiness, was proportionately smaller. It probably was smaller, in that death, sickness and weariness afflicted families more often. Love-making was seldom free from further pregnancies, while the expression of affection between parents and children was often ruined by tiredness and material worries. Yet there still remained the basic human joys of a child's excitement, falling in love and seeing children and grandchildren grow. The things that matter most in life are common to all periods – though they can be wrecked by poor health or a hostile environment.

If on balance there was probably less happiness among the working classes in 1870 than now, belief in an after-life, where the well-intentioned person would know eternal happiness, was a more widespread phenomenon than it is today. And it undoubtedly sustained many people whose lives to the un-believer seemed scarcely worth living. The incurable invalid with no friends, whose life seemed a burden to himself and everyone else, could take comfort in the belief that his patience would bring its reward. Atheist reforming politicians, like René Viviani, were later to boast that they had 'extinguished the stars in heaven', but what they put in their place seemed poor by comparison.

The masses and religion

Although religious observance was stronger in 1870 than it is now, it was weaker than it had been in previous centuries. It could be argued that much of the religious observance of former times was little more than social convention, enforced by fear of employers and local magnates or of what people would think. In so far as it was more than this, love of God probably played a less part than did a vague apprehension of what might happen after death. It is probably true that in all ages only a minority of people are temperamentally 'religious' in that they experience a positive desire for prayer or to 'feel at one' with nature or humanity. Many others have endeav-oured to achieve this state through a sense of duty, based on the conviction that the teachings of religion are true and must be observed. Admitting their failure to achieve much personal 'satisfaction' from prayer, they have taken some comfort in the notion that the merit of their efforts is the greater for not having had the consolations of 'spiritual' experience.

At the same time the nineteenth century had brought many pressures to bear on religious observance especially in western Europe. The destruction of the *ancien régime* had already removed many of the positive compulsions to religious observance. Yet fear of what people would think was still a factor in many rural districts, though church-attendance records show that even there the proportion of church-goers was declining. The growth of industrial cities, however, meant that a large section of the working classes was now living where social conventions had no traditional roots, and where there was little social incentive to go to church. The fact that the working class now lived in one area and their employers in another meant that there was now not even the sordid motive of impressing a devout employer.

There was also, of course, the intellectual onslaught on traditional Christianity, but this scarcely impinged on the working classes, except in so far as they were influenced by the disappearance of some of their social superiors from church. The intellectual arguments had meaning for only a small minority of people in 1870; and even among them the believers and non-believers tended to lead much the same sort of lives. Among the non-intellectual masses, most people lived their lives according to habit, informed by a fairly flexible morality, which had been largely instilled during their upbringing. This morality was generally Christian in its antecedents, but it was often without a consciously avowed point of reference. Then as now, 'fair's fair, that's what I say' was about as far as many would go in rationalising their moral decisions.

Education and social mobility

If the working classes were the majority of Europeans, their comparative lack of education meant that they were less able than the middle class to provide society with a leadership of talented individuals. It must be remembered that 'literacy', as reflected in official records, need mean little more than being able to write one's name and read simple sentences. Only a minority of the officially 'literate' could read as much as the unsophisticated novels that were serialised in working-class periodicals.

TABLE 4
(Mulhall)
(See note to Table 1)

1881 : Percentage of adults able to write		Percentage of total population at school
England	84	15
France	78	13
Germany	94	17
Russia	11	2
Austria	49	9
Italy	41	8
Spain and Portugal	34	5
Switzerland	88	16
Belgium and Holland	86	15
Scandinavia	87	15

The men of intellect and sensibility who left most impression on culture and society were mostly of middle-class origin. At the same time, advantages of wealth and birth still enabled the upper classes to exert an influence out of all proportion to their number or talent.

The middle and upper classes

The society which was shaped by these conditions was a more varied one than we know in Europe today. There existed as always a certain cosmopolitan similarity of tastes and interests in the upper classes and intelligentsia of the various European countries. But this was also true of earlier centuries, having perhaps its clearest expression in the eighteenth century. Yet in 1870 the middle and lower classes of each nation had less in common with their foreign counterparts than is the case today. Modern means of communication have meant more rapid and sustained contact between nations, and this has made for

B

greater uniformity. Whereas the differences between a worker in Manchester and Kiev are still considerable, they are much less marked than was the case in 1870. And if the differences between nations were more striking than now, this was even truer of the differences between classes within each nation. As has been indicated, the standard of living of the manual workers in most western countries has at least trebled since 1870. Yet the buying power of the middle classes in general has altered much less in the last hundred years. Increases in income have been partially offset by increases in tax; and as far as the established upper income groups are concerned, their buying power has actually decreased, owing largely to these all-round increases in taxation. Taking all factors into consideration, the proportion of people today who enjoy a standard of living equivalent to a net income of £10,000 (after tax) at present prices is far smaller than in 1870. The more traditional sources of affluence, such as land-rent and property in general, have been increasingly subject to taxation. Net 'real' income from them is therefore smaller today than it was in 1870 – though exception must be made for land and property in highly-sought-after areas in cities, where the overall increase in capital value has outweighed the increase in taxation. The 'managerial class', as we know it, is largely a twentieth-century phenomenon, and it is difficult to make valid comparisons with 1870. But after tax the net 'real' salaries now enjoyed by top executives in public and private employment compare unfavourably with what their less numerous equivalents obtained in 1870. The increasing taxation placed on private companies, and their increasing reliance on a wider number of shareholders, has kept executive salaries in check. On the other hand it must not be forgotten that the mounting proportion of salary taken in taxation as earnings increase, has encouraged firms to reward key men with 'perks' like cars, free insurance and other untaxed benefits – all of which afford the executive a higher standard of living.

The middle classes of 1870 were also a smaller percentage of the population than now, and contained a greater proportion of self-employed men. There were fewer civil servants, teachers and 'executives', and proportionately more shopkeepers, small businessmen and people living on the proceeds of private investment. The relatively low wages of the manual classes meant that more middle-class people kept servants than is now the case. The absence of washing machines and synthetic textiles meant that there was much more washing and ironing to be done; the absence of kitchen gadgets meant that food preparation took much longer; and the absence of central heating, electric and gas fires meant that there were many more coal fires to be lit. Servants were especially useful – particularly in a period when birth-control was little understood and families were large. At the same time the more limited opportunities for spending money in 1870 encouraged people not only to spend more on servants, but also much more on eating and drinking than they do today. For one thing the dangers of over-indulgence were less appreciated, scientific concepts of balanced diets being still very rudimentary. Indeed as far as the middle and upper classes were concerned, the period might well have been called the Age of Flatulence. Good food and freedom from household chores was what comfort meant in 1870; and since there was a limit to what one family could eat and drink, and to the number of servants they needed, the balance was spent on the upkeep of a solidly built apartment or house, and the accumulation of sound investments.

Yet the composition of the middle class and its relative size differed considerably from country to country, and the familiar picture of the mid-Victorian middle class and its French and German equivalents must not be extended into Scandinavia, eastern Europe and the Mediterranean. Nearly every country had some of its elements, as the plays of Ibsen and Chekhov clearly show, yet the Russian middle class, for instance, represented not only a much smaller proportion of the national population, but was composed in a different way. The element of shopkeepers and self-employed businessmen was relatively weaker in Russia than in western Europe, and the proportion of civil servants and professional men correspondingly greater – not because there were more of them in Russia, but because they had fewer middle-class rivals. At the same time in Spain and southern Italy the middle class was small and largely agricultural, with a sprinkling of business and professional men, and the inevitable civil servants.

The middle classes and religion

Then, as now, only a minority of people, even among the middle and upper classes, were seriously preoccupied with such questions as the nature of man and his purpose, if any, in life. As with the working classes, religious observance was stronger in 1870 than now, but weaker than it had been in previous centuries. It can be argued that fear of social unrest had led many of the French upper bourgeoisie to religious practices which their Voltairian parents had openly despised; but this backwash did not reverse the main tide.

Some of the social factors which brought about the decline in religious practice have already been noted. But for those whose religion had deeper roots, there was the whole onslaught of Positivist and allied thought. The scepticism of the eighteenth-century rationalists had been kept from spreading as widely as it might have done by governmental restrictions and social convention. The Revolution, however, had initiated trends that broke down many of these restrictions, and Positivism was merely the most coherent expression of an attitude which was advancing on a broad front through western intellectual circles.

Positivism owed much to the formulations of Auguste Comte (1798–1857), who reiterated the view of sceptics that mankind could never be certain about the ultimate issues in life – such as whether there was a God or not, or how the universe originated. Since these were issues that were not open to rational enquiry, mankind would be more profitably engaged in studying the laws of science and the observable attributes of the nature of man and society. Most Positivists believed that the study of social science would become increasingly accurate, leading man into a new and better existence, which they called 'the positive state'. Many of the later Positivists not only renounced the search for God, but campaigned actively against belief in God. Their position and that of other agnostic and atheist campaigners was further complicated by the issue of reducing clerical influence in politics.

In many countries the traditional alliance of throne and altar had created a situation where the Catholic hierarchy was consistently pursuing a short-sighted policy of resistance to any change that would weaken the influence of the traditional sources of authority: the monarchy, large landowners and the Church itself. This meant that many desirable changes could only be brought about in the teeth of clerical opposition. The result was that many liberals, who had no quarrel with religion as such, found themselves having to engage in unedifying anti-clerical campaigns. Each side tended to become more extreme in its utterances, the outcome being a political cleavage which caused much heart-searching among people of goodwill who found their loyalties divided.

At the same time nineteenth-century studies in psychology and sociology tended to cast doubts on the traditional Christian view of free will. The insights into the physiological basis of mind and into the importance of sense-impressions, which Pierre Cabanis (1757–1808) and his disciples had achieved at the beginning of the century, had encouraged a growing conviction that heredity and environment were ultimately responsible for most human responses. This seemed to challenge not only the traditional Christian belief in freedom of the will, but also Christian confidence that God would never allow man to be tempted beyond his capacity to resist. These were difficulties which the churches eventually learnt to assimilate, after a fashion: but they created doubts in the minds of many thinking men. The same was also true, in a more publicised way, of the implications of Charles Darwin's theory of evolution.

The Origin of Species had appeared in 1859, *The Descent of Man* in 1871. Apart from buttressing belief in the influence of heredity and environment, it showed creation as a struggle for survival, in which all but the fittest were driven to the wall. The fact that the mechanism of creation itself was based on conflict, in which the wastage and animal suffering was enormous, seemed to put in doubt the very concept of a loving God. Christians had always been aware of the 'problem of evil', but they had tended to regard suffering as an imperfection in creation, not an essential attribute of its basic principle. It is true that once again the Christian churches were gradually to learn to assimilate unpalatable evidence, including that of man's animal origins; but the intellectual casualties on the way were great.

The study of human society was at the same time putting an increasing emphasis on economic conditions. Ludwig Feuerbach had said that 'man is what he eats', while Karl Marx was among the growing number of thinkers who asserted that the whole development of society depended primarily on economic factors. Not only could man not exist without food or drink, but his whole development and character had come about through his struggle for economic advantage. The very aptitudes of human beings had been developed and sharpened by the search for food and warmth, man in this being like the rest of the animal world. The materialist thinkers admitted, however, that man was also activated by all sorts of emotional and idealistic drives, and agreed that a man of feeling and intellect could not live by bread alone. But they emphasised that without bread man could not live at all – and that for the majority of men, the struggle for bread occupied by far the greater part of their conscious lives.

The political pattern

The economic and social pattern of Europe inevitably had its influence on the pattern of political power. Europe in 1870 was much less 'governed' than today. Until the Russian Revolution of 1917, it could be argued that the political state of affairs in each country consistently lagged behind the economic and social realities of the time. With the Bolshevik experiment, on the other hand, it could be held that the political solution that was imposed on Russia was in advance of these realities; and certainly the adjustment in subsequent years was an extremely difficult one. The tendency in 1870, however, was for the political situation to be one or several moves behind the economic and social situation.

On the whole the division between democratic and authoritarian governments was no easier to make than it is now. It is true that there were fewer democratic pretensions to look behind, while democracy as a working reality had not as yet been split into its liberal and totalitarian varieties. Yet the many constitutional monarchies that existed in 1870 represented a wide variety of shades of grey between the off-white of the more democratic north-western monarchies and the near-black of the Russian and Turkish systems. Excluding the freak states of San Marino and Andorra, there was only one republic in Europe in 1870 – Switzerland – until September brought the Third Republic to France. Even the few countries with past republican history, such as Holland, were now under their own kings, or had been annexed by other monarchies.

Yet it would be a mistake to see 'republic' and 'democracy' as synonymous terms. What ultimately counted was how far the government represented the wishes of the majority of the caring population, it mattering little whether the head of state was called king or president. In the nineteenth century the move towards democratic government was generally made by a double process of transferring real power from the head of state to a prime minister, while making this minister accountable for his actions to an elected parliament. Since all important measures required a favourable vote of parliament to become law, the minister could only carry on effective government with the goodwill of a majority of parliament. And so in practice the real measure of a government's democratic nature lay first in how far the parliamentary majority reflected public wishes, and secondly in the proportion of important measures that were submitted to it.

In the early 1860s France had been the only major power in Europe that had a parliament directly based on universal male suffrage. Yet in practice the democratic possibilities of the French situation had been drastically curtailed in two fundamental ways. On the one hand, parliament's powers of criticism and legislation were much more limited than in Britain, while on the other Napoleon III had tried to legislate as far as possible by decree. The result was that Napoleon had been able to appoint the ministers whom he wanted, rather than those who were most representative of parliament's wishes. Parliament had, moreover, been made more complacent by government pressure at elections, though this magic was beginning to wear thin by the late 1860s. Indeed events in the late 1860s were soon to decide Napoleon to give wider powers to parliament.

Crossing the Rhine, the situation in Prussia provided an interesting comparison. In the early 1860s the Prussian franchise had been more limited than that of France. But, as in the case of France, the government tried to free itself from democratic control through the expedient of bypassing parliament. When the Landtag refused to grant money for army reform, King Wilhelm's new Minister-President, Otto von Bismarck, leapt over the obstruction by collecting revenue without its permission – and then tried to suppress hostile newspaper criticism. However, the essential ingredient in Bismarck's handling of the Landtag was his defeat of Denmark (1864) and Austria (1866), which earned him the support of the country as a whole. Parliament thereupon felt obliged to recognise his popularity by retroactively voting the money that Bismarck had unconstitutionally collected in the previous four years. Yet both in Prussia and France such a cavalier attitude to parliament could only be maintained as long as the government's main policies were relatively successful and popular; indeed it was precisely on this question of success that the fortunes of Napoleon III and Bismarck were to divide (see pp. 45–6). In other words, if a government wanted to ignore parliament, it had to show by the success of its policies that it had a better claim than parliament had to public confidence.

The need for governments to reflect the public's wishes, or at least to have the public's acquiescence, was true of all those western countries where there existed some respect for democratic constitutional principles among the public. Clearly the term 'public' in this instance must be confined to those who cared and who were equipped to think about the issue. Yet even in the autocratic monarchies of Russia and Turkey, the same principle existed in a much more primitive form. A monarch could not afford to disregard his subjects' wishes indefinitely – even if only a wealthy minority were politically articulate.

In no European country, however, was the government a direct reflection of the largest social group. Most of the spokesmen of the manual classes were men of bourgeois origin, who were given a hearing in 'respectable' quarters only as long as they promoted plebeian interests with 'moderation'. Furthermore, working-class solidarity was split by the land-holding peasants whose interests were more akin to bourgeois interests than to those of the urban workers. Both the landed peasantry and the bourgeoisie wanted low taxation and respect for private property; so it was therefore not surprising that most land-holding peasant votes went to men who first and foremost represented established middle-class interests. Such men also had a much better chance of influencing governments than someone who claimed exclusively to represent the peasantry.

The urban workers, on the other hand, wanted better living conditions. While it was true that the answer lay in a bigger pay-packet, governments could help in a variety of ways – not only by restricting working hours, but also by providing employment on public works and promoting social legislation. Yet since such help cost the government money, it could be achieved only by increased taxation, which the peasantry, like the bourgeoisie, would resist – land being a heavily taxed item. The urban workers by contrast had little property but their hands, and were thus much less affected by tax increases. A deep divergence of interest was therefore inevitable. The outcome was that the political champion of the urban worker was generally much more of an outsider in politics than the peasants' representative, since the proletariat could expect less profit from making tactical alliances with the bourgeoisie. In any case, even in countries with a fairly wide franchise, the urban working class was still only a minority of the electorate, with little chance of making its will prevail against the interests of other classes.

In the case of the peasantry, however, their numerical importance was offset by the lack of education and political experience of their 'native' leaders. This was yet another reason for basing their political action on those bourgeois or upper-class politicians who were prepared to support peasant demands.

Lack of education was clearly a major obstacle in the political emancipation of the manual classes. In most countries the franchise was based on economic qualifications, illiteracy itself not being a specific bar to having the vote, except in the few countries where an educational qualification was required. But while education must not be identified too closely with literacy, there came a point where experience in life could not compensate for the lack of a formal education. It was this that forced

*

the uneducated to rely on politicians who did not always understand their problems. Indeed what is so striking about many of
the middle-class men who took up the cause of the manual
classes is the feeble grasp they had of the realities of working-
class life.

NOTE

THE FRANCO-PRUSSIAN WAR – A BRIEF SYNOPSIS

For the sixty-five balloonists who left Paris in the autumn of 1870,
the main issue in their minds was almost certainly the Franco-
Prussian War. And so it was with the statesmen of Europe. The war
and its outcome were of enormous importance in shaping the
character of subsequent international relations. Germany was able
to complete her unification and become universally recognised as the
leading European power. The balance of Europe was visibly altered,
while new concerns influenced European affairs. Assumptions
changed, and what were thought to be the lessons of the war and its
diplomatic prelude were to influence the thoughts of statesmen and
strategists for the next forty-five years. Only the mud of the western
front finally swallowed them up.

The war needs first to be seen against the changing pattern of
European national frontiers. In the 1860s the western third of
Europe, with its industry and dense population, was divided into a
number of small but disproportionately powerful states. Eastern
Europe, however, with its sparser distribution of inhabitants, was
largely ruled by three empires, the Russian, Austro-Hungarian and
Turkish. Nevertheless this contrast between the political divisions of
eastern and western Europe was already beginning to soften. The
divisions of western Europe were already being simplified by the
rapid unification of Italy and Germany; while eastern Europe could
be expected to grow more complicated, as the various nationalities
within the three empires became more assertive.

In second place the war must be viewed in the more specific context of German unification. After 1871 Bismarck's achievement acquired in retrospect an inexorable quality that concealed the large
element of opportunism and luck that was involved. Yet what remains surprising is the apparent failure of the powers, even as late
as 1870, to realise how strong Germany had become. Indeed much
of Bismarck's success arose out of the benevolent neutrality of the
other powers, who still regarded France as the main threat to the
peace of Europe.

EUROPE in 1870

This inattentiveness to the reality of German strength was all the more remarkable in that for centuries it had been the policy of Germany's neighbours to keep her weak and divided. They had been consistently helped in their aim by the reluctance of the rulers of the various German states to give up their power and join a united sovereign Germany. By the mid-nineteenth century, however, the cause of German unity had greatly increased its adherents, especially among those sections of the German population who wanted greater economic and military security. At the same time hopes of a united Germany were progressively centring on Prussia, which was gradually usurping Austria's place as the recognised leader of Germany *vis-à-vis* the rest of Europe. The process was nevertheless a slow and difficult one, leaving doubts in the minds of many people as to where their best interests lay.

It was in the midst of these hesitations that 1866 brought a dramatic *mise au point*: Prussia resoundingly defeated Austria in a seven-week war. Not only did it emphasise Prussia's claims to be considered as the leader of Germany, but it gave Bismarck the opportunity of eliminating some states and of bringing all except four into a North German Confederation. Prussia now had every reason to hope that it would only be a matter of time before the others would join.

Even so, the obstacles that remained were difficult. There was first the reluctance of the remaining states to commit themselves to union; and secondly, Bismarck had to recognise the probable hostility of France to the creation of a rival power, equal in strength, just the other side of the Rhine. Traditionally Bavaria, Württemberg and Baden had pursued a policy of gaining advantages for themselves by playing off France against Prussia and Austria; so much so that unless Bismarck could prove to them and to Hesse-Darmstadt that their best interests lay with Prussia rather than with France, it was quite likely that they would prefer to keep an intermediary position.[1]

The Franco-Prussian War was shortly to resolve these problems – and much else. In a book of this size, devoted to Europe after 1870, the sequence of events that led to war and decided its outcome cannot be adequately examined; but the reader who wishes to follow them in outline may do so in Appendix A. There it is argued (pp. 433–5) that if it had been possible for Bismarck to achieve unification without recourse to war, he would have been glad enough to do so. Indeed events in 1869 may well have encouraged him to entertain such hopes. It is likewise argued that the whole issue of the Spanish Candidature (see pp. 433–4) was intended as a prestige venture,

---

[1] Baden, however, was to apply for membership of the North German Confederation in February 1870 – though for diplomatic reasons Bismarck withheld it at that juncture.

aimed at impressing the four southern states. If Bismarck could put a Hohenzollern on the Spanish throne it would demonstrate Prussia's ability to outmanœuvre France, and so encourage the southern states to throw in their lot with Prussia. There is little reason to suppose that Bismarck intended the candidature as a direct provocation to France, as has often been alleged. If Bismarck could attain his ends without war, he would be the first to welcome the saving of men and money that this would represent.

After May 1870, however, it became increasingly probable that France would intervene, if unification ripened. Indeed the appointment of the anti-Prussian Duc de Gramont as foreign minister seemed to threaten an uncompromising line in French relations with Germany. Nevertheless, when confrontation finally occurred in July 1870 (see pp. 434–5), Bismarck was still prepared to leave the choice of war or peace to France. It is true that for France the choice was one between war or humiliation. But for Bismarck either would suit his purpose. He had no fear of war. Helmuth von Moltke, the chief of the general staff, had insisted to Bismarck that the superior state of readiness of the Prussian army made Prussia's chances of an easy victory against France much more likely at that point than later. A military victory over France would convince the southern states that their future lay in union with Prussia. Yet on the other hand, should France choose humiliation, Bismarck would have won a diplomatic victory that would probably have much the same result. As everyone expected, France chose war.

The ease of the German victory in the Franco-Prussian War sprang from France's failure to emulate Prussia in the use of her resources. It is true that if France had had allies the outcome might have been different. But as far as national potential was concerned, the war was really a fight between equals. The total German population numbered 39·5 million against France's 37·5 million; while in time of war France could theoretically muster 1,200,000 men – a numerical match for Germany's 1,183,000.[1] Yet the German total were all trained men, ready within three weeks; while only two-thirds of the French total had received any significant training. Indeed only half of these were in uniform at the beginning of the war.

The shortcomings of the French conscription system were clearly a major factor in the German victory (see pp. 436–7), and it was here that Napoleon III reaped the results of the hybrid regime he had established in France. He himself had wanted a new system of conscription, but the prospects of effective reform had been shipwrecked on largely domestic issues. When far-reaching proposals

---

[1] The southern states mobilised to help Prussia.

were put forward in 1866–7, public opinion and the Corps Législatif were so hostile to them that the reform emerged dangerously weakened.

To understand this widespread short-sightedness, the constitutional position in 1867 must be briefly considered. The limited powers that Napoleon allowed the Corps Législatif gave it a certain obstructive power, but little inducement to behave responsibly. In the first place Napoleon appointed whom he wanted as ministers, irrespective of whether they reflected the wishes of the majority in the Corps Législatif. The deputies in 1867 therefore felt under no obligation towards them – other than their general desire to keep the regime in being, for fear of what might replace it if it fell. Secondly, since Napoleon carried on so much of the nation's business without consulting the Corps Législatif at all, it was understandable that they should try to assert themselves on the issues that were submitted to them.

In the case of army reform, moreover, there were other specific factors. Napoleon had already squandered men and money on inept adventures abroad; and since foreign policy was one of the many spheres of government over which the Corps Législatif had no control, they were scarcely tempted to vote more men and more money for Napoleon to use as he pleased. The government was likewise further to blame in failing to publicise the implications for France of Prussia's victory over Austria. The result was that public opinion in 1867 urged the Corps Législatif to adopt a tight-fisted attitude.

It is worth remembering that the Prussian liberals, for not dissimilar reasons, had been opposed to Albrecht von Roon's proposals for military expansion. Unlike Napoleon III, however, Bismarck had eventually been able to overcome this opposition, precisely because his foreign policy was successful and won the support of the public at large.

Not only did Germany have a larger quantity of trained men than France, but they were brought into operation more quickly. For several years Moltke had been carefully preparing a plan of attack on France, seeing to it that the army was suitably placed to respond at once to a sudden mobilisation. In France, by contrast, the French forces lay scattered over the country in regimental garrisons, each far from the area of its recruitment, and not knowing in what higher formations it would serve when mobilisation came.

The conduct of the fighting itself showed a similar discrepancy between the two sides – though the Germans had their share of bungling and inflexibility. Napoleon III, however, took the disastrous step of assuming his uncle's mantle as supreme commander of the French forces; and, as everyone recognised, his health had been deteriorating for several years, depriving him of his ability to make decisions boldly. What was worse, his waning powers of decision were further sapped by his own realisation of the inadequacies of the French army. The result was that when France lost the opening battles of the war, he made the catastrophic mistake of ordering a general retreat; and it was this decision that altered the whole character of the war from a head-on frontier struggle to a pursuit.

Less than four weeks later, Napoleon was to be a captive in Wilhelmshöhe. Following a saga of mistakes and hesitations, the army he was accompanying was defeated at Sedan, while its twin lay surrounded at Metz. The dismal story is easily summarised. At Metz Marshal Bazaine's army had ineptly allowed itself to be out-flanked and confined to the town (15 August); and there it remained until Bazaine eventually decided to surrender (27 October). In the meantime Marshal MacMahon's army, with Napoleon in tow, had withdrawn north-westwards, until it was brought to battle at Sedan (1–2 September). Here, even more than in previous encounters, the Germans made effective use of their superiority in artillery. Lugubri-ous to the last, Napoleon surrendered to the Prussian king. Little was left of the one-time optimist, who thirty years earlier had invaded France with a paddle-steamer and a caged eagle.

If Napoleon thought France was defeated, however, Paris thought otherwise. When the news of his capitulation reached the capital, a republic was proclaimed (see pp. 134–5) and a new Government of National Defence set up to continue the fight. Nevertheless the out-come of the war could be in no doubt, and although the new govern-ment tried desperately hard to find allies the rest of the struggle was to little purpose. Paris herself fell to the Germans in January 1871, an armistice following in the same month.

The long-term effects of the war are discussed in later chapters. For France, however, the immediate price of peace was heavy, for the Treaty of Frankfurt (May 1871) not only exacted an indemnity of £200 million, but it also gave to Germany Alsace-Lorraine with its rich iron-ore deposits and its thriving textile industry. Germany for her part had already gathered the first fruits of victory in the previous autumn: to Bismarck's immense relief the four remaining independent states of Germany had agreed in November 1870 to join the others in forming a German Empire, with the King of Prussia as Emperor. It was clear to the world that after two centuries France had lost her European supremacy; Germany was now firm in the saddle. And whether the future of Europe would be one of peace or war would depend above all on who held the reins in Berlin.

PART ONE
1870 – 1918

CHAPTER TWO

The Common Factors

'You Europeans look all alike.' *Chinese waiter on bringing food to the wrong table.*

THE CAKE IN SLICES — THE SOCIAL OUTCOME

Population

Perhaps the most important thing that happened to Europeans in these years was that they became more numerous. In 1914 there were about 418 million bundles of consciousness, experiencing the pains and pleasures of life in Continental Europe, instead of about 261 million – despite the emigration of over thirty million.[1] This increase, however, was unevenly distributed. The Russian population grew by about 86 per cent, the French by less than a tenth.

The main reason for the increase was the fall in the death rate, arising from improved medicine and better sanitation. This is borne out by the contrast with Africa, where the population was probably stationary – or with China where it may have actually declined. In India, however, where western medicine and the ability to deal with famine were better established, the population increased as quickly as in Europe. In Europe the benefits had spread from west to east in the course of the century, the last quarter seeing important discoveries concerning typhoid, cholera, rabies and plague. The English death rate in 1890 was only half of what it was in Russia. Furthermore the increasing application of Joseph Lister's methods of hygiene in surgical operations reduced the death

[1] See footnote on p. 25.

rate in amputation cases from about two-fifths to a twentieth.[1] The west, however, was partly compensating for its lower death rate by the increasing practice of birth control, a phenomenon that was slower in coming to the east. This largely took the form of interrupted intercourse, though primitive contraception was spreading among the middle classes. Generally speaking birth control was practised most widely in those countries where the influence of the churches was waning, and where education and the economic or social inducement to limit families were strongest. France led the way, with Britain close behind, followed by Germany.

The business and hazards of living

Improvements in well-being, like the population increase, were also uneven; but the pattern was different. In north-western Europe real wages in the 1870s were double those in many parts of eastern and southern Europe, and were to rise on the average by about a half in the next thirty years. By contrast the rise in eastern and southern Europe was imperceptible in some countries, probably averaging less than a quarter over the whole. Nowadays it is assumed that wages do not represent the whole of the worker's income for there are also the periodic benefits of state social services. But even in the west, social insurance scarcely existed outside Germany until the very end of the period (see Table 5). Insurance against industrial accident was the only facet of social insurance that many countries offered – and this was partly to protect the employers against the risk of court action. In the east, Russia introduced state sickness insurance in 1912, but this could scarcely compensate for low wages and long hours; for whereas in the west, working hours dropped from an average of eleven or twelve hours in the 1870s to nine or ten by 1913, in Russia they only dropped from thirteen to eleven.

For a countryman coming to the towns, any improvement in wages might still leave him worse off, as far as living accommo-

---

[1] Hitherto the dilemma had been that although the advances in anaesthesia in the 1840s had enabled the undertaking of operations which had previously been thought impossible, in most cases gangrene had set in shortly afterwards, causing death.

TABLE 5

Political and social reform before 1914

	Universal male suffrage	Accident insurance or employer's liability	Sickness insurance	Old-age pensions	Unemployment insurance
Germany	1867	1884	1883	1889	
France	1848	1898		1910	
Russia	1906 (qual.)	1903	1912		
Austria	1907	1887	1888	1906*	
Italy	1912	1898		1898*	
Spain	1890	1900			
Portugal	1901	1913			
Belgium	1893	1903		1903	
Holland		1901	1913	1913	
Denmark		1897		1891	
Norway	1898	1894	1909		
Sweden		1901		1913	
Switzerland	1874	1911	1911		
Bulgaria	1879				
Romania		1912		1912	
Greece	1864	1901			
Britain		1897	1911	1908	1911

* Voluntary scheme.

dation was concerned. His water supply and lighting might be better, but his family would be crowded into smaller rooms, and the air they breathed would be much less healthy. There was also little escape that did not involve the expenditure of money. To take small children for a walk in clean air involved a bus or tram fare, which for all the family might cost him two or more hours' wages. Cafés and dance-halls of course cost more. Yet a worker who had only known the towns could only be conscious of improvement.

The bulk of the population in western countries was beginning to enjoy the benefits of improved technology. Ready-made clothes and shoes brought prices down to a fraction of what they had been; though bicycles (viable as a regular means of transport since 1885) did not really come within the reach of the unskilled worker's budget until after the First World War. However, the spread of the horse-drawn omnibus and tram, and the introduction of electric trams after 1881, meant that fewer workers were obliged to walk to work. Most western cities had running water in working-class districts by the end of the period (even if it was only one tap to several families). The water-closet, however, remained essentially a middle- and upper-class perquisite until after the war. An expert has described 1870 as 'the *annus mirabilis* of the water-closet'; but the improvements of that year, like the earlier versions, took time to spread, and so the night-soil man, like the gas-lamp lighter, remained a familiar nocturnal sight in European streets (and the subject of innumerable cheery slum-ballads).

Free medical treatment as such was only available in certain conditions, though there were many voluntary sickness-insurance clubs which enabled people to meet the sudden expense of unexpected illness. In the pre-aspirin age, when so many drugs and medicines that are nowadays taken for granted were unknown or little understood, pain and illness still entailed miseries that are hard to imagine. Dental fillings (and initially many extractions) were carried out without anaesthetics, while the pedal-driven drill was a luxury only invented in 1870. The dentist was an expensive as well as a fearsome beast, and the consequent prevalence of bad breath accounts for the references to sweet breath that are found in eulogies of fair women. False teeth were beyond the working-class pocket, with the result that many faces looked prematurely aged. X-rays were only discovered in 1895 (the very name indicates the mystery that surrounded them); and until their application was developed, bone-setting was a matter of touch and intelligent guess-work. The use of analgesics in child-birth was spreading among the middle class, while perambulators greatly increased in number in the 1880s. But working-class babies in the pre-plastic-pants age were wet and smelly.

Education

Shorter working hours meant more leisure, and the spread of free and compulsory primary education brought about the growth of a literate public who could read the cheap newspapers and periodicals that the manufacture of low-grade paper

was making possible. Nevertheless secondary education remained largely the preserve of the middle and upper classes. A
few scholarships enabled the exceptional working-class boy to
rise to the professions; but success in making money was the
more usual way for a working-class person to break into the
middle class – just as it was for a middle-class man to rise into
the upper classes. The universities continued to equip upper-
and middle-class youths for 'life', offering them the twin
advantages of vocational training and a finishing school. At the
same time in secondary and higher education, science subjects,
geography, modern history and modern languages and literature were continuing to make headway against the traditional
supremacy of classical studies; while at all levels of education
there was a growing if primitive consciousness of the need to
base curricula on the stages of the pupil's psychological growth.
Progress was slow, however, as was shown by the fact that the
major theorists of the educational psychology of the period
belonged mainly to the pre-1870 era.

A major feature of the period was the greater attention given
to women's education. Working-class girls had traditionally been
given much the same education as boys; both were expected
to take basically manual employment, where ability to read
and write and do simple arithmetic was an added if not essential
advantage. In many countries, however, secondary education for
girls was left to private and convent schools. France instituted
state secondary education for girls in 1880, while in Germany
it did not occur until 1908. It was in this period that most west
European countries started awarding university degrees to
women. For the older generation of both sexes, various schemes
for part-time education offered a chance to compensate for the
inadequacies of their childhood education. But most of the
schemes were voluntary, the most remarkable example being
the folk high schools of Denmark.

The purpose of living – doubts and assertions

Intellectual and 'metaphysical' issues remained the concern
of a minority. Religious observance continued to decline, especially in the industrial cities where it had no social buttressing.

The notable conversions to Catholicism that occurred among men of letters in the period 1890–1914 had no counterpart in the mass of the population. Moreover the declaration of Papal Infallibility by the Vatican Council in May 1870 created unease among intellectuals, both inside and outside the Church; the fact that its application was restricted to *ex cathedra* statements on faith and morals softened but did not remove this unease. It seemed to many that the Vatican was compensating for its loss of temporal power by an enlargement of its spiritual power. Indeed this loss of temporal power reached completion only three months later, when in September 1870 the Italian government occupied papal Rome.

It is true that papal infallibility had long been accepted as part of Catholic tradition, but its nature and extent had remained without precise definition. Many Catholic intellectuals feared that a definition in militant terms would alienate other Christians, especially prospective converts. They also feared that it would undo the little that the liberal Catholics had managed to do to demonstrate that the Church and modern society need not be at odds. With Pius IX (1846–78) as pope, their task was certainly a difficult one. But in Leo XIII (1878–1903) they found a pope who was sympathetic to their wishes, and who realised that a church without understanding for the aspirations of modern society would forfeit much of its influence. For the first time, the Vatican took serious official notice of the predicament of the industrial working classes. But as long as the Christian churches continued to regard better living conditions for the working classes as charity rather than social justice, their appeal to the masses was bound to lag far behind that of the secular champions of working-class interests. At the same time much of the goodwill engendered by Leo XIII was to be largely dispelled by the cold if well-meaning intransigence of Pius X (1903–14). Spurred on by the gloomy forebodings of his secretary of state, Raphael Merry del Val, Pius X saw himself as having to defend the deposit of Faith against the encroachments of liberalism both inside and outside the Church. The result was a witch-hunt against liberal clergy which left lingering scars on the intellectual life of the Church for much of the early half of the twentieth century.

The thinkers who were genuinely produced by the period were perhaps less influential than the great figures of earlier years who happened to survive into the period. The Positivists and other agnostics had expelled religious belief from many intellects, but had left an emotional vacuum which both thinkers and poets found hard to fill. The problem was how to give back to life meaning and emotional content. Men wanted the sweet sensation of enthusiasm, but wanted a sound rational basis for their enthusiasm. To enthuse because one was happier enthusing seemed an unsatisfying reason. So poets and thinkers looked for a God-substitute in art, humanity or creation; anything that would give a satisfying answer to the question, 'why bother?'. Friedrich Nietzsche (1844–1900) and Henri Bergson (1859–1941) were among the thinkers who gave hope of reviving enthusiasm. Nietzsche wanted men 'to have life more abundantly'. He wanted them to throw off Christian inhibitions, such as humility and non-violence, and achieve the state of 'Supermen' through 'the Will to Power'.

Nietzsche found disciples in unexpected quarters: liberals like Daniel Halévy who were conscious of the desiccating effects of rationalist philosophies. Many of these, however, were alarmed by the ruthlessness of the Nietzschean ethic, and found in Henri Bergson a man whose ideas combined a humane gentleness with the invigorating force of his concept of the *élan vital*. Marcel Proust and other notable writers of the period were influenced in varying degrees by his thought, while he also had disciples among the young Catholic intelligentsia.

Many people of the time might have assumed that Pavlov's dogs were a circus-turn. But in fact the experiments of Ivan Pavlov (1849–1936) with the conditioned reflexes of animals were opening up a further assault on the notion of free will. At the same time Sigmund Freud (1856–1939) and Carl Jung (1875–1961) were starting to probe the unexplored caverns of the human subconscious. The significance of their work was not widely appreciated until the inter-war years; but for those aware of it their conclusions had shattering implications. It is true that educated people were becoming more used to the idea of personality being the product of heredity and environment; but even in this context, it had been popularly assumed that a man's actions arose from what he rightly or wrongly conceived to be desirable at the time he acted. In other words, however clouded or warped the mind might be, its actions could still be envisaged in basically rational terms. Freud and Jung, however, claimed that human inclination was often the result of subconscious urges of which the man himself was largely unaware. On the nature of these urges Freud and Jung were in disagreement. Freud saw them as basically sexual, and drew attention to the presence in young children of sexual urges in embryo. He laid particular emphasis on the far-ranging psychological effects of suppressing these urges. Jung on the other hand saw human behaviour as largely directed by emotional considerations of power; indeed his conjectures were shortly to give human speech such familiar phrases as 'introvert', 'extrovert', and 'inferiority complex'. Unlike so many contemporary developments in science, these ideas made a profound impression on the lay imagination, their effect in this respect being reminiscent of that of Darwin's theories. The literature of later decades was to exploit them in a frequently uninformed way, much as Emile Zola had made use of Prosper Lucas's (admittedly suspect) ideas on heredity.

For those who could appreciate it, the work of successive scientists from James Clerk-Maxwell (1831–79) to Ernest Rutherford (1871–1937) culminated in the reduction of matter and energy to electrons and protons. Creation was thereby given a comprehensive unity which surpassed even that presented by Darwin's concepts. The theories of Albert Einstein (1879–1955) and Hermann Minkowski (1864–1909) went even further, reducing time to a fourth dimension of space. Although these theories, like Max Planck's quantum theory of 1901, effectually simplified man's view of creation, the layman was to regard them as an incomprehensible complication of the picture that previous centuries had been making clearer and simpler.

> Nature and Nature's laws lay hid in night;
> God said 'Let Newton be!' and all was light.
>
> ALEXANDER POPE

> It did not last: the Devil, howling 'Ho!
> Let Einstein be!', restored the status quo.
>
> J. C. SQUIRE

The practical application of these advances in science to making the world a better place to live in had to wait until the inter-war years. Indeed the consequences of Rutherford's description of the atom (1911) are being reaped only in our own time – for good and evil.

The arts

For many people, these developments in science and contemporary thought seemed to be draining life of all significant 'meaning'. It was therefore not surprising that men of sensibility should turn increasingly to the arts. It would be a mistake, however, to imagine that what we now consider the *chefs-d'œuvre* of those years were typical of cultured tastes in general. The arts that were favoured by the bulk of the middle and upper classes were heavy and sentimental by present-day fashions. The figures that are today regarded as the masters of the period pioneered tastes and preoccupations that only found widespread favour after 1918. This was true of the leading Impressionist and Post-impressionist painters, while some of the Fauve and Expressionist leaders are still beyond popular cultured taste, despite the passage of half a century. The Symbolist poets were likewise only widely appreciated after the war, the same being true of the younger composers like Debussy, Stravinsky and Sibelius (at the level of his fourth symphony).[1] The influence of these painters, poets and composers has done so much to shape present-day popular tastes, that their work seems more in keeping with modern surroundings than with the heavy airless be-knick-knacked interiors of *la Belle Époque* and Wilhelmine Germany. Anyone wishing to find worthwhile music reflecting the prevalent tastes of the time should listen to Saint-Saëns or César Franck, not Debussy, and to Richard Strauss, not Schönberg.[2] Characteristically, one of the most acute sensibilities in literature, Marcel Proust,[3] was largely inspired by Franck and Saint-Saëns to create in his imagination the music

[1] Claude Debussy (1862–1918); Igor Stravinsky (1882–   ); Jan Sibelius (1865–1957).
[2] Camille Saint-Saëns (1835–1921); César Franck (1822–90); Arnold Schönberg (1874–1951); Richard Strauss (1874–1949).
[3] Marcel Proust (1871–1922).

of Vinteuil, the composer in *À la recherche du temps perdu* – rather than by Debussy, whose work he admired and whose sensibility and stature were more akin to his own. Among composers the predominant influences were Brahms and Wagner – though most English composers were still shuffling along in the funeral cortège of Mendelssohn, especially in their choral writing. English music, however, was shortly to be engulfed by an indigenous wave of green-fields-and-decency, hinted at in Elgar and eventually reaching its genial culmination in Vaughan Williams.[1]

The majority of novels and plays of the period were meant to entertain, elevate or shock, novelettes and bedroom farces reaching a much wider public than any literature of lasting worth. Many serious novels and plays showed the influence of the various strands of Realism, with their awareness of social conditions and psychology (however crude). A growing belief in the forces of heredity and environment in shaping personality was seen in authors as widely different as Zola, Hauptmann, Ibsen and Chekhov. In the case of Zola and some lesser figures, the work of pseudo-scientific 'authorities' was used to give a 'scientific' buttressing to their novels and plays – though even here 'scientific verisimilitude' was always subordinated to the requirements of artistic effect and dramatic interest. The 1890s are chiefly remembered, however, for a blossoming of Aestheticism. What had been an attribute of some of the more refined Realists, such as Flaubert and the Goncourt brothers, now became the core of the Aesthetes; and the fashion had its counterpart in the visual arts, notably in an important strand of what is loosely called Art Nouveau (see Plate 7).[2]

The early years of the twentieth century saw a remarkable branching-out of the arts in various experimental forms, which stemmed from a variety of factors. On the one hand there was the growing refinement of sensibility and the continual search for a means of expressing what was too delicate for the customary means of communication. And on the other hand there

---

[1] Johannes Brahms (1833–97); Richard Wagner (1813–83); Felix Mendelssohn (1809–47); Edward Elgar (1857–1934); Ralph Vaughan Williams (1872–1958).
[2] Émile Zola (1840–1902); Gerhart Hauptmann (1862–1946); Henrik Ibsen (1828–1906); Anton Chekhov (1860–1904); Gustave Flaubert (1821–80); Edmond Goncourt (1822–96) and Jules Goncourt (1830–70).

were those like the Fauve painters and early Expressionists who found existing methods of communication too feeble rather than too clumsy for what they had to say. Concurrent with both, however, there were also the seekers of discipline – men like the Cubists who were concerned with geometric and notional concepts of their subjects.

The mainstream of west European architecture was imitative and largely historical in its inspiration. A municipal building, a bank, or even a factory would be given the façade of a medieval *Rathaus* or a renaissance *château* or whatever took the architect's and customer's fancy, irrespective of the purpose of the building. Perhaps only in working-class homes was there a largely functional style, carried over in most cases from the eighteenth century. Farmhouses and peasant cottages were likewise less subject to imitative fashions, and frequently retained the local characteristics that distinguished them from houses in other regions. In America the use of metal frames in skyscrapers encouraged the design of rectangular functional buildings with large windows. But the style was slow in coming to Europe, and there was in the meantime some indigenous competition from the experiments of Peter Behrens (1868–1940) and Walter Gropius (1883–1969). These, however, bore little fruit before 1918 – and the crustacean fantasies of Antoni Gaudi (1852–1926) in Spain were isolated phenomena.

The period also saw the technical foundations laid for art forms that were to achieve significant stature in the inter-war period. The cinema made its début in the 1890s; but it would be hard to make any lasting claims as art for any of the films that were made in this period. Most directors were still thinking in terms of theatre-production methods, and had not realised the enormous potential of the medium. Similarly, negro rhythms from America were making their way across the Atlantic in the form of cake-walks, rag-time and other harbingers of jazz; but it was not until after the war that European composers and executants started to develop them in a markedly indigenous fashion.

Further hazards of living – conscription

Whatever station of life he occupied, the young European was generally faced with the risk of conscription. If drafted to the colours, several years would be taken out of his life, and he would be subjected to the bullying of N.C.O.s and the endless drudgery of kit-cleaning and foot-drill. He could probably have assimilated in a year or less the training that would actually have been of any use to him on the field of battle. But memories of the Franco-Prussian War convinced most high commands that victory lay with the big battalions that were ready for immediate use. And so little consideration was paid to the possibility of giving all able-bodied men six months' military training, and of thereby having an enormous reserve consisting of most of the younger male population. Instead the tendency was to conscript only a minority of young men and give them several years' training, the government thereby always having at its immediate disposal a large number of seasoned troops. In several countries, higher educational or occupational status could reduce the period to a year, but this was only for a fortunate minority of the young population.

MAKING THE CAKE – THE ECONOMIC FACTORS

The economic historian is generally a jolly soul – or so it seems to the sour-faced 'straight' historian. His descriptions of bankers and businessmen radiate a merry sense of purpose, like Disney's seven dwarfs. God-like, standing high above the trade cycles and national boundaries that preoccupy the contemporary economist, he sees that the world economy, despite periodic setbacks, is always growing. Even when analysing periods of depression, he points enthusiastically to where unnoticed toilers are laying the foundations of future growth. He remains, in short, a retroactive optimist to the last.

The 'straight' historian, however, feels obliged to attenuate this contemplation of 'the economy' with anxious looks at the social repercussions of economic growth and the international tensions that it may engender. With furrowed brow, he balances *The Age of Progress* with *The Bleak Age*, and sweating the blood of attempted objectivity, finishes by writing *The Age of Trans-formation* – or, safest of all, *An Age of Transition*.[1]

For the next few pages, however, the reader is invited to confine himself to contemplating the economy. While the telegraph and railways were bringing peoples of east and west closer together, the economic differences between them were in many cases increasing. By contrast in the west itself the economic differences that separated the early industrialised countries from the others (and from each other) were gradually lessening as industry spread. Germany was only the fourth country to become industrialised, yet by 1914 she had taken the lead in European industrial production. The period also saw the entry of Italy and Sweden as small but significant industrial powers. The Jeremiahs of the City chop-houses were meanwhile lamenting that Britain's share of world industrial production had fallen from nearly a third to nearly a sixth, and could take small consolation from the fact that the French share had fallen from over a tenth to a sixteenth. As far as the east was concerned, Russia was the only country to undergo a significant industrial revolution, yet even in 1913 her share of world production was still only a twentieth. No European businessman could ignore the truth: from the 1880s the United States was usurping the world leadership that had hitherto belonged to Britain. At last it was being realised that European primacy itself might one day be called in question.

Nevertheless if Europe now had only about 55 per cent of this particular cake instead of about 70 per cent, the cake itself was five and a half times larger (see Fig. 1). There was also the additional consolation that much of America's industrial growth was absorbed by her own domestic needs. As an industrial exporter she occupied only fourth place, with 12·6 per cent of world exports, while Britain provided 29·6 per cent, Germany 26·4 per cent and France 13·6 per cent.

---

[1] This is not to deny that many economic historians are also social historians, and frequently wear both hats at once.

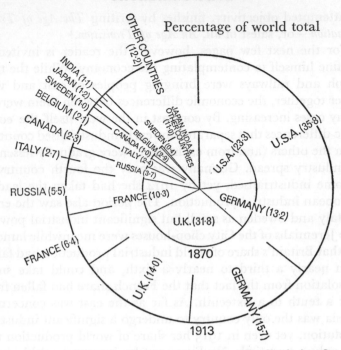

Percentage of world total

OTHER COUNTRIES (12·2)
INDIA (1·1)
JAPAN (1·2)
SWEDEN (1·2)
BELGIUM (1·0)
CANADA (2·1)
CANADA (2·3)
ITALY (2·7)
RUSSIA (5·5)
FRANCE (10·3)
FRANCE (6·4)
U.K. (31·8)
U.K. (14·0)
GERMANY (13·2)
GERMANY (15·7)

JAPAN (1·0)
OTHER COUNTRIES
INDIA (1·1)
SWEDEN (1·0)
BELGIUM (1·8)
CANADA (2·9)
ITALY (2·4)
RUSSIA (3·7)
U.S.A. (23·3)
U.S.A. (35·8)

1870

1913

Fig. 1 *The world's manufactures (percentage distribution) 1870 and 1913 (compare with Fig. 8 on p. 278)*

SOURCE: League of Nations, *Industrialisation and World Trade* (1945).

Agricultural change

Developments in agriculture were much less impressive than those in industry. With a growing population and the practice of dividing land among heirs, the tendency in many Continental countries was towards the fragmentation of holdings rather than their consolidation. Modern techniques were therefore difficult and disproportionately expensive to apply. Furthermore lack of employment, not shortage of labour, was the characteristic of most non-industrial countries, which meant that there was little inducement to install labour-saving machinery. Nevertheless, despite these obstacles, crop rotations and other improvements, pioneered by long-dead innovators, continued their gradual spread across Europe.

Although European society saw some interesting experiments in mixing noble blood with bourgeois wealth ('manuring one's land' as the French elegantly put it), the scientific cross-breeding of plants and animals did not get under way until the end of the period. It is true that the Austrian monk, Gregor Mendel, had published his findings on heredity as early as 1865, but he did so in the transactions of a comparatively obscure natural history society; and it was not until 1900 that another scientist chanced upon Mendel's work and realised its enormous significance. Cross-breeding, as it was hitherto practised, followed the simple empirical methods of the English experimental farmers of the eighteenth century; and within their limitations these methods could have impressive results, a good example being the grafting of indigenous vines on to American vine-roots to combat the phylloxera insect that devastated so many of Europe's vineyards during these years. Indeed this proved an even more profitable admixture than the marriages of *châtelains de premier cru* with the daughters of American millionaires.

By 1910, the motor-tractor had made its appearance, while increasing use was being made of chemical fertilisers, a development that arose from the exhaustion about 1870 of guano supplies from the Chincha islands. It had been guano that had first accustomed European farmers to the idea of commercial fertilisers. But the islands' cormorants and boobies had not kept pace with the enthusiasm of the Peruvian fishermen shovelling up the deposit of the ages, so Europe turned to chemistry.[1] In the poorer countries, however, soil productivity continued to be limited by the fact that animal manure was burnt as fuel, as in present-day India.

For farmers themselves, however, the most significant feature of the period was the import of cheap food and raw materials from abroad. The spread of railways across the rich plains of Russia and America was bringing increasing quantities of grain to the coast for export to Europe, the first full force of which broke on the European farmer in the early 1870s. The next twenty years, moreover, saw shipping freight rates cut by more than two-thirds, as iron and then steel hulls permitted increasing

---

[1] Subsequently other deposits were successfully exploited; and the more northerly Blue-footed Booby joined the Peruvian Booby as the farmer's favourite bird.

capacity. At the same time new land was constantly being brought under the plough in America and elsewhere, with the result that food was now reaching Europe in quantities that largely outstripped the increase in population. Canning methods and refrigerated ships (1877) enabled perishables to be stored or transported for much longer periods, and the 1890s confronted the European farmer with growing cargoes of meat from the New World and Australasia. Silk-growers watched with apprehension the expanding exports of China and Japan, while sheep-farmers saw with equal disquiet the mounting bales of Australasian and Argentinian wool that were filling European ports. All of this undoubtedly meant cheaper food and clothing, and helped to account for the rise in real (as distinct from monetary) wages (see pp. 98 and 126). But it also lowered the income of farmers everywhere – even after landowners persuaded their governments to bring in protective tariffs. The overall price of food fell by two-fifths between 1873 and 1896, and that of raw materials by over a half, with the result that the total number of sheep in France and Germany was itself halved. Even with tariffs, French wheat prices fell by 43 per cent in the same period. Such a situation could only intensify the farmers' role as a battling lobby for protection, setting them yet farther apart from the urban working class with its demand for cheap food.

Governments had a hard choice. The tariffs that they imposed meant that the townsmen could only partially benefit from the fall in prices. But without such tariffs, the rural population could not have afforded to buy the industrial goods that gave the townsmen their livelihood. Food would have been cheaper, but urban wages would not have risen to the extent that they did.

The theoretical solution to such an agricultural *embarras de richesses* was for some of the producers of the surplus commodity to switch to a product in short supply. In practice, however, this was always difficult because such conversions took time and money, demand in the meantime sometimes changing. Yet where a glut or shortage was sufficiently long-term to permit remedial action, such conversions were the only real solution, the Danish and Dutch switch from grain to dairy produce being notable examples. Nevertheless farming was henceforth to be the poor relation of the European economy. Even the sturdy individualism of the western farmer had to accept the idea of more co-operative undertakings, especially in processing, marketing and banking.

Technological change and industry

Railways, refrigeration and steamships were enlarging trade horizons, making it inevitable that the economies of the various countries should become increasingly interdependent. International world trade quadrupled in the period, while world industrial production increased five and a half times.

All countries could potentially profit from the technological improvements that the period brought. Much of the material progress of the period could be attributed to the use of improved forms of steel in manufacturing. Steel and its alloys were tough and resilient, and could be worked with remarkable accuracy. Not only did this permit the making of objects of great strength and durability, but it was perhaps the factor that most facilitated the development of mass production. Separate wings of a factory could each specialise in one component, secure in the knowledge that the various components would fit together. At the same time the strength of steel made possible the building of much more powerful steam engines, accommodating much greater pressures.

Henry Bessemer's process (published in 1856) had already reduced the price of steel from £22 to £7 a ton by 1870 (as compared with £4 a ton for wrought iron); while the Siemens–Martin open-hearth process (1866) was to bring further improvements in the seventies. But both methods were dependent on non-phosphoric ores, which in Europe were only to be found in Spain, Austria and England in any sizeable quantities. However, the process discovered by Sydney Gilchrist Thomas and Sydney Gilchrist in 1878–9 permitted the use of phosphoric ore, thereby releasing the iron resources of Alsace-Lorraine and elsewhere for cheap good-quality steel production, a major factor in German industrial growth. Furthermore Britain and the other countries that had invested large sums in equipment for the earlier processes were slow to change, so losing ground to Germany. Indeed in the years between 1880 and 1910 German steel output rose from 0·7 to 13·7 million tons, whereas that of Britain rose from 1·3 to only 6·5 million, and that of

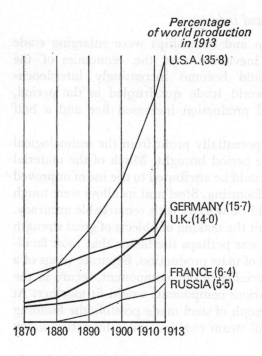

Percentage of world production in 1913

U.S.A.(35·8)

GERMANY (15·7)
U.K.(14·0)

FRANCE (6·4)
RUSSIA (5·5)

1870 1880 1890 1900 1910 1913

Production in 1913 as a percentage of *national* production in 1958:

U.S.A.   22%
Germany* 33%
U.K.   38%
France   44%
Russia   3%

(*1958 total for W. Germany only.)

(The diagram does not attempt to show the fluctuations of production in the intervals between the years specifically indicated. In each of the specified years, production is shown as a percentage of what world production was to be in 1913.)

Fig. 2 *The growth of industrial production in selected countries 1870–1913 (compare with Fig. 9 on p. 278)*

France from 0·4 to as little as 3·4 million. At the same time tungsten and manganese alloys (1868 and 1882) enabled the making of much tougher cutting and breaking tools, while the development of electric furnaces after 1879 permitted more exacting standards in the production of high grade steel and its alloys.

Two notable products of the steel age were the sewing-machine and the motor-car (see p. 71). Although the first recognisable sewing-machine was produced in 1846, it underwent continuous development in the following decades. Its periodic whirring rattle was to be as much the accompaniment of pre-1914 domestic life as the slamming of car-doors has come to be of our own; while by the 1890s its factory counterpart had helped to reduce the production cost of shoemaking to less than a twelfth of what cobbler-made shoes had involved.

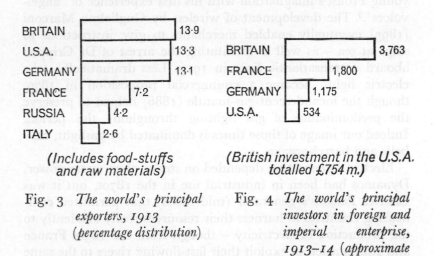

BRITAIN	13·9
U.S.A.	13·3
GERMANY	13·1
FRANCE	7·2
RUSSIA	4·2
ITALY	2·6

(Includes food-stuffs and raw materials)

BRITAIN	3,763
FRANCE	1,800
GERMANY	1,175
U.S.A.	534

(British investment in the U.S.A. totalled £754 m.)

Fig. 3   *The world's principal exporters, 1913 (percentage distribution)*

Fig. 4   *The world's principal investors in foreign and imperial enterprise, 1913–14 (approximate estimates in £ millions)*

These developments in steel represented the latest stage in a long story of growing success. The chemical industry, however, was a relatively new sphere of material improvement. Fertilisers, dyes and cheaper alkalis were among the more important of its early products, later creations including artificial silk (1889), bakelite (1909), and cellophane (1912).

Motive power

The period was also highly eventful in the development of motive power. The 1880s pioneered the use of alternating electric current in factories as well as its long-distance transmission from power stations. This meant that factory lay-out could at last be emancipated from the wasteful tyranny of shafts

and belts that steam and water power had demanded. At the
same time, the invention of the telephone (Alexander Graham
Bell, 1876) gradually increased the whole tempo of life by
replacing the to-and-froing of messenger-boys with a virtually
instantaneous *tête-à-tête* between correspondents – thereby
enabling industry and commerce to respond immediately to the
demands and changes of the market. It was also to provide the
young Proust's imagination with his first experience of 'angel-
voices'.[1] The development of wireless by Guglielmo Marconi
(1895) eventually enabled merchants to give instructions to
ships at sea – as well as facilitating the arrest of Dr Crippen
aboard a transatlantic liner in 1910. Less dramatically, 'the
electric light' became a commercial proposition in 1879,
though the incandescent gas-mantle (1886) helped to preserve
the predominance of gas lighting throughout the period.
Indeed our image of those times is dominated by gaslight, cab-
bells and barrel-organs.

Electrical generation depended on steam, then water power.
Dynamos had been in industrial use in the 1870s, but it was
Charles Parsons's generator (mid-1880s) that permitted coal-
bearing countries to harness their resources really efficiently to
the production of electricity – though from the 1890s France
and Italy started to exploit their fast-flowing rivers to the same
end. Parsons's generator was in fact a modification of his steam-
turbine (1884), which marked a considerable advance in the
use of steam. The turbine worked on a water-wheel principle,
with steam instead of water, thereby dispensing with the piston
system which had governed steam rotary motion since the
beginning of the century. As a result, much greater steam
pressure could be used without the traditional fear of breaking
the piston system. This likewise helped to prolong the dominance of coal as a source of motive power, for as late as 1913 coal
still supplied nearly nine-tenths of world motive power, if
steam-driven electrical generators are included.

From 1902, however, large merchant ships and warships were
beginning to turn to oil, with its saving of space and personnel.
World tonnage in steam-ships had only just overtaken that of

---

[1] *À la recherche du temps perdu* contains many refreshing examples of the response
of a fine sensibility to the changing world of modern technology.

sail (1893), and further conversion was unwelcome to established navies. Indeed Max Pemberton's prophetic thriller, *The Iron Pirate* (1893), probably did more than any serious propaganda to familiarise the British public with the advantages of oil-burning ships. But conversion came slowly.

Meanwhile on land the Benz Company produced a petrol-driven motor-car in 1886, with the result that by 1913 there were nearly 100,000 cars in France alone. In Europe as a whole, however, horse-drawn traffic continued to hold the road. Yet it is often forgotten that cars had already reached speeds of over 65 m.p.h. in the 1890s; and that in fact poor road surfaces were principally responsible for keeping down traffic speeds. The development at the same time of the pneumatic tyre (from the late 1880s) supplied a major contribution to security and comfort. Conversely the aeroplane, pioneered by the Wright brothers in 1903, continued to be a curiosity until the First World War when, as always, military considerations produced the money and courage that enabled its versatility to be demonstrated.

Business organisation

Some of the most far-reaching inventions and techniques in industry were no more than commonsense applications of old ideas. The smooth running of machinery, for example, was greatly facilitated by the use of ball-bearings (1877) and by simple methods of lubricating machinery in motion. Furthermore a neglected aspect of industrial advance in these years was the improvement in lay-out and the deployment of manpower. Time-and-motion studies were pioneered by Frederick Taylor in the 1880s, enabling employers to insist on less time and more motion – or so the unions were to complain. Similarly the increased sophistication of cost-accounting enabled expansion to take place within the limits of carefully gauged budgets. Administration and office work became proportionally more important, developments such as the typewriter (1868) and adding-machine (1888) having a growing influence on the efficiency of industry.

Technical improvement, however, was far from being an

unmixed blessing to mankind. An ominous feature of mass
production was that the regimented semi-skilled worker, trained
to one function, was a more efficient producer than his skilled
and more versatile counterpart, even under identical conditions; for paradoxically enough the habit of making a variety of
judgements was a handicap when only one was required.
Indeed the repeated identical response of a machine was the
ideal that was expected of a worker; and it was one of the many
ironies of a period of growing popular education that less and
less was demanded of the factory-worker's mind and more and
more from his conditioned reflexes.

Moreover some of the ingenuity of business and industry went
into activities that were questionably in the interests of progress.
Falling prices and protective tariffs in the 1880s encouraged
firms making similar goods to try to maintain profits by agreeing
not to undercut each other, an agreement that often involved
dividing the market into spheres of influence. These cartels
became particularly widespread in Germany, Austria, Belgium
and Scandinavia, though France and Italy had a significant
number. Holding companies, trusts and mergers represented
further degrees of consolidation that became more numerous in
the eighties and after. These various combinations had their
vertical counterpart in the *Konzern*, by which a powerful firm,
specialising in a particular process, would establish control over
the other processes involved in making a product. This would
sometimes extend to the mining or growing of the raw material
involved and also to the transport and sale of the finished product. Clearly combinations of this kind could cut production
costs by unifying much of the administration, marketing and
advertising; and it has to be recognised that some of this saving
was passed on to the consumer. On the whole the various effects
of these trusts and cartels tended to counterbalance each other,
with the result that the consumer was generally buying well-
produced goods at a uniform but not unreasonable price.

Despite these developments, it should not be forgotten that
even in Europe's foremost industrial country, Germany, the turn
of the century still found over nine-tenths of industry in the
hands of individual proprietors, while workshops of five or
fewer people employed a third of the industrial labour force.

The dominance of small enterprise was correspondingly even stronger elsewhere. Similarly, although limited liability had been made available to business in the later nineteenth century,[1] the small partnership with unlimited liability continued to be the typical business enterprise for much of the period.

Production and international trade

For the world as a whole, the years 1873 to 1896 were a period of falling prices in manufactures as well as agriculture. Although manufacturers were less hard hit than farmers, industrial prices fell by a third (see Fig. 5). At the same time the pioneers of the

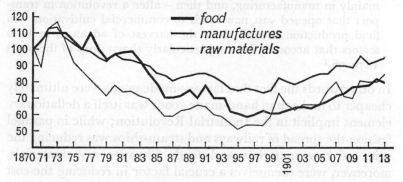

Fig. 5 *The movement of world prices, 1870–1913 (1870=100)*

Industrial Revolution, Britain, France and Belgium, were acutely conscious that other countries had followed in their footsteps, and were not only supplying their own domestic needs, but were annexing an increasing share of the international market. It was not surprising, therefore, that the older industrial nations should see these years in unhappy contrast to what had gone before.

Conversely the last years of the century initiated an upswing in prices, and a remarkable rise in world industrial production, particularly by the second generation of producers, notably Germany and the United States (see Figs 1 and 2). The excitement of these years recalled the optimism of the early seventies

[1] Limited liability, without individual authorisation, became legal in France in 1867 and throughout the German Empire by 1872.
*

(see p. 75); so much so that it was common to think of the intervening period as an aberration, 'the Great Depression, 1873–96', which many saw as the product of an unlucky combination of circumstances. In more recent years, however, economic historians have tended to see 'the depression' as a much shallower and more scattered affair than did their predecessors, and prefer to view it as an uncomfortable stage in a long-term trend, initiated by the Industrial Revolution. To quote Professor David Landes:

> The nineteenth century was marked by a protracted and sharp deflation, stretching from 1817 to 1896 with only one sharp interruption. . . . Over the century, real costs dropped steadily, at first mainly in manufacturing, and then – after a revolution in transport that opened vast new lands to commercial cultivation – in food production as well. It is the harvest of advances in both sectors that accounts for the particularly sharp drop of the years 1873–96.[1]

In other words the fact that factory-made goods were ultimately cheaper to make than hand-made goods was itself a deflationary element implicit in the Industrial Revolution; while in parallel fashion the spread of railways and steam-ships was reducing the price of raw materials and food. Cheaper raw materials, moreover, were themselves a crucial factor in reducing the cost of manufactures, as Figure 5 strongly suggests. Cheaper leather, wool and cotton meant cheaper shoes and clothes, for it was not only the sewing-machine that was cutting costs. As long as there were new markets for manufacturers to tap, increased sales had outweighed the fall in prices. But with the rise of industry in the United States, Germany and elsewhere, the older industrial countries could no longer assume the same increase in their sales. Britain's case typified the dilemma.

> From 1870 on, with the exception of . . . steel, which was transformed by a series of fundamental advances in technique, British industry had exhausted the gains implicit in the original cluster of innovations that had constituted the Industrial Revolution. More precisely, it had exhausted the big gains. . . . Innovation was if anything more frequent than ever. But the marginal product of improvements diminished as the cost of equipment went up and

[1] *The Cambridge Economic History of Europe*, VI, p. 461.

the physical advantage over existing techniques fell. Not until a series of major advances opened up new areas of investment around the turn of the century was this deceleration reversed.[1]

Germany by contrast had not yet reached this stage in the last quarter of the century. With protective tariffs to help her, she still had a large domestic market to exploit, as well as rural neighbours to the east. Indeed when the turn of the century brought Europe new industrial opportunities, Germany was still riding high on the momentum of the old. Apart from a brief set-back in the 1870s (see p. 76), 'the depression' for her had been a period of rapid ascent; and the same could be said, in varying degrees, of other countries that were undergoing industrialisation.

The phenomenon that requires close examination is perhaps not so much 'the depression' as the general rise in prices and production that preceded and followed it. The price-rise of the 1860s belongs to an earlier volume – though it is worth remembering that in these years, wars on both sides of the Atlantic had tended to keep the supply of both raw materials and manufactures below the level of demand. The Franco-Prussian War and its outcome had serious inflationary results. The war had temporarily reduced the amount of French and German goods available to buyers, thereby pushing up prices, while the payment of the French war indemnity to Germany had brought unusually large sums of money into the stock-market, with a parallel inflationary effect. This situation, however, was short-lived. American and other industrial producers had taken advantage of the temporary shortage of Franco-German manufactures to increase their own share of the market. The result was that when French and German goods reappeared in their customary quantity, the market was much more heavily laden than before, and prices started to fall. In Germany and Austria, moreover, the situation had been aggravated by the heavy wave of speculation that had preceded the fall. The most notable casualty was the Viennese Creditanstalt bank, whose collapse (April–May 1873) created a crisis of confidence among bankers everywhere. Both producers and consumers found it harder to get credit, and prices fell further.

[1] Ibid., p. 462.

Nevertheless the crisis itself was of limited proportions when compared with what the world was to see in the following century. Even so, it was to make a lasting impression on the public imagination for two reasons. In the first place, the rapidity with which its repercussions circled the earth was a startling demonstration of how the increasing internationalisation of commerce and finance had its dangers as well as its advantages. Symptomatically the existence of heavy British investment in Germany and Austria had given added impetus to these repercussions, London being the *de facto* capital of the financial world. In the second place, people failed to make sufficient distinction between the aftermath of the crisis itself and the deflation that was to dominate the next two decades. While the crisis of 1873 was undoubtedly a contributing factor, the deflation of 'the depression years' stemmed from much more fundamental reasons – as already suggested (pp. 74–5). On one hand, there was the impact of overseas imports on the price of raw materials and food, already clearly reflected in the prices of 1875.[1] On the other hand, there was the resumption of the long-term deflation of industrial prices inherent in 'the logic' of the Industrial Revolution. Not only were real costs falling, but the industrialisation of more countries was filling the market and lowering prices still further.

The reaction of both farmers and manufacturers was to demand an increase in protective tariffs. Hitherto the sixties had inaugurated a gradual lowering of import duties, but this tendency was now put firmly into reverse. The position of farmers has already been outlined (see pp. 65–7), but that of manufacturers was more complex. They were generally opposed to agricultural tariffs, for fear that dearer food would result in greater wage demands. They likewise believed that reductions in imported food would affect their sales abroad: it would limit the buying power of countries that bought European manufactures with the proceeds of their agricultural sales, and their buying power was already affected by the fall in farm-prices. But manufacturers also had periodic misgivings about protection for each other's goods. The maker of metal goods feared

---

[1] As Fig. 5 shows, raw materials were the hardest hit in the seventies. Food prices, though dropping, were to undergo their major fall in the eighties.

that protection for textiles would mean dearer clothing for his workers: in short each industry saw the others' demands as a potential rise in the cost of living. Nevertheless the need to overcome opposition from other sectors of society generally compelled them to unite their demands and present a common front.

Understandably enough, the first countries to raise their industrial tariffs were those with vulnerable growing industry: the United States (1875), Russia (1876), Spain (1877) and Italy (1878). In 1879, however, Germany followed suit, France doing likewise in 1881. Eventually Britain, Belgium, the Netherlands, Denmark and Turkey were the only countries that continued broadly free-trade policies.[1]

On the whole, however, manufactures suffered less than agriculture. The reduced growth rates of the older industrial countries should not blind one to the fact that their output was still continually rising, if not at quite the same speed. It was the makers of capital goods for export who were most affected, especially in Britain. Moreover the real victims of any depression, the unemployed, remained a relatively small minority. Even in Britain, which lost most ground to foreign competition, over 90 per cent of the labour force remained in work, for monetary wages that were rising 2 per cent a year – and far more in *real* terms, given the falling cost of living.

An increase in demand for manufactures, starting in America, gave rise to a brief resurgence of prices and production in the years 1879–82. But it was not until the later nineties that the long price-fall levelled out and started making a sustained ascent – an ascent that was to continue, despite occasional downward jerks, until the outbreak of war. Industrial production also rose more sharply, though unlike prices it had risen consistently, if soberly, throughout 'the depression'.

Although past generations perhaps attached too much importance to the availability of gold as a price determinant in this period, there is nevertheless a case for supposing that the

[1] The tariff situation was much more complicated than any brief history can indicate. In practice a country's tariff-system generally consisted of a collection of commercial treaties with other countries, each specifying individual terms that were dependent on what was being given in return.

rise in prices was partly initiated by an increased production of gold. From the early seventies, a growing number of nations were basing their monetary systems on the gold standard, instead of on gold and silver, with the result that prices were more directly influenced by fluctuations in gold supply, especially now that improved communications kept the financial world closely informed on the state of gold supplies. In the early nineties, N. Y. Castner's sodium cyanide method of extraction (1887) augmented South African output, while 1896–1903 brought the brief legendary dream-world of the Klondyke gold-rush, when Dawson City allegedly saw imported beauties bathing in champagne – and, most incredible of all – saw no one murdered for his gold, despite the fact that only the first arrivals were lucky. With more gold in the market, it is reasonable to suppose that it made some contribution to the price rise of the later nineties. At the same time, the growing opportunities for profit which these years brought – see below – were to render banks much readier to lend, this itself being an inflationary factor, since producers tended to pass on to the customer their interest-expenses.

Prices however, like production, are primarily stimulated by demand. And demand in the later nineties was expanding. On one hand the exploitation of underdeveloped territory in both hemispheres had already engendered a renewed burst of railway building, which was bringing the steel industry increased orders. On the other hand a whole new sphere of investment opportunities was being offered by what has been termed 'the Second Industrial Revolution'. As David Landes has said:

> these years saw the lusty childhood, if not the birth, of electrical power and motors; organic chemistry and synthetics; the internal-combustion engine and automotive devices; precision manufacture and assembly-line production . . . [They] marked the start of a new upswing, a second cycle of industrial growth which is still in course and whose technological possibilities are still far from exhausted.[1]

As far as increased production was concerned, perhaps the most influential factor of all was the development of the internal

[1] *Cambridge Economic History of Europe*, vi, pp. 462–3.

market. For the older industrial countries this was a major compensation for the markets they had lost through increased competition in the field of exports; though the industries that gained most in the domestic sphere were not necessarily those that had been hardest hit by foreign rivals.[1] The continued rise in real wages had brought more workers into the general market for manufactures, and so expanded demand. It was insufficiently realised at the time that an increase in the working class's purchasing power was potentially a major expansion of the market. It is true that transferring money from shareholders' banks to workers' pockets did not increase the physical amount of money available for purchase. But in fact a sum of money distributed among many men will be spent more quickly than if it remains with a single individual. There is a limit to what the wealthy man of normal appetites can spend on sustenance, comfort and entertainment. He will certainly spend less on clothing, utensils and furniture than thirty men of modest means. The balance of his wealth tends to be put in investments or the bank. Industry certainly requires the capital of rich investors; but investment is of little use if there is only a small demand for the finished product, and in times of depression it is demand that requires particular stimulation, as J. M. Keynes was to point out in the 1920s and 1930s (see p. 275). In short, the gradual transfer of money from the rich to the poor, that was taking place in the later nineteenth century, was on the whole beneficial to production. So much so that employers' profits in many cases outstripped what they lost in paying higher wages.

Such a situation, however, was not only the product of better wages. The habit of buying comforts as well as necessities had to be instilled, especially in rural areas where the kitchen garden and a small village shop supplied the bulk of people's wants. Although the urban working class were accustomed to being dependent on shops for most things, a mounting barrage of advertising impressed on them the variety of goods that

---

[1] Heavy industry, which had less to gain from the expanding home-market of consumers, found some compensation in the mounting arms expenditure of European governments – though the extent of this varied greatly from country to country.

increasingly lay within their budget. The growing number of department-stores and chain-stores were able to cut costs and offer more at lower prices, thereby attracting working-class custom and ingraining new spending habits. At the same time, improved transport to the towns acquainted countrypeople with the flood of goods that were available at prices they could afford – while village shops were spurred into stocking a much greater variety of produce.

These were developments that could be of some cheer to the farmer, as well as the merchant and manufacturer. Indeed the expanding tastes and consumption of the working class were an important factor in temporarily lessening the gap that separated international food prices from those of manufactures. Nevertheless it was an escalator on which both agriculture and industry were rising; and if 1909 was to find the gap between them only 10 per cent wider than it had been in 1871, the industrial spurt of the next four years was to restore it to the old familiar 15 per cent that had separated international food prices from manufactures in the rock-bottom years of the mid-nineties. The situation within particular countries was of course qualified by industrial circumstances, the ratio of agricultural to industrial tariffs being an obvious example. Indeed by 1910 the whole tariff situation was extremely complex, national levels showing a remarkable range of difference.[1] Nevertheless despite growing food-consumption by the working classes, the farmer could have few illusions about the future.

A notable feature of the period was the increasing trade of Europe with the Afro-Asian world. To some extent this reflected the increased imperial activity of Continental Europe. But it was more directly a result of improved shipping and railway communications, and a more systematic exploitation of the regions already under white dominance, notably India. Indeed the areas that were annexed by Europe after 1870 not only contributed very little to world trade in these years, but accounted for only a very small percentage of Europe's overseas

---

[1] Taking industrial and agricultural tariffs together, and calculating them as a percentage of *total* imports (including duty-free goods), the spectrum was as follows: France 8 per cent; Germany 8·4 per cent; Italy 9·6 per cent; Spain 13·4 per cent; U.S.A. 23·2 per cent; Russia 38·9 per cent.

investment. With the exception of Egyptian cotton and the fruit-growing potential and mineral wealth of the south, Africa was not an inviting economic proposition. Palm oil, esparto grass and ostrich feathers were the kind of products offered by the bulk of Africa; and whatever factors brought about partition, the intrinsic economic wealth of the continent was not the foremost. It is often forgotten that the value of the Congo's rubber resources was not really appreciated until after its annexation by Leopold II; while the exploitation of Saharan oil belongs to the period after 1945.[1] Indeed the present predicament of so many of the newly independent African states is a measure of their basic poverty.

By contrast India played a key role in the international economy – and this deserves some explanation. By the end of the period Britain was the one major power to retain free trade, with the result that the only serious obstacle to foreign sales in Britain was British ability to manufacture the same articles more cheaply. On the other hand, the Continental powers excluded British manufactures by protective tariffs, with the result that Britain had an adverse balance of trade with Germany and several others of her European trading partners. It is true that the cost of this situation was partly met by interest on British investments abroad and by such 'invisible exports' as shipping, insurance and banking services. These alone, however, would not have been sufficient; for it was above all Britain's favourable trade balance with her own overseas possessions, notably India, that largely met the cost.

India in fact was a huge market for precisely those British manufactures that found it hard to surmount Continental tariff walls. India spent far more on British goods than Britain spent on India's – and Britain was able to pocket the balance in hard cash. This situation arose partly from the imperial connection. As a British imperial possession, India was prevented from putting up Continental-style tariffs to protect her own nascent industries against cheap mass-produced British goods. Fortunately for India, her raw materials were in great demand in Continental Europe and elsewhere, with the result that they

---

[1] Even cocoa came only as a transatlantic transplant towards the end of the nineteenth century.

could enter these markets duty-free, or relatively so. Consequently, with the money earned by these sales, India could
afford to have an adverse trade balance with Britain, which in
turn enabled Britain to buy more from Continental Europe.

Although Britain's share of international exports fell from a
quarter to an eighth in the 1870–1914 period, her commercial
policy was still a matter of great importance to other countries.
Even in 1914 she was the world's foremost overall exporter,
with the United States second, and Germany third.

The role of the United States in the European economy was
nevertheless becoming more and more ominous in its implications for the future. By the end of the period, the United States
had an overwhelmingly favourable balance of trade with all the
major European powers; indeed only port wine, Swiss watches
and the gastronomic specialities of the smaller countries prevented this excess of American exports being true of every
European country. Germany imported from the United States
nearly twice as much as she exported there, while in Britain's
case it was more than twice as much. The main qualification to
this picture was that Britain and Germany between them had
over £900 million invested in America, and were enjoying the
benefits of this and other invisible exports. Even this, however,
was to be a short-lived situation, for the First World War was to
transform America into the world's foremost exporter of capital.

CUTTING THE CAKE—

COLLECTIVE ACTION AND POLITICAL FACTORS

Trade unionism

The rise in real wages which characterised the 1870–1900
period was not only a result of the fall in prices, but was also
affected by the increasing shift of unskilled labour to semi-
skilled occupations. It is true that the craftsmen, who had been
the élite of earlier times, were being gradually levelled down
with the semi-skilled operatives (whose mechanical response
was better suited to the machines that were dominating factory
life). But at the same time, the ranks of the semi-skilled class
were being filled with newcomers from the other end – unskilled

labourers who, after a few weeks in a factory, could make a sufficiently stereotyped response to be regarded as semi-skilled, and paid accordingly.

However, the fact that the working classes were able to have any share in the increased wealth of the period was largely of their own doing. Economic progress made for a larger cake, but the workers' larger slices came mainly as a result of their own militancy. It must be remembered that nothing remotely resembling working-class control of government was to occur in any country before the Russian Revolution of 1917. It could be argued that *fear* of this possibility may have speeded the various concessions of employers and governments in these years. But even so, withdrawal of labour by means of the strike remained the main weapon of the working class, with demonstrations of violence an occasional supplement. And there can be no doubt that one of the great achievements of the period was the legalising of the right to strike in most European countries.

Most workers would nevertheless have been too dependent on their wages to be able to withhold their labour for more than a few days; and an essential corollary of the right to withdraw labour was the right to form trade unions, armed with strike funds. Indeed a major feature of this period was the legalising of unions, and the banding together of many of them into general unions. This gave the unions far more scope in bringing pressure to bear on the employers. A general union not only had national funds to support a regional strike, but it could also call a strike throughout the country in support of the demands of a particular region. Even so membership remained small when compared with the total working population, subscriptions necessarily matching what workers could afford, with the result that funds were never large. By 1913 Germany had only three million union members, France one million and Britain four million.

In general the unions were working for specific benefits in the form of adequate wages and shorter hours: they were thus much less interested in 'doctrinal' issues than the various socialist parties claiming to represent the working classes in national politics. It was likewise significant that relations with such political parties were closest in situations where the party tended to be empirical rather than doctrinaire in its approach to problems, Britain providing the obvious example. Where trade unionism took on doctrinaire attitudes, the doctrine was usually one of action, as can be seen in the doctrine of the general strike adopted by the French Confédération Générale du Travail (1895), or the anarcho-syndicalism of the Spanish Confederación Nacional del Trabajo (1910). Such doctrine was often at variance with the credo of the main socialist political party in the country, which was often broadly Marxist. Indeed the 'doctrine' of trade unions ranged from Sorellian syndicalism[1] to Catholicism but generally only the leaders were much attached to 'doctrine', the rank and file usually preferring piecemeal benefits to the risk and upheaval of disrupting society.

Socialism

Trade unionism rarely transcended national frontiers, and it was only after the First World War that there was much serious attempt at international co-operation. The socialist parties, on the other hand, put great emphasis on their international ties; though in practice these remained the concern of only the leaders and theoreticians of the parties. National parties tended to go their own way on most practical issues, the First World War finding the majority in each of the main socialist parties solidly behind its country's war effort, instead of boycotting 'a bourgeois war'. The choice between class and country was never so clear-cut as the theorists implied. If the working class of one country refused to take arms, could it rely on the working class of the rival nation doing likewise? As always, lack of confidence undermined adherence to principle.

After 1900, socialism made considerable electoral headway, when its improved organisation combined with the slower growth of real wages to elicit a greater proportion of the working-class vote. Even so, no socialist party came anywhere near to a parliamentary majority – though their political influence

---

[1] I.e. the overthrow of bourgeois society through direct action by the unions. In the early twentieth century Georges Sorel (1847–1922) was the leading literary exponent of this concept.

was probably stronger than their numbers might suggest. It may plausibly be argued that fear of socialism partly accounted for the increase in social legislation after 1900 (just as it had in Germany in the 1880s). And while higher wages and shorter hours were essentially the work of the unions, the parties probably deserve at least some of the credit for the social legislation that was enacted by middle-class parliaments.

Social insurance was in fact the political brain-child of conservatives like Bismarck and liberals like Lloyd George – men who wished to outbid the socialists, or buy the support of the working class with ready-made reform that needed no upheaval. The unions, by contrast, had little or no experience of social insurance. Indeed the German legislation of the 1880s (see pp. 53 and 97–8) had relatively few imitators during the next twenty years, union leaders in other countries knowing little about it. The normal worker was preoccupied with the problem of keeping his family through the next week. He wanted a bigger pay-packet and shorter hours, not a weekly deduction to provide for a remote retirement lasting perhaps only five to ten years. Sickness and unemployment were similarly temporary conditions in the average worker's life; and given the choice of insurance cover or a bigger pay-packet, the pay-packet would probably win every time. It is not easy to be far-sighted on little money. At the same time the socialist parties were primarily concerned with trying to increase their political power, their main contribution to achieving social insurance being the indirect one of panicking governments into making *some* concessions to the working class.

Socialist doctrine

While most socialists were agreed on what they disliked in capitalist society, they were deeply divided on how it should be replaced. By 1870, the only socialist thinkers who could claim a wide international following were Karl Marx (1818–83) and that shambling shaggy monster of a thinker, Mikhail Bakunin (1814–76). Marx passed a large part of his later life in seat K1 of the Reading Room at the British Museum. Much of the rest of it was spent in miserable London apartments, where his poorly dressed children would greet calling creditors with the invariable statement: 'Mr Marx ain't in'. Marx and his collaborator, Friedrich Engels, regarded history as a struggle between exploiters and exploited. Historical change took the form of a series of dialectics. An existing situation ('the thesis') would give rise to active discontent which took the form of a counterforce ('the antithesis'); and the clash between the two would lead to a new situation ('the synthesis'). The 'synthesis' of the first dialectic would then become the 'thesis' of a new dialectic, after which the process would repeat itself. Western Europe, for instance, had undergone such a dialectic when the feudal society of the Middle Ages ('the thesis') had given rise to the powerful discontent of the mercantile classes ('the antithesis'), the ensuing struggle then producing the commercial bourgeois western Europe of the modern period ('the synthesis'). But in its developed capitalist form this bourgeois regime was itself the thesis of a new dialectic, where the discontent of the industrial proletariat provided the antithesis.

Marx and Engels claimed that bourgeois capitalist society would be violently shaken by a series of crises of overproduction, which would drive employers to exploit their workers still further, in their struggle to survive. The proletariat would then combine and forcibly seize power. Gradually a new classless society would emerge in which the age-old struggle between exploiters and exploited would permanently cease. State authority as such would cease to be necessary, and the state would 'wither away'.

It is on this point that many people who accepted the Marxist view of past history parted company with him. Was it not much more likely, they claimed, that the new society that followed the proletarian revolution would itself give rise to new discontents, and a further dialectic? Clearly, however, much of the popular appeal of Communism lay in the prospect of a society without tensions. This prospect encouraged people to throw their weight enthusiastically behind the historical process (even if – superficially – they seemed like railway passengers trying to aid the engine by straining against the carriage walls). If on the other hand the new society was merely to be yet another thesis in a series of dialectics, with tension and misery still existing, there would seem to be less point in trying to aid a process with this less inviting future.

Bakunin and Pierre-Joseph Proudhon (1809–65) were the central figures of nineteenth-century anarchism. But whereas the influence of Proudhon was largely centred on France, that of Bakunin took root in Spain, Italy, Russia and other countries where the peasantry played a significant role in working-class unrest. It must be emphasised that Marxist theory placed the industrial proletariat at the head of the revolution that Marx himself had prophesied would overthrow the capitalist regime. A marked centralism likewise characterised his concept of 'the dictatorship of the proletariat' – the period that would follow the revolution and prepare the way for the ultimate 'classless society'. Bakunin's teaching, however, took the form of a call to arms rather than a prophecy. He claimed that salvation lay in the destruction of existing state institutions, and in the spontaneous setting up of local popular bodies. These bodies would perform basic administrative functions that might still be necessary in the quasi-idyllic unregimented society of Bakunin's imagination. The appeal of this lay in the fact that his revolution needed no suitable preconditions. By contrast most Marxists insisted that the preindustrial agrarian countries must undergo the transformations of capitalism before revolution could occur there. Bakunin waived this, and his ideas had all the appeal of instant soup. They gave hope to revolutionaries in agrarian countries, while at the same time the large degree of local autonomy envisaged by Bakunin had particular appeal to rural and provincial urban communities resentful of the control of the national capital.

Marx and Bakunin had struggled for the leadership of the (First) International Working Men's Association (1864–76). But the remarkable comprehensiveness and cohesion of Marxism ensured its success in the industrialised countries of western Europe. Indeed the Second International, founded in Paris in 1889, was a marriage between Marxists on one hand and the more empirical socialists and trade union leaders on the other. Anarchists were specifically – though not always effectively – excluded. The International's periodic congresses were occupied by heated debate on whether socialists should make tactical alliances with the middle-class political parties to obtain piecemeal reform. Marxists believed that everything should be subordinated to the furtherance of revolution, and were therefore generally opposed to piecemeal reforms, as delaying the great day. Most of the empiricists by contrast thought that much could be usefully achieved by such alliances.

The International managed in fact to survive its differences – partly as a result of the theoretical distinction between 'minimum' and 'maximum' programmes. All were agreed that the ultimate ideal, 'the maximum programme', was the disappearance of the capitalist regime. Indeed many Marxists saw this as the only aim socialists could usefully pursue; but in the meantime they had to decide whether they should refuse or accept the fruits of the empiricists' *liaisons dangereuses* with the middle-class parties. Most of them feared that refusal might forfeit much working-class sympathy. Their answer was therefore to accept these fruits, however contemptuously, regarding them as the fulfilment of a 'minimum programme' of reform (which should in no way slacken their zealous pursuit of the 'maximum programme' of destroying the capitalist regime). On the other hand for those empiricists who saw salvation in gradualism, the concept of two programmes conveniently enabled them to forget the destruction of capitalism by dropping it in a bottom drawer marked 'maximum programme'; this enabled them with an easy conscience to pursue their real aim of a workable 'minimum programme'.

Government

It was nevertheless the activities of the existing governments that directly influenced the lives of the European population. The patterns of political change that occur in the period show two notable trends. On the one hand, universal male suffrage was spreading through Europe; and on the other, there was a steady increase in the power of governments. Superficially this may seem paradoxical, especially in view of the growing constitutional checks on the powers of the central and east European monarchies. But the fact that electoral power was slipping from 'the notables' to the masses did not mean that the new electorate could exercise greater control than the old. Indeed a good case may be made out for arguing the reverse, since a mass electorate is less able to provide the continuous informed criticism of government that had characterised the vigilance of 'the notables'. As men of property and education, 'the notables' were better equipped for this role. The mass electorate on the other hand tended to give a blank cheque for a limited duration to the party or man of its choice; and it is only when government policies touched its pocket or its pride that there was an outcry.

A more important factor in strengthening the executive was the growing complexity of the task of governing greater numbers in an age of increasing speed and technology. The telegraph and telephone made public life move many times faster and multiplied the number of decisions a minister had to make in a day. If government was to be carried on at all, vast discretionary power had to be given to him. Diplomatic negotiations that used to take months now took only days; and wars that had taken decades were now merely a matter of several years at most. Yet paradoxically a debate in parliament on government policy took more time to arrange than before – not less. And the vast increase in parliamentary business meant that an extraordinary debate on government policy could only be secured on major issues. Accordingly a government's critics found it progressively more difficult to comment on the conduct of day-to-day affairs. Politicians thus had to turn increasingly to the Press and non-parliamentary speeches as a means of criticism, this itself giving greater power to the Press and creating a new force with which governments had to reckon. But the Press was not the electorate; and it could be argued that in its attempts, both to influence the electorate and to speak in its name, the growing power of the Press confused rather than helped the attempts of the public to control government. At the same time, the power of the Press, as it was to emerge in the inter-war years, must not be predated. As late as 1898 General Kitchener could walk through a waiting group of journalists, and say: 'Get out of my way, you drunken swabs.'

In these circumstances even the old-style liberals had to revise their ideas of what constituted a tolerable level of governmental power. Not only were governments obliged to act more quickly, but they were also better informed than formerly. Intelligence services and various instruments of enquiry enabled a government to know more about most matters than the majority of critics. This knowledge and power progressively inclined the public to accept the idea that the government was more competent than other bodies to deal with the problems of society. At the same time the very complexity of modern civilisation demanded increased regulation of life, otherwise collisions of interest would have created chaos. Both on a national and local level public authority had to assert itself, if advantage was to be taken of the potential improvements in living standards offered by modern technology. This made for an alarmingly powerful state; but it certainly made for better living conditions.

It must finally be noted that this period witnessed very little change in the surface forms of government. The retreat of Turkey saw new monarchies in the Balkans, while Russia made certain concessions to constitutional government. But otherwise the tally of types of government in 1914 remained much as it had been in the 1870s, it being only the First World War that produced significant change.

OVERSEAS IMPERIALISM

Mention has already been made of European activity overseas; but the significance of this at the time was much greater for the overseas populations than for Europeans. Indeed it is only nowadays that Europeans are appreciating the harvest that has sprung from the dragon's teeth sown before 1914.

The last thirty years of the nineteenth century proved a major turning-point in the history of Africa. Prolonged contact with western civilisation was made for the first time, the frontiers of the present African states being largely determined by the colonial boundaries established in those years. These developments belong to the history of Africa and Asia rather than of Europe; and in so far as they impinged on the lives of the Europeans of the time (as distinct from those of today), they are dealt with in the chapters on specific countries.

France was the only country whose empire could compare in any sense with that of Britain, it being precisely this period that saw the bulk of its acquisition. It was likewise during these years that Germany and Italy obtained what little empire they had, and that Portugal made further important advances in southern Africa. Spain, by contrast, lost most of what was left to her, while the Dutch empire remained largely static. Nevertheless Russia continued in her slow relentless fashion to push her Asian domains southwards to border on Afghanistan and Persia, and likewise continued encroaching upon China and Korea.

The reasons for this expansion varied from power to power. But it is clear that the activities of Europeans overseas were facilitated by a number of common factors. First, advances in medicine and domestic technology enabled Europeans to survive in areas where disease and an unhealthy climate had previously made life either precarious or extremely uncomfortable. Secondly, the invention of the machine-gun meant that the native population could no longer effectively resist a properly equipped European expedition. Indeed the explorer, Henry Stanley, with characteristic sensitivity, described the Maxim gun as 'a bringer of civilisation to Africa'. Thirdly, the telegraph was rapidly joining the extremities of the world, which meant that governments could confer freely with their agents overseas and take more rapid action. Lastly, improvements in ships reduced the time taken by supplies and reinforcements to reach European settlements and expeditions overseas. The sailing time between Britain and Australia, via the Cape, was reduced from 83 days in the 1850s to 42 in the 1890s.

A surprising proportion of the areas annexed in these years had little apparent economic value, issues of national prestige playing a considerable role in their acquisition. Many of these regions were without valuable resources, which meant that they were not only unproductive and unattractive to settlers, but they did not possess the purchasing power to be useful as markets. Nor could financiers see any hope of return on capital invested there. Britain's continental neighbours, however, had long been witnesses – and victims – of Britain's belief in the value of her empire, especially India. They were all too conscious of Britain's jealous concern for her routes to India and the

East, for Britain's hold on the Cape and Suez made her extremely suspicious of any European activity in the regions bordering on these gateways to her eastern markets. This perhaps tended to encourage a feeling among the European powers that these African regions were of value in themselves as recognised status symbols, if nothing else. But the vast majority of these annexations can only be understood in terms of the preoccupations of the European power concerned.

A number of overseas territories were, however, of demonstrable economic value; and the search for markets in this period (see pp. 73-4) cannot be entirely ruled out as an encouragement to annexation. Not only was economic competition growing, but more countries were developing navies of their own. This meant that existing commercial relations between European merchants and independent native communities were being threatened by interlopers from other European countries; and it was therefore arguable that only by annexing the community or establishing a protectorate over it could a European country guarantee its trade relations with it. Nevertheless governments were in general reluctant to annex unless there were pressing reasons. The expense of administering overseas territories was considerable, and might also involve the granting of diplomatic compensation to other interested powers. 'The cabinet do not want any more niggers' was Lord Kimberley's phrase in 1884; but it might have been said by any European statesman of the period. Yet the fact remains that the annexations took place.

The attitude of missionaries varied with circumstance. If they met opposition from the natives, they were generally glad to have government support in the form of annexation. On the other hand, if the natives were docile, and the behaviour of Europeans was expected to be disruptive or corrupting, the missionaries generally preferred no intervention. How far their views were respected by governments depended on how far they came into line with the government's own wishes and whether the missionaries could command a powerful section of public opinion.

Running parallel with the varied relationships between

missionaries and governments were the similar relationships between missionaries and merchants. The old phrase, 'trade and the bible follow the flag', has tended to be recast as 'the flag follows trade and the bible'. But although the twin spearheads of advance into new territory have often been trade and the bible, these have often been in conflict. Understandably so, since trade is ultimately concerned with coming to the most profitable terms with the native population, whereas missionaries have been anxious to convince the natives of their human dignity and the equality of all men before God. These two aims, however, do not necessarily conflict – and it is possible to maintain that they have been complementary. As one writer rather glibly put it 'The missionary has no sooner made the savage ashamed of his nakedness than the trader is there to clothe him'.

TABLE 6

The economics of colonialism

	British (dependent empire only) 1909–13	French (including Magreb) 1910	German 1911	Dutch 1910	Belgian 1910
Percentage of home country's exports to colonies	15%	10%	·6%	4·5%	·7%
Percentage of colonies' imports from home country	43%	61%	25%	44%	77%
Percentage of home country's imports from colonies	11%	8%	·4%	15%	18%
Home country's balance of trade with colonies (£ millions)	+£5·7 m	even	+£·4 m	−£31·6 m	−£2·2 m
Surplus or deficit on administration of colonies (£ millions)	+£2·1 m (incl. milit.)	−£15·1 m (incl. milit.)	−£3·5 m (excl. milit.)	−£3 m (incl. milit.)	−£·2 m (incl. milit.)
Percentage of colonies' exports to home country	27%	63%	35%	75%	48%

(Based on information in *The Statesman's Year-Book*)

To take a final look at the economics of colonialism, the figures in Table 6, drawn from *The Statesman's Year-Book* for those years, put the matter in a contemporary light. Although modern research has somewhat modified these figures, they represent what was readily available to contemporaries. Obviously they do not answer the perennial question: 'Did colonies pay?' The fact that a mother-country had a trade deficit with her colonies could be partly offset by other considerations. It might be that they provided her with produce that was vital to her economy and which would have cost more to import from an independent territory. Similarly trade figures need to be seen in the context of investment and overall military, naval and 'diplomatic' expenditure. For example, Britain's expensive policies in the eastern Mediterranean were part of the price she paid for her empire east of Suez. Nevertheless, despite their inconclusiveness, these figures showed contemporaries that overseas imperialism was no easy road to riches.

CHAPTER THREE

Mütterlich und Militärisch

Germany

AS OTHERS SAW THEM

Foreign visitors are usually intent on noting differences rather than resemblances. And their perceptions by their very sharpness may often result in their leaving with a somewhat unbalanced overall impression. Judging from memoirs and travel books, the visitor to Germany found a country that seemed remarkably divided between male and female spheres, of influence. On the one hand there was the *mütterlich* atmosphere of the home, apparent in varying degrees at all levels of society. To Latin or even Anglo-Saxon eyes, middle- and upper-class German women appeared large and unfashionable. They were simply but comfortably dressed, and apparently always eating; there was no time of day when the rich cakes and pastries would not make an appearance. It was a tired but not unjustified cliché that the three K's seemed the very foundation of their existence: *Kinder, Kirche, Küche*, children, the church and the kitchen. Even the *Federbett* which covered the sleeper at night seemed a capacious sublimation of the *Hausfrau* who owned it. At the same time many German middle-class homes were full of embroidered or poker-work salutations and exhortations to the visitor. A French visitor to a German professor's house counted no less than forty-three; even in the bathroom and beyond 'one never felt alone'.

The outside world by contrast seemed to be the man's domain, where women were expected to accept their inferiority by keeping quiet or acquiescing in what the menfolk said. This was true to some extent of all nations, but it appeared more marked in Germany than in most western countries. Compared with his wife, the middle- and upper-class German, who followed fashion, chose to be tightly dressed with almost military discomfort. The army officer was the prototype of what the ideal German was considered to be; and it seemed to many foreign observers that even the middle-class male affected a military superiority towards working-class people. It should be remembered that the German system of universal conscription meant that most upper-class and a considerable number of middle-class civilians were reserve officers. Only a nobleman could expect to make a career in the guards or cavalry, but the possibility of full-scale war obliged Germany to train large numbers of middle-class officers; indeed in the artillery and engineers, where technical expertise was essential, nearly all the officers were middle-class. Moreover a large number of the teachers in the *Gymnasien* (boys' grammar schools) were reserve officers, with the result that respect for the army was systematically instilled into German middle-class youth. It was also a sad fact that many of the intelligentsia tended to accept with docility the national cult of the officer and all he represented. In a nation that owed its being to blood and iron, this was perhaps not surprising. At the same time the military virtues and the cult of convivial conformity were deep-rooted in the German tradition. It has indeed been argued that in earlier centuries they were a condition of survival. Schools and universities made much of their uniforms and ritual. Duelling and beer-swilling (literally *ad nauseam*) were an integral part of the life of the better-known student fraternities. All in all there was much that might strike a foreigner as primitive and pagan in the German concept of masculinity – even allowing for the fact that responsibility and marriage generally softened the more extreme vestiges of youthful arrogance.

On the other hand, certain aspects of English public-school life might have made a not dissimilar impression on a French visitor, while moving eastward masculine attitudes in Russia contained much that would strike us as barbaric. It was also true that even the most forbidding German male was rarely as inflexible as his outward behaviour suggested. Indeed, anyone who doubts the Wilhelmine German's capacity for compassion and human feeling might usefully read some of the letters and autobiographies that the period produced. Similarly, although it is dangerous to use fiction as evidence, the novels of Thomas Mann and of other close observers of their times depict a society that had an ample share of warmth and understanding.

THE CAKE IN SLICES — THE SOCIAL OUTCOME

This, however, was a world that impinged on the majority of the nation only through the intermediaries of factory foremen, farm bailiffs and N.C.O.s. Conversely, everyone was vaguely aware of the demographic changes outlined in Table 7. For

TABLE 7

	1871	1914
Population	41 million	68 million
Proportion in towns over 2,000	c. 31%	c. 60%
Industrial working day in practice	12–13 hours	9–10 hours

Occupations

	1871	1907
Agriculture and forestry	47·3%	34%
Industry	32·8%	39·1%
Commerce	9%	13·9%
Public service	} 10·9%	6·6%
Domestic service		6·4%
Proportion of peasant land-holders	c. 20–25%	
Working on family-held land	c. 50%	
Landless labourers	c. 25–30%	
Proportion of land held by primogeniture or similar custom	c. 80%	

those in urban occupations, what mattered most about the period was that real wages rose by about a third – though this was still a smaller rise than in France and Britain, where real wages rose by about two-thirds and three-quarters respectively. Furthermore German wages started from a lower base, the average urban wage in the 1870s being only two-thirds of that

D

in France and only half of that in Britain. Nevertheless on retirement they could look forward to a government-guaranteed pension which in the case of the lower-paid workers was equivalent to just under a third of their former wages (law of June 1889), Britain and France following suit only some twenty years later. They were also assured of government-guaranteed sick-pay and accident compensation (laws of June 1883 and July 1884) in which the worker paid a total of about 2 per cent of his wage in premiums, while the employer met the rest of the expense. The old-age pensions were moreover supplemented with a government subsidy.

Fig. 6 *Real earnings in German industry, 1871–1910 (1871=100)*

These figures represent weekly real earnings and do not take account of the shortening working week. Had they been calculated on the basis of the hourly wage-rate, the rise would have been about 6 per cent higher by the end of the period.

1. The fall in weekly real earnings between 1875 and 1879 reflects short-time working during the recession, and reductions in monetary wages in certain industries.

2. The rise in the years 1882–96 reflects both rising monetary wages and a fall in the cost of living.

3. The gradual rise 1896–1913, despite the mounting cost of living, reflects an increase in monetary wages, due to a better organised labour movement and the readiness of the employers to pay more, in the light of growing prosperity.

Although working hours were shortening, there was no legal guarantee of these hours (except for women and children), the law merely assuring one day off in seven (July 1890). Accommodation was a desperate problem, as was reflected in the fact that in 1871 a tenth of Berlin's population was living in what were termed 'cellars' with four to five people in each; while even at the turn of the century 45 per cent of Berlin dwellings contained two rooms or less. Unemployment nevertheless remained low, averaging well below 3 per cent after 1886.

For the peasantry, there was not the constant reduction in the size of holdings that occurred in France – largely because of the inheritance laws (see Table 7) and the expansion of industry. West of the Elbe, most holdings were between ten and fifty acres, these accounting for 40 per cent of the soil in 1907. East of the Elbe, however, the large estates prevailed, over 40 per cent of the land being occupied by estates of over 250 acres. As elsewhere, the peasantry suffered from the competition of cheap imported grain (see pp. 65–7) which caused grain prices to drop by a quarter despite protective tariffs. In consequence the landless labourer's wages fell even further behind those of the urban worker, his only benefit in these years being social insurance (laws of May 1886 and July 1911).

Another dismal truth of the period was that most Germans spent three years of their lives in the regular army[1] though very few were killed. The subjugation of the Herrero revolt in South-West Africa (1904–8) involved several thousand losses (as against tens of thousands of native casualties); but otherwise the only fighting that the German army saw was limited to minor skirmishes in Africa and China. Nevertheless this saving of life was soon to be forgotten in the four years after 1914, when nearly six million Germans would be killed or wounded. Army discipline was harsh; corporal punishment remained a part of it throughout the period (though it might perhaps be remembered that it is still part of the penal system in the Isle of Man; while as late as 1960 a French newspaper could carry the intriguing headline: 'le chat à neuf queues conserve les faveurs du public

[1] Two years between July 1893 and January 1913.

britannique'.) The German conscript had at least the consolation
of being stationed in his home region, which meant that he
could still maintain contact with his family and friends, as well
as follow up adolescent romances. Soldiers also tended to be
better behaved in regions where they were known by the local
people.

Standards of living varied considerably from state to state,
the differences being as great, if not greater, than that between
a Kentish farmer and a Galway peasant. Nor were economic
resources the whole answer, for the progressive states were not
always the richest, as literacy figures showed. Germany in fact
had a higher literacy level than any other country, only 2·5 per
cent of army recruits in the 1870s being classified as illiterate.
Much of the credit for this lay with the initiative of reforming
rulers in Prussia, Bavaria and other states in the eighteenth and
early nineteenth centuries. But the achievement of the 1870–
1914 period was to spread literacy from the 'enlightened'
German states to others – for a poor backward state like
Mecklenburg-Schwerin was two-thirds illiterate in the 1870s.

For the capitalist class, the period was one of remarkable
prosperity, for although the gross national product per head of
population had more than doubled, the real wages of their
workers had only increased by a third. It is true that the
mounting cost of maintaining expensive machinery was an off-
setting factor, and it is true that taxation per head had increased;
but the balance that was going into the owners' and shareholders' pockets was much greater in 1913 than in the 1870s.
Despite this, there was discontent among them – a feeling that
control of German affairs in many spheres still eluded them.
They were well aware that they were reaping the material
profits of a prosperous period, but they had a strong conviction
that their prosperity might have been greater if they had had a
greater control over government. The importance of this discontent must not be exaggerated, for Germany had no democratic tradition, and the middle class mostly shared the German
respect for hierarchy and faith in the 'qualified' man (be he a
Professor, scientist or nobleman destined to rule by upbringing).
It was, however, precisely this belief in the 'qualified' man

which made many of them question the ability of the noble ministers to run government in an age of economic sophistication. Indeed their misgivings were to find full justification in 1914, when most businessmen felt that war would disrupt the international network of trade without bringing definite economic advantage. Although the Franco-Prussian War had brought an overwhelming economic profit to Germany, businessmen as a whole had only indirectly shared in these gains, and as individuals many had suffered from the disruption of trade and the resultant growth of American competition. Another war seemed scarcely to offer better prospects, and understandably many felt their political helplessness. How could they in the last resort preserve their interests against the irresponsible actions of the government?

Nevertheless, they had a share in the feeling of well-being that characterised leisured society in the last years of the Wilhelmine Empire. This was a period of enjoyment for the leisured which had its counterpart in Edwardian England and the French *Belle Époque*; but it holds perhaps a legendary significance in German memories by the contrast it presented to what was to follow in the next twenty years. Its character may now seem autumnal, but at the time must have seemed like early summer. Indeed had it not been for the war, such a feeling could well have been justified. Businessmen might mutter about transatlantic competition, but the German economy was likewise in the ascendant; and only the war was to give America the enormous lead that she was to have in exports.

It has been argued that the reign of Wilhelm II (1890–1918) was less productive in the arts than any equivalent number of years in the previous century. This is perhaps to take too musical a view of the arts – though since music was Germany's main gift to the world this is understandable. Yet some of Thomas Mann's finest work was written in the years before the war; and although few people realised it at the time this period was perhaps most notable for Germany's contribution to painting and architecture, Klee (Swiss-born) and Walter Gropius being explorers from whom other countries had much to learn. In music, however, it must be admitted that the finest German creations belonged to the pre-1890 period. The first decades of the German Empire had been marked by the later works of Wagner and Brahms, these themselves representing the final flowering of the great Romantic movement that had dominated German musical life from the first half of the century. But the post-1890 period had Richard Strauss, the last great German Romantic; and indeed in its swagger and sentiment his music is a splendid evocation of the ebullience of the last years of the Wilhelmine Empire. It has the benevolence that comes with a seven-course meal; and it was to the music of *Der Rosenkavalier* (1911) that the leisured society of Europe waltzed in the last three years before war ended an opulent era.

For the aristocracy the period was not one of enormous change. The material position of the lower and especially the middle classes had improved markedly; yet this had been achieved mainly through increased national prosperity, rather than at the expense of the former ruling classes. The abolition of feudalism had been effected in most German states well before 1850, the period after 1870 seeing no significant alteration in the relationship between landlord and tenant. The competition of foreign grain, however, had a serious effect on the income of landowners, with the result that society was beginning to realise that financial power and entertainment could be offered on a much more lavish scale by the new 'captains of industry'. Nevertheless the higher levels of the Imperial administration and the Prussian administration were still largely staffed by products of the Prussian landed aristocracy; and even in 1914 the aristocracy still exercised an influence on government out of all proportion to their economic strength. This mainly reflected the preferences of the Imperial government; but it also sprang from the fact that electoral divisions had not been changed since 1871. The rural areas were over-represented, while the Prussian landowners could generally count on the votes of their peasantry.

The sovereign families of the twenty-five individual German states were almost numerous enough to deserve treatment as a virtual class on their own; and the limitations which Imperial rule put on their autonomy are dealt with below. The more romantic of them could derive nostalgic joy from the fact that their troops, though part of the Imperial army, still declared allegiance to them; indeed most of the kings, grand dukes and princes soon reconciled themselves to the facts of 1871. Ludwig II of Bavaria is best remembered as the eccentric patron of Wagner and builder of dream castles, literally in the clouds. Bismarck had partially brought Ludwig's consent to the Empire with a pension of £20,000 a year, which Ludwig had promptly invested in the building of his latest project. At the same time the rulers of the lands of the younger branch of Reuss continued to exploit their properties, which covered a major part of the state, while cherishing the Reuss tradition of naming all their male offspring Heinrich, with the result that they had to refer to them by numbers. To make conversation possible, a reversion to the figure 1 was always made at the turn of the century. Thus the reigning prince in this period (who was born in 1832), was Heinrich XIV, but his father and predecessor, born in the eighteenth century, had been Heinrich LXVII. In short, the German ruling families were an interesting menagerie – even if they undoubtedly helped to demonstrate the political bankruptcy of the idea of hereditary monarchy.

MAKING THE CAKE – THE ECONOMIC FACTORS

Every good cake has its cook; and he is often a perspiring figure, stripped to the waist, in a malodorous kitchen – for creating wealth is rarely an aesthetic experience. Germany's relative strength in the European economy and the rate of her growth have already been described (see Chapter 2). Yet it is worth remembering that it was only about mid-century that this industrial giant experienced what economic historians call 'the take-off into sustained growth'.

German industry was aided by rich natural resources and a plentiful supply of labour. The third ingredient, capital, was initially procured from abroad with the help of progressive bankers, to be replenished later with Germany's own profits. At the same time an intensive programme of railway-building linked industry with markets, fuel and raw material. Railways running east–west were particularly important in a country where most of the rivers run northwards to the only coastline, and where southern frontiers were hedged around with high mountains.[1] Already in 1871 Germany produced three times the French amount of coal and lignite – though this was still less than a third of British production. By 1913, in fact, German production was nearly seven times that of France and nearly as great as that of Britain. The acquisition of Lorraine moreover brought Germany large deposits of phosphoric iron-ore which the Thomas and Gilchrist process released for steel-making a few years later (see p. 67). Indeed by 1913 Lorraine was providing three-quarters of Germany's ore-production, which itself totalled nearly twice the British quantity; while concurrently German salt, potash and other deposits helped to contribute to her lead in the chemical industry.

It is worth remembering, however, that although the German chemical industry led the world, it still only employed 3 per cent of her industrial workers in 1913.[2] In reality Germany's pre-eminence here was won in the 1870s, resulting from several factors. First, unlike Britain, France and Belgium, Germany had little money invested in the early techniques of chemical production. Secondly, she had the good fortune to have extensive mineral deposits; while thirdly – and often overlooked – she had managed to acquire remarkably qualified personnel. At all levels the German educational system gave a much sounder grounding in science, one of the many results being that Germany possessed a working-class élite with sufficient scientific training to provide the chemical industry with competent foremen and lower-grade supervisors. Indeed the proliferation of German names in the annals of scientific discovery owed much to German education in the nineteenth century. It also contributed to the growth of the electrical industry, which the Siemens family had so spectacularly pioneered in the second half of the century.

One of the distinctive features of German industrial expansion

---

[1] In 1876 Bismarck took advantage of the economic slump of 1873–4 to push a law through the Prussian Landtag (see p. 110) authorising him to buy the Prussian railways (which belonged to seventy different companies). Other states followed Prussia's example, until by 1913 only a twentieth of Germany's railways were still privately owned. Bismarck would have liked to bring the various state railways under direct Imperial control; but the hostile attitude of the Bundesrat (see p. 110) discouraged him from attempting it.

[2] As compared with a fifth in the metal industry and a sixth in textiles and allied industries.

after 1873 was the active part played by joint-stock banks in organising issues of industrial shares. With contacts throughout the financial world, their respectability and large reserves inspired confidence in buyers and did much to encourage German investment in home industry. At the same time the banks themselves also invested an unusually large proportion of their reserves in German industry – with the result that by the end of the period, a leading bank might be represented on the boards of well over a hundred companies. This itself helps to account for the remarkable number of Jews on the boards of the major companies; by 1913 they held a quarter of the seats.

Turning to business organisation, legal changes in the 1870s had opened the way for the formation of *Kartelle* (see p. 72). The most notable monsters that this movement spawned were the Rheinisch-Westfälisches Kohlensyndikat (1893) and the Stahlwerksverband which by 1913 controlled over half of Germany's coal production and three-quarters of her steel. Indeed after initial uncertainty the Imperial government came to recognise that the financial resilience of cartels enabled them to keep a higher number of men continuously employed than could a multitude of smaller firms; so by 1910, the government was favouring their formation.

In the matter of commerce Germany had followed a relatively liberal trade policy, despite the opposition of manufacturers; but the crisis of 1873 (see pp. 75–6) made protectionist interests more vociferous. In 1874 industrialists formed the Association of German Steel Producers to combat foreign industrial imports, while foreign grain imports caused landowners to form the Association of Tax and Economic Reformers in 1876. Opposing them, however, the textile and chemical manufacturers were afraid that duties on grain imports would lead to dearer food and a consequent demand for wage increases, while the Bremen and Hamburg merchants feared retaliation by other countries. One of the secondary considerations that encouraged Bismarck to come down on the side of protection was the fact that tariffs were one of the few available sources of income that the Imperial government had at its disposal, since most other taxes went into the treasuries of

*

individual states. Nevertheless the benefits for the Imperial treasury turned out to be limited, in that the Centre Party (see p. 113) insisted that the 1879 tariff bill allow revenue over £1 million to be redistributed among the states.

As in most Continental countries, the following decades were to witness a marked if uneven rise in tariffs, especially on grain. Although wheat prices fell in Germany, as elsewhere, the effect of the duties was to keep wheat prices a quarter higher than those in Britain – whereas in the seventies German wheat had been slightly cheaper than British wheat. Inevitably the interests of farmers and manufacturers collided, especially in the early nineties when grain tariffs were modified to accommodate foreign growers who bought German industrial goods (see pp. 118–19 for the sequel).

By 1913 the pattern of German trade was that of a highly developed capitalist economy. Exporting a fifth of her total produce (67 per cent of it finished goods), Germany was likewise a heavy exporter of capital (see p. 69) as well as an international carrier, banker and insurance-broker. The result was that she could afford to import more goods (£538 million) than she exported (£505 million), and still have nearly £30 million in hand, after the balance had been met from her 'invisible' exports (about £65 million).[1]

No one could doubt that Germany was rich. In his portrayal of Hamburg at the turn of the century, Thomas Mann evokes the atmosphere of a prosperous port in a prosperous country.

This great seaboard city: this reeking air, compact of good living and a retail trade that embraced the four corners of the earth. The exhalations from water, coals, and tar, the sharp tang in the nostrils from heaped-up stacks of colonial produce; the huge steam-cranes at the dock-side imitating the quiet, the intelligence, and the giant strength of elephants at work, as they hoisted tons of sacks, bales, chests, vats, and carboys out of the bowels of seagoing ships and conveyed them into waiting trains and scales; the

---

[1] Her best customers were Russia, France and Britain, followed by Latin America and the Ottoman Empire. In fact the eve of the First World War found her conducting six times more trade with her future adversaries than with her future allies. Her heaviest foreign investment was in Latin America (16 per cent), North America (16 per cent) and Austria-Hungary (12 per cent).

business men, in yellow rubber coats streaming to the Bourse at mid-day, where, there was oftentimes pretty sharp work, and a man might have to strengthen his credit at short notice by giving out invitations to a big dinner. . . . Besides it all, there was . . . the confusion of the yards, the mammoth bodies of great ships, Asiatic and African liners, lying in drydock, keel and propeller bare, supported by props as thick as treetrunks, lying there in monstrous helplessness, swarmed over by troops of men like dwarfs, scouring, whitewashing, hammering; there were the roofed-over ways, wrapped in wreaths of smoke-like mist, holding the towering frames of rising ships, among which moved the engineers, blue-print and loading scale in hand, directing the work-people. All these were familiar sights to [the merchant's son] from his youth upwards, awaking in him only the agreeable, homely sensations of 'belonging', . . . Such sensations would reach their height when he sat of a Sunday forenoon . . . breakfasting on hot cuts and smoked meat, with a glass of old port; or when, having eaten, he would lean back in his chair and give himself up to his cigar. For therein especially was he true to type, that he liked good living, and . . . clung to the grosser pleasures of life as a greedy suckling to its mother's breast.[1]

CUTTING THE CAKE — PRESSURE AND POLITICS

The chief beneficiaries of this economic expansion were un-doubtedly the middle class. Yet the working classes also had some share, the size of the portion that each class received clearly depending on the means of pressure at its disposal, and how it used them.

Collective action

As in other countries the workers' power was essentially of three kinds. First, economic and direct, consisting of strikes and the threat of strikes. Secondly, political and indirect, consisting of the possibility of achieving legislation through lobbying and electoral activity. And thirdly, political and direct: namely the use of violence.[2]

---

[1] *The Magic Mountain*, trans. H. T. Lowe-Porter (Penguin, 1960) p. 30.
[2] Some readers may prefer at this stage to take a preliminary look at the constitutional framework of the Empire (pp. 109–12).

The industrial code of 1869, which the Empire took over from the North German Confederation, permitted industrial workers to form unions; but they could not compel their fellow-workers to join, nor could they put pressure on them to strike. The police kept a close watch on the unions, and took advantage of Bismarck's anti-Socialist law of 1878 (see p. 115) to threaten them with dissolution if they attempted effective industrial action. Indeed the prevailing attitude still considered that it was the employer's right to fix wages and working conditions, since he owned the means of production. So it was not until the turn of the century that the German unions began to be recognised in practice as legitimate bodies with whom employers might come to collective agreements; nor was it until after the First World War that this change received legal confirmation. The nature of the unions themselves was part cause, part outcome, of this situation. There was no strong unified union movement which could provide a focus for working-class effort. The unions were divided into broad political and religious divisions, calling themselves 'Liberal', 'Socialist' or 'Christian', and thereby leaving to the workers in each industry a choice of several unions, none of which was sufficiently strong or representative to meet the employers on equal terms.

The first important group of unions to come into being was the Liberal Deutsche Gewerkvereine, or Hirsch-Duncker unions, dating from 1868, which had links with the Liberal Fortschrittspartei. Their aim being to achieve improvement through co-operation with the employers, their number rose only slowly from 10,000 in the early 1870s, to about 113,000 in 1913. A much more dynamic group, however, was the Sozialistische Gewerkschaften, which had close ties with the Social Democrat party, basing its standpoint on the concept of the class struggle. Bismarck's anti-Socialist law of 1878 hit them just as their membership was touching 50,000, forcing them to lead a clandestine existence until 1890. By 1914 their membership was over 2·8 million. These unions shared the anticlericalism of the Social Democrats, with the result that at the turn of the century Catholics decided to form their own unions, the Christliche Gewerkschaften, with a membership of 371,000 by 1913. Like the Liberal unions, they believed in improvement through co-operation with the employers. Nevertheless by 1914 these three groups of unions had only 3·28 million members between them (less than an eighth of the working population).

Like the majority of working men, the unions in practice preferred piecemeal achievements to the apocalyptic vision of the general strike preached by Social Democrats. Indeed by 1906 the Social Democrats had given up their attempt to exercise a controlling influence.

The main achievement of the unions in this period was to have helped obtain a reduction of the average working day by three hours and a rise in real wages of a third. But these were practical improvements that had no legal guarantee. The question therefore arises as to whether working-class political pressure on the Imperial and state parliaments was weaker than their economic pressure on employers.

The regime

German politics were complicated by the divisions of power between the Imperial and individual state governments. The Imperial constitution of April 1871 was an adaptation of the 1867 constitution of the North German Confederation, which had been enlarged to hold a total of twenty-five states. The states in fact kept their traditional autonomy except on the following crucial issues. Individual states were not free to secede from the Empire, while foreign affairs were in the hands of the Imperial government. Their armies, moreover, were at the sole disposal of the Imperial government, the states having to adopt Prussian military legislation including conscription.[1] The Imperial government likewise had complete control over foreign trade and the adjustment of tariffs, while there were also to be standard legal codes. By contrast although certain Imperial taxes provided revenue for the Imperial government, the bulk of taxation was the affair of the individual states. Should the Imperial government run a deficit, the states were to make it up with a *pro rata* payment; though by the twentieth

[1] Bavaria, Württemberg and Saxony retained a certain amount of autonomy in military matters.

century these deficits were so large that the Imperial government was regularly resorting to loans.

The Reichstag or lower house of the Imperial parliament was
elected directly by universal male suffrage, and by secret ballot
which was the price Bismarck had been obliged to pay for the
support of the National Liberals in 1867. Like so many other
conservatives in the nineteenth century, he had previously
hoped that universal suffrage in an *open* poll would create a
solid phalanx of peasant votes for the landlords to command;
and Bismarck now felt out of pocket. With secret voting, the
Imperial system was certainly much more democratic than the
various systems of electing state legislatures. Even in Prussia the
fact of a wide franchise was weakened by the three-class method
of election; while in the wind-swept Baltic duchies of Mecklenburg–Schwerin and Mecklenburg–Strelitz, the legislative was
a largely feudal body, consisting of the proprietors of knights'
estates, supplemented with a few municipal delegates, nearly all
of them burgomasters. This contrast between the Imperial
system and that of the more backward states was a major factor
in encouraging constitutional reform in the states. Even in 1914,
however, a majority of the state constitutions were less democratic in character than the Imperial regime; and in the case of
Mecklenburg–Schwerin the knights persistently opposed attempts to institute constitutional government.

The Bundesrat or Federal Council of the second Reich
consisted of delegates of the various state governments, it being
in this assembly that the individual states had the best chance of
asserting themselves. Prussia held two-thirds of the German
population, this giving her 236 seats out of 382 in the Reichstag;
but in the Bundesrat she had only 17 seats out of 58 – Bavaria
having six, and the others less, according to size. But for Prussia
to be outvoted it required an identity of views between a considerable number of states. Nevertheless the Bundesrat did
periodically succeed in defending what the state rulers conceived to be their interests, the most notorious example being
its defeat of the Reichstag's proposal that every state be obliged
to have a parliamentary constitution. By contrast the Reichstag
was essentially a democratic body, not primarily concerned with
state rights except in so far as particular parties chose to make

state rights a matter of concern. Indeed the growing tendency in Reichstag debates was for the vertical rivalries of states to be submerged by the horizontal conflicts of class interests.

Nevertheless the democratic election of the Reichstag did not of itself guarantee democratic Imperial government. In theory the Emperor could retain the same Chancellor indefinitely, no matter how many times his measures might be rejected by the Reichstag; though had a legislative deadlock of this kind occurred, there would presumably have had to be either a dissolution of the Reichstag or a dismissal of the Chancellor. Unlike Republican France, however, there was no necessity for the Chancellor to resign if an important measure of his was defeated.

At the same time the Chancellor's position was indirectly strengthened by the fact that he was also Minister-President of Prussia, his personal stature being increased by the fact that the Imperial Chancellor had no Imperial ministers as such – only heads of departments who were directly responsible to him, and not to parliament. Yet the dependence of the Chancellor himself on the Emperor's goodwill is often underestimated. The Emperor was 'my only constituent', as Bismarck was forever telling his parliamentary critics. Wilhelm I had first called on Bismarck to break a constitutional deadlock in 1862, regarding him thereafter as indispensable. Bismarck, however, was entirely reliant on the Emperor's esteem, and could not afford to displease him unnecessarily. He had risked this esteem in January 1871 when he forced on Wilhelm the title 'German Emperor', with its vague presidential ring, instead of 'Emperor of Germany', which would have offended the princes. As Bismarck remarked: 'The imperial delivery was a difficult one; and kings – like women – have strange longings at such times, before they bring into the world what they cannot keep to themselves'. Bismarck's dismissal by Wilhelm II in 1890 was to show how vulnerable he was.

As the German economy became more industrialised, so the nature of German government became more anachronistic. The fact that the Chancellor was not primarily the representative of a parliamentary majority meant that he often had to cajole or hoodwink the Reichstag into authorising those measures that could not be enacted by the executive alone. It likewise encouraged the government to bypass parliament as much as possible, especially when the Reichstag became increasingly intractable in the later years of Wilhelm II. Conversely it also encouraged the various sectors of society to bypass parliament in their attempts to make some impression on the executive. Under Wilhelm II the representatives of big business found it more rewarding to appeal directly to the Kaiser's cronies, rather than attempt to achieve their ends through parliamentary pressure. In this way the chances of achieving a proper parliamentary system were betrayed by the very elements that were best fitted to bring it about. Their position was nevertheless far from easy. They all had to compete with the military and naval entourage of the Kaiser, while those who were Jews were inhibited in taking effective political action in a society which regarded them as outsiders.

Bismarck at the helm

Mr A. J. P. Taylor describes Bismarck as 'a big man, made bigger by his persistence in eating and drinking too much'. 'Yet . . . when he spoke, his voice, which one would have expected to be deep and powerful, was thin and reedy – almost a falsetto.' Although he was only fifty-six when he became Imperial Chancellor, 'he looked and acted like an old man – and a shaky old man at that', and suffered much ill-health. 'This was largely due to the nervous irritation which grew on him all the time. But he also smoked too many cigars (at one time fourteen a day) and ate . . . a gigantic supper before going to bed. Then he would lie awake piling up grievances. He once announced: "I have spent *the whole night hating*"; and when he had no immediate object for his hate he would go back over the injuries of twenty or thirty years before.' 'In a life of conflict, he fought himself most of all. He said once: "Faust complains of having two souls in his breast. I have a whole squabbling crowd. It goes on as in a republic." '

The twenty years of Bismarck's Imperial rule were remarkable for five groups of measures that had a direct and farreaching effect on the lives of the population. There were first the social insurance laws of 1883–9; secondly, the series of protective tariffs beginning in 1879; thirdly, the anti-Socialist law of 1878 and thereafter; fourthly, the so-called *Kulturkampf* measures; and lastly the tight hold of the executive on the size of the annual conscription quota. It could at the same time also be argued that the major outcome of German politics in these years was that Bismarck was able to stay in power, exercising a moderating influence on international relations.

Bismarck's freedom of action in the 1870s was limited by two major considerations. First, his chief support came from the National Liberal Party, which approved of his unificatory policies, but differed from him in believing in parliamentary government and a minimum of state interference. He had little sympathy for them, especially the intellectuals. 'They always want to wash the fur without making it wet and so always turn in shame from any naked idea.' Secondly, the inclusion of the south German states had increased Germany's Catholic population to over a third of the whole, their interests being represented by Ludwig Windthorst's Centre Party, which stood for a wide degree of state independence in what was largely a Protestant Empire.[1]

Although a sincere Protestant, Bismarck's religion 'was far removed from . . . the humanitarian Christianity of the twentieth century. There was in it little love, except for his own family. He believed in the God of the Old Testament and of the English Puritans, the God of Battles. . . . He believed that he was doing God's work in making Prussia strong and unifying Germany' (A. J. P. Taylor). Only in this last sense can it be said that his own religious beliefs had any influence on his dealings with Catholicism. Bismarck hoped to take advantage of the pope's loss of temporal sovereignty to strike a bargain: Bismarck would offer the pope some measure of diplomatic support, in return for a papal agreement to muzzle the Centre Party. But Pius IX was not prepared to bargain. Accordingly Bismarck made what is generally regarded as his most serious mistake in domestic politics. He tried to browbeat the Church into submission by a series of étatist measures, on the assumption

---

[1] These denominational figures were of course purely 'official' and took no account of whether the people so described actually practised their particular religion.

that this would also meet with the approval of the Liberal parties and the Protestant Conservatives. Most of the measures in this *Kulturkampf* were confined to Prussia (notably Adalbert Falk's May laws of 1873), while on the Imperial level they brought certain welcome institutions such as civil marriage (February 1875). Nevertheless there was much that was harsh, notably the dissolution of various religious orders in Prussia (May 1875), the abolition of boys' seminaries, the expulsion of the Jesuits throughout the Empire (June 1872) and the imprisonment of bishops and priests who resisted the measures.

The results were sufficiently far-reaching for convinced Catholics never again to feel fully at home in the Empire. Indeed a greater proportion of the Catholic vote went to the Centre Party, which emerged yet stronger as the foremost opponent of Prussian centralising policies. At the same time most of the other parties were alarmed by the autocratic implications of the *Kulturkampf*, so much so that Bismarck began to scale it down from 1876.

The alliance between Bismarck and the National Liberals started to break over the question of parliamentary control over the size and financing of the army. Bismarck wanted a law which would authorise the executive to maintain in perpetuity a minimum peacetime army of 400,000 (without prejudicing its right to approach the Reichstag for more). The National Liberals, however, were only prepared to compromise as far as giving the Reichstag's authorisation for seven-year periods, instead of in perpetuity (April 1874). The Reichstag was thereby ensured of at least one burst of excitement every seven years, just as the French parliament could count on a trip to Versailles at similar intervals to elect the President.

The rift became yet more marked over the anti-Socialist law of 1878 and the tariffs of 1879. An attempt had been made on the Emperor's life in May 1878, which gave Bismarck the opportunity of introducing a bill repressing Socialist activities, a measure which the National Liberals refused to support. Luck, however, favoured Bismarck in the shape of a second attack on Wilhelm in June, Bismarck taking advantage of the public emotion to hold a general election (July 1878) in which, as he expected, the opponents of his anti-Socialist law lost a great deal of ground to the Conservatives. He was then able to get a large majority for a new bill (October 1878) which empowered the government to suppress Socialist meetings and newspapers. Politically the National Liberals had to count themselves as losers with the Socialists. The second attempt on Wilhelm prompted Bismarck to exclaim: 'Now I've got the scoundrels!' – 'Your Highness means the Social Democrats?' – 'No, the National Liberals.'

For the rest of his chancellorship, Bismarck looked to the Conservatives (in so far as he looked to anyone) as his principal *point d'appui* in the Reichstag. As opportunity offered, he made temporary bargains with other parties (even with the National Liberals – whose cohesion had been split by the tariff issue, see p. 105); but, as before, he was above party, his relations with them being largely governed by the tactical demands of getting a particular bill through parliament.

Bismarck was becoming progressively worried by the signs of working-class discontent, arising from the economic depression. Despite police repression, the Social Democrats had twelve successes in the 1877 and 1881 elections, and were to double this in 1884. Since his launching of economic protection, Bismarck no longer needed to be quite so cautious over state interventionist measures; indeed the answer to the social danger seemed to lie in a bold stroke to outdo the Social Democrats at their own game. The result was the social insurance laws of the 1880s (pp. 97–8) which Bismarck at the time ranked next to German unification as his finest achievement. 'Whoever has a pension for his old age is far more content and far easier to handle than one who has no such prospect. Look at the difference between a private servant and a servant in the chancellery or at court; the latter will put up with much more, because he has a pension to look forward to.' Indeed if Bismarck had had his way the government would have subsidised the sickness as well as the old-age benefits. The bills, however, were systematically hamstrung by the *laissez-faire* liberals, in the name of bourgeois concepts of 'liberty', so that it was only the support of the Centre Party and Protestant Conservatives that got them through.

Ironically enough the social question was one of the issues which led to the dismissal of Bismarck. After Wilhelm I died (March 1888), his son Friedrich III only survived him by three months, the Imperial crown passing to his own son, Wilhelm II (1888–1918). Wilhelm, like so many of the catastrophic figures in history, had much to recommend him as far as intelligence and good intentions were concerned. But he was volatile, and disastrously given to making statements without sufficient premeditation. In 1908 for example, a public outcry over Wilhelm's latest *gaffe* obliged Chancellor Bernhard von Bülow to press Wilhelm into agreeing to be more discreet.[1] Yet this did not prevent Wilhelm declaring in August 1910: 'Looking on myself as God's instrument, I shall go my way without regard to the ideas and opinions of the time.' Nevertheless this bold front barely concealed a basic inability to take a firm grasp of affairs, which was to prove disastrous in later years. Since the Chancellor ultimately depended on the Emperor rather than on the Reichstag, it was essential that the Emperor should be a person of firm judgement. Otherwise the only hope for Germany was a rapid evolution into full parliamentary democracy. Wilhelm was fortunate in having inherited Bismarck; but he found the older man's prestige and experience an embarrassing constraint, and he likewise felt that Bismarck was unnecessarily cautious in promoting German interests.

In January 1890 Bismarck tried to harshen the 1878 anti-Socialist law which was expiring. Wilhelm, however, was known to be unfavourably disposed to this – which further encouraged the Reichstag to refuse it. The result was a serious rift between Emperor and Chancellor which widened over an issue of constitutional procedure. Finally Wilhelm provoked Bismarck's resignation (March 1890).

---

[1] Ironically enough Wilhelm had submitted his unfortunate statement to Bülow before publication; but Bülow had neglected to read it.

No one at the helm

Wilhelm was left at the mercy of his own deficiencies. He had neither the ability to keep control himself, nor the judgement to know where best to seek good advice. Throughout his reign his interests and entourage were largely military and naval – with the result that he had a dangerous readiness to accept the opinions of men whose ability and experience were largely confined to the world of land and sea manœuvres. A diplomat of considerable charm, Count Philipp Eulenburg, was especially influential in encouraging him to assert his authority vis-à-vis the chancellor, a process that was unwittingly aided by Bismarck's successor, Georg von Caprivi (March 1890– October 1894) who made an honest attempt to decentralise the accumulated powers of the chancellor. Bernhard von Bülow (October 1900–July 1909) was eventually obliged to restrain Wilhelm, but his successor, Theobald von Bethmann-Hollweg (July 1909–July 1917) failed to exercise real control, and the significant decisions gradually began to depend on other people. Indeed his attitude and role during the international crisis of July 1914 is a striking example of this (see pp. 227–9); and the historian, like Berchtold (p. 229), is left wondering who controlled German policy. In an overall sense the answer was no one.

Wilhelm's reign is chiefly remembered for its repercussions on international relations. It also saw significant changes for the German population, however, well before these repercussions recoiled on to Germany. Lists make dull reading; but only a list of the government's measures, stripped of their political context, can clearly indicate the considerable cumulative achievement that they represent. These were notably: the extension and improvement of the social insurance system (July 1890, June 1899, April 1903, May 1911); the shortening of women's and children's working hours, and guaranteed Sunday rest for all workers (July 1890); improved factory inspection (June 1891); a temporary lowering of tariffs on imported grain (1892–1902); a reduction in military service to two years (July 1893) and a readiness to accept the Social Democrats as a real if unwelcome fact of respectable political life.

Wilhelm was genuinely anxious to improve working-class conditions, while Caprivi was glad enough to make use of this concern in building up a parliamentary majority that would vote for his other more genuine interests. Like Bismarck, Caprivi also intended to steal the Social Democrats' thunder. The lapse of the anti-Socialist law permitted the Social Democrats to emerge from clandestinity and eventually become in 1912 the largest single party in the Reichstag. The Bismarckian repression had driven the party leftwards from the moderate rather old-fashioned Gotha programme of 1875 to a predominantly Marxist position, which the party formally adopted at its Erfurt Congress (October 1891). However, the leaders of the Marxist majority were mainly theorists like August Bebel, with the result that the more practical 'revisionist' minority under Edward Bernstein were gradually able to persuade the party's Reichstag deputies to enter into tactical alliances with the bourgeois parties. Nevertheless their effect on the lives of the working class in this period was really limited to what the government was prepared to grant to outbid them, though this itself was far from negligible, and justification enough for the party's existence. It has to be admitted, however, that the growing strength of the Social Democrats in the Reichstag was a major factor in deciding the liberal parties to drop their demands for a more parliamentary regime.

Under Caprivi, industrialists were prepared to welcome the lower food prices brought about by his reduction in tariffs. But the land-owning Conservatives were alarmed both by the competition of foreign grain and by the reduction in military service. Wilhelm grew restless. Not only were his sympathies openly ranged with the Conservatives, but his attempts to exercise more control eventually led to Caprivi's resignation and the appointment of the elderly and pliable Prince Chlodwig von Hohenlohe-Schillingfürst (October 1894–October 1900). Hohenlohe, a former Bavarian premier, was a ghost from the past, and like most ghosts found it hard to make much impression on a country that had outgrown his traditional concept of what Germany should be. He vanished with the century, leaving Wilhelm to the slippery guidance of Bernhard von Bülow.

Bülow was chosen with an eye to his skill as a smooth conciliator, and in domestic affairs he amply lived up to his nickname of 'the Eel', his chancellorship being characterised by adroit dexterity rather than constructive overall policy. Even Alfred von Tirpitz's vast naval programme served little useful purpose, since it was suited neither to coastal defence nor to long-distance colonial protection. In the words of Mr A. J. P. Taylor, 'Nothing could better express the roaring spluttering energy of Germany, like a ship's propeller out of water, than this vast naval force, absorbing great quantities of economic power, engendering disastrous international friction, destined never to be used to any decisive purpose in war.' But the steel manufacturers were glad enough to have it, while Bülow bought the reluctant support of the landed Conservatives by restoring high grain tariffs (December 1902). However, it was precisely the same landed Conservative interests that drove Bülow to resign (July 1909), when they rejected his proposal for death-duties (the proceeds to go to the Imperial treasury).

The early chancellorship of his unhappy successor, Theobald von Bethmann-Hollweg (1909–17) is chiefly remembered for the increases in the size of the army (see p. 226) and the events leading to war (pp. 227–9).

A civil servant from . . . a family who had supplied the Hohen-zollerns with bureaucrats for generations . . . he was, without doubt, of higher private character than any of his predecessors. . . . All he lacked was any sense of power: and so it came about that this 'great gentleman' . . . became, through his very incapability, responsible for . . . crimes a good deal beyond Bismarck's record, all extremely distasteful to Bethmann, but all shouldered by his inexhaustible civil servant's conscience. . . . Bismarck . . . had been the rider and Germany the horse. Now Bethmann threw the reins on the horse's back.[1]

COLONIALISM

Germany's overseas empire of 15 million people was remarkably short-lived. It was founded in April 1884, when Bismarck declared the German private trading settlements at Angra

[1] A. J. P. Taylor, *The Course of German History* (Methuen, 1961) p. 182.

Pequena to be under German Imperial protection; and it disappeared in November 1918, when the last of the German colonies surrendered to the allies at the armistice.

Bismarck had long resisted suggestions from various quarters that Germany should acquire colonies. With unaccustomed refinement of simile, he likened the idea of Germany needing colonies to the hankering of a Polish nobleman for silks when he has not a shirt to his back; while on many occasions he was to reiterate that he was 'no man for colonies'. Indeed, with the intriguing exception of the years 1884 to 1885, this was an attitude which he consistently maintained. There is something almost dreamlike about 'the aberration' of those years. In eight months he acquired for Germany South-West Africa (August 1884), Cameroon and Togoland (October 1884), northern New Guinea (December 1884) and much of eastern Africa (May 1885). He must have seemed to some like the sober industrious farmer who suddenly makes off with a barmaid on market-day.

There are the simple explanations that assume that Bismarck wanted colonies for their intrinsic advantages. And there are the political and diplomatic explanations that seek to solve the mystery by seeing Bismarck's colonial activity as a mere adjunct to either his domestic or foreign policy. The political explanations point out that Bismarck dreaded the eventual accession of the Crown Prince Friedrich to the Imperial throne, since this would bring the Prince's friends, the liberal (and anti-colonial) Deutschfreisinnigepartei, to power – which would mean his own political downfall. To discredit them in the elections of 1884, it is claimed that Bismarck built up a jingoist feeling in the electorate which would have the effect of putting the anti-colonial Deutschfreisinnigepartei in the embarrassing position of opposing a popular policy. It is true that this explanation plausibly fits in with the chronology and short duration of Bismarck's colonial activity; and it would seem to find some reflection in the electoral results themselves.

On the other hand, others have argued that Bismarck used the colonial issue as an instrument for establishing better relations with France, so reducing the danger of a French war of revenge. Given the rift between France and Britain over Egypt (1882) (see p. 216), they claim that Bismarck sought an ostensible quarrel with Britain which might induce France to look with a friendlier eye towards Germany. What Bismarck needed was an issue that would provoke Britain, but would not lead to a prolonged rupture. Angra Pequena was good in that it seemed to offer an indirect threat to Britain's position at the Cape and to her routes to India. On the other hand, it could not be taken so seriously as Russia's similarly 'diplomatic' advances in Central Asia (see pp. 169 and 217) which pointed towards India and were eventually to lead to a British threat of war.

An equally plausible variant on this diplomatic explanation is that Bismarck was primarily anxious to make Britain feel conscious of her isolation and more ready to fit in with his diplomatic plans. Like the political interpretation, these diplomatic explanations have the advantage of matching the chronology. They also have the testimony of a revealing statement by Bismarck: 'My map of Africa lies in Europe. Here lies Russia and here lies France, and we are in the middle. That is my map of Africa.' Whatever the truth – and the truth could be a mixture of all these – the colonies brought no economic advantage, and little prestige. Wilhelm II undoubtedly saw colonies, like navies, as a source of prestige. But Germany's pre-eminence on the Continent scarcely required the retention of these unimpressive stretches of sand and jungle. Their economic resources only covered three-quarters of their imports, while the administrative costs represented an annual drain of £3·5 million on the German exchequer (exclusive of military expenditure). Indeed until the discovery of diamonds in South-West Africa in 1908, the trade balance of the colonies had been much worse; and none of them was attractive to prospective settlers. Between 1884 and 1914 German colonies attracted scarcely more than 25,000 permanent settlers, while the United States took well over a million Germans.

As far as Germany's impact on the natives was concerned, the first years of the colonial period were particularly bad. Most of the colonies were initially administered by chartered companies which had little regard for the natives, who were simply expropriated. From the mid-1890s, however, various land laws were introduced which endeavoured to safeguard the natives' land and provide for their descendants, though in many areas the laws came too late or were difficult to enforce. In South-West Africa there was no restrictive legislation until 1910, with the result that by 1903 only a third of the land had been left to the natives. Moreover the Herrero rising of 1904–8 led to brutal suppression and the confiscation of further large tracts of land. Yet German colonial rule as a whole was probably no worse than in several other European colonies; and German justice, if harsh, was generally considered to be fair-dealing.

CHAPTER FOUR

La Belle Époque and Before

France

THE SOCIAL OUTCOME

It could well be argued that climate and past generations had endowed many Italians with a more pleasing environment than that enjoyed by the French. Yet there is no doubt that enjoyment of living was cared about in France with an intensity that had no rival elsewhere. The intellectual and cultural life of France in this period was more prolific and more stimulating than that of any country in the world; and a really good French meal came as near to heaven as anyone on this earth was likely to get. Even the less innocent pleasures of Paris could be offered with a refinement and sense of fantasy that softened their less commendable aspects. Although this *douceur de vivre* was within the means of only a small minority of the nation, nevertheless its fame and influence abroad meant that it was a formative influence in the lives of a large section of the upper and middle classes of Europe. No one who was culturally and financially equipped to taste what civilised life could offer could fail to be interested in France.

The blind spots of the French were as intriguing in their way as were their perceptions, and provoked endless questions in the visitor's mind. How was it that a nation that was so rich in intellectual achievement and the art of living should seem to have such difficulty in finding a satisfactory political system? How was it that a nation that prided itself on its humanity could permit the continuance of public executions well into the twentieth century? In an age when the Edwardians, for all their gastronomic philistinism and badly heated homes, enjoyed splendid sanitation, how was it that so many excellent French restaurants were equipped with *cabinets* that required of the user an insensitive nose and the leg-muscles of a gymnast? These were some of the many paradoxes that fascinated the Anglo-Saxon visitor.

For the French manual classes, however, this was a period when living conditions failed to match the superficial promise of France's longest spell of democratic government. In the 1870s just over half the population depended directly on agriculture, and of these nearly half were land-holders.

TABLE 8

	1871	*1906*
French population	36 million	39·8 million
Percentage in agriculture	52%	45%
Percentage of peasantry who		
were owners	30%	50%
Rent payers	13%	} 16%
Share croppers	5%	
Landless labourers	52%	34%

The hard-headed, tight-fisted peasant, tenaciously gripping his independence, was perhaps the most representative figure of nineteenth-century France. Shrewdly calculating to the point of meanness (or so his urban critics thought), his main indulgence was the evening meal and Sunday lunch. In the eighteenth century, British agriculture had undergone the enclosure movement, with its consequent consolidation of big estates and expropriation of the peasantry. France, on the other hand, had undergone the Revolution, with its fragmentation of large estates, much of the land being sold or handed over in small holdings to the peasantry. Furthermore the new inheritance laws stipulated the division of land between heirs – with the result that holdings became smaller and more numerous with the passing of each generation. Such holdings did not require hired labour, many of them barely supporting the owner and his family. The result was that the landless labourer was becoming progressively redundant. When work was available, the weekly wage of the landless labourer in the 1870s averaged about 12s 6d, as compared with about 15s in Britain, but part of this had to be put aside for the months when work was less plentiful. The income of the independent farmer is much more difficult to assess; but since three-quarters of the holdings were under 25 acres, most farmers made a very modest living. Small farms were unsuited to the labour-saving large-scale agricultural techniques that were used on the larger farms of Britain and east Germany, so production was low when compared with the time and effort put into it. However, in a country where the rural areas were already over-represented in parliament, the small farmers by their very numbers were able to exert strong pressure on government; and they were therefore able to obtain heavy protective tariffs against foreign grain imports.

It is true that the increase in peasant owners by 1906 (see Table 8) was to some extent the result of large landowners selling land and transferring their wealth to the Bourse and industry. But it was primarily a remarkable example of the effect of the inheritance laws in subdividing and increasing the number of holdings. The average size of holdings had been reduced by a quarter, despite the practice of younger sons selling their portion to the elder; and nearly nine-tenths of the holdings were now under 25 acres.

The French urban worker, despite his poverty, was superficially less of an inveterate calculator than the peasant or shopkeeper. Directly dependent on his manual skill, his success in life was more simply geared to work or lack of work; the far-sighted purchase or the stroke of luck played a much smaller part in his material fortunes. In most cases his mental agility found its best expression in his conversation and the assortment of imaginative nicknames that he gave to his friends. Often working for small family businesses, his *badinage* with the *patron* tended to give French society a deceptively democratic character, an impression that was likewise reflected in the inter-class *camaraderie* of the bistro.

Industry in the 1870s employed little more than a quarter of the population, weekly wages averaging about 22s 6d in Paris and 15s in the provinces – three-quarters of those in Britain. By 1900, however, real wages had probably risen by about two-thirds, the steepest rise occurring in the 1870s. At the same time the working day in the factories had been shortened in practice from about twelve hours in 1870 to ten or eleven in the 1890s, though it must be remembered that in the 1870s home industry still occupied a quarter of the manufacturing population, and here a fourteen- or fifteen-hour day was still quite common. As far as the law was concerned, a factory-owner could still in theory demand a twelve-hour day until March 1900, while it was not until June 1906 that Sunday was restored as a compulsory day of rest. Ironically enough the guaranteed Sunday holiday had been swept away by the anticlerical high

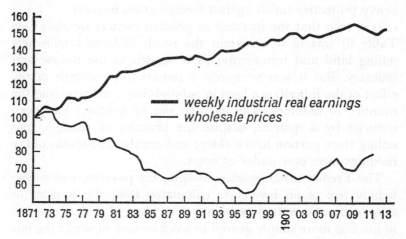

Fig. 7 *Real earnings in French industry, 1871–1913 (1871=100)*

These figures represent weekly real earnings and do not take account of the shortening working week. Had they been calculated on the basis of the hourly wage-rate, the rise would have been about 10 per cent higher by the end of the period.

1. The rise in real earnings during the years 1873–96 was largely the result of the falling cost of living.

2. The continued rise after 1896, despite a rising cost of living, reflects an increase in monetary wages, resulting from a better organised labour movement and the readiness of the employers to pay more, in the light of growing prosperity.

tide of 1880, when, as so often in France, humanity had been unconsciously sacrificed to theory.

The law was likewise grudging on social insurance, though this was still true of most other countries (see p. 53). Long hours meant tired workers and the risk of mutilation in moving machinery, yet it was not until 1898 that industrial workers were systematically insured against accident. Old-age pensions were introduced only in April 1910, when some seven million workers could look forward to coughing out their last years on five or six shillings a week. Unlike the British 5*s* pension scheme, which was non-contributory, the French worker paid 2 per cent of his wage as a premium, the employer adding an equivalent amount, and the state a small subsidy. Sick pay, however, was a matter for the private *sociétés de secours mutuel*, which until 1910 had been the only source of workers' pensions – and membership of these was voluntary. The worker normally paid 2 or 3 per cent of his salary to them; and since this was the society's only regular form of income, the benefits were correspondingly meagre.

By 1906 industry employed nearly two-fifths of the working population. In the early morning the newly-built Métro in Paris was packed with workers, giving it its characteristic smell of blended garlic, tobacco and sweat, perhaps the most evocative of all smells for the foreign Francophile. Outside industry, the rest of the urban working class lived in such varied conditions that it is impossible to generalise about them; but to take an extreme case, at the beginning of the period a maid in the provinces would earn little more than £1 a month, plus food and a bed in the attic or under the stairs, and her time off generally consisted of only half a day once a fortnight. It is easy to imagine the misery of young domestic servants trying to make their time off coincide with that of 'followers' in other households – and it is certainly a common enough ingredient of the popular fiction of the time.

Despite French intellectual eminence, a third of the adult population in France was illiterate in 1871, and the scribe's office was as distinctive a feature of the street or public square as the shops of the basic tradesmen. Desultory attempts had

been made from the reign of Louis XIV to make primary
education universal; but the most realistic step in this direction
came with the law of June 1881 making primary education
free. By 1913 a substantial victory had been won in that
illiteracy among men had now been reduced to well under 5
per cent; but among women it was probably higher, while
few girls had the advantages of a secondary education. State
secondary schools for girls did not appear until the law of 1880
broke the effective monopoly of private girls' schools, most of
them run by religious orders with fees that were generally much
higher than those demanded in state schools. Even by 1914
girls still only represented a quarter of the secondary school
population.

As long as secondary education was fee-paying, it tended to
correspond in some degree to class distinction, a similar class
distinction affecting the incidence of military service. Although
the law of July 1872 theoretically obliged everyone who was
medically fit to perform five years' whole-time service with the
colours, this in effect would have deprived the country's
economy of too much manpower, and would have provided an
unnecessarily large and expensive army. Accordingly the law
exempted widows' sons, the younger brothers of serving soldiers
and students following various forms of higher education. It also
permitted young men of education, who were prepared to pay
for their upkeep, to serve as 'volunteers' for a year only, this in
fact covering the bulk of the middle class. Furthermore, of the
rest only half were to perform the whole five years' active
service, the others, chosen by lottery, leaving after a year,
provided they had learned to read and write. However, many
of the educational exemptions (including those of seminarists)
were abolished by 'democratic' legislation in July 1889 –
though they were still only obliged to perform a year's full-time
service. Apart from the imaginary pleasure of seeing 'le curé
sac à dos', the less educated could at least take consolation
from the fact that the normal period with the colours was now
reduced from five to three years – and was to be briefly reduced
to two, from March 1905 until August 1913. The French
system put some very unlikely people in uniform. What did
the average sergeant-major make of Marcel Proust?

THE ECONOMIC FACTORS[1]

Turning to the dismal science, the most important items in French exports were silks (about 5 per cent) followed by cotton goods, raw wool and yarn, and wine.[2] By the late seventies, however, imports regularly exceeded exports, with the result that by 1913 France had an annual trade deficit of over £60

TABLE 9

	1873	1913
National product	c. £1,000 m	£1,720 m
Agriculture	43%	35%
Industry	30%	36%
Exports	£151 m	£275 m
Manufactures	c. 50%	58%
Raw materials	c. 25%	29%
Foodstuffs	c. 25%	13%

million. Nevertheless this was more than compensated by those faithful standbys of the economic historian, 'invisible exports', which in 1913 converted this deficit into a surplus of £51 million. In fact these phantom-like commodities provided £15 million from the foreign custom of French insurance, shipping, and other companies, £30 million from foreign tourists and £71 million in interest from French investments abroad.[3]

From time to time the French would remember wistfully that they were one of the three pioneers of the Industrial Revolution, and before that the foremost industrial power in the world. Nevertheless their industry was handicapped by a shortage of coal, hydroelectric power being slow in coming as a viable alternative (see p. 70). Indeed throughout the period they were importing a third of their coal requirements.[4] France had been well endowed with iron deposits, but a quarter of these

[1] The position of France in the European economy is outlined in Chapter 2, pp. 63–82.

[2] In 1913 her best foreign customers were Britain (21 per cent), Belgium (16 per cent) and Germany (12·6 per cent). On her colonial trade, see p. 93.

[3] Notably in Russia (25 per cent), Latin America (13 per cent) and the French Empire (9 per cent).

[4] Ironically enough, coal imports were subject to import duty – a splendid example of government schizophrenia.

E

were lost with Alsace-Lorraine in 1871, together with the provinces' other sources of wealth – notably coal and salt mines and the Mulhouse cotton industry. Furthermore, although manpower was cheaper in France than in Britain, modern production methods were not easily applicable to the small-scale structure of the typical French business, with its vesting of all effective power in the hands of the family who founded and still owned it. This was the industrial counterpart of the main problems in agriculture – that many French farms were too small for modern techniques. It can be argued that all of this, like France's principal problems in politics, largely sprang from the individualism of 'the French temperament'. A family used to managing a business was very loath to expand it at the cost of sharing power with shareholders' representatives. In 1870 three-quarters of French workers were employed in enterprises of under fifty men, while even in 1896, 93 per cent of French industrial enterprises employed fewer than ten men each. The inevitable result was that an increasing proportion of French capital went abroad, or into government securities, while home industry remained conservative and slow to expand.

French agricultural riches had been symbolised for the world by such images as the rolling wheatlands of Beauce, and the terraced vineyards of the Côte-d'Or. In the seventies and eighties, however, American and Russian wheat reduced French prices by a quarter, even though the tariffs of the later eighties kept them a third above British prices. Similarly, it was only tariffs that maintained the price of French meat: in the 1890s it was double that of American meat. Moreover, trouble of a different kind had come in the eighties, when the phylloxera insect spread rapidly through the vineyards of southern France, with the result that wine production fell to a third of normal; and, *mirabile dictu*, wine became an import rather than an export. Naturally enough, Algerian, Californian, South African and Australian growers were quick to take advantage of French difficulties, recovery in France coming only at the turn of the century and then at no more than two-thirds of the old selling price. It is true that the fight against phylloxera resulted in the planting of new hardier vines with a greater yield, but it was unquestionably of poorer quality – the only consolation being that the greater yield permitted the transference of a third of the vineyard acreage to other crops.

Silk-farming was another traditional French activity that was hit by pestilence at home and by competition elsewhere, notably from Japan and China and from synthetic substitutes. At the same time falling wheat prices had encouraged a large-scale transference to sugar-beet and cattle raising. But these were themselves commodities that suffered from the competition of colonial sugar and the ranches of the New World, and so the switch did not bring the prosperity that was hoped for.

The troubles of farmers and the uncompetitive nature of French industry were obvious factors in pushing French commercial policy on to protectionist lines. From the first, Napoleon III's policy of relative free trade had aroused little enthusiasm among French producers; and as early as June 1871 it had been clear that the Republic intended to modify it. Even so, it was not until 1881 and 1884–5 that the major increases in tariff levels started to appear. Apart from the economic malaise of these years, the demand for protection had been intensified by the slump that followed the collapse of the Union Générale bank and its subsidiaries in January 1882. Railway improvements at home and economic expansion abroad (see p. 78) had encouraged considerable speculation, Union Générale shares reaching six times their nominal price in November 1881. When the collapse came two months later, not the least of its effects was a revival of that morbid disease of the insecure: antisemitism. The Union Générale had not only had strong Catholic backing but its founder was a business rival to the Rothschilds in Austria, the result being that the main Jewish banks had shown reluctance to come to its rescue. This predictably, if absurdly, started a wave of antisemitism that, although centred on France, served to reawaken indigenous antisemitism in Germany, Austria and elsewhere. The bookstalls of Paris and Vienna were showered with anti-Jewish literature, that at its lowest was not above resurrecting the medieval myth that Jews ritually slaughtered babies, while at its most intelligent, with Edouard Drumont, it still remained basically irrational. The main outcome of the financial crash, however, was another crisis of confidence and a sudden diversion of credit away from French private enterprise into government securities, thereby making it correspondingly more difficult for French producers to compete with foreign goods.

By 1887 the duty on imported wheat was eight times what it had been under Napoleon III, while Jules Méline's tariff of January 1892 systematised those increases so that even favoured nations were faced with a tariff of 5 per cent to 20 per cent on their agricultural produce and 7 or 8 per cent on their industrial goods. Successive tariffs raised the level, until by 1910 the minimum agricultural tariff was 13 per cent and the industrial 11 per cent. This was nevertheless still slightly below the German and Italian averages, and only a fifth of the Russian average.[1]

An unfortunate feature of the period was that men who were dissatisfied with the small profits from farming and industry often drifted into commerce, with the outcome that France progressively suffered from a multiplication of middlemen. Goods passed through a succession of hands before they reached the customer; and since each middleman had to have his percentage *en route*, the result was to keep retail prices high and non-competitive with those of other countries.

COLLECTIVE ACTION AND POLITICAL FACTORS

Despite the limitations of the French economy, it is evident that the standard of living of the poorer French family could have been much improved without unduly burdening the rest. To begin with, taxes on saleable commodities provided nearly half of the ordinary revenue – these hitting the poor purchaser as hard as the rich. Governments, however, welcomed the fact that indirect taxes did not involve prying into the citizen's personal affairs and were easier to impose and cheaper to administer – all this having obvious attractions for governments that were unsure both of their majority in parliament and of the honesty

---

[1] See p. 80 n., though note the different basis of comparison.
[2] Some readers may prefer to have a preliminary look at the regime(pp. 138–41) before embarking on this section.

of their taxpayers. Secondly, the absence of an income tax, and the importance of the land tax, made the peasantry shoulder a greater proportion of the tax burden than the industrial and commercial middle classes. This may seem strange in a country where agricultural interests were politically powerful and respected. But the informed peasant probably shared the generally suspicious attitude of the French middle class towards any tax system which demanded precise statements of overall income. How he made and supplemented his income he felt to be his own affair.

A shift of emphasis from indirect to direct taxation would not only have reduced the financial difficulties of the poor, but if it had been applied rigorously, it should have provided funds for positive schemes of social improvement. It may seem odd that this failed to come about in a country where universal suffrage had potentially given the manual classes control of government. The basic reason was that the manual classes were split between town and country, each of which distrusted the other, perhaps even more than the middle classes above them. Although the peasant land-holder might have little money, he did have land; and like the middle class in general, he feared that if the champions of the urban proletariat came to power, they would establish an expensive programme of social betterment which would result in heavier taxes being put on his land. The main benefits of such a programme would go to the industrial worker, who paid next to nothing in direct taxes; while the peasant, who helped pay for it, would gain little for himself from a programme of factory legislation and slum-clearance. Even when the Socialists advocated measures of social insurance that would benefit the peasantry, those likely to benefit generally preferred to face possible misfortune with the solid strength of a sock-full of gold up the chimney rather than with promises of future help from a government they distrusted. 'Méfiez-vous' was the motto of most Frenchmen, but of none more so than the peasant. At the same time he was scarcely likely to be attracted by the demands of urban socialists for the collectivisation of land. Jean Jaurès was one of the few French socialists who realised that a positive attempt must be made to attract the peasant proprietor, by laying emphasis on collective protection for the peasant rather than collective ownership, and by making it clear that public and private land ownership could exist side by side.

French socialism also suffered from the treatment it received in the early years of the Republic (see pp. 136–8). Government repression on one hand and ostracism by the Radicals on the other meant that organised socialism was to get off to a late start in France. Furthermore the socialists were driven into clandestine habits that later made many of them suspicious or contemptuous of normal parliamentary methods. Legislation of 1884 eventually authorised the principal activities of trade unions, but their previous history of hardship and repression made them even more hostile to the established framework of the regime than were the Socialist party leaders. When the Socialists' parliamentary representatives first entered parliament in force – with fifty-three elected deputies in the 1902 election – they were already losing contact with the more militant trade union leaders. Indeed the Confédération Générale du Travail was to declare in 1906: 'The C.G.T. aims at the expropriation of the capitalist class. It commends the general strike as a means to this end and holds that the Trade Union, which is at present a resistance group, will be in the future the group responsible for production and distribution, the foundation of the social organisation.' With such an outlook, an effective alliance of the type that characterised the British Labour Party and the T.U.C. was impossible – and French socialism was the weaker for it.

It would be an oversimplification to say that the division between 'town' and 'country' was the most important factor in the political events that shaped the early years of the Third Republic; but there is a strong element of truth in it. The peasantry had been fairly solidly behind Napoleon III, as the man who would preserve order and keep the Left in check; conversely, the larger towns had been the stronghold of opposition. There is every reason to suppose that this peasant support would have kept Napoleon III in power for considerably longer, had not his handling of the Franco-Prussian War

thoroughly discredited him. Even so, the Republic came about
with a very large element of luck.

Most of Napoleon's critics in the Corps Législatif would not
have pushed their demands for reform to the point of demanding a republic. But as so often in French history, it was a
journée, not parliament, that had the last word. The day after
the news of the French defeat at Sedan reached Paris, a large
crowd of demonstrators gathered in the Place de la Concorde,
demanding a republic (4 September). Egged on by Blanquist
agitators, they pushed their way across the Pont de la Concorde
and burst into the Corps Législatif, more or less dispersing it.
The Republican parliamentary leaders, Jules Favre and the
young radical fighter, Léon Gambetta, took advantage of the
situation to persuade the demonstrators to follow them to the
Hôtel de Ville where they proclaimed a republic in traditional
revolutionary style. Even then, however, the new Republic
might have been overthrown within a few hours, had not the
Governor of Paris, General Trochu, decided to afford it
recognition by agreeing to become President of a Government
of National Defence.

But if the Republic could survive in Paris for the moment,
there was no guarantee that it would survive in France as a
whole. It is true that it was very unfashionable to be a Bona-
partist so soon after the defeat of Napoleon III, but many
Bonapartists were doing the next best thing, transferring their
allegiance to one of the two Royalist pretenders – either to the
Bourbon pretender, the Comte de Chambord, grandson of
Charles X (1824–30), or to the Orleanist Pretender, the Comte
de Paris, grandson of Louis-Philippe (1830–48). The peasantry,
who had been the backbone of Napoleon III's following, were
completely at a loss now that their man was so discredited. But
their attitude was to be mainly governed by two considerations:
first, by their determination not to let the leaders of the urban
working class get into power; and secondly, by their desire for
a speedy settlement with Germany and an end to the war. Like
the rural middle and upper classes, they thought that the
Government of National Defence was not strong enough to
control the Paris proletariat, should it turn violent; and they
somewhat too readily associated the government with the idea

of a fight to the finish with Germany. In effect they were crediting the government as a whole with the views of Gambetta, its Minister of the Interior, who had made himself the spokesman of the more militant Republicans and of those who were anxious to continue the war. The result was that most of the peasantry were prepared to support the peace-seeking monarchists rather than the Republicans. And this became dramatically apparent in the elections of 8 February 1871 to the new National Assembly, when over two-thirds of the elected candidates were monarchists. The Republic was clearly in danger.

'The Republic in danger' was to be a familiar cry in the years to come. Staunch Republicans were to voice it with the frequency of Victorian heroines defending their virtue. Yet never again until 1940 was the danger to be so real as in 1871. Rescue came, however, in the unlikely shape of the wily, owl-faced Adolphe Thiers, whom the new National Assembly had appointed as head of the new government. He was not the customary hero of melodrama, and indeed entered the scene in several disguises at once, no one, not even himself, quite knowing which was the face and which the masks. Thiers already had a long political career behind him. He had helped to bring Louis-Philippe to the throne in 1830; and most English textbooks still portray him as playing a mildly mephistophelian Gladstone to Guizot's Disraeli. Since Thiers was initially uncommitted as to what form of government he favoured, the monarchists were prepared to let him carry on government until they could decide on a king.

But Thiers's savage repression of the Paris Commune in May 1871 demonstrated to the public that the Republic, however provisional, could be trusted not to let affairs fall into the hands of 'the wild men of the Left'. The Republic became respectable in the eyes of the rural voter, and this, together with the conclusion of a peace treaty with Germany, probably explains why the by-elections of the summer of 1871 showed a violent swing towards the Republicans.

If the Republic was becoming respectable, however, what sort of Republic was it going to be? The episode of the Paris Commune had epitomised the town versus country antagonism

– with counterparts in Lyon, Marseilles, St-Etienne, Toulouse and Narbonne. It is true that the long-term cause of these outbreaks was the failure of previous regimes to deal with the social problems presented by the industrial growth of these towns. But the short-term causes were the decisive ones. The Paris population had suffered greatly during the siege, with butchers reduced to selling dogs, cats and even rats. Many Parisians felt moreover that the government had betrayed their efforts by its half-hearted conduct of the war and by its ignominious armistice terms. Looking to the future they also feared that the National Assembly would attempt to restore the monarchy; while on the level of immediate reality, they were antagonised by Thiers's attempts to restore peacetime governmental control too quickly, notably by confiscating their artillery (18 March 1871). A tug-of-war over the guns led to fighting, which itself became a general insurrection, headed by an elected assembly, the Commune (25 March), which was composed principally of radical Republicans of bourgeois origin with very limited ideas of social reform. Indeed the insurrection could in no sense be regarded as first and foremost an expression of militant socialism, as Marx claimed – despite the presence of a vociferous socialist minority in the Commune.

The days were gone, however, when Paris could hold the country up to ransom. 1848 had given power to the rural majority: it had not only given them the vote but it had demonstrated that Paris could not hold out against train-loads of armed provincials, determined to break the revolutionary arrogance of the capital. (The reversal of roles arising from improved communications was to find its fullest expression in 1958, when the threat of an airborne attack from south-west France and Algeria could topple the Fourth Republic.) As in June 1848, Thiers's troops were greatly augmented by volun-teer bands from the indignant provinces, with the result that 'the forces of order' crushed the Commune by the end of May, killing 20,000, imprisoning 13,000 and transporting 7500 to New Caledonia. Even the annual slaughter on Britain's roads today can equal only a third of this. Not only was the extreme Left in French politics driven underground, but many Radicals became more moderate as a result of the excesses of the

*

Commune. Many were terrified by the burning of buildings and shooting of hostages (including the Archbishop of Paris) which had taken place when the Communards were hard pressed. Léon Gambetta – at one time the bogey of the respectable – was to epitomise the Radical sell-out on social reform when he said: 'There is no social question' (1872).

The growing respectability of the Republic was given the prestige of Thiers's blessing when he publicly advocated a permanent Republic in November 1872. Fear that the Republic might come to stay determined the Legitimists and Orleanists to sink their differences and establish the Comte de Chambord as king, with the Comte de Paris as his successor. The Comte de Chambord, however, had all the splendid idealism of the born failure, insisting that his return should be accompanied by the replacement of the tricolour flag by the white flag of the Bourbons – an impossible demand that symbolised his remoteness from the realities of the 1870s. The royalists realised that a restoration would have to await his death and the succession of the less quixotic Comte de Paris. In the meantime, they made use of their majority in the National Assembly to establish a royalist as President of the Republic (May 1873) whose job would be to keep the throne warm for the Comte de Paris. They chose Marshal MacMahon, of Irish descent, who has since become enshrined in French affections as the subject of hilarious anecdotes, illustrative of the limitations of a melancholy military mind.

In the meantime they felt obliged to establish what was intended as a provisional constitution to fill the gap until a restoration was possible. Designed to support MacMahon, it was also designed to ensure that he remained subject to the wishes of the legislature which they blindly assumed would be composed of royalists like themselves.

'Il n'y a rien qui dure sauf le provisoire' – and what was intended by the royalists as a mere stopgap became instead the basis of a republican democracy that was to last for the next sixty-five years.

The Republic, however, was to suffer greatly from having a constitution that was designed for other purposes, this being a major factor in burdening France with her main political problem: the instability of cabinets. Between 1870 and 1940 there were no less than 109 ministries and only one dissolution of the Chamber of Deputies before its statutory four-year span had elapsed. The average life of a ministry was only seven months, which meant that it was extremely difficult for a government to undertake any reform programme that would take time or would meet with opposition in parliament. In order to preserve MacMahon from attacks by the Republicans in the Chamber and Senate, the constitution laid down that only his ministers should be responsible to parliament. The result of this for the future of the Republic was that when the monarchists were later defeated, the new Republican majority that came to power would only elect harmless individuals to the Presidency – men who could be relied on to do nothing for seven years and who would appoint the ministers the Chamber wanted. Indeed Raymond Poincaré (1913–20) was the first man of any force to be elected President. This would not have mattered, had the prime minister possessed strong executive power. But since he was responsible to parliament, he had to be sure of a majority in the Chamber and Senate. Yet the fragmentation of parliament into numerous parties, together with the absence of Westminster-type discipline within the parties, meant that no premier could ever rely on a stable majority, unless he pursued a negative policy of offending nobody. It is true that the monarchists who framed the constitution had envisaged the possibility of friction between MacMahon's ministers and the Republican elements in a future Chamber of Deputies. Indeed the constitution gave the President the power to dissolve the Chamber before its four-year mandate elapsed, and to hold new elections – provided that the Senate agreed. But in practice this power was more or less abolished after its tactless use by MacMahon in June 1877, as described below.

The monarchists had completely underestimated the progress of Republicanism among the electorate since 1871. The first elections to the new Chamber of Deputies in February and March 1876 gave three-quarters of the seats to the Republicans. Although the Senate elections gave the royalists a majority in the other house, this was to be reversed in the partial Senate elections of January 1879. Conflict soon arose between Mac-Mahon's royalist ministers and the Chamber; so much so that on 19 June 1877 MacMahon dissolved the Chamber, in the hope that new elections would see the return of a monarchist majority. However, despite government attempts to shackle the opposition press, a Republican majority was once more returned. Eventually MacMahon had to capitulate and choose his ministers from among the Republicans. Not surprisingly, disagreement with them finally led to his own voluntary resignation in January 1879 – a land-mark in Republican history in that with him disappeared the last segment of the royalist Republic. After this episode no future President dared dissolve the Chamber before the end of the four-year period, or choose as prime minister anyone who did not have the support of a majority in the Chamber. Within its four-year span, the Chamber could make and unmake as many ministries as it liked.

A further outcome of the episode was that future prime ministers tended to be second-rate. Strong men such as MacMahon's nominee, the Duc de Broglie, had attempted to impose their will on the Chamber; and the Chamber was determined not to let it happen again. That is why Gambetta, the obvious choice for prime minister in 1879, was not invited to form a ministry until 1881, just a year before his death, when he had lost much of his vigour and prestige. Similarly, 'the Tiger', Georges Clemenceau, perhaps the strongest politician that the Third Republic produced, whose influence was to make and unmake ministries during twenty years, had to wait until 1906 before becoming premier. Although he was the obvious man to guide France through the First World War, he was not called to power until November 1917, when the desperate nature of the situation left France no alternative but to invite him.

The prevailing attitude among Republicans towards strong men found its parallel in a remark by MacMahon's successor as President, the drab little Republican, Jules Grévy. Once when making a presidential visit to an exhibition, he was told that there were no outstanding exhibits but that the general standard was good; to which he replied: 'Ah, but that's just as it should be in a democracy'.

Even the most fervent Republican had to admit that parliament was full of provincial mediocrities. France was still predominantly a rural and small-town country, while the electoral system tended to under-represent the industrial cities. The distribution of seats in the Chamber failed to take account of the growth of these towns; while the method of election to the Senate which gave municipal councils a large share of the votes, failed to differentiate sufficiently between the voting power of large and small towns. The result was a disproportionately large rural vote, an unfortunate situation when the country voter was generally more interested in local issues than in national ones. The type of deputy elected was often some local lawyer or small-town mayor with a taste for politics, a man who would promise to get a new bridge built or bring about the extension of a branch line to improve the commerce of the region. Once this scheme was fulfilled, he could live on his constituents' gratitude for life. This predominance of local issues in national politics was to some extent the outcome of the excessive centralisation of France. Many issues which in Britain would be dealt with by county and municipal authorities, were in France the direct responsibility of the central government. The result was that if a district wanted some local improvement, it had to raise the matter at a national level, which might mean competing for the favours of the minister. In the last resort the best chance for a scheme succeeding was for a friend of the district's parliamentary representative to *become* minister. This bore out the sad unspoken truth that for many people the rapid turnover of ministers in France was a desirable thing, since the faster the turnover, the greater chance there was of some acquaintance becoming minister. Between 1870 and 1940 646 men became cabinet ministers, which meant that one deputy or senator in ten achieved cabinet rank at some point or other in his career. Clearly no deputy was going to be tempted to vote for the reform of a system which offered such handsome prizes. Even if the cabinet you were in only lasted a few months, you could build up credit for life in that short time.

After the turn of the century, the Radical Party, despite its name, came to be just as much dominated by these rural mediocrities as were the more conservative Republicans, the so-called Opportunists who formed most of the ministries between 1879 and 1899. The Radical Party had never been very radical. It is easy for the foreigner to be misled by French political labels. On one hand the gradual leftward slide of events tends to leave parties stranded to the right of what their original labels implied; while on the other it could be said that the French Revolutionary tradition favours progressive-sounding titles. All of which contrasts with the Frenchman's passionate clinging to his individuality, and his reluctance to part with his money. As the threadbare proverb says: 'If a Frenchman's heart is on the left, his wallet is on the right.'

The radicalism of the Radicals normally consisted of a pronounced anticlericalism and opposition to strong government. The strong individualism which characterised their political doctrine ran counter to any idea of an ambitious scheme for social reform; and by the time that the separation of Church and State had come about in 1905, and income tax had been established during the First World War, most of their political doctrine was outdated, because already realised in practice. They had, in the early years of the Republic, campaigned for the abolition of the Senate, which was the bastion of Republican conservatism; but General Boulanger's right-wing intrigues in the late 1880s had made the cause of constitutional revision a disreputable one, so they dropped it. The Dreyfus episode eventually helped bring them to power in 1902, and thereafter they were to remain steadily (and negatively) in office for the rest of the pre-war period.

The peasant proprietors on the one hand, and the industrial and commercial middle class on the other, could rely on the Radicals, just as they had on the Opportunists, to oppose any substantial increase in taxation. They feared that an authoritarian government of the Left or Right would embark on expensive programmes of improvement. Indeed the poor record of the Third Republic in the matter of social reform was a measure of their success. Even more strikingly, the general economic record of both the Opportunists and the Radicals showed a similar unfailing solicitude for peasant and middle-class interests. The power of these interests in parliament was a strong unbroken force that lay beneath the succession of political parties, and continued unaffected by the shifts and changes that were taking place on the parliamentary surface. Though from the political angle the Conservatives, the Opportunists and the Radicals were sharply distinct, they developed between them a comparatively coherent economic programme. It was this stability of common economic interests that helped to preserve a political system that seemed to outsiders to be the very essence of chaotic instability. That – and the vested interest of the politicians in a rapid turnover of ministries.

A further obstacle in the way of social reform was the pre-occupation in political life with preserving the Republican victory of 1879. The main political concern of the Opportunist ministries of 1879–99 was to prevent the monarchists regaining power. Taking a long-term view of the problem, the answer lay in the field of education. Many Republicans saw the prime purpose of the Republic as the formation of future generations of Frenchmen who would think rationally and would be equipped to lead society on to a higher level of material and moral well-being. At the same time it was argued that if every child was educated on true rational principles and filled with ideas of civic virtue from an early age, future generations of Frenchmen would see a democratic republic as the only form of government acceptable to an adult-minded nation. The chief obstacle to such a programme was the extensive control of education by the Church. In 1879 two-fifths of the children of France were educated in Catholic schools, over which the state had no direct control. This meant that a large percentage of the future generation was not only cut off from contact with the principles of Republican virtue but was left to the mercy of 'irrationalist' Christian concepts such as Revelation. Further-more since the Church was known to be largely monarchist in sympathy, it was suspected that these children would emerge as bigoted reactionaries, all straining to vote for the monarchists as soon as they were old enough. So the battle of Church and

State under the Third Republic was largely one for intellectual control of the new generation.

The majority of the clergy and many of the practising laity were biased against the Republican form of government for three principal reasons. First they objected to the secular basis of Republican thinking. Secondly, there was the anticlerical record of the first French Revolution and the anti-religious activities of the Commune of 1871, which had declared the separation of Church and State and had turned churches into clubs and dance-halls. Although most thinking Catholics realised that the Commune of 1871 and the ruling Republicans of the 1880s had little in common, many thought that the activities of the Commune indicated what could break out, once a strong monarchical government was replaced by a seemingly weak Republican regime. Thirdly, and most important, many of the Republicans had included in their electoral programmes their intention to press for the disestablishment of the Church and the abolition of Catholic schools. It was therefore not surprising that the Church had broadly sympathised with schemes to restore the monarchy.

In consequence, the ruling Republicans of 1879 considered it essential to close down as many Catholic schools as possible. The new Minister of Education, Jules Ferry, therefore issued decrees in 1880 ordering the expulsion of all religious orders that had not obtained government permission to reside in France. These and other measures increased the anti-Republican attitude of the Church, and partly account for the sympathy which many Catholics felt for the right-wing intrigues of General Georges Boulanger, a former Minister for War, who enjoyed enormous public popularity. With his blond beard and black horse 'Tunis', once the drum-horse of the Russian Imperial mounted guard, Boulanger was all things to all men. Jingoists acclaimed him as the man who made Bismarck tremble, Orleanists and Bonapartists saw him as General Monk who would bring about the restoration, while the masses who voted for him in by-elections thought they were voting for a vigorous national leader who would solve the economic depression and raise wages. In January 1889 crowds gathered outside his headquarters, urging him to take over the presidency. But hesitating to take the final step into illegality, he let the chance go by; and, fearing arrest by a frightened ministry, he fled to Brussels where he eventually committed suicide on the grave of his mistress.

The discredit which fell on all those who had supported Boulanger helped to convince the pope, Leo XIII, that the monarchist cause in France was lost; and in February 1892 he publicly advised French Catholics to proclaim their allegiance to the Republican regime. This Catholic *Ralliement* to the Republic, for all its hesitations, helped to kill French royalism as a serious political force. In fact on the main economic and social questions there was little to choose between many royalists and the conservative wing of the Opportunists.

The royalists, however, were already suffering competition from within the right-wing camp itself, from the Nationalists – extreme right-wing Republicans, who in some ways were forerunners of fascism. Demanding a strong authoritarian form of government, they also preached an exaggerated patriotism, directed mainly against Germany. At the same time their propaganda was laced with a strong dash of antisemitism. Their main spokesmen in the 1890s were the jingo-poet and disillusioned Gambettist, Paul Deroulède, and the distinguished writer, Maurice Barrès, men whose natural panache gave them an appeal far beyond the world of letters. The collapse of Boulangism had been a great disappointment to them, but with incurable optimism they thought that their chance had come again in 1899, when the Dreyfus affair was causing the government embarrassment.

It is difficult for the historian to see the Dreyfus episode in perspective. Basically it added nothing new to French politics – it merely revealed with startling clarity the division that still existed between those on one hand who accepted Republican hopes for a humanity emancipated from 'irrational' beliefs and prejudices, and those on the other hand who felt that Republican policies ran counter to all that was great and good in the French tradition. The Affair drove intellectuals and politicians into taking sharper attitudes, extreme attitudes in many cases, and Dreyfus himself soon lay trampled beneath the wrangling forces of Right and Left. The Affair also represented a personal crisis in the lives of many of the young intellectuals of the nineties, causing some to lose their faith in the existing social order, and causing others to recoil into semi-obscurantism. Both Socialism and the Right thereby received distinguished converts.

The unfortunate man whose predicament was the catalyst for the Affair was Alfred Dreyfus, a Jewish army officer, who had been wrongfully convicted in 1894 of supplying military secrets to Germany. While Dreyfus lay incarcerated on Devil's Island, suspicions were aroused as to the justice of his conviction. But the War Ministry, rather than admit the possibility of mistake, preferred not to reopen the case. In 1898 a number of left-wing intellectuals, including the novelist Émile Zola, launched an attack on the military authorities for sacrificing individual justice to their own public image. The army was a stronghold of right-wing opinion – partly because the Republic had excluded such people from other branches of the public service. The attack on the army over Dreyfus became in consequence a general attack on the army for the anti-Republicanism of many of its members, with the result that the question of Dreyfus's guilt became submerged under a mutual mud-slinging campaign of Right and Left.

In the midst of the controversy, the President of the Republic, Félix Faure, who had been against a retrial of Dreyfus, died of a cerebral haemorrhage – brought on, so rumour had it, while in the arms of his mistress, as a result of his amorous excesses. With devastating if unconscious precision, several newspapers made the traditional lament: 'Ainsi est mort un grand président dans la pleine exercice de ses fonctions.' The Nationalists, however, spread the equally intriguing rumour that he had been murdered by Dreyfusards, and made a ludicrous attempt to stage a *coup d'état* immediately after his funeral (February 1899). Deroulède, rushing in front of the funeral escort, seized the bridle of General Roget's horse, shouting: 'À l'Elysée, mon général, à l'Elysée.' Roget and most of the crowd assumed that he was an unbalanced spectator, over-excited by the martial scene; so much so that it was with considerable difficulty that he got himself taken sufficiently seriously to be arrested. Further incidents eventually brought to power a broad-bottomed ministry under Pierre Waldeck-Rousseau (June 1899 – June 1902) which undertook to suppress right-wing subversion and re-establish public confidence.[1]

The main outcome of the ensuing clean sweep took place under Waldeck-Rousseau's successor, 'le petit père', Émile Combes (June 1902 – January 1905), whose narrow anti-clericalism saw the expulsion of those religious orders that had escaped or evaded the 1880 decrees. In spite of the *Ralliement*, a number of Catholic newspapers had violently attacked the Dreyfusards, claiming that the Republic was progressively falling into the hands of Jews and Freemasons. Reprisals hit the just as well as the guilty, so that a large number of Catholic schools were closed down or could only continue under lay auspices. Combes's anticlerical campaign, however, got out of his control, resulting against his will in the disestablishment of the Church under his successor in December 1905. Combes feared that disestablishment might strengthen the Church, through the freedom it would gain in the nomination of bishops and in the distribution of its personnel; and in the long run he was probably right, since the clergy ultimately gained in self-reliance and public esteem.

The defeat of the extreme Right and the secularising of the state should have left the decks clear for social reform – as the Socialists hoped. But the Radicals had little desire to go further, and became in effect a solid bastion of the *status quo* – the true conservatives of the post-1905 Republic.

COLONIALISM

By 1914 France had an overseas imperial population that was between two and three times the size of her own. In area her empire was nearly fifteen times as big as France, since it in-cluded, among much else, most of the Sahara desert. But economically its value reflected the fact that so much of it consisted of desert and jungle.

---

[1] Dreyfus was retried in August–September 1899, and again found guilty. The government's embarrassment, however, resulted in his being granted a pardon. Nevertheless it was not until 1906 that the court martial verdict of 1899 was finally quashed.

Indo-China was its most lucrative part, playing in a much humbler way an equivalent role to that of India in the British colonial economy (see pp. 81–2). Although Algeria had a greater bulk of trade, it had a trade deficit, whereas Indo-China by 1910 had an annual trade surplus of £2 million. Not only did her exports represent nearly a quarter of the total exports of the French overseas empire, but unlike the bulk of the colonies, Indo-China both had a trade surplus and yet imported more goods from France than France took from her. Like India, she paid for the difference by her exports to other countries. In 1910, for instance, Indo-China exported £11 millions' worth of goods, about two-thirds of which was rice, and imported about £9 millions' worth of goods, most of them being textiles, metal goods and manufactures in general. But a third of these imports came from France whereas France took not much more than a fifth of Indo-China's exports. France therefore enjoyed a trade surplus with Indo-China of about £700,000, which Indo-China was paying for by her rice exports to other countries.

France's trade balances with other colonies were less favourable, and taking the empire as a whole, she just about broke even. At the same time French colonial bonds normally offered an interest of about 3·5 per cent, instead of the domestic French rate of 3 per cent. Companies like the Compagnie Française de l'Afrique Occidentale were admittedly offering upward of 20 per cent on the eve of the war, but this was very exceptional. Nevertheless French overseas trade would probably have been less than it was but for the colonies. British- and German-manufactured goods were cheaper; and had the French colonies been independent, or part of another country's empire, they would probably not have imported French goods. Not only were the French colonies walled with tariffs against non-French manufacturers, but like the British in India, the French 'neglected' the development of colonial industries that would compete with French production. Colonial industry remained geared to simple processing for immediate home consumption. The military expense of empire was heavy, however, and in 1913 the overall cost of military and civil administration reached the unprecedented annual figure of £22·3 million, though

£15 million was a more usual annual figure in the pre-war years. Even £15 million was equivalent to almost a half of French exports to the empire – and some of these goods could have been sold overseas, even if there had been no empire. It must also be remembered that it was the French taxpayer who was directly bearing this cost, whereas the limited trade advantages were largely going into a few private pockets, and only part came back to the government as taxation.

Whereas Britain liked to justify her imperial activities in terms of bringing peace and justice to untutored warring savages, France prided herself on her 'mission civilisatrice'. Given French cultural pre-eminence in the world, this was a plausible line in propaganda. The Third Republic had ostensibly adopted the Revolution's aim of 'assimilating' her colonial subjects, claiming that the black African should become as much a Frenchman as the Breton fisherman or Provençal peasant. This, however, was viewed as an ideal to be obtained in an unspecified future; and in the meantime the legal and electoral rights of French citizenship were restricted to Europeans and to the tiny minority of natives who fulfilled the educational and other qualifications stipulated by the particular colony. Since French citizenship required the renunciation of native customs such as polygamy, even those natives who had the necessary qualifications frequently chose not to become French citizens, this being particularly true of the Muslims. Even in Algeria, where there was most evidence of westernisation, there were only two or three thousand non-white French citizens. Algeria, of course, was nominally regarded as part of France, but this was a fiction that existed only on the level of institutions – and then only just.

A fundamental if not particularly valuable aspect of the theory of assimilation was the right to elect deputies and senators to the French parliament. In 1914, however, only the pre-1870 colonies – Algeria, Senegal, Martinique, Guadeloupe, Réunion, Guiana, Cochin China and the French trading posts in India – had parliamentary representatives. The Indo-Chinese and African protectorates were theoretically ineligible for complete assimilation, yet most of French Black Africa, which was held in complete sovereignty, was likewise without representation. As Afro-Asian nationalists were to discover, however – and as the Irish had already discovered – the idea of colonial representatives in a European parliament has always been a barren experience, and generally reflects the government's reluctance to allow a colony its own effective legislature. As far as their daily lives were concerned, the vast majority of French overseas subjects remained under the local law of the colony, and were liable to forced labour, corporal punishment and the other indignities which only French citizenship averted. Nevertheless, even for the least privileged, colonial rule brought better justice, education and health facilities. Although the massive French expenditure on education and native facilities belongs to a later period, France was already making some effort to justify her claim to a *mission civilisatrice*.

In 1870, the French Empire was limited to the colonies listed above, together with the coastal fringes of Guinea, the coast of Gabon and a loose protectorate over the kingdom of Cambodia. As might have been predicted, the main colonial acquisitions of the next fifteen years were the Tunisian and Indo-Chinese protectorates.

The French presence in Algeria inevitably gave France an interest in the neighbouring territories of Morocco and Tunisia. Although Italy likewise showed interest in Tunisia, the Italians showed few active signs of intending to take it, the upshot being that in 1878 both Lord Salisbury and Bismarck appear to have suggested to France that Tunisia was hers for the taking. Germany was always glad enough to distract France from Alsace-Lorraine, while Britain may have been wanting to reconcile France to the British taking of Cyprus. Nevertheless France, in her diplomatic isolation, was reluctant to take a step that would incur the enmity of Italy and might lead to demands for compensation from other countries. It seems to have been Alphonse de Courcel (a foreign office official, soon to become French ambassador in Berlin) who persuaded Gambetta and, through him, Ferry, of the advantages of an acquisition which would lead to better relations with Germany. Pressure from banking interests seems to have played only a minor role in establishing the protectorate of 1881.

By contrast, private economic interests played a significant role in the acquisition of Indo-China. The Societé des Mines de l'Indochine held coal concessions in Annamite Tonkin, and erroneously believed that France was negotiating a partition agreement with Annam's suzerain, China, in which the coal-bearing parts of Tonkin would go to China. A Societé representative persuaded the commander of the French garrison in Hanoi to take advantage of a dispute with the local Annamite officials to occupy the Red River delta. There is also reason to suppose that French officials in Cochin China were not averse to the move, since on previous occasions they had tried to rush the home government into acquiring further parts of Indo-China. Without attempting to consult the government in Paris, the Hanoi garrison embarked on a campaign which soon ran into difficulties (May 1883), thereby presenting Ferry's government with the invidious choice of sending reinforcements or seeing the garrison wiped out. At the same time French business interests in Indo-China launched a full-scale campaign of pressure on public opinion and the government.

Ferry chose the course of intervention; and this led not only to the occupation of Tonkin, but the establishment of a protectorate over the whole Empire of Annam (August 1883). How far Ferry was the tool of circumstance, and how far he was the high priest of French imperialism is one of the great problems of modern French history. Whatever the truth, his ministry saw the acquisition of Tunis and most of Indo-China. Annam's claims of suzerainty over Laos, moreover, led to Laos becoming a French protectorate in 1895.

The French Empire south of the Sahara owed its origins to the various toe-holds which French trading companies had established on the western coasts from the sixteenth century onwards. After 1870, however, various factors encouraged penetration of the interior (see pp. 91–2). As a consequence, the next forty years saw the piecemeal acquisition of Dahomey, Upper Senegal–Niger, Niger, Upper Volta, the Middle Congo, Ubangi-Shari and Chad; while in the south, Madagascar was similarly acquired between 1885 and 1896.

CHAPTER FIVE

Eastern Empires

Russia, Austria-Hungary and Turkey

RUSSIA

'It is Uncle Mischa trying to shoot himself. It really is degrading how he
fails at everything he puts his hand to.'

USTINOV

THE SOCIAL OUTCOME

One imagines that the picture which the cultured European
had of Tsarist Russia was somewhat coloured by the plays or
novels he encountered. The word 'liberal' might well have
suggested to him a bespectacled figure sitting in the evening
with his friends in the garden of his summer residence. (The
name of the liberal would have escaped him, because although
the theatre programme listed him as Mihail Vladimirovich
Voineghin, each of the characters on the stage would call him
something different, ranging from variants on his three names
to plain simple 'Nish-Nish'.) Most of the time they sat in
depressed silence, gently savouring their ineffectiveness. Then
one of them would suddenly cry out: 'Nish-Nish, teach me how
to live!' A long pause. 'I cannot, Milyushkin. I do not know.'
Another long pause. 'Will it always be like this in Russia,
Nish-Nish?' Pause. 'Yes, Milyushkin, it will always be like this
in Russia.'

To take a broader outlook, however, this period saw considerable change in the lives of most Russians. But it has

additional importance in being the seed-bed of the much greater changes that were to occur in 1917 and thereafter.

TABLE 10

	1870	1914
Population	c. 75 m	c. 140 m
Proportion in agriculture	c. 85%	c. 75%
Proportion in towns	c. 10%	c. 13%
Proportion in manufactures	c. 4%	c. 7%
Proportion literate	c. 10%	c. 40%

These figures include Poland and Finland, but exclude the Russian Empire east of the Urals.

The peasantry

The Russian peasant has at all times been something of a legend to foreigners. The modern film-goer knows him as the broad-faced son of the soil with a screen-splitting smile; while the early Victorian peruser of the illustrated weeklies would occasionally come across engravings of men and women stripped to the waist and suspended by their wrists, writhing under the tax-collector's whip. Certainly the peasant's life was hard. Whipping was widely used by communal courts as a means of extracting overdue taxes, and it was only in August 1904 that it was finally abolished. There was likewise no escaping the fact that by western standards peasant living conditions were appalling. Their dwellings generally consisted of a one-room log cabin, where the head of the household slept over the oven, while the rest of the family slept on piles of rags on the floor.

In times of peace it is rare for the lives of many millions to be profoundly affected by a few pieces of royal writ. Yet this was the case with the emancipation edicts in Russia. It must be remembered that four-fifths of the rural population were either ex-serfs or the children of ex-serfs, of whom more than half had been privately owned. Indeed it was these last who were emancipated by the epoch-making edict of March 1861, which with later decrees gave them the choice of 'buying' or renting the land they had occupied as serfs. Significantly, however, over 85 per cent chose full ownership – a response that indicates the strong attachment of the peasant to the idea of personal property, no matter what the initial hardship.

At this point a few figures are necessary for an understanding of the peasant's problems. To obtain ownership, the ex-serfs gave the landlord a down payment of a fifth of the land value (payable, if necessary, in instalments), while the landlord for his part could claim the remaining four-fifths from the government in 6 per cent bonds. The peasant was now faced with the task of repaying the government, which he could do on an instalment basis spread over forty-nine years. Alternatively he could choose to dispense with the government's intermediary services altogether and pay the landlord direct in labour-services, by working for thirty to forty days a year on his land.

Yet if the edicts represented a tight-fisted justice that made few concessions to the peasant, the reality that followed was much harsher. On the whole the peasant discovered that the land he acquired was officially overvalued by half, thereby obliging him, in many instances, to sell part of it to meet his annual payments and earlier debts. The result was that his farm shrank even smaller than the existing average size of nine acres – already too little in a country of primitive farming methods, where productivity per acre was only a third of western Europe's.

By the turn of the century over half of these peasants were having to supplement their income by working as day-labourers, another quarter turning to cottage industry and other part-time work. It should likewise be remembered that Russian rural wages were only two-fifths of those in England, while subsistence in any case was a much grimmer business in a cold climate.

Indeed there was no doubt that the former private serf had every reason to envy his counterpart from Crown lands. Although Crown serfs had been partly emancipated in the late 1830s, their position was gradually brought closer to that of the ex-private serfs. Yet when their rent was changed to redemption payments in 1886, they were still paying much less than the 'ex-private' majority, the net result being that their farms on average remained two and a half times larger than those of former private serfs.

Nor must it be imagined that the peasant, if poor, was now proudly independent. The fact that he owed indemnity money to the government put him very much under the direct control of the local communal council, which in practice came near to being the real owner of the land. All too often this council or *mir* was controlled by the 'commune-eaters', the more prosperous peasants who were not above demanding gifts from the poorer villagers in return for their support. In over half the communes the land was periodically reapportioned among the peasantry to compensate for varying fertility, with the result that the peasant had little incentive to spend labour and money on improving the capital value of his land. In these communes the size of the allotment depended on the size of the peasant's household. Accordingly young men who wished to leave the commune were frequently dissuaded from doing so, because their fathers feared a smaller allotment at the next reallocation. Furthermore, until 1903, no peasant could leave the commune without a passport, which once again might oblige him to dip into his pocket to curry favour with the 'commune-eaters' of the *mir*.

In November 1906, however, the peasantry were given opportunities for withdrawing their land from communal control. In communes where there was no periodic redistribution, this was immediately possible. But in communes where there was redistribution, a peasant could insist at the next redistribution that his new allocation be given as a consolidated block of strips. In the next nine years at least a quarter of the peasants took advantage of these possibilities. The total proportion of peasant families who had outright control of land was thereby increased to a half.

Apart from their land payments, the peasantry were subjected to fairly heavy taxation, and the commune was responsible for apportioning and collecting it. Although the poll-tax was abolished in May 1885, the 1890s saw an unwelcome increase in indirect taxation, when the Finance Minister, Sergei Witte, was trying to finance industrial growth; and this made a marked difference to the peasant's cost of living. On the other hand, in many provinces, he enjoyed a system of free medical treatment that had no parallel in nineteenth-century Europe (see p. 161).

The industrial workers

By 1914, the Russian industrial worker had acquired a remarkable sense of solidarity. Remarkable in that Russia's industrial revolution did not really start until the 1890s; and remarkable in that as late as 1900 nine-tenths of the industrial workers still had legal links with their former rural communes. Even after the legislation of 1903–7 broke these legal ties, many workers returned there annually for several weeks' harvest work. The solidarity of Russian labour, however, partly sprang from the large size of Russian factories. It is not always realised that by 1913, well over two-fifths of Russian factory workers were employed in enterprises of over a thousand workers, where it was much easier for militants to keep in touch with each other and organise demonstrations. The lateness of Russia's industrial revolution enabled her to profit from the experience of countries that had undergone their industrial revolutions earlier, this experience pointing on the whole to the advisability of large rather than small factories (see p. 163). Not only were factories large, but many of them had free dormitory accommodation for their workers, where the same beds were used alternately for the day- and night-shift workers. For something like one per cent of his wage, the worker could bring his family to share a cubicle with one or two other families; and the result, however unhygienic, was an ideal recruiting ground for militant labour. In some factories, families both worked and slept in individual enclosures, measuring no more than nine by six feet; while in the Moscow district over half of the factory workers either slept on the premises or in adjoining dormitories. The others with families mostly lived in one-room private 'apartments', for a rent of about 2s 6d a week.

Despite improvements in wages, the average semi-skilled wage in 1913 was only sufficient to cover two-thirds of the cost of keeping a family in a rented room; so most wives had to work, women accounting for nearly a third of the factory population, many of them mothers of small children. In the first half of the period, the widespread practice of imposing fines for infringements of factory rules had often reduced the workers' earnings still further. But starting in 1878, a series of strikes had made the government aware of the workers' grievances, so much so that when N.-K. Bunge became Finance Minister (1881–7), he brought in legislation to prevent employers inflicting excessive fines (June 1886). However, all too typically, he was a constant target for the attacks of employers who objected to what they called his 'socialist' measures.

TABLE II

	1870s	1890s	1913
Average industrial daily wage	c. 1s		
for skilled and semi-skilled			2s 8d
for skilled, in engineering and construction		3s or more	

The workers' chance nevertheless came in the 1890s when Witte was launching his campaign to promote Russian industry. This was just the time when the threat of widespread strikes could have the effect of panicking the government into making concessions in defence of its industrial dream-child. And indeed the first dividend came in a law of July 1897, limiting the adult working day to eleven and a half hours and prohibiting work on Sundays and special feast-days. March 1906, moreover, saw a major stride forward with the legalising of trade unions on a local if not on a national level – though clandestine unions, of course, had been in existence since before 1870. Strikes, however, were still theoretically illegal. The last concession of the Tsarist regime, before war overtook it, was the sickness insurance act (June 1912), covering nearly a quarter of the labour force, three-fifths of the cost coming from workers' contributions, employers providing the rest. This was to remain an isolated achievement, however, for the whirlwind of 1917 was to find Russia still without the other main pillar of social insurance, a state pensions scheme.

At the opening of the period, a formidable danger for the working classes was military service. Although only one or two in every five hundred would be designated in peacetime, it literally took the best years of their lives, in that service with the colours was ten or fifteen years, followed by ten or fifteen in the reserve. Those who were unlucky in the lottery were regarded by the rest of the village with the same mixture of awe and sympathy as if they had been struck by lightning. Considerable relief, however, came in January 1874, when the orbit of the lottery was extended to other classes, thereby enabling the government to reduce colour-service to six years, or much less for those with educational or other qualifications.

The landlords

The poor living standards and illiteracy of the lower working class created a much wider gulf between them and the other classes than existed in western Europe. On the whole, the 30,000 noble landowners of Russia did well out of the Emancipation of 1861. Not only was the land over-valued by an average of some 47 per cent, but they still retained 230 million acres, despite being parted from the rest (about 290 million). At the same time, improved rail facilities opened up large markets for grain in other parts of Europe, even if the potential profit was severely curtailed by American competition and the fall in prices. In Russia itself, wheat prices had fallen 15 per cent by the early eighties. It must also be remembered that in 1861 many land-owning families were burdened with substantial debts, and these on the average were to absorb about half the proceeds of the Emancipation. Indeed many tried to solve their difficulties by selling part of their land to the bourgeoisie and richer peasants, so much so that by 1913 the nobility only held half the land they had had just after Emancipation. The work of the official Peasants' Land Bank (April 1883) had speeded the change of ownership, despite the government's creation of a countervailing Nobles' Land Bank in 1885.

Ethnic minorities

As far as the unprivileged masses were concerned, material grievances were not the entirety of their troubles. Well over two-fifths of the population of European Russia belonged to ethnic minorities, many of whom differed from the 'Great Russians' in religion and custom. Half of these were Ukrainians (23 million in 1897) with strong traditions of their own. The Bylorussians by contrast were much less numerous (4·5 million), and less conscious of their separateness. But real difficulties began with the religious minorities. The Poles (9 million) and Lithuanians (2 million) were largely Catholic, while the Latvians (2 million), Estonians (1 million) and Finns (3 million) were mainly Lutheran. There were also over 4 million Jews, who suffered from various legal disabilities, depending on the district they lived in.

The position of religious minorities in Russia can only be understood in the context of the privileged situation of the Russian Orthodox Church. This situation exemplified in extreme form the advantages and disadvantages of being a state church. On the one hand it was entrusted with much of the expansion in primary education that took wing in the 1880s. On the other hand the Holy Synod was traditionally dominated by the government, and had long since ceased to give an intellectual and spiritual lead. The Tsar controlled the appointment of bishops through his lay representative, the Over Procurator, who also exerted a strong influence over the lay secretaries of the diocesan consistories, to which the bishops were largely subservient. Not only were many parish churches and monasteries endowed with state land, but the bishops and numerous lower clergy received state salaries. Nevertheless the intrinsic power of Orthodox Christianity continued to be a source of inspiration for many Russians, as can be seen in some of the great literary masterpieces of the period. Conversely Orthodox Christianity also gained from the growing awareness in cultural circles of Russia's past and traditions.

This awareness, however, had its less fortunate aspects. Both Alexander III and Nicholas II were to cause much misery and ill-feeling by their efforts to Russify ethnic minorities. In Poland Alexander II (1855–81) had already hauled back into the fold those former Orthodox churches that had accepted papal authority; while his son, Alexander III (1881–94), altogether forbade other religions to proselytise. Nicholas II (1894–1917) for his part continued the family tradition by making an all-out assault on Finnish local privileges.

THE ECONOMIC AND POLITICAL FACTORS

In Russia economic and social issues have been much more influenced by government action than has been the case in western European nations. Since the time of Peter the Great, if not earlier, Russian governments have exercised a much more dominant role in the country's life than in western countries. Peter the Great, for example, had endeavoured to reorganise society with a thoroughness that would have been quite unthinkable in the west, even under the absolutism of Louis XIV. Russian society, moreover, both expected and accepted such action. The emancipation of the serfs in 1861 is a case in point, likewise Russia's industrial revolution which, beginning in the 1890s, owed so much to government initiative. For this reason it is more convenient to examine the Russian economy when dealing with government policy in general.

TABLE 12

Annual average

	1876–80	1913
Exports	c. £53 m	c. £153 m
(proportion grain)	(c. 40%)	(c. 40%)
Imports	c. £52 m	c. £138 m

Nevertheless Table 12 perhaps deserves comment at this point. The increasingly favourable balance of trade reflected two major factors. First, grain production had more than trebled as a result of modern crop-rotation and mechanisation on the more prosperous farms. And secondly, Russia's industrial revolution of the 1890s lessened her need to import manufactures in the quantities of past years. It should be realised, however, that this trade balance has to be seen in the context of a heavy public and private indebtedness to foreign creditors, amounting to some £760 million by 1914 (see p. 163). Thus while 1913 gave Russia a trade surplus of £15 million, interest on the foreign debt took away £35 million, while another £7 million was spent by Russians abroad, to say nothing of £2 million in foreign bank and insurance charges.[1]

In Russia, the personality of the Tsar was a prime factor in the nation's life. Until 1905 there was no parliament, the Tsar appointing whom he liked as ministers, none of whom was a prime minister, properly speaking. The reforms of the reign of Alexander II (1855–81) owed most to the hard lessons of the Crimean War, but it was fortunate that this moderate conservative had the good sense to recognise the dictates of necessity. He saw that Russia's defeat at the hands of incompetent opponents was the direct outcome of her domestic backwardness. Most of his far-reaching reforms, however, belong to the 1860s – with the exception of the law on city government of June 1870. This gave every city-dwelling houseowner and trade-taxpayer a vote in municipal elections, even if voting power was proportional to wealth.

Considerable hopes had been raised by the institution of district and provincial assemblies in the ethnically Russian parts of the Empire (Law of January 1864). Consisting of representatives of the peasants, townsmen and landowners, these zemstvos were elected indirectly, the base of the pyramid for the peasant section being the peasant householder. Although the assemblies themselves met only once a year, they were empowered to appoint zemstvo boards to deal with education, medicine, roads, famine-relief and other matters of importance to the locality. And it was these boards, rather than the assemblies, that made such a significant contribution to Russian well-being, especially in the provision of what was in fact a free medical service. The zemstvo system also gave administrative and political experience to men who would otherwise never have found it in Tsarist Russia before the events of 1905 (see pp. 166–7). Nevertheless the power of the zemstvos was severely limited by the authority of the governor, who not only retained control of much of the administration but could also interfere in the zemstvo's work. At

---

[1] Russia's principal creditors were France (67 per cent), Britain (17 per cent), Germany (9 per cent) and Belgium (4 per cent). Her best trade customers were Germany (32 per cent), Britain (19 per cent) and France (6 per cent).

the same time the zemstvos contained too many landowners, the
gentry occupying nearly two-thirds of the seats on the zemstvo
boards.

For many of the middle class, moreover, these reforms in
local government still left unanswered the main question of who
was to guide the nation – and in whose interests. The stock
answer – the Tsar, in the interests of all his people – was no
longer satisfying. The government's suppression of criticism
suggested that it was not prepared to listen to, let alone discuss,
its shortcomings; while the ignorance of the masses prevented
their being aware of these deficiencies. In the view of the more
impatient reformers, the only short-term solutions to the
problem were either violence or a vast campaign for educating
the masses. Given the fact that the bulk of the population
were peasants, it was not surprising that the mainstream of the
revolutionary movement in Russia should look to the peasantry.
This indeed was notably exemplified in 1873, the year when the
government recalled to Russia all students studying abroad,
mainly because it was afraid of the revolutionary ideas they
might pick up. Many of these students on arriving home took
up jobs in the villages in order to make contact with the
peasant masses, their example being followed by many students
from Russian institutions, until a total of some 2500 students
were involved altogether. They intended both to educate the
peasantry and subject them to revolutionary propaganda.
They varied in their political creeds, but many were Bakuninists
(see p. 87), aiming at a peasant revolution, which would take
authority from the central government and vest it in the *mir*
or Russian village-authority. Indeed the whole essence of this
'Populist' or Narodnik movement was agrarian and decentralist. These ideas, however, cut little ice with the peasantry,
who as always were much more interested in obtaining more
private land for themselves. The Narodniks in any case broke
up into various factions, the new groupings making their
presence felt by a series of futile assassinations, notably of the
Tsar Alexander II in March 1881.

The reign of his son, Alexander III (1881–94), bore the
stamp of the new Tsar's mentor, Konstantin Pobedonostsev,
and was one of almost unmitigated reaction on the political

level. Indeed liberals the world over might well lament that the name of 'this best forgotten Tsar' should be perpetuated in one of the finest bridges in Paris – for France paid more than money for the Russian alliance of the nineties (see pp. 218–19). He began in 1881 by giving the government almost complete freedom to deal as it pleased with political undesirables, while his subsequent modifications to local government reduced the municipal electorate in St Petersburg and Moscow by two-thirds. Yet it was Alexander's Minister of Finance, Sergei Witte (1892–1903), who did so much to launch Russia's industrial revolution in the 1890s (see below). Alexander's death gave Russia to the care of his son, Nicholas II (1894–1917), unimaginative and weak-willed, though not without intelligence. But he intensified his father's policy of russifying Finland, and systematically lost what little goodwill was left there. On the other hand it was during his reign that Witte's industrial policies bore fruit.

In the 1860s the government had feared that an industrial society in Russia might lead to a weakening of the monarchy. But the outcome of the Congress of Berlin in 1878 showed that unless Russia became industrialised, her huge army could not preserve her from diplomatic humiliation by more advanced nations. Yet Russia lacked both financial capital and a good labour force, while migration to the cities was limited by the control which the communes exercised over the peasants. Diplomatic tension in the 1880s had reduced the willingness of Britain, then of Germany, to lend to Russia in the 1880s. But the Franco-Russian *rapprochement* of the early nineties brought with it not only French government loans (totalling over £440 million by 1914) but also increased French private investment (£73 million by 1914). Indeed in the 1890s, foreign investment in Russian private enterprise increased from about £20 million to £90 million; while foreign confidence was strengthened by Witte's establishing Russian currency on a firm gold basis in 1897. At the same time the shortage of suitable manpower was partially solved by the installation of the latest labour-saving machinery, which also resulted in the factories being unusually large. The fact that Russia was short of experienced managerial staff similarly encouraged the principle of having a few large factories rather than many small ones. Particular emphasis was put on metal industries. In 1900 textiles still employed nearly a third of the industrial labour force, but metallurgy and mining were already employing a quarter, and metal manufactures about a tenth. Moreover, the rapid increase in the government's railway-building campaign not only provided cheaper and more efficient transport of goods and raw materials, but also provided a growing demand for the nation's metal output. Russian industrial output increased at an average of 8 per cent annually in the 1890s, the class of richer peasants providing a gradually expanding market for clothes and utensils. Russia's Asiatic neighbours likewise provided a growing if impecunious market for manufactures, her overall industrial exports increasing from £1 million to £1·9 million in the 1890s. Nevertheless the main contribution of these industrial developments was still largely that of lessening the need for imports from abroad; for although industry by 1913 accounted for just over a quarter of overall production, it provided only a twentieth of Russian exports.

1900, however, brought a depression. Although partly the result of over-investment and over-production, it also partly came from the inescapable fact that the burden of indirect taxation was lessening the buying power of the peasantry. At the same time peasant discontent had been aggravated by several severe famines – in 1891–2, 1897, 1898 and 1901. Indeed peasant insurrections in the provinces of Poltava and Kharkov in 1902 indicated the depth of economic discontent, while the growing numbers of industrial strikes showed similar feelings in the towns.

Such a situation was bound to encourage revolutionary activity. The mainstream of Russian revolutionary activity was now represented by Victor Chernov's Social Revolutionary Party which in many ways represented a continuation of the Narodnik tradition. Pinning its faith on the peasantry, it took propaganda and violence as its methods. Although it was riddled with police spies, it carried out a series of spectacular assassinations, including those of two successive Ministers of the Interior. Indeed the curious schizophrenic existence of the Russian police spy is well illustrated by the fact that the demise of the second Minister was supervised, if not actually arranged, by one of his own spies, as part of his assumed role.

The Marxists, on the other hand, were represented by the Social Democrat Party of 1903. Having its roots in Georgi Plekhanov's Liberation of Labour, its most remarkable member was Vladimir Ulyanov, alias Lenin, who together with Jules Martov, was on the editorial board of the emigré Marxist weekly, *Iskra*. Lenin was one of the most single-minded men in history. At seventeen his youthful revolutionary zeal had been given emotional depth when his brother was hanged for conspiring to assassinate Alexander III. His energy, the incisiveness of his thinking and the austerity of his life were to make him both a force and an inspiration. There was something almost terrible about his self-discipline, as exemplified in a later remark: 'I can't listen to music too often. It affects your nerves, and makes you want to say stupid nice things.'

The Social Democrats held their first significant congress in the summer of 1903 in Brussels, then London. Martov favoured social action by a broad-fronted popular party, as did another outstanding member of the group, Leon Trotsky. But Lenin by contrast believed in the efficacy of a revolutionary élite. Plekhanov and the majority of those present (hence *Bolshevik*) sided with Lenin against Martov and his minority (hence *Menshevik*). But Plekhanov's subsequent attempts to heal the breach piqued Lenin into forming his Bolshevik followers into a separate group.

The Mensheviks and Bolsheviks, however, were not only divided on strategy. In accordance with traditional Marxist teaching, the Mensheviks believed that the urban workers, not the peasants, would be the executants of the revolution that would finally bring well-being to the people. Most of them likewise believed that there would first have to be a liberal 'bourgeois' revolution to institute a capitalist regime in Russia, from which, and against which, an urban proletariat would rise. Lenin on the other hand, was anxious to see a proletarian revolution in Russia in his own lifetime. He knew that if Russia was to wait until the industrial proletariat became a majority of the nation – as the Mensheviks seemed to imply – then there could not possibly be a proletarian revolution in the lifetime of anyone then living. He therefore advocated a revolutionary alliance between the industrial proletariat and the poorer peasantry, adding that Russia must move straight from the bourgeois to the proletarian revolutions: 'From the democratic revolution we shall begin immediately and . . . make the transition to the socialist revolution. We stand for uninterrupted revolution.'

The liberal bourgeois revolution, which for the Socialists was merely the first rung of the ladder, was the main objective for the Union of Liberation which the Liberals formed in 1902. The Liberals had the advantage of respectability and well-known names. Moreover the government's mishandling of the Russo-Japanese War of 1904–5 created a general feeling of dissatisfaction, which enabled the Liberals to spread demands for a national representative assembly. They also established close relations with a number of trade unions, with the result that the government was faced with an unusual combination of bourgeois liberals and working-class opinion.

The situation became a crisis on 22 January 1905, 'Bloody Sunday'. A procession of demonstrators, carrying a petition to the Tsar, was fired on by the police in St Petersburg, several hundred people, including many bystanders, being killed or wounded. This led to a dramatic wave of strikes, while there were also mutinies aboard several warships, notably the battleship *Potemkin*. (*Potemkin*'s crew were eventually to crown their extraordinary odyssey by being the guests of G. M. Trevelyan and other admirers at a convivial meeting in Whitechapel (1908), where English and Russian songs were sung alternately.) The culmination came, however, in October 1905, when there was a gigantic strike in St Petersburg, where the workers set up a committee or soviet to direct it. The result seemed a triumphant vindication of their efforts. The government agreed to transform itself into a constitutional monarchy and establish a prime minister responsible to a proper legislative assembly. Indeed Paul Miliukov's liberal Constitutional Democratic Party ('the Cadets') prepared to work for substantial reforms within the framework of legality, notably for the expropriation (with compensation) of the large estates.

Yet the reality of the Tsar's offer proved to be much less inviting than the promise. In May 1906 he issued the Fundamental Laws which made it clear that the ministers were to be responsible to the Tsar, not to the Duma or parliament, and that there was to be an upper chamber, half-filled with royal nominees, with the power of blocking legislation passed by the Duma. Furthermore the elections to the Duma which had taken place in the previous quarter were indirect, even though, in theory at least, nearly all men of a year's residence had a vote at some level of the electoral pyramid. Nevertheless the Social Democrats and Social Revolutionaries felt that their distrust of the Tsar's offer had been more than justified, and had largely boycotted the election. The result was that the Duma which met in May 1906 contained few of their representatives, while the boycott brought no compensating advantages.

Even so, the Cadets' demand for land reform decided the government to dissolve the Duma (July 1906). The result was that the Social Democrats decided to fight the next election, as did a number of the Social Revolutionaries – which gave them the reward of a Duma which was over two-fifths left wing.

The prime minister, Peter Stolypin (June 1906–September 1911) was anxious to make constitutional government work, but felt that the new Duma was too hostile to the government for this to be possible, so he agreed with the Tsar to dissolve it in June 1907. Moreover, to obtain a more co-operative Duma, the electoral law was altered on the same day to give much more representation to the gentry. Although no one was actually disenfranchised, the following scale of values was established:

1 landlord's vote = 4 upper bourgeois votes = 65 middleclass votes = 260 peasant votes = 540 industrial workers' votes.

The all-too predictable result was that the government was assured of a majority in subsequent Dumas and the chances of radical reform through constitutional means were effectively buried.

Stolypin accompanied this rough handling of the constitution with firm repressive measures against the opposition outside parliament. Within a few months, over a thousand people

were tried by court martial and executed, while 206 newspapers were suppressed. It is sometimes forgotten, however,
that 1400 people were killed by terrorists in 1906, and another
3000 in the next twelve months. Indeed Stolypin himself was
assassinated in September 1911 – not untypically by a former
police agent. The grotesque mixture of tragedy and farce which
gave many Russian novels their 'Russian' flavour certainly
had its counterpart in the country's political life.

Stolypin's ministry had many positive achievements to its
credit. It is true that his policy of giving the peasants personal
control over their land largely sprang from his belief in creating
a contented peasantry as a bulwark against revolutionary
activity; but the results in terms of human well-being were none
the less real for that. Similarly his law of 1908 for the provision
of many more teachers and schools was another example of the
enlightened quality of much of his administration.

RUSSIAN IMPERIALISM IN ASIA

Russia's non-European territory was three times greater than
what she held in Europe, yet even in 1913 it supported a
population of under thirty million, half of whom were European
settlers or of European stock. The Russian Asiatic empire was
unique among European colonial empires in being contiguous
with the ruling country. Ethnic interpenetration made it
difficult to distinguish between Russians and natives in the
border regions, while the large-scale European settlement that
took place elsewhere further blurred the differences. The result
was that there was no attempt to make legal distinctions
between Russians and natives, the non-racial differences
between them being economic and social.

It could be argued that the principal value of the Empire to
Russia was as a dumping ground for the peasants whom the
process of emancipation had left with too little land. But
Central Asia was also valuable as a cotton-growing region, and
it is perhaps not without significance that Russian advances in
the region had acquired added impetus during the American
Civil War, when American cotton was in short supply. At the
same time, however, punitive expeditions against marauding

tribesmen also played a part, while the proximity of southern Central Asia to India also made it useful as a means of putting diplomatic pressure on Britain (see pp. 216–17).

Broadly speaking, the only significant additions to the Empire that were made in this period were the annexation of the Kars district of Transcaucasia in 1878, and the occupation of what remained of southern Central Asia between 1873 and 1895. The outcome was that the Russian Empire now had a continuous frontier with Persia, Afghanistan and China. Later years, however, brought losses. The Russians lost not only prestige in their war with Japan (1904–5) but also ice-free Port Arthur, which Russia had leased from China since 1898. She was similarly obliged to evacuate the Chinese territory of Manchuria, occupied by the Russians during the Boxer rising of 1900.

Although Central Asia held the most attractive areas for European settlement, the Tsarist government was anxious to make use of the vast expanses of territory to the north-east. The result was a major scheme for state-aided settlement in Siberia, in which the intrepid pioneer, bundled in furs, was offered thirty-six acres of free land, plus a loan, partial tax exemptions and postponement of military service (July 1889). For those who decided to take the plunge, thirty-six acres represented over a fourfold increase in land, since their holdings at home had averaged less than nine acres, but until the building of the Trans-Siberian Railway (1891–1905) the journey was extremely hard, a third of the children dying *en route*. Nevertheless by the outbreak of the war, nearly eight of Siberia's nine million inhabitants were either settlers or of settler stock.

AUSTRIA-HUNGARY

A rather unintellectual Anglican bishop of the nineteenth century once exclaimed: 'I could verily wish all the German philosophers and their German philosophy at the bottom of the German ocean.' A similar exasperation would often overcome foreigners who tried to understand the complexities of the Austro-Hungarian Empire. It was much more satisfactory, at the lowest level, to imagine Vienna as a world of epaulettes and operetta. At a slightly higher level, it was equally pleasurable, aesthetically, to regard the Emperor Franz Josef as some ageing eagle, whom time was overtaking, and whose wide domains would not survive his own demise. Indeed, the Habsburg family itself had a dissolution complex which took the form of indulging in what at times came near to a melancholy pleasure in the prospect of impending doom. But the Empire in fact was much more secure than most of them would admit, and it was only the First World War that brought it to such a rapid end.

TABLE 13

	1870	1910
Total population	36 m	51 m
Germans		24%
Magyars		20%
Romanians		6%
Italians		1·5%
Czechs		13%
Slovaks		4%
Poles		10%
Ruthenians ⟩ 'Slavs'		8%
Slovenes		3%
Croats		5%
Serbs		4%
Proportion of		
population in agriculture	c. 70%	c. 50%
in industry	c. 13%	c. 30%

It has been said, and well said, that there are 'lies; damned lies; and statistics'. But it is hard to avoid statistics when writing of Austria-Hungary so briefly – hence the accompanying tables. The Empire was a strange patchwork of nationalities that had been brought under Habsburg rule during the course of the centuries, with Germans and Magyars outnumbered by the other ethnic groups. The term 'Slav' is about as helpful to the historian as the academic's pet escape-phrase, 'not inconsiderable'. Indeed most of the Slav nationalities were more distrustful of each other than they were of the Habsburg monarchy, so it would be erroneous to envisage 'the Slavs' as a monolithic block of anti-Habsburg feeling.

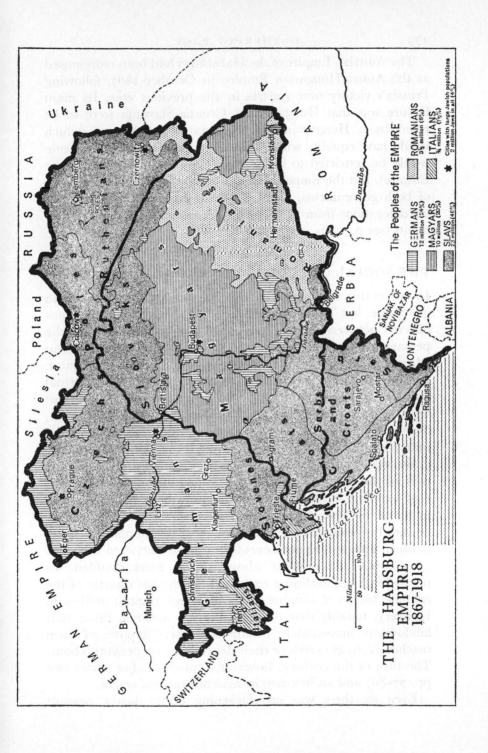

THE HABSBURG
EMPIRE
1867-1918

Miles
0   50   100

The Peoples of the EMPIRE

GERMANS
12 million (24%)

MAGYARS
10 million (20%)

SLAVS
23 million (46%)

ROMANIANS
3½ million (6%)

ITALIANS
¾ million (1½%)

★ Cities with large Jewish populations
2 million Jews in all (4%)

RUSSIA

Ukraine

Poland

Silesia

Czernowitz

Lemberg

Polish
Poles

Ruthenians

Cracow

Slovaks

Czechs

Eger

Prague

Bratislava

Bavaria

Danube

Vienna

Linz

Klagenfurt

Innsbruck

Munich

SWITZERLAND

Trent

Italians

Slovenes

Trieste

Fiume

Zagram

Adriatic Sea

ITALY

Germans

Magyars

Budapest

Danube

Belgrade

SERBIA

Croats

and

Serbs

Sarajevo

Mostar

Spalato

Ragusa

SANJAK OF
NOVIBAZAR

MONTENEGRO

ALBANIA

Hungarians

Szeklers

Kronstadt

Hermannstadt

ROMANIA

Danube

GERMAN EMPIRE

The Austrian Empire of the Habsburgs had been reorganised as the Austro-Hungarian Empire in October 1867, following Prussia's victory over Austria in the previous year. Its main feature was that Hungary and Croatia-Slavonia were to be ruled by a Hungarian 'parliamentary' government, which would have equality with its Austrian counterpart (whose rule would be restricted to the western and northern parts of the Empire). But the Emperor would continue to be the sovereign of both governments, aided by three Imperial ministers and by delegations from the 'Austrian' and 'Hungarian' parliaments (see p. 179).

THE SOCIAL OUTCOME AND ECONOMIC FACTORS

In an entity so diverse as the Empire it is impossible to generalise, but Table 14 gives a rough idea of how conditions differed between the two halves. In both parts, however, the peasant who held land belonged to a lucky minority, while in Magyar 'Hungary' a mere 321 people held a fifth of the land. Indeed the Esterhazy and Schönborn estates were virtual kingdoms. Farmers large and small, however, were badly hit by the European influx of Russian and American grain, despite heavy tariffs and the growing food demands of the industrial regions. Hungary ceased to be an international grain supplier, becoming instead a granary for the Austrian part of the Empire. Timber, wood-manufactures, sugar and eggs were left as the Empire's principal exports. Consequently many of the Hungarian gentry sold their land to their more powerful neighbours, with the result that the number of estates between 1400 and 14,000 acres fell by a third between 1885 and 1914, while the number above 14,000 acres doubled. In parallel fashion, declining real wages in the last quarter of the century led to a number of widespread peasant strikes in Hungary, notably that of 1897, the net outcome being that landowners immediately quadrupled their imports of farm machinery, so as to reduce their dependence on peasant labour. The turn of the century, however, brought higher prices (see pp. 77–80) and an increase in agricultural real wages.

Even so, there was no slackening of the heavy peasant

emigration that had grown during the decades of agricultural depression. From Hungary alone, one-and-a-quarter million had left by 1910.

TABLE 14

The agricultural population in the 1870s

	'Austria'	'Hungary'
Proportion of total who were land-holders	c. 25%	c. 20%
Proportion of land-holders who owned their land	c. 60–70%	
Agriculture wages as proportion of British equivalent	65% or less (e.g. 40% in Dalmatia and Galicia)	60% or less

It must nevertheless be remembered that Bohemia contained one of Europe's most highly developed industrial centres, with textiles, china and glass as its specialities. Its coal production, though insignificant compared with Germany, was over 60 per cent of that of France; while only Germany and Belgium exceeded its glass exports. Taking the Empire as a whole, industrial wages in the 1870s varied from about two-fifths of the British level (Silesia, Bohemia and Dalmatia) to about three-fifths in the German-speaking parts of Austria, with twelve hours as the average working day. The early 1890s, however, saw increased trade union activity (legal since 1870–2), thereby helping to obtain a ten-hour day for most industrial workers by 1907. Nevertheless, accommodation in the towns did not keep pace with the leap forward of the 1890s in industry, with the result that at the turn of the century a quarter of the urban population were living more than five to a room. Before the laws of 1887–8 (see p. 53), social insurance depended on private initiative, about a sixth of the factory population in 'Austria' belonging to factory schemes for pensions and half-pay during sickness. The workman contributed 6 or 7 per cent of his wage as a composite premium, the employer making up the difference. Another third of the factory population were covered by similar factory schemes with lump-sum compensation for sickness, accident and death.

Both in town and country, however, the relatively low level of education impeded personal advancement and the better use of what leisure the wage-earner had. In 1880, over two-fifths of the 'Austrian' population and two-thirds of the 'Hungarian' population could neither read nor write. And despite the efforts of municipalities to increase the number and standard of their schools, 1900 still found the illiteracy level for 'Austria' at between a third and two-fifths, and for 'Hungary' at nearly a half.

All classes were to some degree or other the victims of the Habsburg bureaucratic system. Its endless chains of decision-deferring and its obscurantist worship of the letter of the law often contrasted strangely with the personal kindliness of the officials who ran it. Kindliness, however, was small consolation to supplicants whose livelihood or freedom might depend on a decision lost somewhere in the pipeline or blocked by a literal interpretation of the law. The character of the system is brilliantly suggested in the nightmare novels of Franz Kafka, (1883–1924), *The Trial* (1925) and *The Castle* (1926).[1] Although these works are generally seen as portraying the predicament of man in the modern state, their mood and their perception of the personal side of officialdom owe much to Kafka's experience of life in Imperial Prague.

A not untypical example of Habsburg bureaucracy at work is given by an English observer, Henry Wickham Steed:

> Early in 1911, at a level crossing on one of the State Railway lines in Bohemia, a wagon laden with wood stuck fast between the rails on account of the rottenness of the sleeper. A passing train smashed the wagon, killed one of the horses and injured another. The local tribunal acquitted the wagon-driver of blame and recognised that the fault lay with the railway administration. The wagon-driver consequently demanded from the state £50 indemnity. The first step of the State Railway Administration was to forbid the use of the horse that had been injured but had in the meantime recovered. Then seven different commissions [including] veterinary surgeons from Prague, Eger and Karlsbad made local investigations. . . . The repair of the defective sleeper was forbidden lest the *de facto* situation be changed pending the reports of the commissions . . . [despite the fact that] drays repeatedly stuck fast at the same crossing and had to be lifted out by main force. . . . The sequel is unknown, save that the unfortunate wagoner was ruined by the

[1] Both published posthumously.

loss of his wagon and by the prohibition to use or sell his surviving horse.[1]

The extent of the shortcomings of Habsburg bureaucracy may be gauged from the indignation of even the Papal Nuncio: 'One knows when a document is handed in to an Austrian Department of State; but a young man may grow old before knowing when he will see it again. Accustomed to the business-like methods of the Vatican, I find these eternal delays exasperating.'

Problems of nationality loom large in any history of the Empire. But it was mainly the middle and upper classes who had cause to take them as seriously as the historians. Among the working classes, these issues were really significant only for those who happened to be living where another nationality was predominant, and where prejudice was marked. For them, independence from Habsburg rule would make things worse rather than better, since they would be completely at the mercy of the local majority. It was the children of non-German and non-Magyar people who could be most affected by Austro-Hungarian rule. In mixed areas they might well be forced to speak a different language at school from what they spoke at home. Their parents, however, had few direct dealings with authority, and led their lives largely unaffected by the issue of what was the official language of the province. Nevertheless for the educated, with political or administrative aspirations, the fact of being neither German nor Magyar could put them at a considerable disadvantage, especially in the Hungarian half of the Empire.

The 'Austrian' constitution of December 1867 theoretically guaranteed the equality of the various component nationalities. But the mapping out of parliamentary constituencies was so managed as to give the Germans a disproportionately large representation in the lower house. Even the constitutional changes that came with the law of January 1907 still gave the Germans 45 per cent of the seats, although they were only 35 per cent of the 'Austrian' population. It is true that the representation of the Czechs and Poles was now more in accord with

[1] The Habsburg Monarchy (Constable, 1913) pp. 82–3.

their importance (23 per cent and 17 per cent respectively of the 'Austrian' population), but the smaller minorities were still under-represented.

Although the constitution recognised the right of the various nationalities to keep their respective languages, German continued to be the language used in official publications and, theoretically, in schools. In practice, however, officials, teachers and pupils of the same nationality generally spoke to each other in their native language, although they had to be able to understand and write German for formal matters and examinations. In 1879, however, the government attempted to buy Czech parliamentary support by giving Czech partial equality with German in Czech-speaking areas (see p. 180), while on a general level a larger number of native officials was appointed in the non-German provinces, a number of Czechs even obtaining ministerial office. A further attempt at conciliation came in April 1897, when Count Casimir Badeni's ordinances gave Czech theoretical parity with German in Bohemia and Moravia. Since most non-Germans understood German, while few Germans bothered to master the other languages, this in effect gave the non-Germans an advantage in applying for civil service posts where the languages were interchangeable. However, these latest conciliatory moves foundered on the awkward fact that Germans accounted for a third of the population in Bohemia and Moravia taken as a whole, and it was a sad though not surprising outcome that the Germans wrecked this and other attempts to give the Czechs more autonomy.

The development of Czech industry naturally fostered the growth of an important politically-conscious middle class, which quickly became the principal threat to Habsburg rule. By contrast other non-German nationalities tended to be led by the landowning classes, who in social and economic matters often had more in common with the monarchy than with their fellow nationals of other classes. Another outcome of the growth of industry in the German-speaking parts of Bohemia was that Czech agricultural workers were attracted into these areas, so diminishing the German predominance there. Czech cultural activity in this period contained much that was nationally self-conscious; and it was sufficiently sophisticated to attract notice abroad, especially in music, where Bedřich Smetana (1824–84) and Anton Dvořák (1841–1904) enjoyed an international reputation – though Leoš Janáček (1854–1928) was to achieve fame abroad only after the war.

Looking eastward, Galicia might seem a source of trouble in that its population was three-fifths Pole and two-fifths Ruthenian. But since Galicia had an unusually large degree of autonomy in its affairs, the Poles were fairly favourably disposed towards the Habsburg government, their position being far better than that of the Poles in Russia and Prussia. Lectures were given in Polish at Cracow University, and most official posts were filled by Poles, several Poles achieving ministerial rank, both in the 'Austrian' and Imperial governments. The Ruthenians were the chief victims of this situation, with the result that a considerable number of the politically conscious among them hoped for eventual absorption in a separate Ukrainian state.

Turning to the south, the Empire acquired further problems when Bosnia and Herzegovina were put under Habsburg control in 1878, and finally annexed in 1908. Their population was two-fifths Serb, one-fifth Croat and a third Serbo-Croat Muslim. Not only this, but the Serbs were Orthodox not Catholic, so that religious animosities were added to ethnic differences. The growth moreover of the neighbouring state of Serbia in size and prestige gave the Serbs a focus of loyalty which greatly worried the Habsburg government. Nevertheless the more perceptive Imperial officials recognised that the Serbs were a much less serious threat to the structure of the Empire than the Czechs, since Serb–Croat rivalry was sufficient to make each nationality prefer Habsburg rule to the prospect of being at the mercy of the other.

On balance there could be no doubt that the non-Germans in the 'Austrian' half of the Empire had less to complain about than the non-Magyars in 'Hungary'. Numbering half the 'Hungarian' population, the Magyars thought they could afford to be aggressive. Despite the ethnic distinctiveness of Transylvania and Slovakia, Croatia-Slavonia was the only area to be allowed its own Diet and separate representation in the 'Hungarian' lower house. Even so, the real power there was exercised by the governor, appointed by the 'Hungarian' government. Moreover the mapping out of 'Hungarian' parliamentary constituencies left the non-Magyars with little more than a fifth of the seats that their overall numbers would have justly demanded; while the administration was over 95 per cent Magyar.

Although the 'Hungarian' nationalities law of 1868 guaranteed their right to use their native tongue in schools, the law in practice was not properly observed. Slovenska Matika, the society for furthering Slovak culture, was outlawed in 1875, the 'Hungarian' government declaring that there was no such thing as a Slovak nationality. The number of Slovak-speaking primary schools fell from 1805 to 241 in the next thirty years, while only one Slovak newspaper survived beyond 1900.

One minority often forgotten are the Jews. Eminent in business and the professions, they also controlled a large section of the Vienna press. Most of the Austrian-born Viennese composers of any worth in this period were Jews, while a Prussian diplomat once remarked, with some exaggeration, that 'in most Austro-Hungarian Embassies and legations is to be found an aristocrat with good manners and few brains to do the honours, while behind a screen in the Chancery sits the son of a baptized Jew who does the work'. Antisemitism was strong. Gustav Mahler (1860–1911) had to become a Catholic to direct the Vienna opera, but this did nothing to alter his unpopularity with the performers, which was only partly the outcome of his personality. Antisemitism was likewise a potent factor in explaining the political success of Burgomaster Karl Lueger (see p. 181). As in Germany the consequent insecurity of the Jews was a major factor in preventing them taking a lead in the demand for more democratic government – a role for which their control of the Press would have admirably positioned them.

THE POLITICAL FACTORS

Franz Josef's policy for the Empire was basically one of survival. For him, the Empire and the monarchy were one; he could only envisage an Empire where power lay with the Emperor. As Henry Wickham Steed observed:

Among the scores of ministers and statesmen who had served Francis Joseph, few retired without feeling that they had been mere pawns in a dynastic game of which they might guess the rules but could not control the moves. Titles and decorations were lavished upon them while in office; a supreme honour sometimes bestowed with gracious words on their dismissal or retirement, but, after retirement, they disappeared into the twilight reserved for pensioned officials and were heard of no more.

As he grew older Franz Josef claimed control by right of experience as well as kingship. In old age, he would fob off would-be advisers with the reply: 'En théorie, en théorie, peut-être; mais, en pratique, il faut avoir été Empereur soixante ans.'

His two great fears were liberalism and nationalism; and towards the end of his reign a third could be added: socialism. But, recognising that some concessions had to be made to all three, he quickly saw that a concession to one could serve as a serious brake on the others.

In fact the dual concept of the Empire itself had arisen from Franz Josef's desire to counterweight the liberal elements in the German-speaking part of the Empire, by giving the conservative Magyar landowners a substantial share of government. The Imperial delegations consisted of a two-chambered body, one of which was to be elected by the 'Austrian' parliament and the other by the 'Hungarian' parliament. Nevertheless the Emperor retained full personal control over the choice of his Imperial as well as his 'Austrian' and 'Hungarian' ministers; and the parliaments could unseat them only by systematically blocking legislation. The three Imperial ministers were functional ministers (foreign affairs, war and finance), most of the significant work in domestic matters being done by the 'Austrian' and 'Hungarian' governments. Initially the 'Austrian' lower house consisted of representatives of the seventeen provincial diets, which were themselves elected on a property franchise, while the 'Hungarian' lower house was elected by men paying 16s a year or more in direct taxation (890,000 in 1870). Voting moreover was by public declaration, which left the voters open to intimidation by the Magyar landlords.

The early years of Dualism were difficult for Franz Josef in that the Czechs were demanding either a tripartite or federal Empire, while demonstrating their discontent by boycotting the 'Austrian' parliament. Adolf Auersperg's ministry of German liberals (November 1871–July 1878) managed to lure them back into the constitutional fold by giving them better representations in the lower house, which was now made directly elective on a property franchise (1873). But effective conciliation had to await the ministry of Count Edward Taaffe (August 1879–November 1893).

A boyhood friend of Franz Josef, Taaffe was a conservative landowner of Irish ancestry, with no particular allegiance other than to the Emperor, whose general views he shared. Describing his policy as 'keeping all the nationalities in a balanced state of mild dissatisfaction', his various concessions to the ethnic groups (see p. 176) enabled him to rely on a parliamentary coalition of Czechs, Poles and German conservatives. But the Empire's various nationalities, like saucepans of simmering milk, were hard to keep at the ideal temperature. The elections of 1891 brought into parliament a new intransigent generation of politicians, the Young Czechs, who were much less ready to co-operate with Taaffe than their predecessors had been. Taaffe's balancing act, however, included heavier items than the middle-class demands of the nationalities. As with the Cat in the Hat, that was not all. He knew that the issues which would loom largest in the future would be the economic and social demands of the peasantry and urban workers. His ministry had already seen some mild legislation for improving working conditions, and his consciousness of social reality convinced him that the advent of universal suffrage would see middle-class nationalist demands swamped by the preoccupations of the working classes. On this simple though shrewd analysis, he threatened the new nationalists with manhood suffrage (October 1893). The threat was impressive – too impressive in fact, for it seemed to many politicians that he was calling in the big devil to get rid of the small. Franz Josef sniffed the wind, and dropped him.

There followed seven years of instability, and another seven of futility. In part this was the characteristic outcome of a situation where parliament had a certain degree of obstructive power, but not enough positive power to be encouraged to behave responsibly. Indeed Ernst Koerber's ministry (January 1900–December 1904) was reduced to legislating by decree. So violent were the wranglings of Czech and German deputies that one statistician was inspired to compile an alphabetical list of 1763 abusive epithets used in the debates, ranging from 'ass' to 'zebra'. The aimlessness of these fourteen lost years was finally underlined in December 1906, when parliament accepted the Taaffe solution of 1893 – universal suffrage. The results justified the experiment. The 1907 elections saw the representation of the various nationalities split across by economic and social divisions, the Young Czechs and other militant nationals losing heavily to the Social Democrats and Christian Socialists. The big devil had at last been called in. But what was his price? Like an ageing Faust with more cunning than learning, Franz Josef evaded the issue. His ministers resorted more and more to legislation by decree, and in this way the Emperor kicked himself free of the ball and chain of the new popularly-based majority.

Thereafter Viktor Adler's Social Democrats were the second largest party with a sixth of the seats. The largest, with a fifth, was Karl Lueger's Christian Socialists. Neither group, however, had much hope of a governmental seat as long as Franz Josef reigned. Refused four times by Franz Josef who disliked his demagogy, Lueger had become mayor of Vienna in 1897. With powerful Catholic backing, he claimed to protect the traditional decencies against the onslaughts of liberals, Jews and socialists. Like Pierre Poujade in the 1950s he posed as the champion of the little man against big business, with the result that peasants, shopkeepers and artisans flocked to vote for his representatives. Hitler also learnt a lot from his success.

The Social Democrats were the only party committed to large-scale social reform, but their efforts in parliament were useless as long as a majority remained so far beyond their reach. Like the French Socialists, they could not hope for a massive electoral victory in a predominantly rural country.

Although they preached moderation and avoided denigrating the Habsburg monarchy, they found it hard to make profitable tactical alliances with the bourgeois parties, who were only too aware of the Social Democrats' weakness. If in the long run time seemed on their side, time in the short run brought the war, and all its attendant disasters.

Few historians have kind words for Magyar politics in this period. The two largest parties in 'Hungary', Kalman Tisza's Liberal Party and the Magyar National Independence Party, were both committed to the principle of Magyar dominance. But the very aims of the Independence Party excluded it from any real hope of office under the Habsburgs, and so government was mainly in the hands of the Liberals. Like the Scottish Conservatives of popular imagination, the Liberals despised the apostles of independence, and saw salvation in encouraging the evolution of the Dual Monarchy in a direction which would give Hungary overall control.

The 1905 elections, however, put new heart into the Independence Party. When Louis Kossuth, the Grand Old Man of Magyar independence, died in exile in 1894, his son Ferenc had returned to Hungary where he took over the leadership of the party. Heading a formidable opposition in the 1905 parliament, he pressed for the use of Magyar insignia and words of command in the Hungarian regiments. More dangerously, he refused to recognise the existing ministry which, he rightly claimed, represented Franz Josef not the parliamentary majority.

Franz Josef, however, had heard this sort of thing before, and remembered how Taaffe had proposed to deal with it in the case of 'Austria'. In 'Hungary' the threat of universal suffrage would be much more telling, in that it would undermine the Magyar predominance in parliament. Accordingly Franz Josef put on his war-paint, and the government announced its intention to introduce universal suffrage (October 1905). The masquerade had a fair success. Kossuth dropped his demands and Franz Josef shelved his threat. The losers, as always, were the oppressed minorities.

TURKEY

Statesmen gave enormous quantities of time to pondering what was to happen to south-eastern Europe, now that the so-called 'sick man of Europe' was so obviously getting sicker. Yet the interests of their countries in the outcome of this situation have tended to overshadow the problems of the people living in the area.

In 1870, they probably numbered about fifteen million – eight million of whom were still directly under Turkish rule.

TABLE 15

	1870 (millions)	1914 (millions)
Turkey	8	1·9
Romania	3·8	7·5
Greece	1·4	4·4
Serbia	1·0	4·5
Montenegro	0·25	·5
Bulgaria	—	4·5
Albania	—	·8

Turkey was to lose most of these European subjects in the years to come. Three million went in 1878, when the tributary state of Bulgaria came into existence and when Bosnia and Herzegovina passed under Austrian administration. In 1881, 300,000 were lost when Thessaly became Greek, and 800,000 in 1885–6, when Bulgaria acquired Eastern Rumelia, while 1912–13 saw the creation of Albania, and the loss of 850,000. Finally, and most spectacularly, the Balkan Wars of 1912–13 resulted in another three and a half million being divided between Greece, Serbia, Bulgaria and Montenegro.

The people who remained under Turkish rule probably suffered more at the hands of Christians than of Turks. It is true that their greatest material burden was the payment of half their crop to the Turkish landlord, plus the various taxes in kind and cash which they paid to the collector. But most

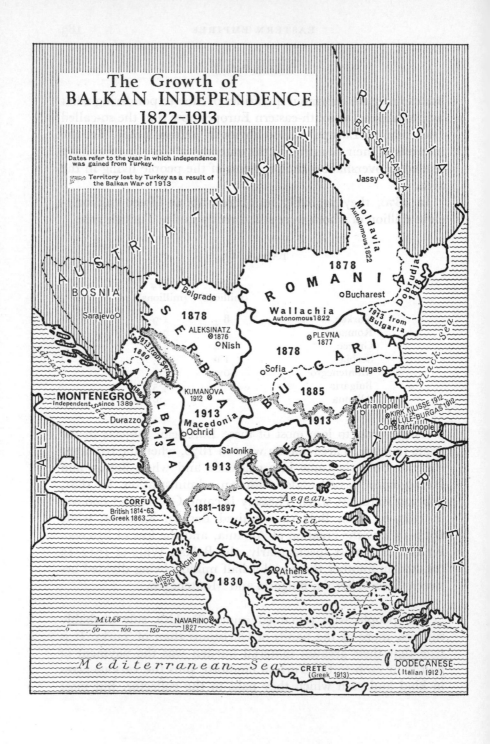

The Growth of
BALKAN INDEPENDENCE
1822-1913

Dates refer to the year in which independence
was gained from Turkey.

Territory lost by Turkey as a result of
the Balkan War of 1913

RUSSIA

BESSARABIA

AUSTRIA-HUNGARY

Jassy

Moldavia
Autonomous 1822

1878
ROMANIA

Dobrudja
1878

BOSNIA

Belgrade

oBucharest

Sarajevoo

Wallachia
Autonomous 1822

1913 from
Bulgaria

1878

SERBIA

ALEKSINATZ
1876
oNish

PLEVNA
1877

1878

Black Sea

1913 from Serbia

1880

oSofia

Burgaso

MONTENEGRO
Independent since 1389

1860

1885

BULGARIA

Durazzo

ALBANIA

KUMANOVA
1912

1913
Macedonia
oOchrid

1913

Adrianople
KIRK KILISSE 1912
LULE-BURGAS 1912

Constantinople

ITALY

Adriatic

Salonika

TURKEY

1913

CORFU
British 1814-63
Greek 1863

1881-1897

Aegean

Sea

Smyrna

GREECE

MISSOLONGHI
1826

1830

oAthens

Miles

NAVARINO
1827

0   50   100   150

Mediterranean   Sea

CRETE
(Greek 1913)

DODECANESE
(Italian 1912)

complaints of injustice were directed against the *millet* or village authorities, which were themselves directly controlled by the Christian ecclesiastical authorities of the region. It should be understood that the Turkish government exercised what was more or less a partial system of indirect rule through the local representatives of the three principal Christian exarchates; and these controlled education and much of the social life of the area. The inhabitants would certainly have seen nothing humorous in the fact that Shaw's Scottish missionary in *Captain Brassbound's Conversion* should feel honoured by being called 'the Christian who is not a thief'.

The rule of the Turkish government itself was nevertheless inefficient and corrupt by most European standards. A group of would-be reformers, led by Midhat Pasha, brought Abdul Hahmid II to the throne (1876–1909) in the hope that he would institute a progressive constitutional reign.[1] But although he called a parliament in March 1877 he used the war with Russia as an excuse to prorogue it, and it never met again until after the revolution of 1908.

In July 1908, however, a reformist military organisation, the Ottoman Society of Liberty, won over the Turkish army in Macedonia, and threatened to march on Constantinople unless Abdul Hahmid restored the short-lived constitution of 1876. They eventually replaced Abdul Hahmid with Muhammad V (1909–18), making the office of Grand Vizier equivalent to that of a European prime minister. The leader of these 'Young Turks', Enver Pasha, proposed that the various nationalities within the Empire should be offered integration and equality, somewhat on French lines. But the *millet* system and tradition of local autonomy within the Empire made such a solution unrealistic. The 'Young Turks' certainly had no intention of relinquishing Turkish control over the subject nationals. Indeed their determination and firmer grasp created great opposition among the Europeans, which itself contributed to the outbreak of the Balkan Wars, thus helping to bring about the virtual exclusion of Turkey from Europe.

[1] Although known to history as 'Abdul the Damned', his many faults have been redeemed in the eyes of Conan Doyle addicts by the fact that he died (1918) clutching a copy of *The Hound of the Baskervilles*.

CHAPTER SIX

The South-West

Italy and Spain

ITALY

THE SOCIAL OUTCOME

If Italy had more to delight the eye than any other European country, she also had a fearsome quantity of problems. Most of the major issues that agitated Europe in the nineteenth century had their counterpart in Italy, where they were often found in accentuated form. If the central event in Italian politics was the fusion of eight states into a single nation, it was a union that had yet to be made on the level of social and economic reality. Antagonism between the developing north and the poverty-stricken south continued to be a dominant feature of Italian politics, while the traditions and antipathies of thirteen hundred years of disunity were not to be effaced by the mere fact of a uniform system of law and administration. Similarly, the way unification had been achieved created a host of new grievances. In effect Piedmont (the Kingdom of Sardinia) had progressively extended her frontiers to include the rest of the peninsula, with the result that the discontented elements in the new Italy were frequently to condemn the unification as a piece of thinly disguised Piedmontese imperialism. The popular enthusiasms of the Risorgimento were easily forgotten amid the unsolved troubles of later decades.

At the same time the seizure of Rome, which completed unification in 1870, greatly deepened the gulf that already divided the Church from the Italian government. For a nation containing a large number of practising Catholics, this was a serious situation. It is true that the Church and liberal government were at odds elsewhere in the world. But in Italy the Church in the 1860s was both a large landowner and a sovereign power – a power moreover that held Rome. For many politicians an Italian nation without Rome was a body without a head, and it was not only the Left that urged its occupation as essential to Italian unity. Indeed it was a ministry of right-wing liberals that eventually ended the temporal power in September 1870.[1]

Even so these issues were small when compared with the grim reality of Italy's social problems, starkly reflected in Table 16. Goodwill alone could not overcome the grinding poverty of so much of the country; indeed goodwill itself was often in short supply, especially between north and south. It was easy enough for parliament to declare primary education compulsory (1877), but the heartbreaking burden of converting hope into reality fell on the unhappy communes who had to try to scrape up the money. Similarly it cost the government little effort to secularise £20 millions' worth of church land (1873); but it was quite another task to spread it fairly and usefully among the peasants. When split up among so many, the plots were small and often situated at a considerable distance from the peasants' own holdings. In consequence wealthy landlords and speculators found it only too easy to buy the land secretly from the peasants at fairly low prices. Predictably enough the clergy were quick with wry suggestions that the nation should follow the example of Pilate's soldiers and cast lots for Christ's garments, instead of dividing them.

Indeed the period was one of continual dilemma for the practising Catholic. On one hand many recognised that the temporal power (see above) had been an obstacle to social progress, and thought it pointless that the Vatican should keep an old wound open. A proportion were prepared to concede that a distribution of church land could be socially desirable. But the orthodox nevertheless found it hard to ignore Vatican directives with an easy conscience. The Vatican not only refused

---

[1] Napoleon III, the reluctant guardian of papal Rome, had been obliged by the Franco-Prussian War to withdraw his garrison to France, thereby leaving the city virtually undefended.

to recognise the Italian occupation of Rome (1870), but demonstrated its displeasure by forbidding Catholics to participate in Italian politics (1874). Apart from the usurpation of the Papal States, however, and the expropriation of religious orders in 1873, the functioning of the Church proceeded unimpeded. Indeed, it was increasingly apparent to thinking Catholics that

TABLE 16

	1871	1913
Total population	28 million	38 million
Non-returning emigrants	5 million	
Percentage of total population		
dependent on agriculture	c. 68%	c. 57%
dependent on industry	c. 13%	c. 23%
Percentage of agricultural population		
landless labourers	c. 57%	
owners	c. 18%	
tenants	c. 7%	
share croppers	c. 17%	
Rural wages as proportion of		
British equivalent	c. 33%	
	(less in the south)	
Industrial wages as proportion of		
British equivalent	c. 50%	
Increase in industrial real wages		c. 100%
Industrial working day		10–11 hours
		(exceptionally 8)
Illiteracy	c. 65–70%	c. 38%
(in south)	(c. 85%)	(c. 70%)
Compulsory worker's compensation	1898	
Pension scheme	1898	
	(voluntary only)	

many of the Church's difficulties in Italy sprang from the Vatican's own attitude. Now that the pope's territorial sovereignty had gone, the main concern of the Vatican was to make it unmistakably clear to the world at large that he was not under the influence of the Italian government, otherwise other states might affect to believe that he was, and declare themselves absolved from dealing with him over the position of the Church in their own territories. At the same time, however, the Vatican probably hoped that its policy of rejecting the Italian government's concessions would acquire for it a certain aura of martyrdom.

The pope therefore not only rejected the concessions of the Law of Guarantees of May 1871, but no longer appeared in public, thereby acquiring the inappropriate if romantic title of 'the prisoner in the Vatican'. The situation was later well summed up in the daily patter of an Italian guide to English tourists: 'That there the Vatican. That where the pope live. He called "the prisoner in the Vatican". He could come out if he want to. But he no want to.' The Vatican may or may not have hoped that the role of 'prisoner in the Vatican' would bring the pope some sympathy – which he certainly needed after the difficulties surrounding the proclamation of Papal Infallibility in 1870 – but, as Queen Victoria likewise discovered, people rapidly lose interest in a figure they never see.

THE ECONOMIC FACTORS

Italy's ambitions were constantly frustrated by her lack of material resources. Predominantly an agricultural country, with very little coal or iron, her only significant mineral deposits were sulphur and borax. Although hydroelectric power was pioneered in 1898, it was only towards the end of the period that she began to make real use of her fast-flowing rivers. Even her agricultural wealth was extremely uneven in its distribution. The Lombardy plain might be a by-word for rich fertility; but the arid uplands of the south came to symbolise for the European liberal all that most offended his clean rational soul: poverty, ignorance and superstition. Indeed, one had to go to Portugal or North Africa to find similar conditions of misery.

Yet the Italians were slow to develop what few resources they had. The peasantry, illiterate and ignorant, were reluctant to change their methods, especially in the south, where farming techniques remained medieval; indeed in Sicily the wheat yield in the mid-nineteenth century remained the same as in Roman times. Nor were the moneyed classes much more given to adventure. Rather than invest in Italian industry, they preferred to invest in land and government securities, with the result that many Italian enterprises were financed by foreign capital. The government, for its part, failed to give a lead; instead of developing the country, especially the south, it squandered

money on futile colonial enterprise and on augmenting the
army (see below and pp. 197–9). All too often, it was only when
the government wanted to buy the votes of a particular region
in a forthcoming election that subsidies were given to improve
local facilities.

The country's trade balance grew steadily worse. Whereas in
the 1870s exports just managed to cover about nine-tenths of
imports, by 1910 they scarcely covered as much as two-thirds.
Raw silk represented about 5 per cent of the total, with cotton
and silk products in second and third places; but the bulk of the
rest were raw and processed foods, together with other agricultural products. Even promising enterprises such as FIAT motors
(1899) and Olivetti typewriters (1908) brought significant
returns only after the First World War. Fortunately this trade
deficit was increasingly compensated by the money sent home
by Italian emigrants in America and by the profits of the tourist
trade, so much so that Italy's overall balance of payments was
actually on the credit side in the last decade of the period. At the
same time the exchequer managed to improve its own balance,
though mainly at the expense of the poor who bore the brunt of
heavy indirect taxation. Indirect taxes and government mono-
polies brought in twice the proceeds of direct taxation, income
tax included, until by the twentieth century revenue was
beginning to cover expenditure. If in terms of hardship the poor
paid the bill, they saw little in return for it. A seventh of the
budget was spent on the army alone while, conversely, the cost
of the Risorgimento had saddled Italy with a vast national debt.
In the 1870s the mere servicing of the debt had accounted for
half the government's expenditure, with the result that expenditure regularly exceeded revenue by 12 to 20 per cent. Nevertheless by the twentieth century the debt took only a fifth of the
budget, so that the government could only blame its own
mistaken order of priorities for its failure to spend more on
social amelioration.

COLLECTIVE ACTION AND POLITICAL FACTORS

If the conditions just described largely explain the low
standard of living in Italy, a further factor was the difficulty of

the working class in acquiring effective bargaining power. Following the Po Valley strikes of 1884-5, the courts ruled at long last that striking for higher wages was legal; while 1889 saw trade unions freed of former prohibitive legislation. It was not, however, until the pre-war decade that the main coalitions emerged.

At the same time, national politics offered no clear route to social improvement. It was only in 1882 that the first socialist was elected to parliament; while even the coming of universal male suffrage gave them only a quarter of the vote and an eighth of the seats (October 1913). Nor did the ruling parties make realistic efforts to improve conditions. Successive governments appeared obsessed with establishing Italy as a great power, irrespective of the cost of the standard of living (see pp. 197-9); while Italian politics as a whole seemed bedevilled with various intrusive problems that impeded the pursuit of social improvement.

The first of these was the patent fact that parliament could in no way claim to represent the people. Italy was a constitutional monarchy, governed by ministers who were dependent on the support of parliament, the whole system being based on the old Piedmontese constitution of 1848. Not only did the Senate consist exclusively of government-appointed life peers, but the Chamber of Deputies was elected for five years on a severely restricted franchise of only half a million. Admittedly the electorate was increased in 1882 to nearly two million by lowering the tax and educational qualification, but this still only represented a tenth of the total adult population. It was always argued that illiterate peasants would have been incapable of using a vote intelligently, and would merely have followed the lead of the local landlord. Consequently, although the gradual spread of literacy and rising incomes increased the electorate to three million by 1911, universal male suffrage was only exercised for the first time at the general election of October 1913.

A small, propertied electorate ensured that government would be conducted in the interests of the 'haves' rather than the 'have-nots'. Yet in practice the electorate had been even smaller, on account of the Vatican's refusal to allow Catholics to vote or stand as candidates in general elections. Many, of course, ignored such a short-sighted prohibition, the Vatican eventually conceding that the Church itself was probably the main victim of such a policy. From 1904, in fact, Catholics were gradually permitted to reintegrate themselves into national politics; but the lesson learnt had been long and expensive.

Secondly, Italian politics were overlaid by antagonism between north and south. Since the worst poverty lay in the south, many of the northern politicians regarded it as none of their business, and refused to make sacrifices to help it. Conversely powerful elements in the south had been opposed to integration in a unified Italy, with the result that full-scale civil war had continued until 1865 – and unofficially thereafter. More people in fact had died in this 'pacification' than during the whole of the Risorgimento. Understandably enough the bitter feelings that were left were exploited by conservative elements, and also by the secret societies and brigand bands. The Camorra virtually governed Naples in the 1870s, while the Mafia remained a dominant force in Sicily throughout the period. They had their own taxation and judicial systems, for in the remoter districts they were much better placed than the state to make their will felt. Politically most of them were conservative, being pro-Bourbon or pro-papal in many instances, since their former rulers had tended to play King Log, owing to the difficulty of suppressing them.

Yet even among the important elements that had welcomed unification, there was strong resentment against the indifference of the north to the economic difficulties of the south. They had looked forward with pathetic optimism to the financial aid which they thought Italian unity would bring; while on the other hand many of the politicians of the north had failed to realise the extent of southern poverty – some even imagining that the south would bring riches not liabilities. Inevitably both sides were bitterly disillusioned. As A. J. Whyte remarks, '[during the Risorgimento], the Italians had climbed a mountain in order to find a terrestrial paradise, and all they found was a building site'.

The economics of vote-catching was another blow to southern

hopes. Since the franchise was dependent on a property or educational qualification, the bulk of the electorate lived in the north, where literacy and wealth were more widespread. Not only did the membership of cabinets reflect – and exaggerate – this northward bias, but governments were naturally tempted to concentrate their improving activities on the north where there were more electors to be impressed. It has been claimed that as far as public works are concerned the south generally received a numerically fair return for the amount of taxation it paid. But a large proportion of this was railway-building – undertaken in much the same spirit as the British railways in India, to keep the country subdued as well as supplied. And a proportionately fair return was not enough. The needs of the south were much more pressing; even the most elementary sense of national solidarity should have dictated a more generous programme of aid. It has been claimed that between 1862 and 1896 only 2 per cent of the money voted for agricultural improvement was given to the south. This was particularly galling for people who found themselves subjected to much higher taxes than they were used to before unification. They were now also subject to military conscription on the German model, which in 1872 was made compulsory for all Italians. Resentment was further aggravated by the fact that the new Italy became little more than an enlarged Piedmont; for instead of new codes of law and administrative machinery, the Piedmontese system was merely extended to the rest of Italy.

In a more indirect way, the improvement of society was obstructed by the shortcomings of the political system itself. Cavour had been an admirer of the British constitution; but his personal conduct must bear much of the blame for the irresponsible traditions of parliamentary behaviour which had become established by 1870. And none of his successors had his redeeming genius.

The right-wing ministries of Domenico Lanza (December 1869–July 1873) and Marco Minghetti (July 1873–March 1876) had been comparatively honest, if unimaginative. The

G

Law of Guarantees would have been a sensible solution to the religious issue, had the Vatican accepted it. Their military expenditure, however, was unnecessarily high, despite the civil war; and their attempts to pay off the public debt by indirect taxation weighed heaviest on the poor. Indeed the grist tax on grain (1869) led to Minghetti's resignation in 1876, and to the coming to power of the Left under Agostino Depretis (March 1876–March 1878; December 1878–July 1879; May 1881–July 1887).

Such a long run of office immediately suggests a politician with a gift for manœuvre.

> Pareto wrote of [Depretis] as someone with a sceptical turn of mind, who never embarrassed himself with principles or convictions and never bothered much about the truth. Always ready to follow any route which would assure him of a majority, he enjoyed in the later years of his life what Pareto called the most absolute dictatorship possible under a parliamentary regime. [Yet] Depretis personally was one of the most respectable in modern Italian history. Even when prime minister he continued to live in a top-floor apartment one hundred and twenty steps up.[1]

Depretis in fact was to systematise with remarkable thoroughness the growing tradition of dubious political behaviour and bad habits that had marked Italian parliamentary life since Cavour. He confirmed his power by holding a general election (November 1876) in which the worst types of local influence were used to ensure a governmental majority, methods that were to become typical of most of the ministries which followed. As a result the new Chamber consisted largely of new men with little experience of politics and whose only recommendation was their willingness to support Depretis. The Right was unable to make a come-back until the 1890s.

The virtual disappearance of the Right in the Chamber and the disorganised nature of Depretis's following stopped the growth of any effective two-party system, without which no liberal democracy can properly work. The state of the Chamber moreover gave further encouragement to the Italian practice of

1 Denis Mack Smith, Italy. A modern history (Michigan U.P., 1959) p. 108.

transformismo – the transforming by favours of various parliamentary groups into a government coalition. Although the
term was new, *transformismo* had its roots in the political
practice of Cavour and his successors. The next thirty years,
however, were to see it systematised to a remarkable degree.
When Depretis was faced with the possibility of parliamentary
defeat, he would forestall it by resigning, and then reform his
cabinet with the addition of men from the groups that needed to
be conciliated. In this way cabinet would follow cabinet, with
a nucleus of familiar faces, flanked by new ones, which
brought with them outside interests that had to be reconciled
with the old. Thus government policy tended to be the same
mixture as before, plus or minus the ingredients that had to be
added or subtracted to please the government's new supporters. The result was that important but divisive issues, such
as the condition of the poor or Church–State relations, were
generally avoided, so as to preserve the coalition. Politics
seemed to many observers to be little more than a game of
'ins' and 'outs'.

Nevertheless the Depretis era did have a number of important
measures to its credit, despite the fact that 'while in opposition,
the Left had possessed not so much a programme as an accumulation of grudges' (Mack Smith). Its most notable achievements were the institution of compulsory primary education
(1877), the extension of the franchise (1882) and the final abolition of the grist tax (1884). Its forays into foreign policy, however, were more controversial (see p. 215). Although entry
into the Triple Alliance helped to put an end to the Italian
feeling of insecurity, it was dearly paid for in the alienation of
France. France was Italy's best customer and the commercial
treaty signed with France in 1881 was an important source of
income. But cooling relations between the two countries eventually encouraged Italy to inaugurate a disastrous tariff war,
which she, as the poorer nation, could ill afford. It probably cost
a fifth of Italy's potential exports, and was only resolved by an
eventual trade agreement in November 1898. The withdrawal
of French capital from Italy was an important factor in the
series of bank failures in 1889–90. At the same time, Italy's
membership of the world's main power bloc encouraged her to

waste her resources further, by trying to cut an impressive figure in the world, her disastrous colonial policy being but one outcome of this (see pp. 197–9).

It was a tribute to the political skill of Depretis that death, not an election, should remove him from office. There then burst on Italy the Sicilian bomb-shell, Francesco Crispi (August 1887–February 1891; December 1893–March 1896), whose long spell as premier likewise suggested no mean ability as a manipulator. His gifts were different, however. While using all the weapons in the Depretis political armoury, his own particular asset was a flair for creating and exploiting public emotion. Indeed his miraculous power to make the winds and waves obey him tempted him to treat parliament in a progressively cavalier fashion. Up to a point he could do this with limited risk, for 'the deputies themselves were usually grateful when a man of action cut through their interminable debates, arbitrated their hopelessly conflicting views, and relieved them of responsibility for unpopular decisions' (Mack Smith). But later developments were to show him as the sorcerer's apprentice rather than the sorcerer.

In order to raise his prestige in the country still higher, he tried to build up a head of steam by lighting a fire under popular jingoism. It was this that led him to propel Italy along the barren track of African imperialism. At best he only had part of public opinion with him in this venture; and when the essential ingredient, success, was ineptly lost at Adowa (see pp. 198–9) the drum-beaters were among the first to turn on him and secure his resignation.

His role in furthering colonial ambitions has tended to obscure his more positive achievements in internal affairs. Denis Mack Smith has written: 'he was indeed . . . always to remain a volcanic revolutionary by temperament, but he partly matured into a political conservative once he had to defend the position which his great talents and energy had won him'. Yet his past career as a radical bore fruit in several of his measures as premier (despite parliament's rejection of his land reform): confirmation of the right to strike and more freedom for trade unions; the Public Health Act of 1888; more democratic procedure in local government; and reform of the prisons.

The dominant figure in the immediate pre-war years was Giovanni Giolitti, a man of the Centre, who, with the eclipse of Crispi, was the obvious leader of the liberals and those to their left. 'A crafty and masterful parliamentarian . . . he was particularly adept at manipulating any controversial issue to make it seem a simple matter of administration on which most people could agree' (Mack Smith). While premier (November 1903–March 1905; May 1906–December 1909; March 1911–March 1914), he attempted to take the sting out of socialism with a number of mild social reforms. The voluntary pensions scheme of 1898 became compulsory for certain occupational groups, while he also set up a National Employment Office (1907) and an extended system of factory inspection (1911). Giolitti combined impeccable 'respectability' with a readiness to make concessions to the Left, notably the granting of universal male suffrage (June 1912). Indeed when he resigned in March 1914 it was only to safeguard his popularity against the difficult decisions that had to be taken in the immediate future.

His premiership had seen the completion of Italy's diplomatic *volte-face* from 'the Alliance' to 'the Entente' (see p. 222), as well as the occupation of Libya. Had he remained in office, however, it is very questionable whether he would have brought Italy into the First World War. It was perfectly clear that in 1915 he was opposed to participation; but for reasons of personal self-interest he preferred not to take office when it was offered to him. In this way, his customary concern for his political image prevented him making what might have been his major contribution to Italian well-being.

COLONIALISM

Italy's bid for colonies in the late nineteenth and early twentieth centuries is perhaps the best example of the prestige motive at work. The territories involved were of very little economic value, while their strategic value was lessened by the fact that the neighbouring territories were already in the hands of more powerful European states. Given Italy's geographical position, however, it was logical that she should choose the Mediterranean as the area in which to exert her authority. Prestige-seeking requires a utilitarian basis, for even status symbols must have some outward utilitarian justification. And defence of Italy and her trade routes was a plausible pretext for the interest she took in various Mediterranean islands and above all in the North African coast opposite Italy.

Yet to be fair to Italy she had realised in the 1870s that she had more pressing needs than colonies; and her activities in Africa had been accordingly confined to the economic penetration of Tunis. Nevertheless the establishment of a French protectorate there in 1881 had humiliated her, so much so that she was determined not to let the same thing happen in Libya. Yet her activities there remained at first largely commercial, until the Agadir crisis of 1911 made Italy suspect that both Germany and France wished to increase their influence in North Africa. Giolitti had hitherto been against colonial expansion; but he knew that if he allowed Libya to fall into foreign hands his political career would be finished. The outcome was that he unleashed the dogs of war on Turkey – and not only the dogs, for the war was remarkable for the first use of aerial bombing (1911–12). Victory and the Libyan sand-pit fell to Italy.

However, Italy had parallel if subsidiary interests in the southern entrance to the Red Sea. Not only did they result in the piecing together of Eritrea (1882–90) but they also saw the establishment of a protectorate over much of Somaliland (1885–92) and a disastrous attempt to do the same to Ethiopia in the 1890s. Looked at in detail these acquisitions largely stemmed from clashes with the natives, which indirectly had their origin in the occupation of Assab (March 1882) as a revictualling base for Italian shipping. Italian reverses resulted in demands for military proof of Italian superiority, and it was a defeat by dervishes at Dogali (January 1887) which transferred Francesco Crispi's interest from the Mediterranean to the Red Sea. Nevertheless nothing obliged Italy to take these defeats so much to heart; Crispi undoubtedly saw in colonialism a means of winning the support of prestige-hungry politicians. Nemesis came, however, with the Ethiopian victory of Adowa (March 1896), which scotched Crispi's attempt to assert a protectorate over Ethiopia. Whatever the wishes of politicians, it was very questionable whether the Italian people at large had much interest in prestige-seeking in the sands of Africa.

Italian statesmen liked to justify their Red Sea activities by saying that the Red Sea was the key to the Mediterranean. But given British control of the Suez Canal and Aden, and given Britain's vastly superior naval power, it was absurd for Italian statesmen to claim that Italy would now be able to control movement in and out of the Mediterranean – despite the fact that Britain's position in Egypt was in principle only temporary (see pp. 213–14). What mattered for them ultimately was that part of Africa was painted green, for then Italy could pose as an imperial power.

Economically her colonies were a liability. The information which Italy supplied to *The Statesman's Year-Book* in 1912 spoke of 'a very promising trade . . . in palm nuts' in Eritrea; and the same phrase was still being used in the 1930 issue. The total exports of the colonies in 1912 amounted in fact to little over £600,000, while their imports were over £2 million. Moreover three-quarters of the colonies' expenses had to be met by Italy.

SPAIN

The appalling poverty of much of Spain and Portugal could only be matched by that of southern Italy and the Balkans. It is nevertheless hard to generalise about Spanish life, in that conditions varied enormously between the fertile belts of the northern and eastern seaboards and the arid plateau land of the interior.

Yet in a country where poverty and ignorance were so widespread it is at first sight surprising that the population did not undergo the same increase as eastern Europe (see p. 51). The relatively slow growth reflected two things: first a high infant mortality rate that was twice the European average; and secondly, heavy emigration to Latin America, which removed a third of the natural increase in population.

The land problem was particularly acute in the southern half of Spain, where over a third of the land was exploited by a small group of families totalling only 11,000 people. Conversely less than half of the land had to support over four-fifths of the remaining population, two-thirds of whom had less than two and a half acres for each mouth in the family.

TABLE 17

	1870	1914
Population	c. 16 m	c. 20 m
Proportion in agriculture		c. 65%
Proportion in manufactures	c. 10%	c. 20–25%
Peasants' income as proportion of British agricultural wages	c. 40%	
Industrial wages as proportion of British wages	c. 50–60%	(after 1900) c. 50%

The root trouble of Spain's economic difficulties was the relative infertility of her soil. It was only in 1902 that the Spanish government seriously undertook irrigation and other schemes to improve the land, while private investors took little interest, because agriculture did not offer quick returns like mining or industry. Indeed, less than 1 per cent of Spanish and foreign organised investment went into soil improvement. This affected industry, in that, if agriculture remained backward, there was little chance of developing an internal market for Spanish manufactures. It is true that the mounting tariff wall, encircling Spain and her Caribbean empire from 1891, obliged the colonies to take about a third of Catalonia's textile produce. But the loss of the colonies in the Spanish American War of 1898 left Spain even more dependent on her internal resources. In fact the only outward-looking spheres of the economy were mining and wine production. Spain was not only the leading copper-producer of Europe, but her iron-ore, with its low phosphorous content, was in great demand. Spanish sherry was likewise a reliable export; but the success of her other wines was a short-lived affair, based on the French misfortune of phylloxera (see p. 130). Many farmers improvidently turned from grain to grapes, nemesis coming in 1885–6, when demand fell off – then phylloxera invaded Spain. Indeed for areas like the

Costa Brava the brief prosperity of the wine boom was only to be regained with the tourist boom of the 1950s and 1960s.

At the same time ignorance helped to prolong poverty. While less than a third of the population could read and write in 1870, the proportion was still only about two-fifths in 1914. Yet Spain had to wait until 1902 before the government began to give significant aid to education; primary schooling becoming compulsory only in June 1909. Lack of education moreover meant that the peasant voter was easy prey to the many landlords who were prepared to exploit the advantages of universal male suffrage in an ignorant population (June 1890). There was no doubt that Antonio Maura's Conservative government knew what it was doing when it made voting compulsory in August 1907. The tradition of government interference in elections was a further obstacle to achieving reform through a wide franchise.

Since the expulsion of the loose-living slack-shaped Queen Isabella (1868), Spain had experienced a particularly troubled political history. Indeed the first concern of any government was to remain in office. It is true that the 1870s saw the gradual establishment of a rudimentary two-party system, in that both the conservative and liberal parties were prepared, out of self-interest, to concede to each other a fair crack of the whip when in office. At the same time the king tended to encourage this arrangement in the interest of a quiet life; but the losers as always were the Spanish people, for while cabinet stability had its advantages, the tacit agreement between the two parties resulted in the party in opposition observing a gentlemanly silence about the country's social and political problems. Politics therefore tended to avoid the real issues of the time.

These problems moreover were themselves obscured by the issue of regionalism. While racial and linguistic differences distinguished the Catalans and Basques from other Spaniards, their desire for greater autonomy was increased by their progressive economies. It was a patent fact that their interests were often at variance with those of the rest of Spain. To take just the most obvious example, the poorer agricultural areas wanted cheap imports, while the Catalans and Basques wanted protective tariffs.

By 1907 Spain had the rare distinction of being the only

significant European country without a working-class deputy in parliament. Since parliament did not effectively represent them, working-class political activity tended therefore to look to violent methods. There was no shortage of revolutionary doctrines to choose from in the late nineteenth century but, as any social thinker might have guessed, the rural nature of Spain was more congenial to the ideas of Bakunin than of Marx, with their emphasis on decentralisation and the village community (see p. 87). At the same time the migration of landless Andalusian labourers to Barcelona helped to make this urban community the centre of Spanish anarchism, despite its theoretical suitability for Marxist propaganda. Predictably enough, when placed in an industrial context, anarchism became anarcho-syndicalism, with the workers' union replacing the village community as the armature of the golden future system. A further factor was that the decentralist aspects of anarchism had a particular appeal to Catalan sentiment, just as conversely the centralist nature of Marxism had more success in Madrid, the Spanish capital, where Andalusian immigration was in any case less marked. Yet the overall Spanish preference for anarchism was reflected in the membership of working-class organisations. When the anarcho-syndicalist Confederación Nacional del Trabajo came into existence in October 1910, it acquired 30,000 members in under a year; whereas the Marxist Unión General de Trabajadores, which had been in existence since 1882, could still only boast 44,000 in its pre-war peak year of 1904.

Given the remoteness of parliament from working-class aspirations, it was not surprising that organised strikes and periodic assassinations were the main form of working-class action. Deaths to date included three prime ministers.

CHAPTER SEVEN

From Sedan to Sarajevo

International relations

The common cormorant or shag
Lays eggs inside a paper bag.
The reason you will see, no doubt,
It is to keep the lightning out,
But what these unobservant birds
Have never noticed is that herds
Of wandering bears may come with buns
And steal the bags to hold the crumbs.

ANON.

To many people today the preoccupations of the great powers before the First World War seem as unrealistic as those of the cormorant and its observer. It is tempting, for instance, to dismiss much of Britain's foreign policy during the nineteenth century as governed by fears that were largely of her own making. It is likewise hard to feel much sympathy for the other far more dangerous illusions and neuroses. In the light of what was to happen by the autumn of 1918, it seems extraordinary that a ramshackle empire like Austria-Hungary should feel that war rather than peace would best guarantee her stability in 1914. And it seems equally extraordinary that Germany should be so confident of success in 1914 that she could willingly accept the prospect of a major European war.

The modern observer looks at these and other international issues across the twenty-one million dead of the First World War[1] and the many million more who were permanently disabled. He also sees the time, money and energy that pre-war statesmen spent on safeguarding what now seem unnecessary

[1] Including the civilian victims of famine and disease.

positions or positive liabilities. How could issues like these lead nations to spend and risk so much? Yet these preoccupations did exist, seeming very real to the governments that held them. And the more the historian examines them, the closer he comes to the paradoxical conclusion that the action of the great powers was both grotesque and eminently understandable.

At the same time it must be recognised that the air of un-reality that shrouds pre-war diplomacy is something that belongs in varying degree to the diplomacy of all periods. Indeed the risks that have been run in the course of the Cold War would stretch the credulity of any generation. But what never fails to strike the lay imagination is the disproportion between the language of diplomacy and the ultimate sanctions at its command. The understatements of diplomacy conceal a merciless self-seeking that is prepared to use death and destruc-tion as 'legitimate' methods. On a diplomat's lips, the phrase 'seek satisfaction' can be infinitely more terrible in its implica-tions than the exterminating zeal of the most fanatical warrior-sect. And in the world before 1914, when diplomats were aristocrats, and the ranting of dictators had not yet been heard, the seeming contrast between the soft words of diplomacy and the cold steel of reality appears to our generation much more marked than that of later times. Moreover, at a time when the aerial bombardment of capital cities was not yet envisaged as a direct consequence of declarations of war, the large landowners who occupied the foreign ministries of Europe seemed utterly remote from the slaughter and filth of war. Lord Salisbury, for example, was as tough a statesman as any of his time, a realist whose 'settled and sardonic belief' was 'that things are as they are in the most ironic of possible worlds',[1] a man whose decisions were to involve the deaths of thousands. Yet in 1888, when a visitor to Number Ten collapsed and died in his presence, Salisbury could write: 'It was a very painful scene. I had never happened to see anyone die before.'

The monstrous fact of the First World War has nevertheless tended to overshadow the less dramatic fact that in the forty-

---

[1] R. Robinson and J. Gallagher, *Africa and the Victorians. The official mind of imperialism* (Macmillan, 1961) p. 256.

three years before 1914 relatively few Europeans lost their lives through military action. Of those who died, most were east Europeans engaged in the Eastern Crisis of 1876–8, the Russo-Japanese War of 1904–5 or the Balkan Wars of 1912–13. The rest, including nearly all west Europeans, were mainly casualties of colonial or semi-colonial enterprise. Avoiding war, however, is only the negative side to diplomacy – even if in human terms it is by far the most important. The positive gain diplomacy achieved for Europe is much more difficult to measure, for the simple reason that one nation's advantage is generally another's loss. During the period as a whole, eight million Europeans came under new rule, most of them former subjects of the Ottoman Empire who tended to regard themselves as better off for the change.

Paradoxically this period of peace is often described as 'the international anarchy'. The phrase is largely inspired by the apparent contrast between the 1856–1914 period, and those that preceded and followed it. For many, the first half of the nineteenth century seems characterised by a certain identity of interests among the European governments – a period when Metternich was foreshadowing John Foster Dulles, shoring up every tin-pot reactionary regime that might fall victim to 'the forces of Revolution' – a period when governments regularly held international congresses to concert their policies, or so it is claimed. On the other hand, the post-1918 period, for its part, saw the setting up of the League of Nations and its successor, the United Nations. By contrast, the 1856–1914 period seems one where there was much less identity of interest between governments. Congresses were fewer and generally the outcome of specific crises or problems, the only common motive between members being a desire to achieve their separate aims without recourse to war. Even the alliances between nations were mostly of a defensive kind, resulting from very different preoccupations on the part of those who signed them. These treaties characteristically contained no agreement to follow a common policy; and once they were signed, the signatories tended to continue their separate existences, with little continuous regard for their partners, rather like members of a ratepayers' league. Although nearly five hundred private international organisations were founded between 1875 and 1919, public international organisations were restricted to the administrative and technical fields. And symptomatically when Britain and America tried to bring about an arbitration treaty in 1897 it fell through, since from the first it was dogged by the fact that Britain wanted to leave out all questions of 'national honour or integrity', while the American senate insisted that its government do likewise. Even then it refused to ratify the treaty, for as one senator put it: 'We will be purblind if we put a paper guarantee of peace in place of the moral and military forces that are the supreme elements of strength in our splendid republic.'

It is perhaps significant that it was Russia who astonished Europe in 1898 by denouncing war and inviting other governments to meet and set up a procedure for the peaceful arbitration of disputes. For among the great powers it was precisely Russia who first discovered that she could not afford to keep up the arms race. The outcome was scarcely surprising. Although a Court of International Arbitration was eventually set up at The Hague, it was extremely limited in its powers; Lord Salisbury, for example, summed up the British attitude to it by saying that the court should not be taken 'too seriously' while the Kaiser said that most of its objectives were 'utopian'.

Yet for all its 'anarchy' 1870–1914 was a period of comparative peace. This was to some extent the product of a fairly delicate balance of power, where each nation felt, in some degree, that war would bring it more harm than good. Recent advances in weapons and military techniques not only made war much more destructive and expensive, but it required much more preparation. Nations did not indulge in it unless the objective was really worth the outlay, and unless they felt certain of winning. And until 1890, and probably later, most influential statesmen felt that their schemes depended on peace rather than war for their fulfilment.

PAX BISMARCKENSIS

After the Franco-Prussian War, no one could doubt that Germany was the strongest continental power. Bismarck was in charge of German policy until 1890; and Bismarck's all-absorbing aim in these twenty years was to preserve his past achievements and protect Germany from the risk of 'a war of revenge' by France.

In some ways Bismarck's position was rather like that of the unscrupulous businessman who having made his millions becomes a philanthropist and chairman of innumerable charitable boards. People are aware of the change of circumstance, yet still look for the moral thug behind the podgy hand-shake. Indeed, perhaps the main irony of Bismarck's career was that when he was still rapaciously extending Prussian power, other governments, with their eye on Napoleon III, treated him indulgently. Yet when he had achieved what he wanted by 1871, and desired nothing more than his pipe, his beer and the *status quo*, every foreign minister was henceforth looking for the fish-hook in any morsel that he might offer him. They were right to be vigilant, in that Bismarck never gave something for nothing, but their ultra-vigilance would have been even better placed in the 1860s.

Bismarck knew that the *status quo*, like cream, is not an easy thing to preserve. The chances of friendship with France were uncertain, the only viable alternative being the prevention of France achieving a position of military strength. Put at its crudest, France had to be kept without allies; and to do this Germany had to be on good terms with everybody else, a goal that obviously had its own superior intrinsic merits. Accordingly it was both politic and a statement of truth when Bismarck declared in 1871 that Germany was satiated, with no desire to round off her unity with further annexations. Broadly speaking, Bismarck believed that the preservation of German gains was best guaranteed by favouring the existing international balance, a belief that was further strengthened by his suspicion of 'popular' movements. Socialism in western Europe and nationalism in eastern Europe were movements that both offended his authoritarian concept of government, and promised all kinds of uncertainty. Whatever reservations he held about the Habsburg monarchy, it did at least keep popular nationalism in check, and he was accordingly prepared to contribute to its preservation. For Bismarck, violent outbreaks and uncertain developments were dangerous, partly because one of the nations involved might invoke the aid of France as an ally – and France with an ally could rapidly become a danger to Germany.

The chances for peace were therefore good as long as Bismarck was in control of the strongest Continental power, and as long as his successors were prepared to regard war as something to be avoided. Without allies, France could not even consider the possibility of war against Germany, her main preoccupation being to safeguard herself against the possibility of a second German attack. Bismarck was determined to keep France isolated – and diffident; and it was partly to maintain her diffidence that he manufactured the 'war-in-sight' newspaper-scare of April 1875. The scare, however, was also intended to discredit the German Centre Party (see p. 113), whom he imaginatively accused of participating in an international Catholic conspiracy against the German Reich. It was thus both part of the *Kulturkampf* and a sharp warning to France, who was actively rebuilding her army. The scare had at least the effect of revealing that Austria-Hungary was not prepared to help France. But it also revealed that Russia and Britain would oppose any further attempt to humiliate France – while nevertheless remaining unsympathetic to any French attempt to regain Alsace-Lorraine.

In the east, however, the situation was uncertain. Austria and Russia were rivals for control over south-eastern Europe; but the ambitions of each were confined by certain basic aims. Austria-Hungary was primarily interested in self-preservation, having no desire to bring fresh complications into her domestic difficulties by expanding for expansion's sake. On the other hand she wanted guaranteed access to the port of Salonika, which would give a permanent outlet for the produce of her eastern territories. It could furthermore be argued that certain annexations would enable her to deal more firmly with troublesome minorities at home; and if this seemed likely, she was prepared to consider them. But, what was more important, Russian expansion in south-east Europe might encourage Slav troublemakers within the Empire.

It is true that for her part Russia had considerably modified her ambitions since the Crimean War. Hitherto she had specifically aimed at acquiring a large part of the Ottoman Empire for herself. After her defeat, however, she was primarily interested in preserving herself from the danger of another British or foreign attack via the Black Sea, a concern that became more acute after 1878 (see pp. 216–17) and this in practice still meant trying to substitute Russian for Turkish control of the Straits – for the international Convention of 1841, prohibiting non-Turkish warships from using the Straits, was a guarantee of Russian safety only as long as the signatories chose to observe it. At the same time, since a considerable proportion of Russia's grain exports passed out through the Straits, it was disquieting to have them dependent on the good-will of Turkey, or whatever power controlled the Straits. It was like having a neighbour's garden dividing one's door-step from the street. It must also be remembered that Russia's intentions in the Balkans were frequently embarrassed by the demands of Slav nationals. A considerable number of Slav nationals within the Austro-Hungarian and Ottoman Empires looked to Russia for support, which meant that Russian prestige was in constant danger of being brought into issue – irrespective of Russia's convenience. Good intentions on Russia's part might not, therefore, be sufficient to keep the peace.

At the same time the basic consistency of Russian policy was often obscured by the eccentricities of her governmental system. Salisbury was to exclaim in 1885:

> . . . it is very difficult to come to any satisfactory conclusion as to the real objects of Russian policy. I am more inclined to believe that the Emperor is really his own Minister, and so bad a Minister that no consequent or coherent policy is pursued; but that each influential person, military or civil, snatches from him as opportunity offers, the decisions which such person at the moment wants.

There was a certain element of truth in this, as far as the day-to-day decisions of diplomacy were concerned; but fundamentally Russian policy was quite as consistent as that of Britain.

Britain, at the other extreme of Europe, continued to occupy her chosen role of non-alignment. It could be argued that such a role was unfortunate now that Germany had vastly increased in strength. Britain still imagined, however, that she could subordinate her European policy to her overseas imperial interests, so basing her attitude to the various powers on the extent to which they appeared to threaten or benefit her overseas possessions. Her hostility to Russia rested on the fear that Russian naval access to the eastern Mediterranean could threaten British communications with India – hence her opposition to all idea of Russian control of the Straits. Yet it was questionable whether Russia ever had any serious designs on India, or on Britain's routes thereto. Indeed Britain's concern for her routes to India had become an even bigger bore to Europe than the pope's desire for territorial sovereignty or Queen Victoria's public cult of the memory of her husband – infinitely bigger in that it was dangerously obstructive as well as tedious.

Britain was still to remain unattached at the turn of the century. She saw her interests as lying mainly overseas, where she still tended to regard France and Russia as the principal enemies. Nevertheless it was a general truth of this period that no Continental power was prepared to go to war with another power about an overseas issue, since the possible repercussions in Europe were too momentous to be worth risking. Only Britain, protected by the sea and her navy, felt able to afford the luxury of putting her imperial interests first, the result being that whenever it came to a confrontation overseas, Britain generally got her way.

At this stage, despite her anxiety to be accepted as such, Italy scarcely counted as a power. Materially her initial diplomatic preoccupation was with the Italian-speaking parts of the Habsburg Empire, though prestige and other factors were soon to cause her to push irredentist claims into the background and encourage her to pursue larger if less appetising game overseas (see pp. 197–9). Italy as a nation was not only very young, but painfully conscious that her unity had been achieved largely through the help of France and Prussia. She was therefore anxious to prove to the rest of Europe that she was a fully-fledged European power, able to stand on her own feet. Indeed there was something very adolescent about her desire to demonstrate her strength. 'Italy needs a blood-bath' 'to test her virility' was admittedly the remark of a right-wing journalist, but 'Italy must make herself feared' was a royal statement, doubly dangerous for a country that was so desperately poor.

The 1880s saw her launched on an imperial career. Not only was it widely felt that overseas territories were necessary to put Italy in the same class as Britain and France, but Italian statesmen such as Crispi wanted a series of easy victories over poorly armed natives to show that her armies were invincible.

The risk of an Austro-Russian conflict in the east had nevertheless been slightly reduced by Bismarck's creation of the Three Emperors' League in May–June 1873. Bismarck's main purpose in linking Austria and Russia with Germany was to forestall any possibility of either allying with France. However the league was soon to be rudely put to the test by the so-called Eastern Crisis of 1876–8. There was a time when the episode would have loomed large in any book on the period; but as Mr A. J. P. Taylor has commented, even to some contemporaries

> the interminable Eastern crises seemed so many manœuvres, where great skill was displayed and everyone went home unhurt in the evening. . . . The diplomatists pointed to the deadlock as evidence of their sustained skill. Cynical radicals retorted that nothing happened because nothing serious was at stake and that the Eastern Question was kept going to provide 'out-door relief' for members of the foreign services.

It would be tempting to suggest that historians have likewise been added to the pay-roll. Yet although the outcome of this particular crisis was something of an anticlimax as far as it concerned the major powers, from the viewpoint of the local population its origins were violent enough.

Disturbances in the Turkish province of Bosnia (July 1875) had encouraged the Bulgarians to revolt (May 1876), the outcome being that the Turks tried to suppress the revolt with great brutality, killing some 30,000 Bulgarians in the process. Nowadays the phrase 'the Bulgarian Horrors' may suggest the penalty of over-addiction to slivovitz, but at the time these massacres understandably occasioned a great outcry. Serbia and Montenegro declared war on Turkey (June–July), and Russia, fearing that her prestige would suffer if she did not aid the Slavs, followed suit in April 1877. The eventual outcome was that by January 1878 her troops were within a few miles of Constantinople.

Russia was thereby holding Britain's sacred cow by the tail; and Britain was not slow in responding. Until then Disraeli – 'the flamboyant Disraeli' of the historians – had been sufficiently embarrassed by the public outcry against Turkish misrule to refrain from checking the Russian advance. Russia had indeed already told Britain before the campaign that she would not occupy Constantinople – though with what sincerity it is hard to know. The arrival of a British fleet, however, forced her to be sincere, and she had to make peace. Russia nevertheless exacted a heavy if short-lived price. She forced 'the hapless Turk' to accept the Treaty of San Stefano (March 1878) which obliged him to recognise the independence of Bulgaria, Eastern Rumelia and Macedonia, which together were to form a massive unified state ('Big Bulgaria'). Neither Britain nor Austria would accept the treaty, however, since it created a large Russian client state with frontiers only a hundred miles from Constantinople.

The situation was clearly one of undisguised confrontation, and it was with considerable sense of occasion that an international congress met in Berlin to try to settle the issue (June–July 1878). Predictably enough victory went to British and Austrian interests, as Russia's case was weakened by her earlier promise to Austria not to create a 'great compact state' like Big Bulgaria. The result was that Bulgaria was now stripped of Eastern Rumelia (which became an autonomous Turkish province) and of Macedonia which was restored to direct Turkish control. By contrast, however, Bosnia and Herzegovina were transferred from Turkish to Austrian administration. In many ways the Berlin settlement was a poor substitute for San Stefano. The inclusion of more Serbs under Habsburg rule increased rather than diminished the Empire's difficulties, as Sarajevo was to show. Furthermore Macedonia was restless under Turkish rule, becoming a prime issue in the Balkan War of 1912. As for Eastern Rumelia, it took only seven years for the San Stefano solution to be adopted in any case. It could in fact be argued that the interminable Eastern Question would best have been solved along the lines that Nicholas I had suggested as far back as 1844 when on a visit to Windsor: Russia should have had Constantinople, and Britain should have had Egypt, since

Egypt would have given Britain control over the short route to India. Bismarck held similar views, maintaining that Austria could profitably have been given Salonika and the intervening Ottoman territory. However, Bismarck's role throughout the crisis and the congress had been that of 'honest broker', with peace between the powers as his prime objective; and he was not prepared to risk this success by pushing a solution that would meet with antagonism in Britain and other circles.

As far as Egypt was concerned a British, or at least an Anglo-French, occupation was becoming progressively a greater reality. The Egyptian government was bankrupt as a result of the Khedive's extravagance on one hand and the cost of building the Suez Canal on the other. Ismail's predecessor, Said, had granted over-favourable terms to the French canal company, partly because of his liking for Ferdinand de Lesseps, who in earlier days had furthered a firm friendship by giving Said huge clandestine meals of macaroni, at a time when Said was suffering under his father's directive to get rid of his 'hateful fleshliness'. Ismail's liking for gold plate and his refusal to institute economies had worsened a desperate situation, while the ceremonial opening of the canal in 1869 had been an excuse for further extravagance, 1871 seeing a sumptuous first performance of *Aïda* in Cairo's new opera house. Britain and France, acting on behalf of the creditors, had subsequently undertaken to help the Khedive put his finances on a sound basis. But Ismail embodied to perfection that splendid mixture of indolence and cunning that only the life of an oriental potentate can bring to full fruition; and he had characteristically evaded Anglo-French prescriptions by instigating riots against his European advisers. In desperation Britain and France decided to depose him (June 1879).

The enforced subservience of the new Khedive, however, called into being a new devil, which was potentially much more dangerous to Anglo-French control than the old. Colonel Arabi's revolt of June 1882 was not only the first clear demonstration of Egyptian nationalism, but it can also be regarded as the first example of the radical Afro-Asian nationalism that was to take full shape in the twentieth century. The immediate result was that Gladstone decided to occupy Egypt. The French government would willingly have participated, had not the Chamber refused to finance a joint expedition, the outcome being that Sir Garnet Wolseley (Gilbert's 'Modern major-general') occupied Egypt on Britain's sole behalf (September 1882). Gladstone seems to have been sincere in claiming that Britain was there merely to enable Egypt to pay her debts, and to have been genuinely anxious to leave Egypt as soon as possible. Yet it was all too easy for foreign critics to call this self-elevated man of principle high-handed rather than high-minded.

In the minds of enemies, there was plenty of room for ambiguity. The longer Britain stayed, the more indispensable Egypt came to seem for the defence of the route to India. The opening of the Suez Canal in 1869 had vastly increased the importance of Egypt, while the expanding interests of the other European powers in Africa and Asia during the 1880s made Britain correspondingly more sensitive, so that the uncertain duration of her presence in Egypt made her continue to oppose Russian control of the Straits. It would be easy to suspect Britain of hypocrisy in this instance, but successive British governments were genuinely uncertain how long Britain would be there. And as late as 1887, even the imperially-minded Salisbury attempted to negotiate a withdrawal from Egypt with Egypt's nominal suzerain, Turkey. Symptomatically it was Russia who sabotaged this attempt – for fear that a Britain without Egypt would be more difficult on the Straits question. The British were in fact the victims of their initial protestation that they were in Egypt merely to collect debts. They felt obliged to keep to this explanation – even partly believing it, long after the strategic value of Suez had become the predominant motive – which resulted in a dog-in-the-manger attitude towards Russia over the Straits. It would have been much more comfortable for everyone, including the Egyptians, if Britain had followed earlier advice and put an unashamed protectorate over Egypt, allowing Russia what she wanted.

The Eastern Crisis had thwarted Bismarck's aim to keep Russia and Austria on good terms. Indeed the crisis had brought

Austria, Britain and France closer together in mutual opposition to Russia. France had large investments in the Ottoman Empire, so it was clearly in her interest to support Turkey against Russian encroachments. Bismarck's double concern was to prevent France finding a friend in Austria – and to control Austrian behaviour towards Russia. Paradoxically this led him to offer Austria a defensive alliance against Russia (October 1879). Yet the terms of this alliance clearly represented the smallest possible bait that Bismarck could offer Austria – and significantly enough Bismarck was shortly to revive the Three Emperors' League with Russia. The new Austro-German document stipulated that if either was attacked by Russia, the other would come to her rescue; while if either was attacked by another power without Russian help, the other would remain neutral.

Curiously enough this Dual Alliance was enlarged to include Italy in May 1882; as before it was to remain purely defensive, to run initially for five years only. Italy's entry largely arose from her disappointment in Tunis, where France had forestalled her (see p. 150), thereby convincing her that she could realise none of her ambitions without the help of more powerful countries. On the other hand, Austria had encouraged her entry in order to nullify the growth of Italian irredentist claims to the Italian-speaking parts of the Empire. Italy's active obligations under the treaty were restricted to the event of a French attack on Germany, or of an attack by two powers on either of her partners – while her partners' obligations were to help her if she was attacked by France, or by two powers in combination. Characteristically, however, Bismarck was at great pains to keep on good terms with Russia; indeed somewhat to Austria's disappointment, he had revived the Three Emperors' League in June 1881, in an agreement that pledged the signatories to benevolent neutrality, should any of them be engaged in a war with a country other than Turkey.[1] The general public was unaware of the contradictions contained

[1] This agreement of 1881 also pledged each of its signatories to make no changes in the Turkish territorial *status quo*, without consulting the other league partners. It was therefore in effect a self-denying ordinance imposed by Bismarck on Austria and Russia.

in these secret treaties – so much so that Anton Bruckner was persuaded to describe his Eighth Symphony as a triumphal evocation of the meeting of the three emperors at Skierniewice (1884). It could be argued that from Bismarck's point of view the parallel existence of the Triple Alliance and the Three Emperors' League would seem to ensure a salutory jamming of the war-machine, should events get out of his control – though in fact Bismarck, like most able opportunists, counted on being able to deal with awkward events as they arose.

The mid-1880s were nevertheless disappointing years for Bismarck in that they began with bright prospects, none of which materialised. Initially he received notable help from the estrangement of Britain and France following the British occupation of Egypt in 1882 – for France was resentful that Britain should exclude her from the subsequent management of Egyptian affairs. Bismarck probably saw here a double opportunity; by causing trouble for Britain, he would be indirectly siding with France, so inducing France to look on Germany with less disfavour. At the same time, however, it would make Britain conscious of the dangers of isolation, and readier therefore to listen with less indifference to Bismarck's suggestions. His launching of a programme of colonial activity in 1884 (see pp. 119–21) certainly had the effect of antagonising Britain, and of lessening French hostility – while concurrently Britain was made to feel the price of isolation especially during the Penjdeh crisis of April 1885.

The local reasons for Russian expansion towards Afghanistan are described elsewhere (see pp. 168–9); but a possible factor of major importance was Britain's attitude over the Straits. At the Congress of Berlin, Britain had greatly alarmed Russia by claiming the right to enter the Black Sea should the Sultan be under duress. It should be remembered that the Convention of 1841 had put the Straits out of bounds to warships of all nationalities, except those of the gate-keeper, Turkey. But Britain maintained that her claim was both reasonable and in the interests of preserving the Convention, arguing that after all someone must protect the impartiality of the gate-keeper.

To Russia, however, it seemed that Britain was wanting the best of both worlds, namely a universal restriction that did not apply to herself. The outcome was that all Russia's fears of a Crimea-type situation were intensified.

By 1885, Russia's imperial advance in Central Asia had reached the Afghan border. Perhaps Russia hoped that her proximity to India might eventually enable her to extort concessions from Britain over the Straits. In April Russian and Afghan troops clashed at Penjdeh. Salisbury, then in opposition, summed up British fears: ' [the real danger] would not be a direct attack of the Russian Army coming through the Khyber and Bolan passes. It would be the undermining of British strength in India by the production of intrigues and rebellions among the natives of India.' Gladstone in fact prepared to strike at Russia through the Straits. But the other powers, led by Bismarck, refused to allow this violation of the Straits Convention, their unanimous stand helping to convince Russia that her fears of a Crimea situation were perhaps unfounded, and that the Straits Convention could work to her good as well as her detriment. At the same time the powers' refusal persuaded Britain to opt for a peacefully-negotiated settlement of the Afghan issue.

It was clear, however, that the crisis had not taught Britain the lesson that Bismarck had hoped for. The episode had clearly shown (to those prepared to see it) that a policy of non-alignment would severely limit the courses of action open to Britain in Europe. It is normally unnecessary for a member of an alliance to remind a troublesome opponent that his obstinacy could lead to severe reprisals; but an isolated country is more likely to be obliged to make its threats explicit. Significantly, therefore, Britain was the only power between 1871 and 1904 to resort to a specific threat of war against another – and this she did three times, twice against Russia (in 1878 and 1885) and once against France (1898). But Britain was still not prepared to abandon non-alignment.

Bismarck was scarcely more successful with France. Well before the appointment of General Boulanger as French war minister (see p. 144), the *détente* which had been growing under Ferry had already largely evaporated.

Furthermore dissolution likewise befell the Three Emperors' League, which was ruined when Austria and Britain opposed Russia's attempts to make Bulgaria a client state (1885–8). Indeed the only salvage from the League was the Reinsurance Treaty of June 1887, by which Germany and Russia each pledged herself to remain neutral if the other was involved in a war with a third power.

The year was nevertheless not entirely fruitless in that it did at least see the Triple Alliance with Austria and Italy renewed for a further five years. And so, despite the disappointments of the mid-eighties, Bismarck was at least managing to preserve reasonable relations with two powers that were fundamentally hostile to each other.

THE DIVISION OF EUROPE

When Bismarck fell from power, his successors were more ambitious. Both Wilhelm II and his Chancellor, Caprivi, thought that they could do what Bismarck had failed to do, and pull Britain into the Triple Alliance. Since Britain regarded Russia as her principal rival, Caprivi thought it good policy to break off friendly relations with Russia; so when Russia asked for a renewal of the Reinsurance Treaty, he neglected to give it (June 1890). The new rulers of Germany felt at the same time that Bismarck had been unnecessarily cautious in the support of German interests, and that it was no longer necessary for German safety to maintain an arrangement with Russia. In this way they unwittingly made it possible for France and Russia to come together. France wanted an ally, and Russia needed money (see p. 163) and once Caprivi's tactless handling of Russia caused them to look in each other's direction, they each saw the advantages of a Franco-Russian alliance. It must be emphasised, however, that the treaty which was eventually signed in January 1894 was purely defensive. It stipulated that if Russia were attacked by Germany or by Austria aided by Germany, France would attack Germany. Conversely if France were attacked by Germany or by Italy with German support, Russia would attack Germany. However, no time limit was set, for unlike Bismarck's treaties it was not merely designed to keep in touch with the powers that might drift away, but seriously designed to meet the possibility of attack.

Other than that of defence, there was very little sympathy or common interest between France and Russia, and there remained much that divided them. But the alliance transformed the character of European international relations. The effect was to create in the minds of the military leaders of Europe (if not in the minds of the civilian governments) a picture of Continental Europe divided in two: an axis-bloc of Germany, Austria and Italy, with a potential enemy on either side. Once again, however, it must be emphasised that for either the Triple Alliance or the Franco-Russian Alliance to be operative, it would require an aggressor on the other side to take the initiative – since both treaties were only concerned with defensive wars. Even then, there was no guarantee that an ally would stand by her treaty obligations. It required some motive, even if only a desire for mutual security, before a power could be relied on to honour her obligations; so the existence of these treaties did not of themselves create a dangerous Europe. It has indeed been argued that the balance which the two alliances created could be a major peace-keeping factor. A war between the two could be very costly, neither side being able to claim with any confidence that victory would certainly be theirs.

Nevertheless the peace-keeping possibilities of the situation were to be slowly and indirectly eroded by two factors: the neuroses and long-term ambitions of the new rulers of Germany, and the military preoccupations of the general staffs.

Economic and military reality had made Germany the leading European power; and Bismarck, who had done so much to make her internationally accepted as such, had been content to preserve the *status quo*. Wilhelm II, however, had been a child of seven when Bismarck defeated Austria, and had little realisation of the labour and risks that had gone into achieving what Germany now enjoyed. He felt that it was not enough merely to exploit the domestic benefits of primacy, but that to remain great Germany must assert her greatness by playing a thrusting role in international affairs. Lacking Bismarck's stability and strength of will, he was dangerously vulnerable to the pressures that came from his entourage. In the next twenty years the mushroom growth of the United States and Russia was to make many Germans conscious that their newly won Continental supremacy might one day seem sadly parochial in a world dominated by these future giants. In the case of Russia, there was still time to stunt the giant's growth; and the years before the First World War were to hear much talk in the Wilhelmstrasse of the coming 'struggle between Teuton and Slav'. Indeed by 1914 an influential group of bankers and industrialists saw Germany's survival as a world power in terms of a *Mitteleuropa* economically subservient to Germany. They believed moreover that this project could best be protected against Russia by a bulwark of new client states, made up of Poles and other liberated peoples of the Russian Empire. This concept was to make a considerable impression on Chancellor Bethmann-Hollweg, and was in fact to influence Germany's subsequent war aims. At the same time another object of industrialists' dreams was the mineral wealth of French Lorraine.

Conversely men like Bülow were to favour the prestige and supposed economic advantage of an overseas empire; and there can be little doubt that the French colonies were to be a tempting consideration in July 1914, when Germany was weighing the pros and cons of a European war. Others, notably Alfred von Tirpitz and Georg Alexander von Müller, were to visualise huge extensions to the navy. As shown elsewhere (pp. 119–21), neither the type of navy envisaged nor the colonies that were coveted offered much that was of obvious material advantage to Germany (and both threatened to cause friction with Britain); but to have said so would have been like questioning the value of Vesuvius or the Matterhorn. More dangerously, some of the partisans of naval and mercantile expansion were to see Antwerp and its Belgian hinterland as an essential springboard for German ambitions – a belief that was also to find reflection in later German war aims.

It is true that the existence of these covetous dreams and ambitions was dangerous only in so far as the government was prepared to be influenced by them. But recent evidence on what was to happen in 1914 suggests that neither Wilhelm nor his advisers were to have the perception or the self-control to resist jumping at the illusory opportunity of fulfilling these dreams, when it eventually appeared.

Turning to the military preoccupations of the general staffs in Europe, strategists in all countries were claiming that victory in the next war would lie with the side that was quickest off the mark, and this consideration was to be particularly strong in the case of Germany.

The chief of the German general staff, General Alfred von Schlieffen (1890–1905), was faced with the problem of having an enemy on each side. Accordingly he had completed by 1905 a war plan which envisaged an initial all-out effort against France, which would crush her in four to six weeks. This would then be followed by a sudden switch of Germany's forces to the east, where in the meantime a few German troops and the Austrian army would have been holding Russia in check. Then, reinforced from the west, the combined Austro-German forces would proceed to pulverise Russia. It is essential to realise that all subsequent German military thinking was dominated by this concept, and by the necessity for speed – and also by the obvious need to crush France before Russia could mobilise in strength.

The wartime strength of the Russian army alone was greater than that of the combined Austro-German armies – though it would take time to become a reality, in addition to which the Russians were notoriously inferior in equipment. Furthermore the German need for speed and the problem of transporting vast numbers of men and material over long distances meant that all the details of the plan had to be worked out in advance, there being no room for modification once the machinery was set in motion. The German general staff as a result were constantly impressing on the civilian ministers the need for striking the first blow. The nature of the plan moreover strengthened the assumption that any war with Russia would also automatically mean war with France. Indeed so dominant was the plan that the general staff would have been positively embarrassed if France had dissociated herself from a Russian war. All this began to colour the thinking of statesmen as well as soldiers, so that the nicety of the balance between the alliances had an ambivalent effect. On the one hand it acted as a deterrent to war; but on the other it put a premium on speed, and fostered a temptation to strike while a temporary advantage was available.

These alliances were far from being the monolithic blocs that are popularly imagined. Since 1898 Italy had been looking with growing favour on France, for not only was France Italy's best customer, but Italy wanted French support for her plans for eventually annexing Libya. The result was that in November 1902 Italy secretly undertook to remain neutral if France were attacked or indirectly provoked into declaring war. In October 1909, moreover, she secretly gave Russia an assurance that she would oppose any attempt by Austria to alter the *status quo* in the Balkans, provided that Russia recognised Italian interests in Libya. Italy nevertheless continued to be a member of the Triple Alliance – though Germany was under no illusions as to her worth as an ally. Similarly – though much less seriously – it is often forgotten that in July 1905 Wilhelm II managed to persuade the Tsar to sign a secret undertaking at Björkö that each would support the other if attacked by a European power. Indeed, the refusal of the Russian foreign minister to ratify the treaty arose not so much out of loyalty to France, as out of his feeling that under existing circumstances the treaty gave too much to Germany and too little to Russia. Lest, however, too much importance be given to this episode, it should likewise be noted that Chancellor von Bülow was equally firm in rejecting his master's initiative, though his objections were mainly based on the restriction of the treaty's terms to Europe.

The British enigma

In this strange and largely aristocratic world of real and imaginary dangers, the strength of the Franco-Russian camp became more difficult to assess because of the shadowy presence of Britain. The agreements which Britain made with France in April 1904 and Russia in August 1907 were essentially settlements of overseas differences; and as far as European issues were concerned, Britain was still pursuing a policy of relative non-alignment. Britain was nevertheless prepared to seek help with her overseas interests; and from the late 1890s she made periodic attempts to obtain a German partnership against Russian expansion in the Far East. The German terms, however, were too high, and, as Lord Lansdowne put it, they threatened to draw Britain 'into disputes which do not concern her' (1901). She therefore turned an ear to Japan.

The alliance she made (January 1902) was primarily aimed at preventing a possible Russo-Japanese *entente*; and from the British point of view the terms of the commitment were minimal. Indeed when war broke out between Japan and Russia in February 1904 (see p. 169), Britain was not even called on to participate. It was likewise significant that Britain had already partially insured herself against the danger of being called on, by improving her relations with Russia's ally, France – for Japan could call on Britain only if Russia was aided by France or another power.

Britain in fact had found a receptive audience in the French foreign minister, the sly but eminently sensible Théophile Delcassé. Despite optimistic moments during the Boer War, Delcassé's memories of the Fashoda crisis of 1898 had convinced him that France could consolidate her position in Africa only with the co-operation of Britain. In July of that year a tiny French expedition had arrived at Fashoda on the headwaters of the Nile, which Britain regarded as within her sphere of influence. Captain Marchand and his 127 men had crossed 'darkest Africa' from the west coast, bringing with them a steamboat, which they had carried in pieces over the more difficult parts of the route, the boiler being rolled on logs. After two months at Fashoda they were confronted by General Kitchener, fresh from crushing the dervishes at Omdurman, and backed by three battalions of infantry, a strong force of artillery and five gunboats. The ensuing threat of war had been sufficient to secure the French withdrawal, for France could expect no help from Russia, since the situation did not come within the terms of the Franco-Russian alliance, and the risks for Russia of a war against Britain were too great. At the same time the Anglo-Japanese alliance made Delcassé aware that France would now have to behave with particular tact in the Far East. Consequently in April 1904 an Anglo-French convention was signed, resting on an intrinsically attractive bargain: France recognised Britain's interests in Egypt, in return for British recognition of French interests in Morocco. It also eased the way to an Anglo-Russian *entente* in August 1907, in which Russia notably recognised British interest in Afghanistan and south-east Persia, India's neighbours.

It is true that Britain's concern for the Straits has slowly decreased since the 1880s. In fact Britain's growing hold over Egypt had led Salisbury to admit as early as 1895 that Britain had no further reason to oppose Russia having possession of the Straits, as long as they were open to all. Nevertheless Britain would expect a fair price for this concession; and until Russia had an adequate Black Sea fleet, Russia had no desire to see the Straits open to all.

It must be emphasised, however, that for Britain the *entente* with France and Russia was only intended to have relevance outside Europe. Paradoxically enough it was precisely Germany's efforts to prove this point that gave the *entente* its relevance in a European context. In March 1905 and again in July 1911, Germany tried to humiliate France by challenging her special position in Morocco.[1] The German aim was to try to prove to France that Britain would not come to her rescue when she was in trouble. The challenge had precisely the opposite effect, however, convincing Britain that she could not afford to ignore Germany's increasingly domineering attitude on the Continent. As it turned out, only Austria was prepared to stand by Germany, and in view of the opposition, Germany was obliged to back down on both occasions. The incidents furthermore led to the opening of Anglo-French military and naval discussions, in 1906 and 1911–12. But although this resulted in mutual agreement over the deployment of their navies, and although it doubtless raised French hopes of closer ties with Britain, these discussions did not of themselves contribute a pledge by Britain to help France if she was attacked by Ger-

---

[1] Bülow and Holstein had browbeaten Wilhelm into making a visit to Tangier, where he had extolled the principle of equal opportunity for all comers to Morocco. Germany hoped that the subsequent Algeciras Conference (January–April 1906) would reveal France in all her nakedness. The second Moroccan crisis occurred when Germany sent a gunboat, *Panther*, to Agadir, allegedly to protect German interests, but in reality to demonstrate British reluctance to support France.

many (as Grey pointed out to the French ambassador in November 1912). What Britain would actually do in the event of a German attack on France was still a mystery, both to Europe and to the British government itself. The naval and military discussions merely planned *how* Britain would help France, should she decide to do so, yet this itself remained highly problematical. Nevertheless it could be argued that the naval agreement did give the *entente* a strategic logic, which, when the final crisis came, could have been evaded only with difficulty and embarrassment – despite the hostility of several cabinet members.

Danger in the Balkans

How great was the danger in this somewhat ambiguous confrontation of powers? It is easy to be mesmerised by the armaments programme and the military plans, and assume that a general war was an overwhelming likelihood, even before the assassination of the Habsburg heir at Sarajevo. There was also the race in naval armaments between Britain and Germany (see p. 119); but Britain was managing to keep her advantage over Germany in battleships at a ratio of eight to five. There were likewise misgivings in Britain about Germany's scheme for a Berlin–Baghdad railway, though these were partially allayed by a mutual settlement in June 1914.

The most dangerous area of conflict seemed to be the Balkans. The Young Turk Revolution of July 1908 had resulted in Austria annexing Bosnia and Herzegovina (October 1908), for fear that the Turks might withdraw them from Austrian administration. As the majority of the inhabitants were Serbs, Serbia was prepared to resist the annexation by force, but such resistance would only be possible with Russian support. Germany was annoyed by the annexation, but would not allow her only certain ally to be humiliated. She therefore demanded that Russia accept the situation – which she did, rather than risk war (March 1909). But the inescapable significance of the episode lay in the apparent destruction of any hope of reconciling Austria and Russia – and, perhaps more important, it left Russia very sensitive on matters of prestige.

H

A further crisis came with the Balkan Wars of 1912–13, when the Balkan states took advantage of the Turko-Italian War to mount an onslaught on Turkey (see pp. 183–5). The net result was that when the victors fell to quarrelling over the spoils, Serbia eventually emerged vastly strengthened; and indeed would have gained even more, had not Austria objected to some of her earlier demands in Albania. Predictably enough, Russia had wanted to back Serbia's demands; but being unprepared for war she had been obliged to accept a second humiliation. Clearly, however, there was a limit to the slights that Russian prestige could bear, and it was in everyone's interest that Austria should avoid humiliating Russia a third time.

The difficulty lay in Austria's mounting fear of the disruptive effect of Serbia's successes upon the Serbs within the Empire. Serbia had grown enormously in prestige, and was therefore in a much stronger position to encourage them to revolt, which in turn might trigger off revolts among the other subject nationalities – or so Austria feared. Nevertheless whatever Serbia's ambitions may have been, it was highly questionable whether she was prepared to do anything that would risk war with Austria, though it is true that she could probably rely on Russia's determination not to risk another humiliation, and that she would therefore probably get Russian military help. But even if Serbia could count on Russia, she had no desire to become a battlefield. Indeed she knew all too well that in the event of war Austrian troops would certainly occupy Belgrade before Russia could arrive in strength.

The swinging tiller

Danger, however, was not confined to the east. There was the German army law of January 1913, which in turn gave rise to the French army law of August 1913. The French law extended the period of conscript service from two to three years, which meant that the number of conscripts with the colours would be increased by a half in 1915. The immediate significance of this was that the relative advantage which the Germans derived from their January law would not last beyond 1914. Clearly, as far as the German general staff were concerned, if war was going to come, the sooner it came the better. And it may be significant that the general staff asked the government for an extra £50 millions' worth of armaments, to be ready by the summer of 1914. It must nevertheless be remembered that a general staff's function is to be ready for all eventualities, and that even if preparations were being made for a war in the summer of 1914, this did not necessarily mean that the government intended to go to war, either then or later.

Even so, there is no denying a disturbing readiness on the part of Germany's rulers to envisage at least the possibility of war. In October 1913 the Kaiser told the Austrian chief of staff, Franz Conrad von Hötzendorff, that he was no longer opposed in principle to the idea of a major war. He likewise urged both Conrad and the Austrian foreign minister, Leopold von Berchtold, to take the earliest opportunity of teaching Serbia a lesson. Austria was certainly Germany's only reliable ally, and it may well be that the Kaiser now genuinely regarded the prospect of irredentist propaganda from the newly victorious Serbia as a threat to the integrity of the Austro-Hungarian Empire. He may at the same time have seen a blow against Serbia as a necessary stimulus to Austrian morale.

The assassination of Franz Ferdinand at Sarajevo on 28 June was the work of a Bosnian Serb working for a Serbian secret society, the Black Hand; but neither the evidence nor commonsense suggests that the Serbian government as such had anything to do with it. It is true that the Black Hand happened to have as its head the chief of the Serbian military intelligence – but it is, after all, a small world. The Austro-Hungarian government, however, either believed or wanted to believe that the Serbian government had *something* to do with it; and both Conrad and Berchtold thought that Austria should seize this opportunity of crushing Serbia as a centre of anti-Habsburg propaganda, provided that German protection was forthcoming.

Nothing could better illustrate the absence of firm control in Berlin than the events of the next few weeks. The chief of the German general staff, Helmuth von Moltke, and his subordinates consistently urged that Germany should seize this double opportunity of strengthening her ally and crippling Russia and

France, should they come to Serbia's rescue. Chancellor Bethmann-Hollweg and the foreign minister, Gottlieb von Jagow, likewise tended to this view, but their wishes were tempered by fear of British reactions. While hopes existed that Britain would not intervene, the Chancellor was happy enough to urge Austria to force war on Serbia. Indeed on the occasions when he changed to an attitude of caution, this was dictated each time by the necessity of making Austria's behaviour appear reasonable to Britain. This would thereby make any possible Russian intervention seem to Britain like an unwarranted interference in a local quarrel. It was not fear of Russian intervention, but fear of Britain seeing right on Russia's side that moderated the Chancellor's bellicose advice to Austria. There were even times when he hoped that France might likewise take an unsympathetic view of Russian intervention, and fail to back her ally. If this happened, the Austro-Serbian conflict would have brought about the long-dreamed-of prize of splitting the Franco-Russian alliance.

The German general staff, however, were ruled by the Schlieffen Plan, and preferred not to entertain such inconvenient hopes. The Kaiser for his part acted with characteristic volatility. He assured Austria (4–5 July) that Germany would support her, even if Russia declared war. He emphasised that if Austria felt that Serbia was a real danger to imperial integrity, Austria should take advantage of the assassination to thrash her. Having given Austria the go-ahead, he then departed on his annual cruise with the German fleet, 'in order not to alarm world opinion'.

But when he returned to Potsdam three weeks later he discovered that Serbia had accepted most of the terms contained in Austria's belligerent ultimatum. His reaction was typical; 'a great moral victory for Vienna', 'that eliminates any reason for war' (28 July). It was just such a *volte-face* that his ministers feared. Knowing that Austria was about to declare war, they delayed sending Wilhelm's views to Vienna. Indeed the Chancellor told the German ambassador that 'you must most carefully avoid any impression that we want to hold Austria back'.

Yet the decisive step had in fact already been taken. Continuous German promptings had borne fruit: Austria declared

war on Serbia on the same day (28 July). The readiness of the
German general staff to entrust themselves to a partnership
with Austria appears the more remarkable when their contempt
for the Austrian army is remembered. As Professor Gordon
Craig has pointed out, it always seemed to Germany that the
Austrians had a tendency to take a certain melancholy pride in
their own inefficiency. 'The ability of the Austrians to regard
some incredible foul-up with a mixture of resignation and
aesthetic enjoyment must have brought many a narrow-gutted
Prussian close to apoplexy.' Yet when Chancellor Bethmann-
Hollweg's lurking fears materialised and Grey told Germany
that Britain might well be obliged to enter a Franco-German
war (29 July), Moltke tried to outmanœuvre the Chancellor's
requests for caution. In the small hours of 30 July the Chancellor had telegraphed Vienna advising them to give serious
consideration to British suggestions for a mediated settlement.
But the same afternoon Moltke telegraphed Conrad, urging
him to 'mobilise at once against Russia. Germany will mobilise.'
This drew from Berchtold the obvious comment: 'Who gives the
orders, Moltke or Bethmann?' Predictably enough Bethmann
quickly gave way to the generals' insistence on swift action.

If the Kaiser was volatile and irresponsible, Nicholas of
Russia was weak-willed. In 1909, largely as a result of Rasputin's scheming (see p. 298), Nicholas had given the war ministry to one of Rasputin's entourage, General Vladimir Sukhomlinov (1909–15). Sukhomlinov not only opposed all proposals to
modernise the army but proceeded to make impossible promises
to France concerning the Russian army's role in a future war.
The Tsar for his part knew perfectly well that war with Austria-
Hungary would mean war with Germany, since Germany was
well aware of the chaotic condition of the Russian army.
Moreover, like Napoleon III in 1870, Nicholas himself had no
illusions about the state of his own forces. Yet despite this he
feebly yielded to his generals' demands for full mobilisation. A
strong-minded Tsar would either have modernised the army
when there was time, or he would have refused to play the role
of champion of Serbia.

When Russia ignored the German demand to cease

mobilisation, Germany handed her the formal declaration that made the war a general war (1 August). Contagion lay in the fact that the assault on Russia depended on the Schlieffen Plan – and the plan could not go into operation without a further declaration of war between Germany and France. On 31 July, therefore, Germany asked France to state officially within eighteen hours whether she would stay neutral in the event of a Russo-German war. In the unlikely eventuality of a conciliatory reply, the German ambassador was to demand the temporary cession of Verdun and Toul as a guarantee – a humiliation which France could be relied on to refuse. As Germany expected, France rejected the initial demand; and Germany declared war (3 August). At the same time, however, it must not be overlooked that France had already given Russia assurances that she would honour the alliance if Germany attacked Russia; so it would be difficult to claim that France might have remained neutral, if Germany had not prejudged the issue.

Crossing the Channel, it is open to question whether the British cabinet would have agreed to back France had not the question of Belgian neutrality entered into it. It is true that the Schlieffen Plan envisaged a thrust through Belgium, as France and Britain well knew. But the nature of the Anglo-French naval and military arrangements had been known to the cabinet since 1912; and since these arrangements did not themselves constitute a pledge to France, a section of the cabinet might conceivably have refused to listen to arguments based on moral obligation, had not Belgium been involved. However, the issue was by-passed when Germany ignored Grey's request (31 July) that Belgian neutrality be respected – for the German silence effectively persuaded the British cabinet to grant France defence of her Channel coast. Events soon justified the commitment. Early on 4 August, when the bells of Liège and Namur were sounding eight, the first German troops crossed the Belgian frontier. Grey went through the vain formality of demanding a withdrawal, but by the end of the day Berlin and London were at war – for the first time since 1748.

By way of postscript, it is perhaps worth asking whether the economic rivalry between Britain and Germany played much part in encouraging the British government to back France. Most of the evidence tends to point the other way. Both in Britain and Germany many businessmen petitioned their respective governments not to declare war, for Anglo-German trade was far too valuable to be sacrificed to the long-term possibility of eliminating an industrial rival. The militant advocates of a *Mitteleuropa* (see p. 220) were only a small if influential minority in the German business world. As always most businessmen wanted a steady income, and were extremely reluctant to abandon the existing network of trade for the prospect or mirage of a highly dubious long-term objective. It is sufficient to see what happened to European stock-market prices in July 1914 to realise the deep hostility of most of the business world to war. The obvious beneficiaries – the armaments manufacturers – were likewise only a small minority; and even they had their fears in war, government control being but one of them.

CHAPTER EIGHT

Disaster

The First World War

So Abram rose, and clave the wood, and went,
And took the fire with him, and a knife.
And as they sojourned both of them together,
Isaac the first-born spake and said, My Father,
Behold the preparations, fire and iron,
But where the lamb for this burnt-offering?
Then Abram bound the youth with belts and straps,
And builded parapets and trenches there,
And stretched forth the knife to slay his son.
When lo! an angel called him out of heaven,
Saying, Lay not thy hand upon the lad,
Neither do anything to him. Behold,
A ram, caught in a thicket by its horns;
Offer the Ram of Pride instead of him.
But the old man would not so, but slew his son,
And half the seed of Europe, one by one.

WILFRED OWEN

To have avoided the war, or cut it short by negotiation, would not have been as simple as the poem suggests. Statesmen thought that more was at stake than the 'Ram of Pride'. But whatever was at stake can only appear absurdly trivial when compared to the slaughter and misery of the next few years. It could moreover be argued that the war claimed most of its victims after 1918. As a result of the war, the world was to suffer twenty years of economic upheaval, while the social improvement that the pre-war period seemed to promise was indefinitely postponed. Not only were dictatorships of Right and Left to spring up as a direct or indirect consequence of the war; but a second world war was then to break out which owed much of its origins to the inadequacies of post-war reconstruction. This is not to deny that even if the war had not taken place, some of these disasters might still have occurred in some form or other; indeed there would possibly have been others that in fact did not occur. The historian can only survey what actually happened.

TABLE 18

Casualties in the armed services

Countries	Total mobilised forces	Killed and died	Wounded
Allies and Associated Powers:			
Russia	12,000,000	1,700,000	4,950,000
France	8,410,000	1,357,800	4,266,000
British Empire	8,904,467	908,371	2,090,212
Italy	5,615,000	650,000	947,000
United States	4,355,000	126,000	234,300
Romania	750,000	335,706	120,000
Serbia	707,343	45,000	133,148
Belgium	267,000	13,716	44,686
Greece	230,000	5,000	21,000
Portugal	100,000	7,222	13,751
Montenegro	50,000	3,000	10,000
Total	42,188,810	5,152,115	12,831,004
Central Powers:			
Germany	11,000,000	1,773,700	4,216,058
Austria-Hungary	7,800,000	1,200,000	3,620,000
Turkey	2,850,000	325,000	400,000
Bulgaria	1,200,000	87,500	152,390
Total	22,850,000	3,386,200	8,388,448
Grand total	65,038,810	8,538,315	21,219,452

As reported by the United States War Department in February 1924.

The more immediate harvest of war was the elimination of one in twenty of the entire European population, and the disablement of one in fifteen. Since only fourteen of Europe's twenty-seven nations were involved, the swathe that was cut through the people of the belligerent countries was much wider than these overall figures suggest. Added to this were the broken lives of their bereaved families. Nor must the men be forgotten whose minds were permanently scarred by the sight of suffering on a scale unthought of – not only the thousands in mental hospitals, but the many millions who had to live with unspeakable memories. There were also the indirect victims of war.

*

Many marriages and careers were wrecked, while one British soldier in five went home with venereal disease.

Ultimately, the most important question that can be asked about the war is why was the cost so great? Nor must one lose sight of the second issue – why the Central Powers were defeated. The historian can only hazard guesses as to what Europe would have been like had they won. Germany and Austria-Hungary would presumably have enlarged their frontiers to take in part of Belgium, Poland and the Balkans. Austria-Hungary would have prolonged her mildly agonising existence, with perhaps greater ethnic problems; while Germany would have added some to hers, though additions would still have remained a small percentage of her population. It is not known precisely what financial and economic reparations they might have extracted from the Entente Powers, or whether these would have made life so much more difficult than the reality that followed the pyrrhic victory of 1918.

THE ECONOMIC FACTORS

If the resources of both sides are examined, the balance appeared to lie in the Entente's favour. Russia, France and Britain had between them just under eleven million trained men, either with the colours or in the reserve; while Germany and Austria-Hungary had seven-and-a-half million. During the course of the war, however, Russia, France and Britain were able to mobilise a total of over twenty-nine million troops, against the nineteen million of Germany and Austria-Hungary. Furthermore the allies that the Entente picked up during the war were to increase the total of mobilised Entente troops to over forty-two million, nearly twice the combined strength of their opponents (twenty-two million). Similarly, in terms of economic resources, it is worth remembering that the exports of Germany and Austria-Hungary were less than two-thirds of those of Russia, France and Britain. Germany, however, had the advantage in armaments and training. While the French had the best light field-gun (the 75 mm.), Germany had the best medium and heavy artillery. Nevertheless, given the nature of the overall balance, time was clearly on the side of the

Entente; and a victory of the Central Powers would depend on speed and luck. Yet, despite their superiority of readiness, they began the war with only about 150 infantry divisions to the Entente's 170.

No country had foreseen the economic upheaval that the war would entail. In France mobilisation left the home economy with a skeleton staff, thereby closing nearly half her business concerns, and putting two million unconscripted men out of work. Moreover in most countries the military requisitioning of railways severely restricted the ability of producers to supply their markets, so creating the paradoxical situation of acute shortage side by side with mounting accumulations of unsold stock. Within a year, enemy action and the switching of industry to war production had cut German exports to a third of their pre-war level and her imports to two-thirds. Russia suffered worst in that the Central Powers' control of the Baltic and Constantinople reduced her exports to a seventh and her imports to two-fifths; while in the west German submarine warfare had cut Anglo-French shipping to almost two-fifths by the autumn of 1917. Indeed by 1918, the war was costing the world over £2 million an hour, with German war expenditure in 1917 already equivalent to two-thirds of the average annual pre-war national income. This enormous expense was largely met by borrowing and by printing more paper money – all of which stored up trouble for the future. In fact some two-thirds to four-fifths of the expenditure was met in this way, the rest largely coming from increased taxation. France doubled her tax revenue during the war, while Britain trebled hers. And inevitably this all contributed to a marked reduction in the standard of living, which rising prices had already depressed.

Most belligerents followed Germany's example of setting up co-ordinating bodies to manage the national economy. Germany likewise inaugurated the requisitioning of foodstuffs in February 1915 and the rationing of bread a few weeks later, to be followed by other comestibles. France did not introduce food rationing until 1917. Within a fortnight of hostilities Britain and France had established mutually co-operative methods for food purchase, but Austria and Germany only did so at times of crisis. Even Austria and Hungary had bitter differences over mutual economic support, largely because Hungary was reluctant to supply Austria with her food demands. And it was difficulties of this sort that frustrated German ideas of some sort of economic union for the Central Powers.

Conscription of troops was eventually followed by varying degrees of conscription of labour. In Germany all civilians between the ages of seventeen and sixty were obliged to work as directed (December 1916), while in France the number of working women increased by a third. Morale at home, however, was noticeably raised by the coming to power of Lloyd George in Britain (December 1916) and Georges Clemenceau in France (November 1917). Both men were prepared to conduct the war with much more drive than their predecessors, and their enthusiasm and ruthlessness made the home population feel that their sacrifices were being put to some purpose. In Germany, on the other hand, government seemed to be falling progressively into the hands of the high command, whose military prestige was sinking with the fortunes of war.

THE MILITARY FACTORS

The western front

The whole German gamble hinged on the shattering effect of the opening. The massive Schlieffen Plan (see p. 221) depended on a quick envelopment of the French army; for without this the rest could not succeed. Yet it was precisely on this first stage of the plan that Germany lost her best chance of victory. The original plan for the western front had envisaged a clap-net technique rather like a turning page. The pivot of the net had been fixed in Alsace and Lorraine, while the leading edge of the net consisted of a very strong right wing which was intended to sweep through Belgium and fall shut to the west of Paris. In the meantime the French were expected to try to advance against the pivot in Alsace and Lorraine, thereby enmeshing themselves in the pocket of the net. However, Schlieffen's successor, Helmuth von Moltke, had ill-advisedly modified his plan. The German right wing that was to sweep through

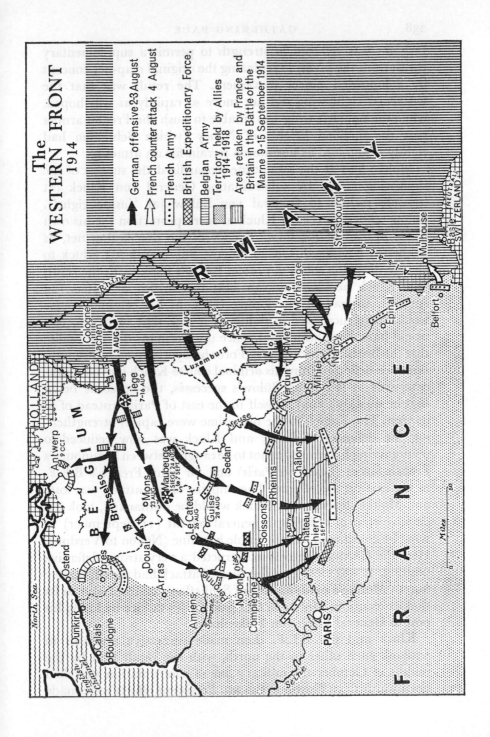

The WESTERN FRONT 1914

Legend:
- German offensive 2-3 August
- French counter attack 4 August
- French Army
- British Expeditionary Force
- Belgian Army
- Territory held by Allies 1914-1918
- Area retaken by France and Britain in the Battle of the Marne 9-15 September 1914

GERMANY

HOLLAND (NEUTRAL)

BELGIUM

Antwerp 9 OCT
Brussels
Ostend
Ypres
Mons 23 AUG
Maubeuge SIEGE 24 AUG to 7 SEPT
Le Cateau 26 AUG
Guise 28 AUG
Sedan
Rheims
Châlons
Soissons
Château Thierry 4 SEPT
Douai
Arras
Amiens
Noyon
Compiègne
PARIS

Liège 7-16 AUG
Aachen
Cologne
Luxemburg
3 AUG
2 AUG

Rhine
Moselle
Meuse
Marne
Oise
Somme
Seine

Verdun
St. Mihiel
Metz
Nancy
Morhange
Strasbourg
Epinal
Belfort
Mulhouse

Lorraine
Alsace

Basle (NEUTRAL) SWITZERLAND

FRANCE

North Sea
English Channel
Dunkirk
Calais
Boulogne

Miles 0 50

Belgium was reduced in strength to permit a supplementary thrust from the pivot, so replacing the original clap-net concept by a lop-sided pincer movement. The result was that the weakened right wing did not move so rapidly as was hoped, while the new left wing was unable to push the French armies past the fortified heights of Nancy (which Schlieffen had rightly recognised as unsuitable terrain for an attack).

Moltke had at the same time jeopardised the success of the right-wing sweep by subordinating General von Kluck (at 'outside right') to General von Bülow (at 'inside right'). Bülow tended to regard Kluck as mere protection for his own flank, instead of the forward edge of the descending net, as Schlieffen envisaged. On 20 August Bülow ordered Kluck to change direction south to protect Bülow's flank, with the result that Kluck accidentally ran into the British at Mons (23 August), instead of enveloping them, as his original course would have succeeded in doing. It is true that such a success would have been accidental, since the Germans did not realise that the British Expeditionary Force had yet arrived in strength. But once deflected from his original course Kluck moved south-eastwards to follow up Bülow's successes, the outcome being that he quickly found himself to the east of Paris, instead of to its west. The French in the meantime were rapidly strengthening the defences of Paris; and Kluck was now reduced to manœuvring his army so as not to be caught between Maunoury's French forces (based on Paris) and Sir John French's B.E.F. to the east on the Marne. The impetus of the attack was lost; and Moltke, fearing that Kluck would be outflanked, took the decisive step of ordering a general retreat (11 September) to what he considered a more viable base line (Noyon to Verdun). Here the Germans rapidly constructed a very strong defensive position. It was clear that the plan of attack had failed, largely due to Moltke's modification of Schlieffen's concept and to its shaky execution. Moltke in fact paid for his failure by losing his post to General Erich von Falkenhayn.

Kluck and the B.E.F. then made successive attempts to outflank each other to the north, with the result that by the middle of October the military line of confrontation stretched northwards from Noyon to the sea. Persistent efforts were made by both sides to break through this line, but the onset of winter weather on 11 November brought the year's campaigning to an end. Both sides dug in – the Germans more effectively than the allies, for the Germans recognised the situation for what it was, a type of siege warfare, while the Entente seemed to regard it as 'open warfare at the halt'. But few then realised that the front line, as then established, was to remain little changed for four years. Trench warfare gave the advantage to the weapons of defence, the machine-gun and barbed wire. And until an armoured assault weapon was invented that could smash through barbed wire and withstand machine-gun fire, there was little that an infantry or cavalry attack could do. Millions were to die, however, before the tank and American intervention were to resolve the issue.

The eastern front

Failure in the west meant that there could be no steam-rollering of Russia, since Germany could not spare sufficient forces from the western front. Nevertheless Moltke had placed an army in East Prussia, which managed to counter the first Russian offensive. Indeed it might have victoriously outflanked the Russian First Army, had it not decided on a direct assault, which the Russians were able to stem after hard fighting (20 August). The Russians had nevertheless placed themselves at a continual disadvantage by their failure to put their wireless communications into code; and it was knowledge of their movements that enabled the Germans to envelop the Russian Second Army at Tannenberg (29–31 August). A similar German flanking movement could well have caught the Russian First Army a second time (9–14 September), but the Germans failed to carry the attempt through, thereby enabling the Russians to retreat.

The German campaign in East Prussia was weakened, moreover, by the need to reinforce the Austrians in Galicia and Poland. Once again, Austro-German successes were spoilt by failure to complete outflanking movements. The fighting resulted in the creation of an extended front in eastern Europe that ran roughly parallel to the Russian frontier – about twenty miles inside it in the north, and a hundred miles inside it in the centre; whereas in the south the front lay about a hundred miles within the Austrian frontier. It was much more flexible than the western front, and was not accompanied by extensive digging-in operations. Nevertheless it symbolised the failure of either side to make really significant advances. It is true that the Central Powers could scarcely have hoped for a walk-over in eastern Europe, with such limited forces at their disposal, but they had lost several good opportunities of encircling Russian armies which, had they been taken, might have persuaded Russia to come to terms. It now seemed clear that the key to the war lay on the western front.

Seen in retrospect the failure of the Central Powers to achieve the essential swift victory in 1914 arose from a repeated loss of faith in flanking movements, this being true of both the western and eastern fronts. Admittedly it can only be guessed how far the original flanking intentions would have fared in practice, but it is hard to imagine them having less success than what replaced them. Indeed this loss of faith was an important factor in changing a war of movement into a static war. It was moreover a dangerous change, since their enemies' superiority in resources seemed to promise them victory in the long run.

The Entente, however, had increasing cause to be worried about Russia. Russia lacked modern weapons and machinery, while Turkey's entry on the side of the Central Powers (29 October 1914) made it difficult for Britain and France to supply Russia. The fact that Britain clearly admitted her willingness to let Russia have Constantinople was small consolation in the present circumstances, for British attempts to break through the Straits met with repeated failure, including the expensive and short-lived occupation of the Gallipoli peninsula (April 1915–January 1916). In fact it was precisely Russian shortages that encouraged the Central Powers to launch an all-out attack on the eastern front (2–4 May 1915) which eventually pushed the Russians back two hundred miles into the Pripet Marshes. As Russia retreated, however, her front line contracted, so shortening her lines of communication and improving her ability to resist. By contrast, Germany and

Austria faced increasing transport problems as they moved deeper into Russian territory. Indeed this problem of supplying advancing armies (and the relative ease of supplying retreating ones) was a major factor in creating the pendulum character of the war.

In 1916, however, the pendulum was swinging the other way (May–September) though the net Russian advance was only forty miles, both sides suffering about a million casualties each. The Russians had been helped to some extent by the entry of Italy (May 1915), who eventually provided some distraction on Austria's southern frontiers; while the entry of Romania (August 1916) and Greece (July 1917) more than offset the recruitment of Bulgaria by the Central Powers (October 1915). However, the war potential of all these Balkan states was very limited, making little difference to the outcome of the war.

Paradoxically, the Russian Revolution of March 1917 gave hope to both sides. The Germans saw it as an opportunity to disrupt the enemy, and with unusual prescience helped Lenin on his way to Petrograd; while on the other hand the Allies hoped that it would mean a more efficient conduct of the war, especially as the best Russian general, Brusilov, had been made commander-in-chief. But the Russian army was now hamstrung by insubordination and desertions, many soldiers returning home in hopeful anticipation of a redistribution of land. The Bolshevik revolution of November brought Lenin to power, and one of his first acts was to seek a peace with Germany.

The circumstances of the Russian withdrawal are examined in a later chapter (see pp. 297–302). But it should be noted here that the eventual peace of Brest-Litovsk (March 1918) reflected a break-up of Russian territory that was already taking place. The Provisional Government of the previous year had already recognised Polish independence (March 1917) and granted varying degrees of autonomy to Finland and Estonia. Predictably enough Lithuania, then under German occupation, had declared its independence in the summer, to be followed by the Ukraine in November 1917. Only the vain possibility of a German socialist revolution could have saved the Soviet government from signing away a large part of Russia's western empire. As it was, the failure of these hopes obliged Russia to abandon Congress Poland, Lithuania and Courland to the Central Powers, who were empowered to decide on their future. She was also forced to recognise the independence of the Ukraine and Finland, and to agree to a temporary evacuation of Livonia and Estonia. In the Caucasus, she was stripped of Kars, Ardahan and Batum, which were given to Turkey. March 1918 was indeed a grim month for the Allied cause – and not only in the east.

New elements

It was extremely fortunate for the Entente that the United States was ready to fill the gap. The United States had entered the war in April 1917 (see p. 247), but it was not until the summer of 1918 that American forces started arriving in France in significant quantity. When they did, they settled the outcome of the war.

Prior to this, the stalemate on the western front had become a slaughterhouse, as each side believed that its own powers of endurance were the greater. The Allies rightly believed that time was on their side; but the Central Powers were sustained by the fact that they already occupied considerably more enemy territory than they could reasonably expect to keep at a negotiated settlement. If they could merely stay where they were for the duration of the war, they would have the stronger position at a peace settlement. And in so far as they wanted to push beyond the *status quo*, it was mainly to secure themselves against counter-attack and to be in an even better bargaining position at the peace.

An added obstacle to peace was the absence of precise material war aims on either side. Each wished to eliminate the other as a threat to its security, but such a wish could not express itself in material terms that would be acceptable to the other side. Once war was started, the British wanted the destruction of the German fleet, while the French wanted the return of Alsace-Lorraine. But these would not of themselves provide the 'security' that both sides wanted. Russia for her part had been primarily interested in curbing Austrian influence in the Balkans and obtaining effective control of the

Straits; yet her difficulty had been that any territorial gains would embarrass her with further ethnic problems. Like her allies, moreover, she had also been concerned with 'destroying German militarism' – however that might be done.

The German war aims were now mainly negative: a refusal to give up the iron-ore of Lorraine or the maritime advantages of Antwerp, as well as a desire to control Russian territory at least as far eastwards as Riga. Austria, as always, had her ethnic problems in the forefront of her preoccupations, even to the point of still believing that the humiliation of Serbia would help to solve them. Nevertheless she made secret overtures for peace in February 1917. The Allies insisted, however, that Germany must return Alsace-Lorraine to the French; and stalemate was inevitable as long as Germany insisted on the terms just mentioned. Italy for her part had joined the Entente on the understanding that she would receive among other substantial gains the South Tyrol, Trieste, Istria and part of Dalmatia; while in the east Romania expected to receive Transylvania, Bukovina and the Banat. In the same way, the Central Powers had promised Macedonia to Bulgaria.

On the western front, the misery of the trenches continued, subjecting millions to a constant interplay of wretchedness, fear and boredom.

> Our brains ache, in the merciless iced east winds
>   that knive us . . .
> Wearied we keep awake because the night is silent . . .
> Low, drooping flares confuse our memory of the
>   salient . . .
> Worried by silence, sentries whisper, curious,
>   nervous,
>   But nothing happens.
> Watching, we hear the mad gusts tugging on
>   the wire,
> Like twitching agonies of men among its brambles.
> Northward, incessantly, the flickering gunnery
>   rumbles,
> Far off, like a dull rumour of some other war.
>   What are we doing here?
>   WILFRED OWEN, *Exposure*

At dawn the ridge emerges massed and dun
In the wild purple of the glow'ring sun,
Smouldering through spouts of drifting smoke that
      shroud
The menacing scarred slope; . . .
. . . .
The barrage roars and lifts. Then, clumsily bowed
With bombs and guns and shovels and battle-gear,
Men jostle and climb to meet the bristling fire.
Lines of grey, muttering faces, marked with fear,
They leave their trenches, going over the top,
While time ticks blank and busy on their wrists,
And hope, with furtive eyes and grappling fists,
Flounders in mud. O Jesus, make it stop!

SIEGFRIED SASSOON, *Attack*

In 1916 Falkenhayn made an all-out effort to force Britain and France to negotiate a settlement while Germany still had the diplomatic advantage of occupying so much of France. With monstrous calculation, he reckoned that a gigantic onslaught on the French fortresses at Verdun would result in the French bleeding themselves white to defend this symbol of French national integrity. It must be remembered that Britain did not institute conscription until January 1916, and that France had consequently been left to bear the brunt of the fighting with all the strain that this entailed. The German attack launched on 21 February had the desired result of goading France into bringing up hundreds of thousands of reinforcements. By the time that the Germans had to reduce pressure (11 July), the French had suffered 315,000 casualties, but the Germans themselves lost 280,000, leaving them with a net gain of only 35,000 – plus five miles of shell-torn ground. Not surprisingly the failure of the Verdun offensive resulted in Falkenhayn being replaced by Paul von Hindenburg (who together with Erich Ludendorff had been systematically scheming against Falkenhayn).

Even these meagre gains were to be partly eroded by the end of the year. The French launched two counter-attacks (24 October and 15 December), in which they expended some 47,000 men to eliminate 55,000 Germans and regain most of the five miles which the Germans had bought so dearly.

The grotesque enormity of this kind of warfare was perhaps best exemplified on the Somme. In order to relieve the pressure on the French forces at Verdun, a Franco-British attack had been launched along the Somme valley on 1 July 1916. The British had 57,000 casualties on the first day and by the time it was over (18 November) they had suffered 420,000 and the French 195,000. The Allies could at least boast that the Germans had lost 650,000 (and about six miles of land); and what was more to the point they had forced the Germans to admit that a policy of 'attrition' was likely to exhaust Germany first. German policy thereafter on the western front was to sit tight, unless a suitable occasion for a breakthrough presented itself. But this Allied victory of nerves had its corresponding price – with terrible implications for the future. The Allies were now readier to exert massive pressure, despite the appalling loss of life; so the slaughter on the Somme merely paved the way for more.

Significantly the rising hopes of the high command found little response in the trenches; and the growing bitterness of the serving soldier is clearly mirrored in a poem like Siegfried Sassoon's *They*.

The Bishop tells us: 'When the boys come back
They will not be the same; for they'll have fought
In a just cause: they lead the last attack
On Anti-Christ; their comrades' blood has bought
New right to breed an honourable race,
They have challenged Death and dared him face to face.'

'We're none of us the same!' the boys reply.
'For George lost both his legs; and Bill's stone blind;
Poor Jim's shot through the lungs and like to die;
And Bert's gone syphilitic; you'll not find
A chap who's served that hasn't found *some* change!'
And the Bishop said: 'The ways of God are strange!'

Indeed the incompetent handling of French offensives in April and May 1917 led to mutinies in the French army, in which 23,000 men were convicted by courts martial (though only 55 were actually shot). The Germans, had they known of the situation, could possibly have made a decisive breakthrough at that point. But it was then that the British attempted to give the French time to reorganise themselves by launching an offensive on the northern sector of the front (7 June–6 November).

This Passchendaele offensive cost each side about 240,000 casualties, many of whom were drowned in rain-filled shell craters. The only hope for the future was given by a British demonstration near Cambrai of what massed tanks could do (20 November) – though a canal prevented this particular attack achieving its objective. Nevertheless it was these monstrous tortoises on wheels that were to break the deadlock in the west.

In the meantime, however, the withdrawal of Russia from the war enabled Germany to transfer large numbers of troops to the western front, so that by the spring campaign of 1918, she had a 10 per cent advantage. The Germans moreover had also introduced the rolling barrage technique, which had been used effectively on the eastern front and in Italy. The customary method had been to pound the enemy lines for days with a preliminary barrage, the disadvantage being that advancing troops had to pick their way through a lunar landscape of mounds and craters. The rolling barrage, however, consisted of a bombardment that advanced with the infantry, the shells falling just a kilometre in front of them. With the help of this, the Germans in March advanced forty miles in under a week – though their most spectacular offensive was to come in May and early June, when they made a desperate clutch at Paris.

In the words of John Terraine:

> The German bombardment opened at 1 a.m. on May 27th; it was 'of a violence and accuracy that in the opinion of the most seasoned soldiers far outdid any other barrage they were under.' The forward positions were obliterated by howitzers and mortars; the defending artillery was overwhelmed by fire searching back into the rearmost areas. Then, at 3:40 a.m., 17 German divisions moved forward to storm the Chemin des Dames Ridge. In a matter of minutes the astounding message was received at one British brigade headquarters: 'Can see enemy balloons rising from our front line.' The breakthrough was complete; the Aisne bridges behind the front had not been destroyed, so that by

evening the Germans had crossed the river, swept over the next ridge, and reached the river Vesle. 'This was roughly an advance of ten miles. No such day's work had been done in France since trench warfare began.' By June 3rd the Germans were once again on the Marne, near Chateau-Thierry, only 56 miles from Paris. The most equivocal victory of the War had been won.[1]

The Germans were, however, already outrunning their supply lines, while the heavy casualties of the spring campaign were not being replaced sufficiently quickly. This was the time, moreover, when American troops began to arrive in large numbers.

America's entry was neither that of Fortinbras nor the crocodile in *Peter Pan*. It was the predictable outcome of previous events, but had nothing inevitable about it. America had become involved in the war largely as a result of U.S. ships lost to German submarines. Tension had mounted in the spring of 1916 when Germany had intensified her attack on Britain's supply lines, though American rumblings had decided her to adopt a more cautious policy towards merchant shipping after May 1916. In January 1917, however, she announced her resumption of unrestricted submarine warfare, underlining the intention by sinking several American ships in the next few weeks. It was this that decided the American entry in April. American help was at first primarily naval, U.S. destroyers being particularly useful at a time when the British economy was hard-pressed by the submarine blockade. Furthermore Britain's large surface ships were unsuited to hunting submarines, their main function being to ensure that the German surface fleet remained in hiding (as it had done since the indecisive battle of Jutland in May 1916).

The summer of 1918 brought the decisive American contribution to the war on land. By the end of June the steady arrival of American troops had tipped the balance of manpower on the western front in favour of the Allies. A last German offensive started on 15 July; but General Ferdinand Foch (who had been given overall command of the Allied forces since April) had advance knowledge of it through German deserters and aerial

[1] *The Great War 1914–1918* (Hutchinson, 1965) pp. 340–2.

observation. The French counter-offensive which checked it became the start of a massive Allied drive to clear France of the enemy. The Germans had few resources to fall back on, and with the relative strength of the Allies growing daily they had no option but to make a fighting retreat. Foch for his part was anxious to inflict as heavy losses as he could on the Germans before they left France, and therefore attempted to cut off their retreat by taking the important rail junctions of Aulnoye and Mézières. But the bulk of the German forces escaped before the French pincer attack was completed, obliging Foch to be content with an armistice signed by an enemy (11 November) who was still strong and still on French soil.

The fact that the Germans were ready to sign an armistice at all reflected not only the changed balance of forces in the west, but also conditions at home (see pp. 320–1) and the collapse of their allies in the east. General Franchet d'Esperey's swift penetration of the Balkans and Sir Edmund Allenby's Palestine campaign eliminated Bulgaria (29 September) and Turkey (30 October); while the news of Foch's final offensive encouraged the Italians to strike north-east at Vittorio Veneto (24 October). By the time an armistice was made with the Austrians, the Italians had taken half a million prisoners, a success which helped Italy to forget her traumatic defeat at Caporetto in the October of 1917.

THE PEACE SETTLEMENT

The conference

It was tempting to be bitter about the peace settlement, especially for those countries which profited least from it.

JANUARY 18, 1919, in the midst of serried uniforms cocked hats and gold braid, decorations, epaulettes, orders of merit and knighthood, the high contracting parties, the allied and associated powers met in the Salon de l'Horloge at the Quai d'Orsay to dictate the peace.

but the grand assembly of the peace conference was too public a place to make peace in
so the High Contracting Parties

formed the Council of Ten, went into the Gobelin Room and
surrounded by Reubens' History of Marie de Medice
   began to dictate the peace.
But the Council of Ten was too public a place to make
peace in.
   so they formed the Council of Four.
Orlando went home in a huff
and then there were three:
Clemenceau,
Lloyd George,
Woodrow Wilson.
Three old men shuffling the pack,
dealing out the cards;
the Rhineland, Dantzig, the Polish corridor, the Ruhr,
self-determination of small nations, the Saar, League of
Nations, mandates, the Mespot, Freedom of the Seas,
Transjordania, Shantung, Fiume and the Island of Yap:
machinegun fire and arson
starvation, lice, cholera, typhus
oil was trumps.

JOHN DOS PASSOS, *1919*

The defeated nations were not represented in the discussions;
their role was merely to receive the Conference's decisions.
Russia, in the throes of civil war, was likewise unrepresented.

The type of person who enjoys reading about peace con-
ferences is often the type of person who enjoys courtroom
dramas or playing bridge. The same interest (or lack of
interest, depending on taste) arises out of seeing what each
member of a small group of strong or influential personalities
can do with the powers put at his disposal. But what drama there
was at the Paris peace conference largely stemmed from the
failure of the European leaders to realise what a weak hand
President Wilson was holding. American military strength had
brought peace, and American loans were counted on to help
Europe survive the peace; so it was natural that Europe should
listen to American wishes with respect. But what the European
leaders failed to weigh was how far Wilson represented American
wishes. Even before the conference, the mid-term elections of
1918 had destroyed Wilson's majority in Congress; and
retrospectively, the European leaders appear as men who were

paying unusual deference to a private individual's opinions. Essentially it was the cards that Wilson was thought to be holding, rather than Wilson himself, that made him such an influence on the outcome of the conference.

Even when full allowance has been made for the force of personalities, it is fairly clear that the will of the various victors prevailed in direct proportion to their national strength. It was America's strength that persuaded Clemenceau and Lloyd George to accept from Wilson such seeming eccentricities as the League of Nations. Neither of them had much faith in what seemed a naïvely utopian venture: a venture, moreover, which had the potential danger of obscuring the necessity for tangible safeguards of national security. At the same time, American strength persuaded the Allies to respect Wilson's refusal to be bound by the European Allies' secret treaties of the early war period, before America's entry into the war. Wilson had progressively adopted the stance of a Wagnerian hero, whose physical strength was yet further augmented by his purity of purpose; he clearly saw his role in Europe as a cleansing wind passing through the cobwebbed corridors of European power politics, leaving the way clear for the spread of democratic ideals. Unfortunately Lohengrin's swan called for him much sooner than he expected – in the shape of a Senate disavowal (March 1920) – and he was obliged to depart with his work not only incomplete, but potentially dangerous, through not having the assurance of America's active participation.

The terms

Some of the Central Powers' losses were already foreshadowed in the armistice terms at the end of the war, and as such were only to be expected in the final peace settlement. Germany had bought a cessation of fighting by agreeing, among much else, to evacuate not only Alsace-Lorraine, the left bank of the Rhine and East Africa, but also territory that lay on the right bank of the Rhine within thirty kilometres of the main crossing points. The Austrians had similarly agreed to evacuate the South Tyrol, the Dalmatian coast, and the territory claimed by the Yugoslavs; while the Turks had undertaken to open the Straits, and surrender their garrisons in the whole of the Empire outside Turkey itself.

Clearly the nature of this armistice put the Allies in a strong position to dictate harsh terms in the final peace settlement. Indeed the Germans for their part had already attempted to off-set this possibility by declaring (4 October) their readiness to consider peace along the lines of President Wilson's Fourteen Points of 8 January 1918. They were determined to make the most of America's suspicion of Allied war aims, which had been symbolised during the war by her insistence on being only an Associated Power.

The Fourteen Points stipulated either complete independence or absolute opportunity for 'autonomous development' for separate nationalities. Wilson had likewise advocated that frontiers correspond to the distribution of nationalities – though this had been potentially qualified by the insistence that Poland and Serbia have access to the sea. Moreover, 'a general association of nations must be formed under specific covenants for the purpose of affording mutual guarantees of political independence and territorial integrity to great and small states alike'. Henceforth 'adequate guarantees' should be 'given and taken that national armaments will be reduced to the lowest point consistent with domestic safety'; 'diplomacy shall proceed always frankly and in the public view'; there should be 'absolute freedom of navigation upon the seas outside territorial waters alike in peace and war', and there should be 'the removal, so far as possible, of all economic barriers'. It was understandable that Clemenceau, Orlando and Lloyd George in their worldly wisdom should smirk at the apparent naïvety of some of these stipulations; Wilson himself came to recognise the impossibility of achieving some of them. America's strength, however, meant that they could not be ignored; and it was in fact an American draft which formed the basis of the covenant of the new League of Nations. This covenant moreover was incorporated in each of the peace treaties, thereby saddling Europe with this strange new contrivance.

The Treaty of Versailles of June 1919 gave back Alsace-Lorraine to France: thereby putting 1·9 million people under

French rule, and depriving Germany of three-quarters of her iron deposits. Furthermore the Saar was put under the administration of the League of Nations for fifteen years, after which a plebiscite would decide whether its three-quarters of a million inhabitants should become German or French. In the meantime France was to enjoy the produce of its coal mines, which had provided Germany with 8 per cent of her coal. Should the eventual plebiscite go in favour of Germany, France was to receive extensive compensation for the loss of this coal, which itself was regarded as compensation for the wartime destruction of French mines. The Allies were meanwhile to continue to occupy the German territories west of the Rhine and also the bridgeheads of Cologne, Koblenz, Mainz and Kehl (the entirety to be vacated in three five-year stages – or sooner, if Germany paid her reparations promptly). Germany moreover was to keep the east bank of the Rhine clear of military installations to a depth of fifty kilometres. Wilson and Lloyd George had had reservations concerning Allied occupation, but they realised that Clemenceau had resisted great pressure at home for the setting up of a Rhineland buffer state, and therefore felt that these more moderate French claims should be granted. Finally, as far as the west was concerned, the 65,000 people of Malmédy and Eupen became Belgians; while, as a result of a plebiscite, the northernmost 166,000 inhabitants of Schleswig became Danes.

For centuries, the common people of central and eastern Europe had regarded the successive wars and peace settlements as a grotesque game of musical hats. As an outcome of the Versailles treaty and subsequent plebiscites, nearly four million German subjects became Poles when Posen, West Prussia, the rest of 'the Polish corridor' and part of Upper Silesia changed hands. In fact, the 330,000 people of Danzig (90 per cent of whom were of German stock) would have become Poles as well, had not Lloyd George advocated that they be given the status of a Free City, thereby throwing a new hat into the game. The real influx of bright new hats, however, came farther south with the break-up of the Habsburg Empire (see pp. 255–7). As far as Germany was concerned, 48,000 Upper Silesians became Czechs, while the 141,000 people of Memel

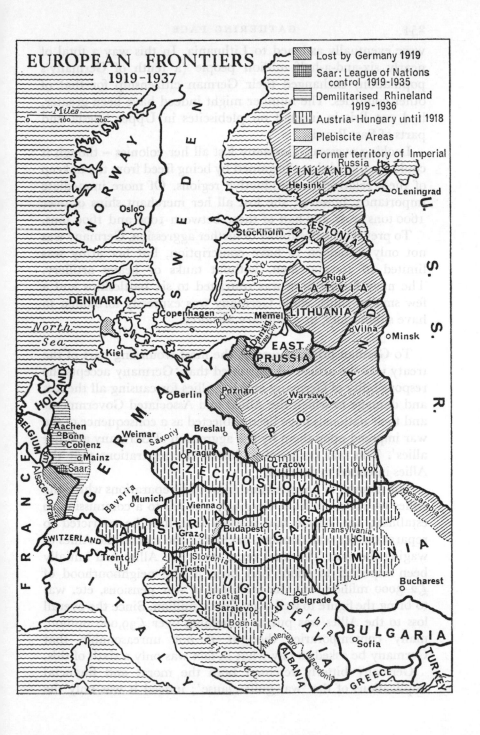

EUROPEAN FRONTIERS
1919-1937

Miles
0   100   200

Lost by Germany 1919

Saar: League of Nations
control 1919-1935

Demilitarised Rhineland
1919-1936

Austria-Hungary until 1918

Plebiscite Areas

Former territory of Imperial
Russia

NORWAY

SWEDEN

FINLAND

Helsinki

Oslo

Leningrad

Stockholm

ESTONIA

DENMARK

North
Sea

Baltic Sea

Copenhagen

Kiel

LATVIA

Riga

Memel LITHUANIA

Danzig
Free City

Vilna

Minsk

EAST
PRUSSIA

HOLLAND

BELGIUM

Aachen
Bonn
Coblenz
Mainz
Saar

Alsace-Lorraine

GERMANY

Berlin

Poznan

Warsaw

POLAND

U. S. S. R.

Lvov

FRANCE

Weimar

Saxony

Breslau

Prague

Cracow

SWITZERLAND

Bavaria

Munich

CZECHOSLOVAKIA

AUSTRIA

Vienna

Graz

Budapest

HUNGARY

Transylvania

Cluj

Bessarabia

ROMANIA

Trento

ITALY

Slovenia

Trieste

Croatia

Sarajevo

Bosnia

YUGOSLAVIA

Serbia

Montenegro

Macedonia

ALBANIA

Belgrade

Bucharest

BULGARIA

Sofia

GREECE

TURKEY

Adriatic Sea

were eventually assigned to Lithuania. In this way a total of nearly six-and-a-half million people (a tenth of Germany's population) exchanged their German citizenship for that of other countries. The number might indeed have been greater, had not Britain insisted on plebiscites in Upper Silesia and parts of East Prussia.

Looking overseas, Germany lost all her colonies – though it could be argued that she gained by being freed from the upkeep of these relatively unproductive regions. Of more immediate importance, however, she lost all her merchant ships of over 1600 tons gross, and half of those between 1000 and 1600 tons.

To prevent the possibility of further aggression, Germany was not only forbidden to have conscription, but her army was limited to 100,000 men, without tanks or heavy artillery. The navy furthermore was restricted to six battleships and a few smaller ships, while Germany was expressly forbidden to have submarines, or a military air force.

To German pride, however, the most wounding part of the treaty was the article which stated that 'Germany accepts the responsibility of Germany and her allies for causing all the loss and damage to which the Allied and Associated Governments and their nationals have been subjected as a consequence of the war imposed upon them by the aggression of Germany and her allies'. This was designed to justify the reparations that the Allies intended to demand.

The amount of financial and industrial reparations which the Allies would claim from Germany was left to a commission to establish; but Wilson had insisted that they be restricted to reparations for war damage, excluding the cost to the Allies of waging the war. The total reparations the Allies had initially been expected to claim had been in the neighbourhood of £2–3000 million, but the inclusion of war pensions, etc. was to bring the figure to well over £6000 million. Since the overall loss to the Allies was put at something over £39,000 million, many contemporaries thought it not unreasonable that Germany be asked to pay what in fact was only a sixth of this.

Germany bitterly resented both the moral and financial implications of the 'war-guilt clause'; indeed it was only the

threat of an Allied invasion of Germany that permitted the
signature of the treaty. The German Chancellor, Philipp
Scheidemann, resigned rather than sign it – 'the hand that
signs such a treaty must wither'. At the same time the treaty
condemned the exiled Kaiser 'for a supreme offence against
international morality', and stipulated that German war
criminals be handed over for trial by Allied military tribunals.
The Netherlands government, however, refused to hand over
Wilhelm, while the Germans for their part managed to evade
the war-criminal issue.

Significantly, the Treaty of Versailles had also enforced a
German renunciation of union with Austria, despite the fact
that the Austrian Republic that had come into being on the
Emperor Charles's abdication (November 1918) had declared
itself 'a component part of the German Republic'. The peace
treaty of Saint-Germain-en-Laye with Austria (September
1919) similarly prohibited this union, thereby clearly demonstrating that fear of Germany was stronger than the principle of
ethnic self-determination in the peacemakers' minds.

Otherwise the Treaty of Saint-Germain was a remarkable
expression of this principle, since it gave independence to
Czechoslovakia, Yugoslavia, Poland and Hungary. It is often
forgotten, however, that the break-up of the Habsburg Empire
had only become in effect an Allied war-aim after it had become
clear that a separate peace with Vienna was not possible. The
Fourteen Points had initially recommended no more than 'the
freest opportunity for autonomous development' for 'the peoples
of Austria-Hungary'; indeed the British Foreign Minister, Arthur
Balfour, had seen the maintenance of the Empire as a guarantee
against the fusion of Germany and Austria. Yet it was clear that
the Allied wartime promises of territory made to Romania,
Serbia and Italy meant that the Empire would be considerably
shorn at the peace.

The real threat to the existence of the Empire had come
when the Allies discussed national independence with Czech
emigré leaders during 1917–18, though it was largely an accidental
result of a war-aims wrangle between Italy and the other Allies.
More specifically the subsequent work of the Czechoslovak

Legion in Russia encouraged France and Britain to recognise Thomas Masaryk's National Council 'as trustee of the future Czechoslovak government' (summer of 1918), Wilson following suit in September. The Serbian premier, Nicholas Pašič, had meanwhile conferred with the Croat leader, Ante Trumbič, and agreed on a kingdom of the Serbs, Croats and Slovenes under the Serbian dynasty (July 1917). Italy in fact had taken this enterprise under her wing in April 1918; and by the last weeks of the war they were receiving active if unofficial encouragement from the Allies as a whole. So it was very much within the logic of events that when a Czechoslovak Republic was proclaimed in Prague on 28 October, a Yugoslav state should be declared in Zagreb on the following day.

Galicia followed a similar pattern. The Habsburg government had already potentially weakened its hold on Galicia when it had joined with Germany in recognising the independence of Poland in an attempt to encourage the Poles to support the Austro-German war effort against Russia (November 1916). The question of boundaries had been left vague; yet it came as no surprise when the Galician Poles declared their union with Poland (October 1918) while wanting to keep control over the Ruthenians. Similarly the Hungarians, while obtaining their independence from Austria (November 1918), were anxious to keep their grip on the Slovaks and Romanians. Ironically enough, however, Allied promises to Czechoslovakia and Romania were to deprive Hungary of precisely the sort of domination that Allied fear of Bolshevism was to give all too readily to Poland (see p. 304).

The Habsburg Empire had disintegrated, as the Austrian Germans themselves recognised when the German members of the Reichsrat proclaimed the state of 'German-Austria' on 30 October. In effect the Treaty of Saint-Germain merely consecrated what had already happened. Even in respect of Italy, it was partly influenced by the armistice terms, for Italy obtained the South Tyrol and also Trieste. Wilson, however, refused to honour the early wartime secret treaties by which the Allies had promised Italy territory in the Balkans and Africa, and it was this 'betrayal' which occasioned so much indignation in Italy.

The corresponding Treaty of the Trianon with Hungary was not signed until June 1920 on account of disturbed conditions in Hungary (see p. 450). Its most remarkable feature was the cession of large tracts of territory to Romania, Czechoslovakia, Yugoslavia and Austria (compare maps 1 and 5). In the meantime, however, the Treaty of Neuilly had been made with Bulgaria (November 1919) which notably deprived her of Thrace, which was given to Greece. And as in the case of Germany, these treaties imposed reparations, limitations on the size of armed forces, and the punishment of war criminals (though the former Austrian Emperor was not personally named).

The territorial settlement by no means settled the ethnic problem, which in view of the scattered nature of some minorities was insoluble by frontier adjustment. A sixth of the Yugoslavs were neither Serb, Slovene nor Croat. A quarter of the Czech population were Germans, and a twentieth Magyars, while in Poland more than an eighth of the population were Ukrainian and 4 per cent Germans. Moreover Romania in doubling her population found that a quarter of her subjects were now of different nationalities, and the overall situation would have been still worse if the Allies had honoured their wartime pledge to Italy. As it was she now had half a million Slovenes and Croats, to say nothing of nearly a quarter of a million German-speaking Austrians.

The danger of this 'Balkanisation' of Central Europe was that these separate states were not only vulnerable to aggression by larger powers, but some of them were economically barely capable of standing on their own feet. Schemes such as that for a 'customs union from Danzig to Sicily' (August 1919) were discussed at the peace conference; but Britain discouraged them, since she feared the erection of a common tariff wall against her manufactures – while Wilson himself had been forced by Congress to admit that his principle of tariff-abolition was more or less utopian.

There finally remained the peace settlement with Turkey at Sèvres (August 1920). This not only deprived Turkey of Eastern Thrace and all her Asiatic and African dependencies, but it subjected her also to the same demands for reparations,

I

demilitarisation, and punishment of war criminals. The treaty moreover empowered inter-Allied commissions to remain in Turkey to supervise the treaty's fulfilment and the navigation of the Straits, and to reform the judicial system. Smyrna and its hinterland was to be administered by Greece for five years, after which it was free to opt for incorporation in Greece.

The Turkish territories of Syria and the Lebanon were put under French mandate, and Mesopotamia (Iraq) under British. The oil-wells of Mesopotamia were certainly a major factor behind Britain's wish to exercise control there, just as the activities of the Anglo-Persian Oil Company (1909) further increased her involvement with Persia. But British concern for these regions dated from Napoleonic times, being traditionally connected with problems of Indian defence. It was only after the Second World War that Kuwait and Saudi-Arabia revealed their wealth. Even in 1938, Persia and Iraq produced only 10 million tons and 4 million tons of oil respectively, as compared with America's 165 million tons, Russia's 29 million and Venezuela's 28 million. Kuwait was then no more than an insignificant sheikhdom, protected by Britain since 1899 on account of its fine natural harbour.

Perhaps deservedly, the Treaty of Sèvres was the first of the peace treaties to be forcibly modified – and in less than three years. The initiative in this modification came from the nationalist reform movement in Turkey, which refused to accept the Sultan's signature of the treaty. When Greece unsuccessfully attempted a military intervention, the reformists both deposed the Sultan and obliged the Allies to accept a compromise, by which the demand for reparations and the Smyrna issue were dropped and Turkey recovered Eastern Thrace (Treaty of Lausanne, July 1923). While this modification had much to recommend it, it was an unhappy augury for the future, in that it had clearly been force rather than common sense that had first obliged the Allies to temper their harshness. Indeed other more dangerous men were shortly to apply the Turkish lesson, and show that when it came to obtaining results, the big stick was worth more than twenty arguments from justice.[1]

---

[1] The future of Russia's frontiers was settled outside the Peace Conference – partly by war – and is dealt with in Chapter 10 (see p. 304).

PART TWO
1918 – 1945

PART TWO
1918 – 1945

CHAPTER NINE

Paying the Cost

THE SOCIAL OUTCOME

The total cost to mankind of the First World War has been conservatively estimated at £67,516 million, the rough equivalent of the world's total exports from 1922 to 1938; and most of the loss was European. Largely as a result of the war, Europe in the twenties entered a period of economic stagnation which cost her the equivalent of eight years' economic growth (assuming that the pre-war rate of growth would have continued). The subsequent depression of the 1930s (which indirectly stemmed from the war) saw world trade in 1934 reduced to a third of what it had been in 1929 and little more than a half of what it had been in the immediate pre-war period. If the overall economic losses of those years cannot be precisely calculated, they were clearly several times as great as the more direct costs of the war itself.

While all classes suffered from the economic malaise of the inter-war years, the impact on the urban working classes was somewhat softened by the welfare legislation of the period. Dissatisfaction and upheaval in the defeated countries and their former territories brought to power governments or coalitions of social democrats; while in all countries, there was pressure to provide returning soldiers with more tolerable working conditions in civilian life. In more specific fashion the information service of the newly created International Labour Organisation made the leaders of the working classes aware of what had been achieved in neighbouring countries, thereby making it more embarrassing for governments with poor records of social legislation to resist demands for similar benefits. The

TABLE 19
Unemployment

Country	1926	1928	1930	1932	1934	1936	1938
United Kingdom	1,062,000	980,000	1,467,000	2,272,000	1,801,000	1,497,000	1,423,000
Germany	2,011,000	1,353,000	3,139,000	5,579,000	2,718,000	1,592,000	160 000
France	11,000	15,000	13,000	308,000	345,000	431,000	375,000
Italy	113,000	324,000	425,000	1,006,000	880,000		

(League of Nations, *Statistical Yearbook*.)

growing strength of trade unionism, moreover, and the greater representation of socialists in national politics made it less easy for employers to resist wage demands. All, however, were

TABLE 20
Coverage of public unemployment insurance, 1931

Compulsory Plans

Country	Adopted	Percentage of gainfully employed
Great Britain	1911	63·5
Italy	1919	23·0
Austria	1920	38·0
Poland	1922	9·0
Bulgaria	1925	12·0
Switzerland (9 cantons)	1925–30	
Germany	1918–27	48·7

Voluntary Plans

Country	Adopted	Percentage of gainfully employed
France	1905	1·5 (underestimate)
Norway	1915	3·3
Netherlands	1916	16·0
Finland	1917	5·0
Spain	1919	
Belgium	1920	20·0
Denmark	1921	21·0
Czechoslovakia	1921	28·0
Switzerland	1925–30	

(U.S. Bureau of Labor Statistics, *Monthly Labor Review*.)

prisoners of the economic situation, while the reality of the working-class predicament can be seen from the accompanying tables both in terms of wages and of unemployment. It was above all the unemployed who paid the price of the Depression;

and the demoralising effect of being without work is well suggested by Christopher Isherwood in this description of Berlin in the winter of 1931–2.

And morning after morning, all over the immense, damp, dreary town and the packing-case colonies of huts in the suburb allotments, young men were waking up to another workless empty day to be spent as they could best contrive; selling boot-laces, begging, playing draughts in the hall of the Labour Exchange, hanging about urinals, opening the doors of cars, helping with crates in the markets, gossiping, lounging, stealing, overhearing racing tips, sharing stumps of cigarette-ends, picked up in the gutter, singing folk-songs for groschen in courtyards and between stations in the carriages of the Underground Railway. After the New Year, the snow fell, but did not lie; there was no money to be earned by sweeping it away. The shopkeepers rang all coins on the counter for fear of the forgers.[1]

On the other hand, for a considerable number of those fortunate enough to have work the Depression resulted in higher real wages, because prices were falling more rapidly than their pay. Even for these, however, the period was fraught with uncertainty and anxiety.

Cheap contraception undoubtedly eased poverty and frustration in many working-class families. In some countries, however, notably depopulated France, specific legislation attempted to discourage contraception altogether; but the findings of Ogino and Knaus on the 'safe period' in 1930–1 provided a form of birth control which was acceptable to Catholics and to others who found contraception morally or aesthetically objectionable.

At the same time working-class children benefited from the general improvement in primary education, which even the most casual observer could see reflected in the fact that the rude words chalked on walls were now nearer to the ground. The financial barriers surrounding secondary education were lowered for an increasing number of children; and education at all levels was progressively accompanied by a growing range of ancillary welfare services, including cheap school-meals, systematic medical care, and more enlightened physical training.

Preventive medicine made similar progress in the adult

---

[1] *Mr Norris changes trains* (Penguin, 1961) p. 90.

TABLE 21

Real weekly earnings in seven European countries and the United States 1924–36
(index numbers: 1913 = 100)

	1924	1928	1932	1936
U.K.	111	117	129	134
Germany	70	108	94	106
France	100	99	109	133
Switzerland	116	123	142	140
Sweden	148	161	183	178
Denmark	118	129	151	135
Czechoslovakia	115	114	131	124
U.S.A.	131	138	122	144

(Largely based on Svennilson, *Growth and Stagnation*.)
N.B. Unlike Table 22, this is *not* a comparative table internationally, since the pre-war base-line of 100 is different in each country.

TABLE 22

Purchasing power of hourly wages in terms of food, U.S.S.R. and selected other countries, 1928, 1936–8, 1950
(U.S.S.R. = 100)

Country	1928	1936–8	1950
U.S.S.R.	100	100	100
Austria	90	158	200
Czechoslovakia	94	142	329
Hungary	—	121	193
Italy	92	108	171
France	112	283	221
Germany	142	213	271
Netherlands	170	188	271
Sweden	176	250	450
Finland	—	204	279
Norway	—	283	600
Denmark	216	304	521
Switzerland	—	204	329
Great Britain	200	192	443
United States	370	417	714

(Janet G. Chapman, *Real Wages in Soviet Russia* [Harvard U.P., 1963].)
N.B. Since these wage-values are calculated in terms of food only, they differ from those (in later chapters) that are based on the general cost of living.

world, and was accompanied by significant advances in curative medicine. Many of these were to find much fuller application after the Second World War, when the financial help of government health services and the technical experience of seven years of slaughter were to bring these sophisticated medical benefits within easy reach of the working classes. Penicillin and 'M and B' were among the products of the inter-war period, while the Second World War was to generalise blood transfusion, skin grafting and other important developments.

TABLE 23
Occupations
(percentage of active population)

	North-western Europe			Eastern & southern Europe		Europe as a whole	
	1920	1930	1940	1920	1930	1920	1930
Agriculture	27	24	22	62	57	40	37
Industry	44	44	44	20	24	35	36
Services	29	32	34	18	19	25	27

Turning to agriculture, many of the peasants in eastern and central Europe were the beneficiaries of land-distribution schemes which indirectly arose from the political repercussions of military defeat. Most eastern countries were 'defeated' countries, in that they were, or had belonged to, countries that had either shared in the Russian defeat of 1917 or the Austro-Hungarian and Turkish defeat of 1918. Taking Europe as a whole, however, the period was one of low agricultural prices and depression (see p. 271). Even in 1939 there were still only 200,000 tractors in Europe – no more than twice the number that Sweden alone was to have by 1950. Some western governments made an effort to help farmers by subsidies and indirect aid, while nearly all countries raised agricultural tariffs; but, as always, help of this sort had to be paid for out of the pockets of the taxpayer, and in dearer food for the townsman.

Those of the upper and middle classes whose wealth lay in savings or fixed securities were hit by the inflation that affected Europe as a result of the overprinting of money during the war, plus the influx of American capital (see p. 274). Similarly

*

all the middle and upper classes were affected in varying degrees by the increase in taxes on wealth which came with the leftward swing of politics in many countries in the immediate post-war period. Their profits moreover were being eroded by higher wages and the increasing cost of capital equipment and maintenance. The profits themselves, of course, were to be catastrophically reduced by the Depression.

Yet if fewer of the middle class could afford to keep servants, the need for servants was being lessened by the growing number of gadgets that reduced the drudgery of housework and the business of living. Central heating, refrigerators, vacuum-cleaners and mass-produced motor-cars came within the reach of middle-class men of the teacher or shopkeeper income level and upwards, while electric and gas fires and wirelesses were to be found in a large number of working-class houses in western Europe.

The wireless and the gramophone were to transform the lives of large sections of the population, especially those of limited income, or those who were bed-ridden or confined to the house. The wireless brought people in contact with a wide range of subjects which they would never have bothered to read about – and which, in many cases, first impinged on their minds accidentally, as a result of being too idle to switch off the set. Waiting for sports results obliged people to hear news-bulletins which made them at least aware of events that were outside their normal sphere of interests, though it was only with tele-vision that this awareness was later transformed into something approaching interest.

Music was perhaps the greatest beneficiary, in that it was now brought to people who had never been in a concert-hall, and whose knowledge of music had been restricted to parlour-ballads and the brass-band repertoire. Many suddenly found a new dimension added to their lives. This moreover was the period when improved standards of electrical recording made it possible to listen to orchestral music on record with something approaching the illusion of listening to an orchestra. Indeed some of the most satisfying recordings of orchestral and operatic performances date from the early thirties. Toscanini, Beecham and Weingartner were at the height of their powers, and the 78s of those days are perhaps the most precious legacy of the period. There is much that is evocative in the paper record-covers of the time, depicting some eminent performer sitting listening attentively to his walnut or mahogany cabinet-de-luxe gramophone, his hands on his knees and his head turned with a mildly apprehensive smile towards the double-doored loudspeaker.

What was especially important about the gramophone was that it enabled people to become properly acquainted with little-played works. It is often forgotten that before 1914 it was only the best known works that the average musical layman was likely to hear more than two or three times in a lifetime, unless he was an unusually avid and widely-travelled concert-goer. The effect of the gramophone on listener and composer alike has been enormous. Modern composers are no longer obliged to make the greater part of their impact on first hearing. They can proceed on the assumption of several successive hearings, and like the poet and painter can hope for the gradual appreciation of their work. This has inevitably encouraged the existing tendency for music to be less immediately accessible to the innocent ear.

In varying degrees this was true of all the arts. Yet what present-day critics consider the great artistic achievements of the inter-war years were mostly the work of men who had already made some mark in the pre-war period. To some extent this reflected the general truth that most men produce their greatest work in middle age, and that in the case of men of lasting significance their stature is usually hinted at in earlier works. Thus Picasso, Matisse, Stravinsky, Sibelius, Schönberg, Berg, Gide, James Joyce, D. H. Lawrence, Mauriac and Thomas Mann had all produced significant work before the war; and in the case of Proust and Kafka much of the substance of their post-war publications had already been assembled before 1918. But it also reflected the fact that a considerable proportion of the trends and schools of artistic achievement that were most productive in the inter-war years were already delineated, at least in embryo, in the pre-1914 period. Thus man as both victim and beneficiary of the irrational is a broad theme that is already apparent in the pre-war writing of several of the men just listed; though it was essentially with the publication of Kafka's *The Trial* in 1925 that this theme was first popularly recognised as also underlying the relationship of the individual and society. This recognition inevitably increased as governments increased their control over individuals, and as more regimes became totalitarian.

But the irrational was also in the process of being rationalised. The broad implications of the work of Freud and Jung (see pp. 57–8) were being gradually assimilated and often distorted by novelists and the reading public. At the same time surrealist art explored or pretended to explore the subconscious; and for people with a little learning the visible world became full of phallic and uterine symbols. Surrealism found a streamlined showman in Salvador Dali, whose clear-cut craftsmanship enabled his pictures with their essentially sexual preoccupations to find their way on to the walls of some very unexpected places.

It was also the irrational that inspired some of the most remarkable films of the inter-war years. The German cinema of the 1920s brought film-making into the world of serious art; and from Robert Wiener's *The Cabinet of Dr Caligari* (1919) to Joseph von Sternberg's *The Blue Angel* (1930) the most memorable German films were characterised by an obsession with moral or physical 'abnormality' or degeneracy – but the 'abnormality' that supposedly lurks somewhere in everyone. In Russia, however, Sergei Eisenstein's camera-work was revealing the latent dramatic force in everyday faces and natural objects when viewed from unaccustomed angles or in close-up. Yet perhaps the films which future generations will remember with most gratitude are the comedies of René Clair and Jean Renoir, and the fast moving transatlantic slapstick of Charlie Chaplin, Buster Keaton and the Marx Brothers. At the same time the lush Hollywood film-scores of the 1930s were indirectly to develop among many cinema-goers a liking for Tchaikovsky, Dvořák and Liszt, to whom the film-composers owed so much; and it was through this initial and involuntary encounter with orchestral music in the cinema that many were induced to listen to the more popular type of broadcast concert.

Exploiting the irrational or rationalising the irrational was not all that dominated artistic activity in these years. Yet irrationalism was often to appear even in the search for concrete solutions to problems. Various writers, from Gide in the immediate pre-war period to Jean-Paul Sartre in the late thirties, were preoccupied with the problem of living in a world without God and a world without any apparent reason for being. In the nineteenth century the loss of faith of so many writers had not as yet led to an open questioning of the Christian morality that still underlay many of the moral assumptions of society. But in the immediate pre-war period, Gide had brought the issue into the open. Sartre had stated the problem at its most acute in *La Nausée* (1938), but it was not until four years later, in *Being and Nothingness* (1943), that he proposed a solution. This solution in fact was largely based on work of Martin Heidegger and Karl Jaspers written in the 1920s; but until Sartre modified and simplified their existentialism, and made it eminently palatable in his plays of the 1940s, most laymen would have thought the word Heidegger was no more than an Australian form of greeting. In effect existentialism offered whole-hearted commitment to *something*, no matter what, as the solution to the problem of living in uncertainty; and in so far as it was primarily concerned with promoting a feeling of self-fulfilment, and bypassed the insoluble problem of the ultimate 'truth' of the way of life adopted, its critics might have had some grounds for calling it irrationalist. Not surprisingly it was a philosophy that had considerable attraction in a period of upheaval like the forties, when inaction could so easily pass as indifference or cowardice.

The real measure of popular taste, however, was to be found in the paper-back novels and popular songs of the period. Detective stories, westerns and romantic love-stories were the staple fare of people whose desire to read had not yet been tempered by television, for the wireless, unlike television, was rarely on non-stop; and if it was, it was generally to provide a musical background to other activities, including reading. Popular music was dominated by America, though each country was beginning to adopt transatlantic styles to its own idioms. Nevertheless there was at the same time a growing gulf between popular music and the more sophisticated forms of jazz which, like 'serious music', were becoming a cult for *cognoscenti* rather than a part of everyday life. Popular songs, however, were mainly about love, going back home and occasionally current events: 'They wanted a song-bird in heaven, so God took Caruso away' was not untypical.

The fact that most workers now had more leisure helped to transform Europe into a continent of games-watchers. Football increased its hold because of the speed, simple rules and observability of the game, even at a distance; while the spread of holidays with pay enabled large sections of the working classes to have seaside holidays for the first time.

This was also a period when the churches began to take realistic measures to establish contact with the secular world that was growing up outside Christianity. It is true that awareness of the problem had grown during the late nineteenth century (see p. 56), but the inter-war years saw the widespread establishment of lay-people's organisations whose function was to spread Christian attitudes (although not necessarily Christian faith) in the milieux of their working life. Religious observance nevertheless continued to decline. The war had had an ambivalent effect on people's attitude to religion. The slaughter and apparent pointlessness of the struggle had indeed convinced many that the idea of a benevolent deity was absurd, while others were led to see belief in God as the only salvation for a mankind otherwise hopelessly lost. It is true that it was only in January 1939 that Otto Hahn and Fritz Strassmann discovered how to split the atom, and that it was only in August 1945 that the public at large realised the earth-shattering potential of nuclear energy. Nevertheless people were coming to realise that the idea of total war could become a reality; and the distribution of gas-masks in the late thirties brought the fact home even to the most unthinking.

THE ECONOMIC FACTORS

The economic malaise of the twenties and the depression of the thirties have already been briefly outlined (see p. 261); but both require a somewhat closer look.

Although a variety of factors was involved, the malaise of the twenties was at bottom agricultural, and like so many of the troubles of these years, its roots lay in the war. Trench-digging, bombardment, and fear of enemy occupation had driven farmers from the battle areas, while much of the hinterland had been geared to feeding armies. At the same time the traditional exchange of west European manufactures for east European grain had been shattered by the basic fact that central Europe was at war with the perimeter; and communications were broken or extremely hazardous. The overall result was that Europe became much more reliant on imports of foodstuffs and raw materials from overseas. Prices rose, and overseas growers responded to the situation by bringing more land under the plough. It might be thought that peace would bring a return to more familiar conditions; but 1919 was dominated by the necessity of providing food for the semi-starving peoples of central Europe, which meant that overseas growers continued to enjoy a ready market for their goods. So much so that world prices rose still more sharply, until in March 1920 they were three times what they had been at the outbreak of war.

This farmer's paradise, however, was an artificial situation, arising from a short-term emergency, with little prospect of lasting. The shell-torn fields of Europe grew food once more, and for a smaller market. Years of slaughter, famine and disease had reduced the population, and in north-western Europe an increasing knowledge of birth control was limiting the speed of demographic growth. At the same time the spread of new agricultural techniques made for a higher yield per acre.

Freed from the risk of mines and torpedoes, overseas produce poured into Europe in even greater quantity. Once the demands of post-war relief were met, the bottom fell out of the market. From March 1920 world prices began to fall dramatically. By the autumn of 1921 they were already half those of 1920's peak, while 1934 was to find them at only a quarter. Even those farmers who remembered the 1870s and 1880s (see pp. 65–6) had to admit that this was a blow without precedent. Agriculture seemed permanently condemned to be the poor relation of the world economy.

Whatever the effect on farmers, the fall in agricultural prices was also to bring hard times for industry and commerce. Initially the immediate post-war period had seen an industrial boom. Demand and employment had risen, as the former belligerents of Europe laboured to replace the means of production that had been destroyed – £6000 millions' worth, according to some estimates. Inevitably this work of reconstruction had largely to be undertaken on borrowed money, and, predictably enough, the principal lender was the United States, the financial saviour of the war years to whom the world was already indebted to the tune of £3000 million on public and private account.

By 1920, however, a considerable part of this reconstruction work had been completed, except in France and Belgium where destruction had been particularly heavy, and in Germany which, though physically undevastated, was working hard to meet her reparations commitments. There was unfortunately no comparable demand to which Europe's industrial energies could be quickly turned. The traditional market in overseas countries for European manufactures had partly shrunk, since a number of these territories had speeded up the development of their own industries during the war, at a time when much of European industry was geared to war production. The post-war collapse of agricultural prices was likewise to limit their capacity to buy European manufactures. In Europe itself moreover there had also been a tendency for countries to attempt to become more self-sufficient during the war.

Even before March 1920, financiers and financial authorities had observed that the immediate post-war boom had little chance of continuing, especially in view of the uncertain future of agricultural prices. If farm prices dropped, growers could no longer buy manufactures in the same quantity. 1920 was therefore marked by various measures in Europe and America to restrict credit. Prospective purchasers now found it harder to borrow money, while business enterprises had difficulty in obtaining loans to tide them over the sudden slack period. Many workers found themselves on the street; and for every wage-packet that was stopped, the market was deprived of a potential buyer. International prices fell catastrophically from the (admittedly inflated) level of 1919–20. Indeed 1921 already

1 *The Franco-Prussian War*

a. *above:* Making balloons in the Gare d'Orléans during the siege of Paris

b. *left:* Hunger in Paris, December 1870: shooting Castor and Pollux, the young elephants of the Jardin des Plantes (sketch sent by balloon-post to the *London Illustrated News*)

2a *Prussian officers – as the occupied French knew them*

2b *Lunchtime in Budapest, summer 1904: the Franz-Josef Quay*

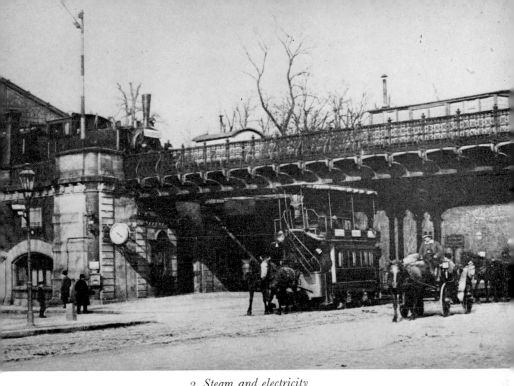

3 *Steam and electricity*

a. *above:* Public transport in Berlin, 1896: a steam suburban train and a horse-drawn tram

b. *below:* An electrical power-station, 1887. Before the use of the steam-turbine, steam-driven dynamos like these were wasteful of space and a potential danger to workers

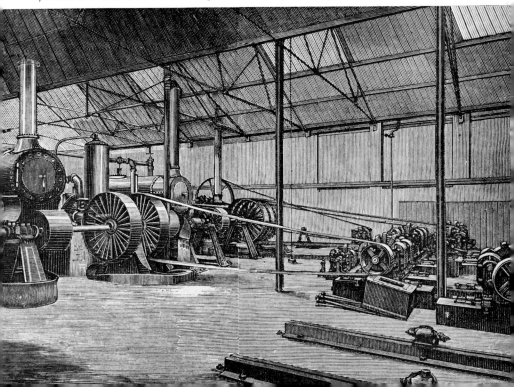

4 *Two sides of Wilhelmine society*

a. b. *above:* Male elegance and female solidity, seen by Rudolf Wilke and Olaf Gulbransson

c. *below:* Home – for the urban masses

5 La Belle Époque *on wheels*

a. Cycle-racing at the Parc des Princes

b. *La Jamais Contente*, 1899 – at 65 m.p.h. the world's fastest car

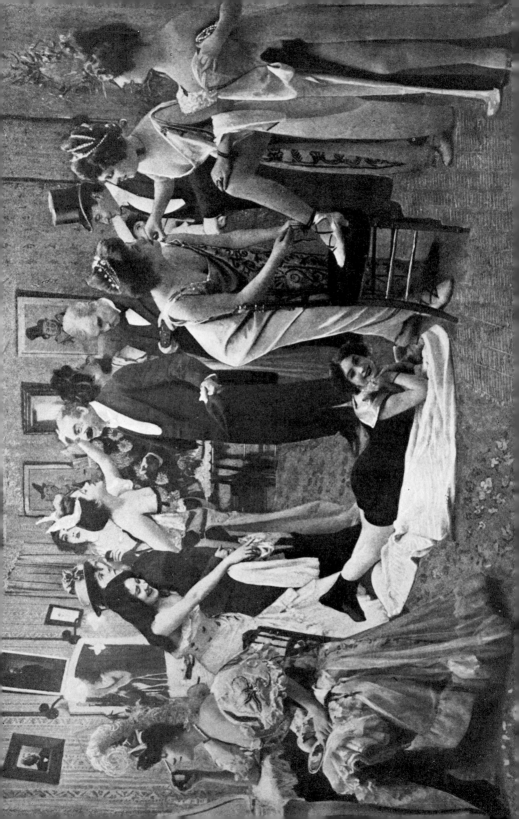

facing page: 6. *Grand Horizontals of* La Belle Époque
Emilienne d'Alençon, horizontal, flanked by Lavallière and Germaine Gallois

above and right: 7a, b. *Art Nouveau – and its influence*

A piano by Louis Majorelle, and the candelabra style in women's dresses.
Majorelle's work made a deep impression at the Paris Exhibition of 1900.

8a. *Daily work at −12° C.: washerwomen on the River Moskva, 1874*

b. *Church and State officiate at a hanging: the execution of the Tsar's assassins, 1881*

9 *Travelling in Russia, 1877*

10 *The far east of Europe*

a. *above:* Merchants in Nijni-Novgorod, 1905

b. *below:* Romanian peasant-dwellings

11 *In training for the naval arms-race? Nephew and uncle take healthful exercise*

a. *above:* Early morning on the *Hohenzollern* (Wilhelm II is marked with an X)

b. *below:* Edward VII when Prince of Wales

13 *A dream come true – the new Chancellor takes power*

12 *Germany 1919–20 – Georg Grosz's vision of a demoralised nation haunted by war cripples and profiteers*

The top right-hand quarter probably depicts the army executing civilians in Munich, following the abortive Communist take-over of 1919. The figure immediately below may belong to one of the *Freikorps* brigades that adopted the swastika.

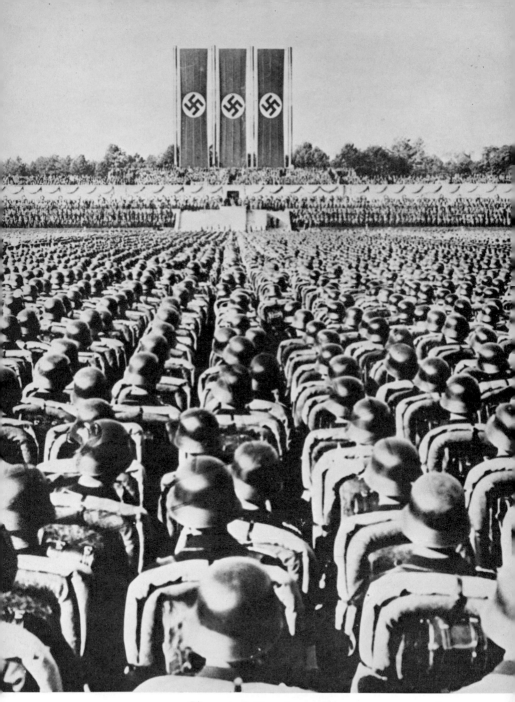

14 *The annual Nuremberg rally*

ama molto i bambini.
I bimbi d'Italia amano
molto il Duce.

VIVA IL DUCE!

Saluto al Duce:

A noi!

15 *Four faces of propaganda*

a. *top left:* Mussolini shown to the children: a page from a primary school textbook

b. *top right:* Saint Joan of the Third Reich: the official art of Hubert Lanzinger

c. *bottom left:* The antisemitic film: Werner Krauss as Rabbi Loew in *Jud Süss*

d. *bottom right:* A poster for *The Eternal Jew* in occupied Holland

Heckenschützen

16 *The home front in Germany*

a. The great enemy, 1941

b. After an air-raid – Mannheim, 1944

found them at less than three-fifths of what they had been in the previous year – though it must be admitted that 1920's peak had been artificially high.

The effect of this overall drop in prices was to encourage many countries to adopt an ultra-defensive attitude in trading matters. Tariffs rose to protect home industry against foreign competition. Perhaps the most striking result of this situation was to destroy the possibility of economic co-operation between the less developed countries of eastern Europe. In more favourable circumstances the successor states of the Habsburg and Romanov Empires might have learnt to overcome their chauvinistic and highly costly desires to be economically self-sufficient. They might have sought instead to complement each other economically. Moreover these states should ideally have been encouraged to confine their development of industry to the newer and lighter industries, where the headway of the western industrialised countries was less marked. East and west might then have complemented each other. The east would thereby have escaped its heavy dependence on low-priced agricultural produce, and been able to industrialise at less cost and with more chance of profit abroad.

The problems of eastern Europe had been further increased by the fact that the American immigration laws of 1921 and 1924 had severely restricted the number of immigrants to be taken from outside north-western Europe. Yet it was precisely in these eastern countries, where modern techniques of birth control were little known among the manual classes, that population was growing fastest and the achievement of a reasonable standard of living so difficult. Furthermore the break-up of big estates by the new governments resulted in a fragmentation of land that made many holdings unsuited to new agricultural methods.

The dramatic fall in world prices at the beginning of the twenties must, of course, be distinguished from the fortunes of individual national currencies, which in many cases underwent rapid inflation. Austria, Hungary, Poland, Germany and Russia all suffered astronomical inflation (see later chapters), while only the currencies of Britain, Holland, Denmark,

Norway, Sweden and Switzerland managed to return to their pre-war parity with the dollar. Much of this inflation stemmed from the continuation of the wartime expedients of living on credit and settling domestic debts by printing more paper money. In addition the promise of reparations from the Central Powers encouraged some of the former Allies to meet current difficulties by drawing in advance on their future expectations with the result that more and more bank-notes were rolled off the printing presses. Although all European currencies were eventually to return to the Gold Standard by 1928, only the six just mentioned succeeded in regaining their pre-war status.

Amid this blizzard of paper money, it was the U.S. dollar that represented solidity. There can be little doubt that even if there had been no war, America's vast resources would have widened still further the gap that separated her from her nearest competitors, Germany and Britain. But the war had vastly accelerated the process. American industry had expanded greatly in the war years for much the same reasons as it had expanded, in microcosm, during the Franco-Prussian War (see p. 75): the military preoccupations of European industry had left American industry an open field. Moreover the American mass-production techniques, pioneered before the war, further helped the United States to make a vast inroad into the world market. It was true that European industry was being modernised, but a sizeable proportion of this modernisation was being carried out with American money. Whatever the future held in store for Europe, it was clear that the fortunes of the dollar would play a major role.

The industrial slump of the infant twenties did not last long in America. The visions conjured up by mass-production techniques encouraged investors to pour money into modernising American industry on the pattern initiated by Henry Ford and other kings of the conveyor-belt. Industrial productivity per worker increased by two-fifths between 1919 and 1929, the emphasis being on 'consumers' durables', such as cars and electrical appliances, rather than on 'non-durables'. There was similarly a vast increase in building, following a housing shortage inherited from the war, while the middle twenties continued to see a mushrooming of factory and office construction. The potential danger of the American expansion was that cars and other durable goods were particularly vulnerable to the risk of over-production. Unlike non-durables such as clothing, these products were still slightly more dependent on new purchasers than they were on existing owners replacing worn-out possessions, important though this market was. In times of recession these were precisely the goods that the population was most prepared to do without. There were moreover various reminders that the market could not expand indefinitely. The steep rise in industrial real wages that had marked the war period and its aftermath in America, flattened out in the twenties (see Table 21), which meant that no great store could be set by an increase in workers' spending. At the same time, the world-wide impoverishment of farmers, following the collapse of agricultural prices, weakened a whole segment of the potential market; and although tariffs and other factors enabled American farm prices to maintain a respectable level in the 1920s, they tended to lag several points behind other prices, especially after the overabundant harvest of 1928.

One way of expanding the market was to increase the manual workers' purchasing power. J. M. Keynes, the English economist, was tirelessly to point this out both in the twenties and during the Depression of the thirties; but many governments were still partly influenced by the traditional view that modest wages enabled business to employ more men and reduce unemployment. Keynes's advice was to seem rather like exhorting society to raise itself by its boot-straps; and his critics were insufficiently appreciative of the sort of argument outlined in earlier pages (see pp. 78–9).

In the meantime, however, the market continued to expand on credit. Between 1925 and 1929 America lent other countries over £600 million, the German 'boom' of the mid-twenties being largely based on American capital and the real if unwelcome stimulus of reparations obligations (see pp. 318–19). In Europe as a whole, moreover, the gradual rise in real wages *did* create a larger domestic market, which in turn encouraged greater industrial productivity. European industrial production (excluding Russia) increased by three-fifths between 1923 and 1929, though it is important to realise that this peak still represented an increase of less than a third on the pre-war level of 1913.

The precarious nature of American expansion in the late twenties became more evident when 1928–9 saw a spate of speculation in which holdings changed hands for prices far in excess of their potential value. Indeed the attractions of home speculation led to a gradual withdrawal of American money from Europe. But given the limitations of the market for durable goods (outlined above), businessmen began to ask how long the industrial boom could last. By March 1929 it was clear that production was outstripping demand, with the result that American producers began to think about cutting back on their output. By July there was already a drop in production, while factories were showing reluctance in taking on new labour. Indeed it looked as though this plateau might well turn out to be a downward slope. This was what many businessmen had been expecting, and the rush to sell became a stampede.

The resultant Wall Street Crash of October 1929 was initially no more than a belated recognition by speculators of the facts of the situation; it followed rather than created the break in the twenties' boom. But this panic among speculators must bear a lot of the responsibility for the steepness of the downward plunge and the excessive caution that was to characterise financiers for the next few years. With credit hard to come by, it was difficult to stimulate demand into life again. Maintaining or raising the workers' purchasing power depended on availability of funds or credit. If a business could not sell its goods, it could raise wages only by borrowing – and this supposed the existence of credit. In fact the very reverse was happening: factories were dismissing their workers in millions; and every worker on the street meant another buyer lost to the market. Governments on the other hand were better placed to provide work and wages, in that they had some power to increase their funds through selective taxation, and they were also in a stronger position to borrow than most private enterprises. F. D. Roosevelt's government (March 1933) was to show some appreciation of this fact in its 'New Deal' policies, when it attempted to provide public works to absorb the unemployed, and also did its best to raise wages. Unfortunately, it likewise tried to stimulate investment by raising prices – which, of course, largely offset the beneficial rise in wages.

The main problem facing the economic historian is to explain why the depression turned out to be a much deeper and more prolonged affair than was initially anticipated. Arthur Lewis expresses the view of many economists when he says:

What was probably the most important factor emerges if one concentrates attention on the year 1930. In the earlier part of that year there was some revival, and the experts announced that the recession was over; conditions on the contrary deteriorated rapidly in the second half of the year. The principal cause seems to have been the surprisingly rapid fall of agricultural and other raw material prices, which checked confidence in recovery, and persuaded business men to 'wait and see' rather than make new investments. Next year confidence was further shattered by the collapse of the international monetary mechanism [see p. 279]. . . . From 1929 to 1930 the average price of wheat fell 19%, cotton 27%, wool 46%, silk 30%, rubber 42%, sugar 20%, coffee 43%, copper 26%, tin 29%. . . . In most of these commodities the collapse was due to over-investment. Wheat and sugar were war-casualties; but others, notably tin, rubber, and coffee had expanded in the 1920s beyond the level justified by demand even at the height of the boom, and the fact that their position was already shaky before 1929 made the collapse of prices all the greater.

The collapse of primary product prices was decisive because its ramifications were so wide. . . . Primary producing countries were placed in difficulty; some were driven off the Gold Standard in 1930, or forced to take other measures to curtail their international payments, measures which started a train of restrictions on international trade, and harmed industrial producers as well.[1]

The bottom of this downward spiral was not to be reached until the summer of 1932. American wholesale prices fell by nearly a third, while industrial production was cut by more than half. By March 1933 America had over fourteen million unemployed.

Given the importance of America in the world economy, it was inevitable that the slump should have profound repercussions in Europe. Between 1929 and 1932 the amount of American money flowing to the rest of the world, in payments and

[1] *Economic Survey 1919–1939* (Allen & Unwin, 1949) pp. 56–7.

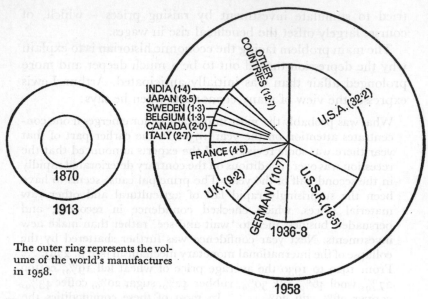

The outer ring represents the volume of the world's manufactures in 1958.

Fig. 8 *The world's manufactures (percentage distribution) 1936–8 (compare with Fig. 1 on p. 64)*

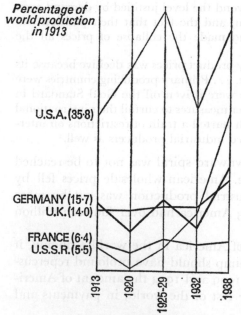

Percentage of world production in 1913

U.S.A. (35·8)

GERMANY (15·7)
U.K. (14·0)

FRANCE (6·4)
U.S.S.R. (5·5)

1913 1920 1925-29 1932 1938

Production in 1938 as a percentage of *national* production in 1958:

U.S.A.	34%
Germany*	51%
U.K.	55%
France	50%
U.S.S.R.	18%

(*1958 total in W. Germany only.)

(The diagram does not attempt to show the fluctuations of production in the intervals between the years specifically indicated. In each of the specified years, production is shown as a percentage of what world production had been in 1913. Note that the last year shown is 1938, not 1936–8 as in Fig. 8. Figures 8 and 9 are based on different statistical series.)

Fig. 9 *The growth of industrial production in selected countries 1913–38 (compare with Fig. 2 on p. 68)*

investment, dropped by more than two-thirds. European financiers followed the lead of their American counterparts and sat heavily on what money they had, the result being a repetition of the American pattern of depression. As borrowing became more difficult and the number of unemployed grew, the market contracted and business found it yet more difficult to sell goods. Industrial production in Europe (excluding Russia) fell by over a quarter between 1929 and 1932, while world trade in manufactures was cut by two-fifths.

The Depression hit the various European countries with differing intensity and timing (see Table 24), as is explained in the later chapters on individual countries.

TABLE 24
Industrial production in 1932 as percentage of 1929 level
(1929 = 100)

U.S.A.	53	Italy	67	Britain	84
Germany	53	Belgium	69	Holland	84
Poland	63	France	72	Sweden	89
Czechoslovakia	64	Hungary	82	Norway	93
		Romania	82	Russia	183

(N.B. These figures are not internationally comparative, production in 1929 being different in each country.)

The situation was made yet more complex by a European financial crisis, beginning with the insolvency of the Creditanstalt bank of Austria (May 1931). Early in 1931 Germany and Austria had publicly broached the matter of a customs union, with the result that France, haunted by the spectre of 'Greater Germany', had retaliated by withdrawing funds from Austria. The Creditanstalt was merely the first victim. Its demise provoked a panic-stricken run on German banks, which in turn resulted in a withdrawal of German deposits from London.

The immediate effect of this was to cause Britain to abandon the Gold Standard (September 1931). By the end of the following year, twelve countries followed suit, bringing to 32 the total to do so since 1929. This today may seem no more than the belated slaughter of a sacred cow; but that the cow was sacred was all too clearly the belief of many financiers. The division of

the world into a 'gold bloc' and what might be called 'outsiders' further restricted the movement of money, financiers
being even more chary about whom they dealt with. It was not
until America abandoned gold (April 1933) and other gold
blocards devalued (1936) that international transactions became
less inhibited. Even so, the release was perhaps one of despair
rather than confidence. In a world where devaluation had
become a legitimate expedient, money no longer seemed safe
in banks and 'guaranteed' securities. Investment in profitable
enterprise seemed the only realistic alternative, apart from the
barren resort of buying gold. It is true that America, France and
Britain, followed by some smaller countries, agreed in 1936 not
to alter exchange rates unilaterally, but financiers had long
since learnt not to place much faith in good intentions.

The later stages of the Depression were notably marked by a
preference for national rather than international solutions.
Tariffs had been rising throughout the depression years, and by
1932 even Britain had substituted imperial preference for her
traditional free-trade policies. Attempts at international co-
operation met with very limited success. In June 1931, when
German banks were under heavy pressure (see p. 279), President Hoover had proposed a year's moratorium on all inter-
governmental debts, in order to rescue Germany, which was,
after all, America's principal debtor. Other countries eagerly
accepted the proposal, since rising American tariffs had made
it even harder for them to pay off their debts to America in
exported goods. When the moratorium elapsed, an international conference met at Lausanne (June 1932), where representatives of Germany, France, Belgium, Britain, Italy and
Japan agreed to cancel what was left of German reparations
(see p. 319) in return for £150 million in 5 per cent bonds.
But America – which was not represented at the conference –
refused to accept the scheme and insisted on its entitlement
under the Young Plan (see p. 319). After Hitler came to power,
however, he not only repudiated German liability, but also put
a complete moratorium on all repayments of foreign loans (June
1934). On the other hand America showed no sign of intending
to cancel the debts of her former allies. Given the size of American loans, it was understandable that America should stand

firm. But the apprehension of her debtors was also understandable, for they now had no hope of receiving the German reparations that they needed to pay off their own debts to America.

In practice, however, America accepted the fact that her debtors would be slow in paying, and ultimately less than a third of the total outstanding amount was actually repaid.

Towards the end of 1932 production and trade began to pick up slowly. As Arthur Lewis has commented:

> It is doubtful whether recovery is to be attributed to any particular national policy. The economic system usually recovers from slumps. During the depression prices fall, marginal firms go bankrupt, investment is curtailed, and confidence recedes. After a while it is felt that prices have fallen too low; depreciation has accumulated, confidence returns, and reinvestment begins. There would have been recovery in Germany or the United States without Hitler or Roosevelt or their spectacular policies; and indeed the indices show that recovery had begun before such policies were initiated.[1]

Progress was slow, however, until the first half of 1937, when a short sharp boom in America drove prices artificially high. Impatience after eight years of playing safe, plus the disillusioning effect of the recent devaluations (see p. 279), may have helped to encourage the boom, though the immediate cause was the sudden payment of heavy bonuses to American war veterans. These stimulated demand and raised prices. Once the demand had been met however prices fell, and 1938 saw a decline in production in many countries.

Ironically enough, it was to be the distant rumblings of another general war that 'came to the rescue' – with an industrial boom in the instruments of death and destruction.

Economic stagnation and the colonies

Colonial activity in the inter-war period was largely one of consolidation, with attempts to give some sort of overall direction to what was a confused and sometimes aimless process. There were very few new acquisitions. Italy's conquest of

[1] *Economic Survey*, p. 69.

Ethiopia in 1935–6 left Liberia as the only independent African
state; while Japan, China, Siam, Afghanistan, Persia and
Saudi-Arabia were the only significant areas that remained
un-'protected' or unmandated in Asia. Indeed Japan was
doing her rapacious best to simplify Asia still further. No
colonial power was thinking as yet of granting colonies independence, the furthest limit of progressive action being the
granting of a measure of self-government.

Nevertheless the example of Japan was not being wasted on
the colonial peoples of Asia. From the time of her victory over
Russia in 1905, Japan was living proof that Europeans could be
beaten with their own weapons and with their own tools.
Although she still accounted for only 3·5 per cent of world
industrial production in 1938, this had no parallel among non-
white countries; while her navy was the third largest in the
world. It is true that it needed her initial victories in the Second
World War to show the full extent of European weakness in
Asia. But in the meantime everyone had noted the reluctance of
the white nations to restrain Japanese expansion in China (see
pp. 384–5). White people were clearly no stronger than their
technology; and they were gradually losing their monopoly
even of this.

The economic stagnation of the inter-war period hit the
colonies hard, since they were nearly all producers of primary
goods. At the same time the fact that some had nascent industries of their own was of little use in a period of industrial over-
production. Given the state of the international economy, it
was perhaps inevitable that Europeans should focus their
attention on the value of their colonies as potential markets
rather than as suppliers of raw materials, important though this
latter function was. Unfortunately a market can only function
in terms of its buying-power, and in the twenties and thirties
the colonies were not able to sell enough to be sufficiently
absorbent markets to help the mother-countries significantly in
their difficulties. It is true that rising tariffs threw colonies and
mother-countries closer together economically, and it must also
be admitted that the mother-countries derived considerable
advantage from controlling their colonies' tariffs in a period
when the nations were glowering at each other over mounting

tariff walls. But the hostile protection-spirit of the thirties was one of desperation. Their possession of colonies was rather like having a private kitchen-garden: it was splendid in times of shortage or hostility, but a confounded nuisance when prices in the shops were cheap. Indeed the labour and upkeep of colonies had much in common with the gardener's double penance: back-breaking work from winter to summer, and indigestion in the autumn when grimly eating mountains of lettuce and cabbage.

THE POLITICAL FACTORS

The Europe that emerged from the First World War was politically much more complicated than the Europe that marched into it. Whereas the European population (excluding Russia) had actually decreased by over three million during the war years, the total number of sovereign states had increased from twenty-seven to thirty-five. Indeed the degree of internal political disturbance that took place can also be gathered from the fact that among the sizeable states the number of monarchies had dropped from sixteen to thirteen (plus two 'regencies'), while the number of republics had increased from three to thirteen.

The immediate post-war period brought universal male suffrage to those countries that did not already have it, and direct forms of election to the countries where universal suffrage had been qualified by complicated procedures. In many countries women received the vote, though this reform was markedly absent in those 'Catholic' countries ruled by liberal anticlerical governments, who feared that women would increase the conservative Catholic vote.

The leftward swing in many countries in the immediate post-war period has already been noted (see pp. 261–2). But in most cases the early promise of social democracy foundered on inflation and the general economic malaise of the time, with the result that right-centre coalitions took over with mandates to achieve financial stability. Although the inter-war years are chiefly remembered for the dictatorships and the growth of

Communism, there is still a tendency to think of the dictatorships as something exceptional, a bright red gash, as it were,
across the normal greyness of democratic Europe. But in fact,
of the twenty-eight sizeably-significant states of Europe, only
twelve managed to pass through the inter-war period without
having several years of undisguised dictatorship. All the other
sixteen underwent significant periods of dictatorship, and half
of them had already succumbed to dictatorship by the end of
the 1920s.

There were, however, dictatorships and dictatorships. There
was a world of difference between the violent racialism of Hitler
on one hand and the rather weary paternalism of Salazar on the
other. And in some of the east European countries like Albania
and Romania, dictatorships could take the form of royal
dictatorships which had many of the features of earlier centuries.
In fact only a minority of the dictatorships fully corresponded
to what is normally envisaged by the word. 'Dictatorship'
usually suggests authoritarian government based on the outward appearance of popular support; and in the most developed
cases it not only endeavoured to create the illusion of popular
support by forcibly suppressing all opposition, but it also
attempted to exercise what, for want of a better word, might be
called some sort of mass hypnosis of the public: a mass hypnosis
which both tried to inculcate a veneration of the nation-state,
and also tried to create a cult of the personality of the dictator
himself. Hitler was the supreme example of this, though there
have been less spectacular examples in Latin America and the
Far East. By Hitlerian standards Mussolini was a fairly easy-
going dictator, but he is of great interest in that he was the first
of the demagogue-dictators to take power in a sizeable country
in western Europe. It was also Mussolini who did so much to
create the brand-image of dictatorship, and whose party gave
the word 'fascist' to Europe's political vocabulary. Franco, by
contrast, scarcely conformed at all to the popular image of
dictatorship. The really 'great' dictators were men of imagination. They were showmen, who not only had propaganda and
publicity experts to project their image, but who themselves
knew better than anyone precisely what image it was that they
wanted to project. Hitler played a very large part in working

out the visual details of the great Nuremberg rallies; and Mussolini had a vivid if somewhat vulgar sense of the dramatic, which was apparent in all that he did, both before and after seizing power. These, moreover, were men with a passionate desire for power; men whose obsession was politics, and who before they came to power had no serious hope of making a significant career for themselves in other walks of life. Franco and Salazar, however, were eminent men in non-political fields, who were only encouraged by circumstance to assume power. For them government was a stern necessity of life, not something to be relished. Neither was a demagogue, and unlike Hitler and Mussolini, they were basically unimaginative men.

Yet Franco and Salazar present a special interest in that they were the only pre-war dictators still in power in the 1960s. Their example suggests certain broad generalisations about dictatorship. Broadly speaking dictatorships have good chances for survival, provided that they are reasonably efficient; and provided that they avoid alienating powerful sections of society, notably the owners of the means of production, and the army. Another proviso, of course, is that the dictator himself should be either long-lived or find a successor with similar qualities. Most of the other dictators of the 1930s fell as a direct result of their participation in the Second World War. Had Hitler and Mussolini avoided large-scale war, they might conceivably be ruling in the 1960s – albeit as very aged men. Indeed looking to the nineteenth century, Napoleon and Napoleon III would almost certainly have ruled for much longer, if it had not been for their defeat in war. Franco and Salazar were very careful not to become involved in the Second World War; and that undoubtedly is the major reason why they survived so long.

Turning leftwards, 'the emergence of Communism' can be a misleading phrase when applied to the inter-war years. For what had happened was that a minority of European socialists had exchanged the old umbrella of the Second International for the new umbrella of the Third International based in Moscow (see pp. 438–9). It is, however, important to realise that the Communists outside Russia were numerically very weak – assuming for the moment that the term 'Communist' comprises only those Marxist socialists who accepted the control of Moscow. As might be expected, Communist numbers were highest in industrial areas, reaching their peak during periods of unemployment and economic difficulty. They were most numerous in Germany, where the German Communists had their most spectacular success in the elections of November 1932, when the Depression gave them a fifth of the total vote and well over a sixth of the seats in the Reichstag. But 1933 saw them driven underground by the Nazis; while in any case distinction must be made between party members on one hand, and, on the other hand, those members of the general public who happened to vote Communist at a particular election. Clearly the German Communist party was only a tiny fraction of the six million Germans who decided to vote Communist in the November 1932 elections.

In France the Communists reached their peak in 1936, when as part of the Front Populaire, they polled nearly a seventh of the votes in the May elections, obtaining an eighth of the seats in the Chamber of Deputies. But this was an isolated triumph, which they themselves failed to exploit when they refused to join Blum's government. In Italy, as in Germany, the Communists were driven underground by a fascist government; but in the last free elections to be held (May 1921) they polled little more than half a million votes and received only fifteen seats.

Moving westward, numbers in Spain were more difficult to ascertain. The Spanish police in the 1930s maintained that there were over 100,000, but this was almost certainly a gross exaggeration, though it is conceivable that Communists and their sympathisers might have come somewhere near this number at the height of their influence during the Civil War. In the other western countries, however, the relative strength of the Communists was even smaller, and there was no country in the west where Communists were anything more than a small minority. Although they made many converts, they also suffered many defections. Men like Jacques Doriot in France rejected the Moscow line, and in Doriot's case took their supporters not only out of Communism but led them over to the extreme Right. Violent switches such as this are a recurrent feature in politics; Mussolini is a case in point. And it is always disconcerting for other people who must feel rather like Romans confronted by Queen Boadicea's chariot. (Her chariot-wheels had scythes projecting from the hubs; and legend has it that, like many women drivers, when she seemed to be going to the left she would suddenly switch to the right – with painful results for even the wiliest Roman.)

It is true that the small number of Communists outside Russia did not in itself rule out the possibility of a Communist take-over, in that the Bolsheviks in Russia had themselves been only a very small group. But it did mean that the western Communists would have to be as ruthless in their methods as the Bolsheviks if they were to succeed, and that they would also have to be helped by a large element of luck. Yet it was only a minority of western Communists who were prepared to be as ruthless as the Bolsheviks. Most of them had too many personal ties with the established features of their homeland to indulge happily in the destructive tactics that Moscow often demanded of them. After all, what they were called on to overthrow was much more familiar to them than the transitory regime of Kerensky in Russia, which had had no claims to the loyalty or affection of the Bolsheviks. At the same time the western Communists were always vulnerable to the charge that they were not so much the apostles of international Communism, but rather the tools of Russian foreign policy. This was perhaps their greatest disability, since there was a strong element of truth in the accusation.

There is no doubt that the issue of democracy versus dictatorship was a dominant issue in the inter-war years; indeed many Europeans in the 1930s saw it as the issue that most divided Europe. For many intellectuals the whole significance of the Spanish Civil War was as a microcosm of the great struggle between democracy and dictatorship which they saw as imminent in Europe. Nevertheless the international politics of the 1930s and the Second World War itself were primarily a conflict of national policies, not a matter of democracy versus dictatorship. What caused the Second World War was the fact that Hitler was an aggressor, not the fact that he was a dictator. There was nothing new about dictatorship in the late 1930s,

even though the unpleasant aspects of it had never been so
marked as they were in Nazi Germany. But no government,
however democratic, was prepared to invade another to rescue
an oppressed minority, or even a majority, unless it felt its own
security to be at stake. Although for many intellectuals the
Spanish Civil War symbolised the whole issue of democracy and
dictatorship at a crucial time in public thinking on the issue,
the number of foreigners who either participated in it or sent
financial support was a very small percentage of the thinking
public. It would have needed some direct threat to other countries for there to have been more widespread and tangible
concern among foreigners – such being the self-interest of
nations and the men who compose them.

CHAPTER TEN

The Great Experiment

Soviet Russia

'Very like a whale'
HAMLET III 2

When Lenin was in exile before the First World War he spent part of 1902 and 1903 in London. On Sundays he would occasionally visit Karl Marx's grave in Highgate Cemetery, or more often Speakers' Corner in Hyde Park to amuse himself listening to the revivalists. Most weekdays he spent in the Reading Room of the British Museum, where he became a fairly familiar figure. Some thirty years later the historian, E. J. Passant, happened to ask one of the older doorkeepers at the museum whether he had any recollections of Lenin in his London days. The reply was: 'Oh, yes. Nice quiet gentleman. Used to come here quite often. And then the war came, and he stopped coming, and we haven't heard of him since.'[1]

But such refreshing innocence was not the lot of the better-read sections of the European population, who were very much aware that Lenin was at the centre of momentous events. It was generally recognised that Russian society was trying to transform itself by its own efforts in a way that had no parallel in previous modern history. Only a return to the millennia when primitive societies were changing into civilisations would find similar attempts at breakthrough. It could be argued that the political regimes of other countries were hard put to it to keep up with changing economic and social reality, whereas in Soviet

---

[1] The years 1903–14 were in fact to see very little of Lenin in London. Geneva, Paris and Cracow became his principal footholds. (E. J. Passant related his experience to Dr David Thomson, to whom I am grateful for the anecdote.)

K

Russia there was for the first time in Europe a gigantic attempt to take this economic reality by the scruff of the neck and make it conform to the government's wishes. Yet it should of course be remembered that since the time of Peter the Great, if not earlier, the Russian government has traditionally exercised a much more dominant role in the people's lives than any western government (see p. 160).

THE SOCIAL OUTCOME[1]

The years 1917–41 brought violent changes in the lives of most Russians; so much so that the western mind ceases to be able to register the enormity of such change. Some thirty-three million lost their lives or their personal freedom; and not far short of a hundred million peasants passed from private landownership (in many cases newly won) to the communal ownership of the collective farm, with its severe restrictions on economic liberty. Moreover nearly all property owners of any substance lost the greater part of their possessions. If the new regime brought power to new men, it remained instrumental power, and did not give them extensive possessions. Indeed by the thirties the Soviet state controlled three-quarters of the gross national product (as compared with just a fifth in the United States in the 1950s).

For the rest, the benefits the Revolution brought were far from striking in the inter-war period, since among other factors the Soviet government was working for long-term results, and hardship in the early years was fully expected. Even in 1928 when real wages were at their highest, they were little more than half of those in Britain, while in 1932, when they were at their worst, they probably sank to a quarter of British real wages. It is moreover important to remember that western Europe was then suffering from the Depression which affected Russia only slightly. Even in Russia's foremost steel works, the workers dined mainly on bread, cabbage-soup and 'grits'; while former members of the middle class were known to have their gold fillings removed to provide their teeth with something more appetising to work on. Foreign visitors complained of the

---

[1] The reader with no knowledge whatsoever of the Revolution may at this point prefer to read 'The political and economic features' first (pp. 297–312).

complete absence of lavatory paper and the scarcity of soap, while the only substitute for a missing bath-plug was a raw potato. Yet these privations were trivial compared to the sufferings of the famine-stricken villages of the Ukraine in the early thirties, where anything from a tenth to a quarter of the inhabitants died. It was rumoured in Poltava that there was a thriving black-market in human flesh, which was only brought to an end when the organisers were arrested and shot.

By the late thirties Russian real wages had risen to something over two-fifths of those in Britain, a proportion that was slightly worse than the comparative situation *vis-à-vis* Britain in 1913 under the Tsar. On the other hand, in marked contrast to the west European slump situation, there was full employment by 1930, so that in October of that year the Soviet government felt able to drop unemployment benefit from its social insurance scheme. The premium on manpower, however, brought savage penalties for absentees. One day's unauthorised absence from work entailed instant dismissal and the confiscation of the worker's food-card, which was virtually his permit to live in such times of shortage. It was also significant that Russia's full employment encouraged very little immigration, even by the desperately poor of eastern Europe. Indeed the term 'full employment' becomes grimly humorous when the reader recalls the 20 million lives lost in the civil war of 1918–21 and the famine of 1921, the million *émigrés*, the 5 million members of kulak families deported or dead during the collectivisation of the late twenties, and the 7 or 8 million arrests during the purges of the late thirties. Nevertheless the Soviet European population contrived in its familiar way to increase from about 115 million in 1920[1] to about 138 million in 1939.

It was inevitable that the government's ambitious schemes for economic expansion should result in hard working conditions and a considerable amount of state direction of labour. A seven-hour day and one day off in six were the legal norm; but piece-work payment and compulsory overtime made for a much harder day in practice. Everything was subordinated to increased production, while inadequate health and safety precautions led

[1] The post-war frontier changes are outlined on pp. 253 and 304.

to a high casualty rate in industry. The comrade who lost his hand in moving machinery or his sight in a blast-furnace was a familiar if less numerous counterpart to the war cripple, whose presence in the streets was a constant reminder that the reward of self-sacrifice is as often as not a look of disgust rather than gratitude. However the Labour Code of November 1922 entitled all state-paid workers (and many privately-employed workers) to pensions of 50 to 60 per cent of their normal pay, and to full pay during sickness. The workers themselves paid no insurance contributions; and for them direct taxation was low, rising on the average from 0·5 per cent to 5 per cent in the 1928–40 period. It could of course be argued that the state covered the cost by paying low wages; and indeed it was not until the early thirties that pensions and other benefits were paid at the full legal rate. Certainly in all spheres welfare was sacrificed to the immediate goal of modernising the nation's economy, as was notably reflected in the poor salaries of doctors compared with those of engineers, the result being that by the 1950s three-quarters of Russian doctors were women. Although theoretically the Labour Code of 1922 and subsequent additional regulations entitled most workers to about a fortnight's holiday with pay, this was dependent on whether the factory could spare workers at the time in question – a rule which applied even to sick leave. Moreover the bargaining power of the workers was greatly weakened by the fact that since 1930 the trade unions had had no real separate existence from the state; while conversely Soviet workers were constantly subjected to propaganda and other pressures to encourage them to accept the state's terms concerning wages and working conditions.

There was nevertheless no denying the impressive nature of the results. The government's policy of rapid industrialisation had increased the urban population from less than an eighth of the whole in 1914 to nearly a third in 1941, the proportion of people dependent on agriculture falling from just under four-fifths to three-fifths.

Although state direction thus restricted the individual's freedom in choosing work, the improved educational system gave able men from poor families better chances of obtaining work that was worthy of their talents. In 1917 only 45 per cent of the population were literate; by 1927 the proportion had reached 55 per cent and in the mid-thirties Russia dared to claim complete literacy – though the claim was highly questionable. Nevertheless for the able person, education became the main criterion for advancement, assuming always that he was politically conformist and ready to take personal advantage of the mistakes of others. The 1930s saw the first main influx of technocrats and administrators from working-class backgrounds. Before that, Lenin and his successors had been obliged to keep on many Tsarist functionaries, precisely because there were not enough qualified people to take over their jobs. Yet by the time the Soviet educational system was producing people of the required calibre, the new élite was already trying to consolidate itself and prevent further infiltration from below. Their children were often given favourable educational opportunities; this, of course, affording them a great advantage when they came to seek state employment.

In this way a new class structure came into being that had depressing affinities with the old – though unlike Tsarist times, latent ability still remained an Open Sesame to occupational and social preferment. It is instructive to see how the class divisions of Soviet Russia were reflected in such things as the hierarchy of dining facilities in a major steel-works. There were at least five different classes of dining-room, regular meat dishes being restricted to the top three – for the management, the technicians and the *udnarki* or outstanding workers. Symptomatically one of the most popular of the many tired jokes that went the rounds of Russia was the ironic comment of a worker in a tram-queue seeing members of the management pass by in comfortable cars: 'I'm the boss. Those people are just my clerks.'

Opportunities nevertheless multiplied as bureaucracy grew; and between 1914 and 1941 the white-collared classes grew to four times their former size, in a population that had only grown by a fifth. While income difference between management and workers had greatly lessened since Tsarist times, the disparity at the extremes was still very marked. It is often forgotten that in the late 1930s the difference between the pay of the lowest-paid worker and the top executive was considerably greater than in the United States. And there was likewise a marked disparity between industrial and agricultural wages. The industrial worker had a wage geared directly to his skill and effort; whereas the collective farm-worker was simply entitled to a fixed proportion of the profits of the farm (and was therefore dependent on both the whims of the weather, and the price that the government chose to pay for farm produce).

Social mobility, however, was offset by government insistence on intellectual conformity. The Communist party was the only authorised political party, membership of it being essential for any responsible office seeker. A man's ability would get him nowhere, if he did not also show himself an active apostle of current doctrine, and (what involved more contortion) a zealous disciple of the government's current application of doctrine. An illuminating parallel can be drawn between the wording of Zinoviev's 'confession' of 1933 and that of Galileo three centuries previously. This atmosphere had a marked effect on humanities and social sciences, where since the early thirties creative thinking had been stunted by the continual effort to impose government views on intellectuals and artists. The finest artistic achievements of this period were often contrary in spirit to government wishes, and accordingly condemned; although the worst period of cultural dictatorship was to come with the Zhdanov decrees of 1946. Stravinsky preferred to live abroad and eventually become an American citizen – an event immortalised by the officiating clerk who, according to legend, concluded the formalities with the stock question: 'Now that you're an American citizen, Mr Stravinsky, would you like to change your name?' Of those who stayed behind, Prokofiev and Shostakovich were at their least inventive when conforming to government artistic policy. Those writers and artists who accepted the regime were often bullied into giving their work an optimistic character that was in marked contrast to the (admittedly excessive) fatalism of that of the late Tsarist period. A revealing example of the conformism of cultural life was the omission of Brahms's *Variations on the St Anthony Chorale* from a concert programme, exception being taken to the religious character of the basic theme.

At the same time the office-seeker had also to be personally pleasing to the rulers of the time. In the Great Purge of 1936–8 three-quarters of the old Bolshevik element in the All-Union Party Congress disappeared, as well as all the surviving members of Lenin's Politburo with the obvious exception of Stalin himself and Trotsky (who was in exile until his murder in 1940). Moreover, the majority of high-ranking army officers were arrested, including three out of five marshals and thirteen out of fifteen army-commanders. In theory, too, members of the Communist Party had to profess atheism, even if in practice it was not uncommon for minor party officials to have their children unobtrusively baptised. Although the Russian Orthodox Church was never proscribed, it was nevertheless disestablished in January 1918; and after 1929 religious instruction could not be given to anyone under eighteen, except in the privacy of his own home. The result was a gigantic drop in the practising membership of the Church. Whereas in 1914 Orthodoxy could probably claim over two-thirds of the population for the faith, by 1941 it is unlikely that it could claim even a quarter – and this in a population which still had a peasant traditionalist majority. As one worker's wife put it: 'Before the Revolution everyone told me that I ought to go to church, so I went. Now everyone tells me that I shouldn't go, so I don't.'

Militantly atheist youth organisations like the Young Pioneers were particularly busy at Christmastime trying to eradicate vestiges of the traditional Christian feast, including its pagan antecedents. As was explained by a publication of the Library of the Young Atheist, 'The struggle against the Christmas tree is the struggle against religion and against our class enemies. Behind the back of Uncle Frost hide the priest and the kulak.' Traditions die hard, however, and visually it would be hard to choose between processions carrying ikons and those carrying portraits of Lenin and Stalin.

There was likewise no doubt that Soviet ideology and practice had weakened the family as a social unit. Communism regarded the Russian patriarchal family as part of the structure of bourgeois capitalism; and as such it had to be weakened and subordinated to the larger interests of society. The nationalisation of large sections of the Russian economy inevitably brought

about the break-up of family farms and family businesses; the
head of the family lost his pre-eminence; and with the provision
of state nurseries and other facilities, women were encouraged to
go out to work. In support of this the government supported a
national cult of the strong woman, the industrial or athletic
heroine becoming a familiar symbol of Soviet life; the process
culminating in the man–woman dynamos of the 1960s, who
present athletics medical boards with such difficulties of diag-
nosis. Divorce in the twenties had been easy, the development
of state welfare lessening the individual's reliance on the family.
The rapidity of marriage and divorce formalities had much to
astonish the western observer. At the registry office a young
clerk would ask the happy couple: 'You are to be married?
Please show your documents and pay two roubles.' The registry
office did not concern itself with the grounds for divorce. One
clerk told a western visitor: 'We don't ask for them. Any
married person may come here, apply for a divorce, and get it
after paying two roubles. We then inform the other party to the
marriage by post that he or she is divorced. . . . If there are
children, they are usually left with the mother, while the father
must pay a quarter or a third of his earnings for their support.'
But the government soon discovered that transitory marriages
led to social irresponsibility, the thirties therefore seeing greater
difficulty in obtaining a divorce. In parallel fashion the granting
of family allowances in 1936 likewise implied a certain recognition of the family's responsibility for rearing children.

The momentous changes in Soviet society brought inevitable
tensions between old and young, as was reflected in the announcement columns of provincial newspapers which regularly
published declarations by young people that they had broken
off relations with their parents. Indeed the differing points of
view were well exemplified in a parents' debate at a Moscow
high school, where one father declared: 'We of our generation,
reached our convictions with blood and tears. Now the young
man is given ready-made beliefs in school. . . . They are dry,
crude rationalists. They talk excitedly about the mating of
rabbits, but they cannot dream. They are insolent cynics, new
business men, Soviet Americans. I can perhaps admire some
traits in them, but I cannot love them.' To which a girl indig-

nantly replied: 'You say we don't dream. Here is Pavel Ivanov, who is absorbed in organic chemistry and can quote fifty complicated formulas from memory. He pronounces them with the inspiration of a great poet. He dreams of making protein. ... Our epoch is so full and varied; there is so much to dream about.'[1]

THE POLITICAL AND ECONOMIC FACTORS

The Revolution

The changes in Russia are so staggering, that the historian must continually stand amazed at the apparent simplicity of the chain of events that precipitated them. Compared with the Revolutionary decade in eighteenth-century France, the two decades of the Russian Revolution seem at first sight to present remarkably few problems of explanation. Undoubtedly part of this impression is created by the gigantic roles played by Lenin and Stalin; whereas in the 1790s, before the rule of Robespierre, the neophyte finds it hard to associate the driving forces behind the French Revolution with particular persons or even groups. The concealed complexity of the Russian situation, however, becomes more apparent when the historian starts asking himself unorthodox questions – such as what would have happened if Lenin and Stalin had not lived.

A book of this length has nevertheless to stick to more visible issues, and however reluctant the reader may be to retrace his steps to the years before 1917, this is necessary, for there can be no doubt that the momentous changes described in previous pages were nearly all to some degree the indirect outcome of military defeat in the First World War.

It will be remembered that the Russian army suffered somewhere between 1·7 and 4 million deaths, the wounded and captured numbering at least 4·9 and 2·5 million respectively. Much of the responsibility for such losses undoubtedly lay with the government. Although at least 12 million men were mobilised they were very poorly equipped, the incompetence of the war minister, Vladimir Sukhomlinov, eventually leaving no

[1] W. H. Chamberlin *Russia's Iron Age* (Duckworth, 1935) pp. 242–3.

alternative but his dismissal in 1915. Shortly afterwards the
Tsar took personal command of the army, despite the misgivings of his cabinet. Civil government was virtually left in the
hands of the Tsarina and her confidant, the unsavoury mystic
Gregory Rasputin. Part of Rasputin's religious way of life was
the search for complete contrition through sensual excess and
subsequent sorrow – a method not without its attractions,
especially as there was no shortage of women who were prepared to help him along his chosen spiritual path. The Tsarina
Alexandra regarded Rasputin as a holy man sent by God to
steer Russia to salvation; she also imagined that Rasputin
was the only man who could save her son from haemophilia.
Rasputin fully exploited her illusions with the result that his
own peculiar mixture of seedy piety and open self-seeking gave
the court an atmosphere that scarcely seemed possible in a
major European power. It was hardly surprising that a reforming court faction finally murdered him in December 1916 – a
macabre business in that it took two poisoned cakes, a glass of
Madeira laced with cyanide, a bullet, and many kicks and blows
to release his tenacious grip on life. But any good that might
have come from this Grand Guignol incident was overtaken by
the epoch-making events of 'the February Revolution'.

    In March 1917 (western calendar) the shortage of food and
fuel led to riots in Petrograd. Not only did the military fail to
control the situation, but an increasing number of soldiers
mutinied in support of the rioters. Fearing a national revolution,
Nicholas tried to dissolve the Duma, which violently reacted by
forming a provisional government under Prince George Lvov.
Seeing 'all around nothing but treachery, cowardice and
deceit', the Tsar decided to abdicate, Lvov's government thereupon taking control of the country. This cabinet was mainly
composed of liberal Cadets (see p. 166), socialism having only
one representative, Alexander Kerensky.

    But the most remarkable feature of the next few months was
to be Lenin's rise to power. In April Lenin represented no more
than a minority view within a minority revolutionary group;
yet by November he was in control of government. March had
actually seen him an exile in Geneva, wondering how he was
going to pay his landlady; but the German government,

hoping that his presence would cause Russia further trouble, had for once backed the right horse, and, in Churchill's words, 'transported Lenin . . . like a plague bacillus from Switzerland into Russia'. On arrival in Petrograd (April) Lenin condemned the current Bolshevik policy of tolerant neutrality towards Lvov; but he made few converts. Close friends denounced his policy as 'the delirium of a lunatic' and declared that 'Lenin the Marxist . . . is no more. A new Lenin is born, Lenin the anarchist.' It was essentially a combination of the Provisional Government's mistakes and Lenin's careful planning of the November *coup* which finally brought him to power.

The government made the error of shelving important issues like the promotion of peace and the break-up of large estates until a constituent assembly could be called. It accordingly decided to go on fighting the war until elections could be held and a more representative government could take over, while it likewise proposed to pass on the land question to a new representative government, despite the fact that the peasants were already seizing land. In this way the government lost two golden opportunities of making itself popular.

At this time the two main socialist groups in Russia were Victor Chernov's Social Revolutionaries on the one hand and the Menshevik wing of the Social Democrats on the other. Paradoxically the Bolsheviks now represented only a minority view within the Social Democrats. Yet the mistake of the Social Revolutionaries and Mensheviks was to support Lvov's government. True to their past, the Social Revolutionaries pinned their faith on the peasantry, hoping that Lvov's government could be steered into bringing about the break-up of the big estates and the distribution of land among the peasantry. The Mensheviks on the other hand supported Lvov's government out of loyalty to the 'orthodox' Marxist view that a social revolution could not take place until Russia had shaken off the last vestiges of her pre-capitalist economy and entered the full stage of capitalist bourgeois society. The Mensheviks regarded Lvov's government as the body that would take Russia through the full capitalist stage of her development, believing that it was only after this capitalist transformation that the urban proletariat would be large enough and sufficiently conscious of its needs to rise up and establish its own control over society. At the same time even the bulk of the Bolsheviks adopted a similarly co-operative attitude towards Lvov.

Lenin's genius was to think and act otherwise. As early as 1898 he had questioned the belief that a period of liberal bourgeois rule was necessary before a socialist revolution could take place. By 1905 he had elaborated the view that the industrial workers, helped by the peasantry, should take over power from whatever government was in office; and that they should bulldoze Russia through its liberal capitalist stage themselves, before taking their country right through to her ultimate socialist stage. Lenin hoped that revolution would break out in western Europe, spreading across the continent so that Europe would become one huge proletarian community, in which Russia, alongside the other communities, would become co-heir to the industrial west. This was in fact a partial telescoping of the Marxist pattern, with the leaders of the proletariat and not the liberals as the operators from the start – but only a partial telescoping, since unlike his collaborator, Trotsky, Lenin did not think that the bourgeois and socialist revolutions could be effected simultaneously. The appeal of Lenin's analysis was that it implied action by the Social Democrats right from the start; but the process of converting his fellow Bolsheviks was nevertheless slow.

In July 1917 the premiership of the government passed to the mild socialist, Kerensky – a man to whom history gave a central role in momentous events, and whom historians have since preserved, alive and productive, in the Hoover Institution on War, Revolution and Peace at Stanford University. Perhaps Lenin's corpse, embalmed and on show in the Red Square Mausoleum, registers a half-ironic smile of fellow-feeling from time to time. In September 1917 Kerensky was faced with rumours of an intended *coup* by Lavr Kornilov, commander-in-chief of the army, 'a man with a lion's heart and the brains of a sheep', as a colleague called him. Kerensky thereupon tried to counterbalance this threat from the Right by releasing many Bolsheviks from prison and giving them weapons. This added unexpected strength to Lenin's following, with the result that a few weeks later, on 7 November, Lenin's sympathisers in the armed forces joined him in a dramatic overthrow of the government, known to history as 'the October revolution'.

But victory in Petrograd did not of itself ensure victory elsewhere; and it was here that dividends were reaped from Lenin's previous work among the soviets – revolutionary committees which the Social Democrats and Social Revolutionaries had set up all over Russia. While the urban soviets were mainly dominated by Mensheviks, the rural soviets were largely in the hands of Social Revolutionaries. And it was only Kerensky's release of many Bolsheviks in September that gave the Bolsheviks a majority in a number of key soviets. Lenin was also aided by his own ruthlessness. 'Do you really think we shall be victorious without using the most cruel terror?' he once asked. 'How can one make a revolution without executions?' David Shub describes how Petrograd was purged of opposition:

> At night his men moved from the dark streets into apartment houses. . . . The prisoners were generally hustled to the old police station not far from the Winter Palace. Here, with or without perfunctory interrogation, they were stood up against the courtyard wall and shot. The staccato sounds of death were muffled by the roar of truck motors kept going for the purpose.[1]

The rule of Lenin

Lenin's capture of nation-wide support for his new government came mainly from his immediate handling of the two vital issues of peace and land. On his first day in office he ordered the break-up of the large estates and their distribution among the peasants (8 November), while in December he negotiated an armistice. Unfortunately Kerensky's government had chosen 25 November for the general election to the Constituent Assembly, which meant that these measures came too late to bear immediate fruit. Even the news of Lenin's land-decree of 8 November only reached a minority of the electorate, with the result that the massive peasant vote gave an overall majority to the traditional upholders of peasant interests, the Social Revolutionaries, who were likewise committed to land reform. The Bolsheviks came a very poor second.

[1] *Lenin* (Penguin, 1966) p. 347.

With Napoleonic ruthlessness, however, Lenin dispersed the Assembly on its second day (19 January), for he correctly calculated that the promise of peace and the land settlement would prevent any large-scale popular protest. As Trotsky later remarked: 'The simple, open, brutal breaking-up of the Constituent Assembly dealt formal democracy a finishing stroke from which it has never recovered.' In March, however, Lenin's popularity underwent a severe test with the Peace of Brest-Litovsk (see pp. 241–2), in which the territorial changes demanded by Germany involved a loss of a third of the Russian population, a third of her agricultural land, and nearly four-fifths of her coal-fields. Indeed only the victory of the western allies saved Russia from having to make the whole of this sacrifice (see pp. 253 and 304), though the Russian civil war that had already started was to reopen the possibility once more.

It was disappointing but scarcely surprising that the peace which was bought at such high cost should bring so little respite to the Russian people. From January 1918 to October 1920 Russia was to be torn by civil war, in which the Bolshevik government was challenged by both counter-revolutionaries and Social Revolutionaries. This opposition moreover received support, albeit limited, from the western powers. Lenin and his foreign minister, Trotsky, believed in the necessity of revolution in the west (see p. 300) and the western powers, being well aware of this, were not only predisposed to view Lenin with great hostility, but were ready to intervene in Russia should occasion arise.

From the historian's point of view, the civil war itself was inextricably bound up with Lenin's policies. On economic and social matters, Lenin seemed to be oscillating between two radically different views. There was his own well-known view that the government must push Russia through a capitalist stage of economic growth before she could embark on socialism. And there was Trotsky's opposing view that the two stages could be telescoped. Yet much of what Lenin did between 1918 and March 1921 would seem to show him inclined to Trotsky's view. Management of the factories was put in the hands of workers' committees (November 1917) and although peasant land was not collectivised, farmers were not allowed to hire agricultural

workers or lease land to tenants (February 1918). This meant
that no one could farm more land than he and his family could
cultivate themselves. It could indeed be argued that this was
giving Russia the worst of both worlds – twenty-five million
smallholdings, all too small to be farmed by modern methods,
and yet legally prohibited from amalgamating into larger viable
units. Either collectivisation or peasant 'capitalism' would have
enabled the agricultural economy to find its proper level; but
Lenin's solution ensured that no advantage could emerge, other
than a barren concept of equality. At the same time the banks
were nationalised and the contents of private bank accounts
confiscated (November 1917). This meant that any counter-
revolutionary movement could expect a lot of support among the
upper and middle classes – though it was arguable from Lenin's
point of view that this consideration was outweighed by the
enormous financial advantage to the government. Not only was
heavy industry nationalised (June 1918), but wholesale commerce was quickly brought under state auspices, while even
retail trade came progressively into government hands.

There can be no doubt, however, that the government's
increasing hold over trade was largely the result of shortages
arising from the Civil War that began in January 1918. Fortunately for Lenin the leadership of the opposition was divided
between dissident army leaders and Victor Chernov's Social
Revolutionaries, the rank and file consisting of the economic
victims of government policy, together with discontented
national minorities like the Ukrainians. Predictably enough
Lenin's government managed to keep a firm control over the
central regions of Russia, where the land settlement helped to
preserve peasant loyalty. Conversely opposition was greatest in
the frontier marches, with their ethnic minorities and vulnera-
bility to foreign intervention. In the autumn of 1919 White
armies actually came within thirty miles of Petrograd and a
hundred miles of Moscow. But supplies and troops from western
governments were very limited, and it was not until the Soviet–
Polish war of April–October 1920 that they could be said to
have affected the outcome in any way. The White armies were
constantly handicapped by disputed leadership; while, under
Trotsky's vigilance as minister for war, the Red Army was

steadily better equipped. In spite of this, the Poles in the Soviet–Polish war were able to take advantage of Russia's domestic difficulties to seize part of western Bylorussia and part of the western Ukraine – which they managed to retain at the peace (March 1921).[1]

It was hardly surprising that the war had led Lenin's government to requisition crops; but many peasants preferred to leave their land fallow rather than have their crop requisitioned. No western mind can really register the catastrophic results of the devastation of the civil war and the droughts of 1920–1. The harvest yield was only a third of normal, while the output of mining and industry had now fallen to a fifth of what it had been in 1913. In addition, the toll of human life was probably about twenty million. As Lenin admitted in March 1921, 'the poverty of the working class was never so vast and acute as in the period of its dictatorship'. And it was only in 1928 that Russia reached once more the level of overall production that had been achieved under the Tsar in 1913.

The period had also suffered from the effects of galloping inflation, as the government printed more and more paper money to meet its mounting expenses. By December 1922 the rouble was down to a 1,680,000th of its pre-war value, stabilisation being achieved only in February 1924. The only people to find a certain bitter satisfaction in the situation were the middle classes, whose bank balances had been confiscated by the government. Their former deposits were now worth precious little to anyone.

The immediate post-war period, however, saw a remarkable change in government economic policy, March 1921 witnessing the inauguration of what Lenin later called 'state capitalism'. This New Economic Policy openly allowed the expansion of private retail trade, likewise permitting private industry on a small scale. By 1923 three-quarters of the retail trade and an eighth of the industrial labour force was in private hands. 1925 moreover saw the removal of restrictions on the farmers' freedom to lease land and employ hired labour. The N.E.P. was

[1] In the previous year the Soviet government ratified the independence of Estonia (February), Lithuania (July), Latvia (August) and Finland (October).

clearly something much more than the relaxation of wartime emergency measures; and it was arguably a return by Lenin to his earlier belief in the necessity for a 'capitalist' stage in the Russian economy. On the other hand it can also be argued that this represented a realistic appreciation of what Russia needed after the upheaval of the civil war. Since two problems confronted the government – shortage and discontent – Lenin undoubtedly realised that the state could not undertake on its own the whole revitalisation of the national economy. And Lenin also knew that hungry and war-weary people could not be driven along uncongenial paths without regard for their reaction. It is perhaps significant that the N.E.P. began at a time of public discontent, exemplified by the Kronstadt naval mutiny of March 1921. At the same time the issue was further complicated by the decline in the hopes Lenin had entertained of revolution abroad; for this removed the alleged factor that revolution in the west would enable Russia to push straight on into the full socialist stage, without going through the full capitalist stage herself (since Russia could thereby rely on the west for its industrial impetus). It is argued that in the years 1917 to 1920, Lenin was sufficiently confident of revolution abroad to feel able to make an advance start on socialism in Russia; but that by 1921 it was clear to him that revolution was not coming. Russia could rely only on her past and her own efforts, so that there was now need for a capitalist stage to the economy.

This period of comparative economic liberalism was accompanied by a contrasting political development in the prohibition of independent groups within the party. The government had already launched an all-out persecution of non-Bolshevik parties in the autumn of 1920; but from March 1921 variation within the party itself was forbidden. 'The Party is not a debating society' is one of Lenin's best-known remarks; and on other occasions he has described 'free speech' as 'a bourgeois prejudice, a soothing plaster for social ills. In the Workers' Republic, economic well-being talks louder than speech.'

The hierarchy of authority that had evolved in Russia was of a dual nature in practice – governmental on one hand,

and party on the other. But the governmental aspect was further complicated by the fact that Russia was technically not a single state but rather a union of several states. In fact the Union of Soviet Socialist Republics which emerged in its definitive form in December 1922 consisted of four states, though the majority of the population belonged to the Russian Soviet Federated Socialist Republic, stretching from Petrograd to the Bering Straits. However, the Ukrainian S.S.R., the White Russian S.S.R. and the Transcaucasian S.F.S.R. were later matched by other states, as various regions subsequently acquired statehood; there being by 1941 eleven states altogether. The actual base of the political pyramid in the individual states was provided by the local soviets, which were often self-perpetuating bodies that owed their particular form to the upheaval of the early months of the revolution. Indeed many of the small factory or village soviets consisted of the entire adult population, but others were elected according to individual systems. The basis of the *Union* pyramid on the other hand was universal male and female suffrage, though this was limited to those engaged in productive work. In this way it was implicitly recognised that Russia was still in the stage of the dictatorship of the proletariat, where remnants of bourgeois opposition remained to be eliminated.

It was in practice the party hierarchy that controlled the direction of government, in that it had selected the candidates whom the public elected – generally unopposed. Moreover the work of ministers and important government officials was examined and criticised by their opposite numbers in the party, this being the logical if curious outcome of the belief that the government must be subordinate to the party as to the most enlightened section of the people. Yet in practice the party could scarcely claim to be democratic, for elections at its lower levels tended to be held by acclamation, the candidates usually being nominees of the higher echelons. Party membership was still little more than a million in the mid-twenties, while even in the 1950s only one Russian in thirty-nine was a party member.

The Stalin era

After almost superhuman efforts on behalf of Communism, Lenin had a stroke in 1923, and died in the following January. There were several men who had reasonable claims to the leadership: notably Leon Trotsky, Gregory Zinoviev, Leo Kamenev, Nicholas Bukharin and Joseph Stalin. Trotsky, Zinoviev and Kamenev represented what might loosely be called 'left-wing' opinion. They believed that the success of socialism in Russia depended on world revolution abroad, insisting therefore that the Russian government should do all in its power to bring this about. In the meantime, however, they held that Russia should follow a policy of thorough-going socialism at home – instead of the compromise regime of Lenin's N.E.P. They nevertheless supported the principle of free speech within the party, Trotsky being particularly opposed to any attempt to dragoon the intelligentsia. Bukharin by contrast represented 'right-wing' opinion. Believing that it was useless for Russia to disperse her energies trying to bring about world revolution before the time was ripe, he felt that Russia should meanwhile content herself with a domestic policy of state capitalism of the N.E.P. variety. Stalin's position, however, was a compromise between these extremes. Arguing that Russia was so large a country that it was possible to have socialism in Russia without having to force a world-wide revolution elsewhere, he advocated a single-minded policy of socialising Russia without too much concern about what was happening elsewhere.

Stalin as a person combined cunning with a seeming impassivity – though his inveterate enemy, Trotsky, claimed to have discerned in 'his yellow eyes' his capacity for 'deep and lasting hatred'. Even in the early thirties, when Stalin's policies were put to their cruellest test, there was, as Isaac Deutscher says, 'something almost incomprehensible in the mask of unruffled calmness which Stalin showed in those years'. As far as methods went, Stalin represented a ruthless approach to problems. He regarded opposition as something to be eliminated, and unlike Trotsky had little or no regard for the creative possibilities of free speech. His great gift was skill in manipulating the party machine. During 1924 he sided with Zinoviev and Kamenev, using them to force Trotsky's resignation in January 1925. But when Zinoviev and Kamenev broke with Stalin in the summer of 1925 to resume contact with Trotsky, Stalin gradually discredited all three, his triumph coming in December 1927 when the All-Union Congress of the Party expelled them, together with seventy-five of their supporters. The Congress furthermore specifically endorsed Stalin's plans for the economic future of Russia. Having thus eliminated his 'left-wing' rivals, Stalin proceeded systematically to eliminate his 'right-wing' rivals, a process that was complete by 1930.

Under Stalin the Soviet government fully accepted the assumption that revolution abroad could not be envisaged in the immediate future. Accordingly Stalin's First Five-Year Plan represented a switch from the N.E.P.'s 'state capitalism' to the pursuit of 'socialism in one country'. Its main purpose was to develop Russia's industrial capacity, particularly capital goods, 86 per cent of the Plan's investment going into heavy industry. But apart from laying a foundation for the domestic economy, Stalin intended that it should provide a basis for armaments – for if the prospect of world revolution had been temporarily shelved, it was arguable that Russia's survival in a hostile capitalist world was all the more dependent on modernisation.

Although the Plan failed to achieve its goal of trebling the production of capital goods, steel production nevertheless rose from 4·3 million tons to 5·9, coal from 31·7 million to 54·6, oil from 11·6 million to 21·4 and electric power from 5 billion kilowatts to 13·5. By 1940 indeed these figures were to be raised to 18·3, 151, 31 and 48·3 respectively. At the same time the relative significance of the advance is perhaps better appreciated when it is remembered that the United States in 1929 was producing 55 million tons of steel, 546 million tons of coal and 137 million tons of oil. During the Plan, Russia's industrial labour force had doubled, though such emphasis on capital industry was inevitably made at the expense of consumer goods, despite the Plan's aim to double their production. The parallel fall in real wages and worsening of working-conditions has already been indicated (see p. 290), while it could also be argued that many of the ideals of the early Revolutionary period were sacrificed to industrial expansion. Everyone was aware that wage differentials were increasing, Stalin himself describing equality of wages as 'alien and detrimental to Socialist production' (June 1931). 'Equality in the sphere of consumption and personal life', he later commented, 'is reactionary petty bourgeois nonsense, worthy of some primitive sect of ascetics, but not of a socialist society.' 'Marxism proceeds from the assumption that tasks and needs are not and cannot be the same as regards quality or quantity either in the period of Socialism or in the period of Communism.'

The most remarkable social outcome of the Plan was the collectivisation of agriculture. Since industrial growth would mean a large urban population to feed, the government was acutely aware of the shortcomings of an agricultural economy split into twenty-five million smallholdings. The initial intention was to limit collectivisation to 14 per cent of peasant holdings, to be effected on a voluntary basis. But since in practice the process had to be imposed by force, the impetus needed to overcome peasant opposition prompted the authorities to advance further than Stalin intended, with the result that by March 1930 55 per cent of the agricultural economy was collectivised. Stalin was alarmed, however, by the bitter hostility this aroused among the peasants. Nor could the immediate economic consequences be ignored, many of the more wealthy peasants preferring to destroy their property rather than see it fall into the hands of the state. As a result of this and other aspects of the general disruption, the amount of livestock in Russia fell by over a half. Human suffering was inevitably enormous: some five million members of peasant families either died or disappeared, or were sent to labour camps. Accordingly Stalin decided to permit those collectivised households who wished to withdraw, to do so. But when two-thirds of the total proceeded to take advantage of the offer, he took fright at the reaction, launching a firm if gentler campaign to reverse the tide. Eventually a mixture of pressure and concessions brought the percentage back to 55 per cent.

The collectivisation process had nevertheless revealed undreamed-of financial advantages for the government, collectivisation turning out to be a major means of financing Russia's industrial expansion. Russia's initial difficulty had been that foreign countries were unwilling to lend capital to Russia, understandably so, since the Soviet government had repudiated the foreign debts of Tsarist Russia (1918). But the government found that by buying the produce of the collective farms at something like an eighth of its normal market price, it could sell food to the public at 700 per cent profit, using the proceeds to finance industrial development.

The period of the plan was the most testing time in Stalin's career. Even his characteristic impassivity was unable to conceal the anguish that assailed him in the autumn of 1932. In Deutscher's words:

> Memoranda about the need to depose him circulated in his immediate entourage. . . . His own wife . . . hitherto blindly devoted to her much older husband, began to doubt the wisdom and rightness of his policy. . . . [She] spoke her mind about the famine and discontent in the country and about the moral ravages which the Terror had wrought on the party. Stalin's nerves were already strained to the utmost. In the presence of his friends he burst out against his wife in a flood of vulgar abuse. . . . The same evening she committed suicide.[1]

The Second Five-Year Plan (1933–7) put more emphasis on the training of skilled labour, and less on sheer quantitative production. Stalin's fear of Nazi Germany, however, led him not only to divert considerable energy into arms production, but also to site new industrial enterprise in the remote eastern parts of Russia, where invasion risks were smaller. Nevertheless, taking industrial output as a whole, Russia's share of world production had probably risen from about 3·7 per cent to about 18·5 per cent between 1929 and 1937, production being second only to that of the United States in certain classes of capital goods. As in the first Plan, everything was done to encourage greater efforts by the individual worker. When in 1935 a coal-hewer, Alexis Stakhanov, became a national hero by producing fourteen times the daily quota, the Stakhanov movement led to a quantitative increase in piece-work standards – although conversely some of the more zealous pace-makers were quietly disposed of by their less enthusiastic fellow workers.

[1] *Stalin* (Penguin, 1966) p. 133.

The Third Five-Year Plan (1938–41) was of course cut short by the German invasion, but followed principles that were similar to those of the second. Collectivisation of agriculture was more or less completed; and from 1928 to 1941 the whole process saw some twelve million people leave the country for the towns.

Despite its phenomenal advance, the Russian economy remained a highly introspective one, exports accounting for little more than 2 per cent of the world total. To a large extent this reflected the growing self-sufficiency of a nation that stretched from the Baltic to the Pacific; and to a much smaller extent it was a legacy of the initial political isolation of Soviet Russia, though this factor is often exaggerated. Britain, Germany and the United States were her best customers. Two-thirds of Russia's exports were industrial goods, though the largest single items were timber (5–20 per cent), grain (4–20 per cent), petrol (11–19 per cent) and furs (10 per cent), grain being exported even during the Ukraine famine of the early thirties.

Stalin has been most heavily criticised for the increasingly repressive character of the Soviet state. Marx had predicted that when the proletariat stamped out the last vestiges of bourgeois opposition the repressive functions of the state would wither away. Hopes were raised in the late 1930s when it was officially stated that the enemies of the proletariat had been eliminated. Symptomatically the constitution of 1936 gave the vote to all adults, thereby implicitly recognising that the parasites had gone. More explicitly Stalin declared in 1939 that: 'There are no more bourgeois classes'. Far from relaxing its grip, however, the state was becoming increasingly dictatorial, the purges of the later thirties seeing the systematic elimination of nearly all Stalin's possible rivals and party opponents. A case could be made for maintaining that the purges were but part of an overall attempt to strike terror into the whole population – possibly with the aim of silencing discontent with the low standard of living. It was certainly grotesquely clear that the arrest of some seven or eight million people went far beyond the elimination of the leaders of discontent.

It began with the execution of a hundred members of the

'left-wing' opposition alleged to be implicated in the assassination of a party leader, Serge Kirov, in December 1934. But the
first major climax came in 1936 when sixteen major party
figures, including Zinoviev and Kamenev, 'confessed' to
having connections with Trotsky and foreign governments.
1937 and 1938 then saw 'confessions' from thirty-eight others,
including Bukharin; and like their predecessors, they were all
executed or died in prison. As Trotsky wrote, 'Stalin is like a
man who wants to quench his thirst with salted water'. Moreover the purging of the army (see p. 295) was so thorough that
it was later to play a major role in the early Soviet reverses of
1941.

The formidable difficulty of reconciling all this with Marx's
prophecy was theoretically answered by Stalin in 1939. He
explained that the apparatus of the state would continue to be
necessary until 'capitalist encirclement is liquidated and the
danger of foreign military attack has disappeared'. In other
words the external enemy had replaced the internal one as the
major factor preventing the withering away of the state. It was
obvious, however, that the police-state had become such a convenient short-cut to 'popular rule', that no Soviet leader was
likely to relinquish it. Stalin moreover had become the victim
of his own intensely suspicious mind. By punishing all criticism,
he transformed his entourage into a silent body of poker-faced
men. He ceased to be able to know what his subordinates were
thinking; and frustration at his ignorance further deepened his
suspicion. Ultimately Stalin's predicament seemed to have only
one logical solution: the liquidation of everyone of any consequence.

SOVIET ASIA

The history of Soviet Russia's relations with her Asian subjects
is theoretically a history of relations between equals. The total
population of Russian emigrants and Russian emigrant stock
was becoming far greater than the native Asiatic population,
while theoretically there was no distinction between the Soviet
institutions of Asia and Europe.

Communists had consistently denounced what they termed

capitalist imperialism; but with the Revolution the Communists of Russia had found themselves heirs to the Tsarist Asiatic Empire. What had seemed a new era dawned in April 1917 when the All-Russian Party Congress had spoken of the right of non-Russian nationalities to secede from Russia. But, as Zinoviev was to point out in 1922, the sad fact was that 'we cannot do without the oil of Azerbaijan or the cotton of Turkestan' – though he hastened to explain that 'we take these products which are necessary for us, not as the former exploiters, but as older brothers bearing the torch of civilisation'. In fairness to Moscow, however, it must be admitted that independence would have posed difficult problems, given the large proportion of Russian settlers and given the empire's contiguity with Russia. Only in the frontier regions was there a cast-iron case for giving the inhabitants the chance of deciding their future by plebiscite. But even there it could also be pointed out that Russian treatment of Asiatics came much closer to giving them equality than was the case with other colonial empires. It is true that conditions in European Russia provided a much lower standard for comparison than was the case in Britain or France. But official wage rates were the same as in European Russia. And if the average standard of living was a quarter below the European level, that was because there was a greater proportion of unskilled workers among the Muslims.

It must likewise be conceded that under Soviet rule literacy rose among Asiatic Muslims from about 3 per cent to nearly a quarter of the population (nearly half by 1955), though inevitably they were at a disadvantage compared with the better educated European Russians who held nearly nine-tenths of the professional appointments in Central Asia. And there was no doubt that the key positions in Asiatic administration were controlled by Europeans – primarily for political rather than educational reasons. Generally speaking the First Secretary of the local Party Committee was a native; but the Second Secretary was nearly always a European Russian and in practice the real power in the Party Committee. Moreover the key departments within the Party Committee were nearly always held by Europeans.

Yet the Asiatics trod the same *via dolorosa* to Soviet fulfilment

as the Europeans. They passed through the same stages of land-
tenure and collectivisation, reacting in similar fashion. As in
Europe, many slaughtered their cattle rather than see them
collectivised. Furthermore, although Lenin had accused the
Tsarist governments of making Central Asia 'a cotton appendix
of Russia', the Soviet government continued in the same way to
subordinate the Central Asian economy to cotton. Nevertheless
the Soviet government did attempt to develop the industrial
potentialities of the area – though it was the German invasion of
European Russia in 1941 which really established Central Asia
as an important industrial region, which in the 1960s produced
over a tenth of the Soviet Union's steel.

The totalitarian nature of Communism was bound to come
into conflict with indigenous ways of life sooner or later. The
history of the official Soviet attitude to Islam corresponded
roughly to that of the Soviet attitude to Christianity, the initial
period being tolerant, but the 1930s seeing increasing intoler-
ance. By 1941 less than one in twenty of the Tsarist mosques of
the Soviet Union survived as places of worship; while not
surprisingly the government complained that Islam helped to
preserve unproductive attitudes. An Uzbek man of substance
once said to a Russian visitor: 'We have been happy in
Samarkand for many, many years. Allah is good, the soil is
rich, and one is blessed with many children. Why have discontent and all these meetings and reading and writing? It is not
necessary.' And again, another Muslim pointed to the women
picking cotton in the fields and said: 'These need no spare
parts, no maintenance and work well. Why have machines?'
Traditionalism moreover had its positively dangerous aspects.
In the late twenties literally hundreds of women were killed
by their own relatives for no longer wearing veils. At the
same time many Muslim party officials at the local level were
remarkably traditional in their domestic life. Some had several
wives, and there were cases of women directors of co-operatives
or even women presidents of the local soviet who at home lived
in harems with their husbands' other wives.

CHAPTER ELEVEN

Humiliation and its Price

Germany

To speak of Soviet Russia as 'the great experiment' and inter-war Germany as 'humiliation and its price' might seem to betray a strong political bias. The overall loss of life and material hardship that occurred in Russia had no parallel in Germany; while compared with Stalin's purges, Hitler's 'Night of the Long Knives' might seem a very slight affair. Yet however questionable the motives of many Soviet activities have been, and however dubious in practice many of the benefits of Communism have turned out to be, there was a genuine underlying intention to improve the lot of the masses, in the long if not in the short run. In theory, at least, the 'benefits' of Communism were to be extended to everyone who did not resist them. By contrast Nazi Germany intended to improve living standards at home by the indirect benefits of a thriving capitalist economy, and more ominously, by subordinating 'inferior' peoples to the German purpose. It was of no avail for Jews or Slavs to applaud National Socialism and expect to share in its success; the fact that they were Jews and Slavs automatically designated them as the victims of German intentions. It is true that Soviet Russia also had its persecuted nationalities; but it could at least be argued that unlike Germany's victims it was open to them to be assimilated in the Russian monolith, provided they made their willingness clear enough. This is not to deny that many suffered without their attitude even being ascertained; nor is it to deny that the whole situation of minorities in Russia was inhuman.

Developments in Germany in the inter-war period were to affect not only the Germans and their neighbours but the world as a whole. Hitler's expansionist policies led directly to the Second World War; and whereas it could be argued that the main causes of the First World War had their roots in several countries, the Second World War owed its origins first and foremost to events in Germany. Conversely, however, it cannot be denied that events in Germany owed much to the mistaken policies of other countries.

THE WEIMAR REPUBLIC

The social outcome

It would be tempting to say that the hardship of Germans under Weimar was primarily economic, while under Hitler it was to be principally 'moral'. But 'moral' issues are not easily measured; and it may well be that historians have underestimated the 'moral' effect of military defeat on Germans in the 1920s. Nevertheless the following statistics of real wages and unemployment (Table 25) are the most eloquent evidence that is likely to emerge on life under Weimar.

In most western countries, real wages had regained their pre-war level by 1924 at latest; but in Germany this was not so until 1928. Hardship in particular months often went further than annual averages show, especially in the inflationary period of the early twenties when real wages were scarcely more than half of what they were in 1913 (e.g. December 1922). Although unemployment insurance and an eight-hour day were established in November 1918, the eight-hour decree was soon suspended in the interests of economic recovery, while the workers' insurance contributions rose as the demands on funds increased. By 1932, in fact, contributions were taking an eighth of the worker's wage.

The middle classes were affected in varying ways by the events of the twenties. By the end of 1923 the paper mark had fallen to the ludicrous fraction of a trillionth of a gold mark, retired people living on fixed incomes being literally reduced to beggary. Wage- and salary-earners rushed to the shops and spent all their wages as soon as they got them, because their value was falling every hour. But landowners, factory-owners and merchants were able to sell their produce at the current prices, or slightly ahead of them, and so were much less affected. Moreover, people who had loans to pay back were positively helped by the inflation, since by 1923 the value of their debts had fallen to a trillionth. Indeed the government's pre-war debt of 40 billion marks was now worth less than a tenth of a glass of beer. Exporters of goods, for their part, left the proceeds of their foreign sales in foreign currency and waited for the

TABLE 25

	Industrial real wages as percentage of British wages	Industrial real wages as percentage of 1913 level	Percentage of working population unemployed
1920		78	4
1921		89	3
1922		70	1·5
1923		70	10
1924	55	70	14
1925	63	87	7
1926	70	90	18
1927	71*	97	9
1928	77*	108	8
1929	77*	110	13
1930		105	22
1931		100	34
1932		94	44

*These percentages are probably 5 to 10 per cent over-optimistic.

German mark to regain its stability before converting them back into marks; in this way they were often able to buy up their less fortunate rivals. Hugo Stinnes, for instance, eventually controlled firms totalling 600,000 workers – which meant that one German in twenty-two worked for Stinnes. Nevertheless 1925 was to find him in difficulties, and the profits of most businessmen were to fall disastrously with the Depression of the early thirties.

The inflationary period is sometimes portrayed as a whirling *Totentanz*, in which a demoralised middle class abandoned itself to a joyless riot of loose living. Certainly the desire to hang on to the last shreds of material comfort drove many women to prostitution, while novelists were not romancing when they spoke of the leather-booted ladies who made a living off the masochistic tendencies of Berlin businessmen. But immorality in the twenties was not a monopoly of the Germans, nor was the level in 1923 so markedly above that of other times.

The economic factors

The economic causes of these social changes largely stemmed from the war. The German government during the war had tried to cover the enormous military expenditure by borrowing at home, and not surprisingly had then succumbed to the temptation of printing more bank notes to pay the interest on its debts. About four-fifths of the war expenditure was covered this way, with the result that by the end of the war severe inflation had set in. Moreover German difficulties were vastly increased by the victors' demands for reparations. In May 1921 the Reparation Commission presented Germany with a net bill for £6300 million, to be paid in thirty annual instalments plus 6 per cent interest, in the form of gold and produce. The capital alone of each instalment was equivalent to a third of the German revenue and four times what Anglo-American economists thought Germany could afford. To pay these reparations, Germany required large quantities of gold and foreign currency; and to get it quickly and in sufficient quantity she was having to pay a higher price in German paper marks than would otherwise have been the case. The result was that the value of the paper mark dropped very rapidly. The situation was made worse by the fact that there was not sufficient ready capital in Germany to finance the expansion of industry; so the banks tried to meet the situation by printing vast quantities of paper money. Furthermore in January 1923 France and Belgium retaliated against the non-payment of reparations by occupying the Ruhr, a gesture that did no good and much harm. The Ruhr industry, far from profiting the occupants, benefited no one since the German workers immediately embarked on a campaign of passive resistance; and in order to finance the strike, the government resorted to printing yet more paper money, with catastrophic social results (see p. 316).

The inflation came to a stop after Chancellor Gustav

Stresemann brought in a new mark which more or less struck twelve noughts off the old one (November 1923). Stresemann and his successors had the confidence of big business, and the new mark held steady. But the main reason for the success of the new mark was the easing of German reparation payments with the international Dawes Plan of 1924. Although this plan did not reduce the total amount to be paid, it changed the annual payment from a fixed sum to whatever Germany could afford in the particular year.[1] Indeed the plan more or less marked the general acceptance of the plain truth that it was very much in the world's interest that a big market and skilled producer like Germany should be taken back into the family of nations, and that reparations must not be allowed to hinder Germany's economic recovery. German exports doubled in the next five years, though they still had not surpassed the level of 1913. Her prospects seemed to brighten still further with the Young Plan of 1929 which cut down her reparation debts to less than a third of the original assessment, making them payable over fifty-nine years. By 1932, however, the Depression cut German exports to little more than two-fifths of what they had been in 1929, while in June of that year the Lausanne Conference decided to cancel reparations in return for £150 million in 5 per cent bonds (see p. 280). Ironically enough the suspension of reparations meant that many German exporters now lost their best foreign customers, with the result that, like other manufacturers, they had to dismiss large numbers of their workmen and subsist on marginal profits.

The political factors

The weight with which these economic facts fell on the various sections of society was in part determined by political factors. There can be no doubt that the industrial workers would have come off much worse than they did, if the employers had not been so scared of social revolution in 1918. Fear impelled the bosses to recognise the trade unions as the sole representatives of the workers (November 1918), with the result that by 1922

[1] For the first five years, however, the plan laid down a rising scale of annual charges, to reach £125 million by the fifth year.

over two-thirds of industrial workers were covered by collective agreements – a tenfold increase on 1913.

The political history of the Weimar Republic poses three major questions that were of great import to the Germans and their neighbours. First, why did Germany not become a socialist state at the end of the First World War? Secondly, why did parliamentary democracy fail to take permanent root in Germany? And thirdly, why did the Nazis succeed in coming to power?

The Social Democrats came to power in November 1918 as a direct outcome of the war. Their co-operative attitude towards the government during the war made them a much less radical party than they had been in the pre-war period; so much so that their left wing had broken off in disgust to form the Independent Social-Democratic Party, the U.S.P.D. (April 1917). The pure essence of the extreme Left, however, was to be found in the Spartacists, a quasi-Leninist group under the leadership of Karl Liebknecht and Rosa Luxemburg.

They had consistently denounced the war, Rosa Luxemburg condemning 'the mass slaughter of the European proletariat . . . our hope, our flesh and blood, which is falling in swathes like corn under the sickle'. They believed that 'the madness will cease and the bloody product of hell come to an end only when the workers of Germany and France, of Great Britain and Russia . . . extend to each other the hand of friendship and drown the bestial chorus of imperialist hyenas with the thunderous battle cry . . . "workers of the world unite".' By comparison with the Spartacists the Social Democrats were the very essence of respectability; so much so that they were eventually invited to join the government (October 1918).

The army high command had had effective control of government throughout the war, and when at last it decided that an armistice was unavoidable, Erich Ludendorff had suggested that a few tame Social Democrats in the cabinet might create a good impression for Allied consumption. Since the Social Democrats had always insisted that a victorious Germany should evacuate non-German territory, it was just possible that the Allies might remember this and be more lenient at the armistice. The result was twofold: a coalition cabinet under Prince Max of Baden, and the establishment of parliamentary democracy, a government directly responsible to the Reichstag.

It soon became clear, however, that the United States and a growing section of the German population wanted the resignation of the Kaiser. The war had brought the public into prolonged contact with the Wilhelmine military autocracy; and dislike of its bullying and disillusion with its blunders prompted a popular demand for the resignation of the man who was its most representative figure. Tension mounted further when it was known that Ludendorff had rejected the Allied demands and was thinking of a last-ditch stand. The result was dramatic: widespread mutinies, with many towns taken over by so-called workers' and soldiers' councils. The culmination came, however, on 9 November, when the Social Democrats called a strike to force the abdication of the Kaiser. Faced with disorder on all sides, it was at this point that Prince Max decided that the only solution was to hand over power to the good boys among the Social Democrats.

As a firm believer in constitutional monarchy, Friedrich Ebert fitted the bill; though by now it was clear to everyone that the Kaiser would have to go – clear to everyone, that is, except the Kaiser. Nevertheless he was bundled off to Holland, indignant and bewildered to the last, leaving Ebert at the head of a short-lived coalition with the U.S.P.D.

In its first weeks, the coalition brought in a series of important social measures (see p. 316). But the U.S.P.D., feeling that the Social Democrats were moving too slowly in the matter of social reform, resigned. In the meantime, outside the pale of respectable politics, the newly-formed Communist party was remembering what Lenin had managed to do in Russia in 1917 with his small body of followers and resolved on bold direct action. They forgot, however, the essential fact that Lenin had managed to acquire support among the troops. And when they attempted a *coup d'état* on 6 January 1919, the Social Democrat government easily suppressed it with the help of the *Freikorps* – irregular bands of soldiers which the high command had patronised to counter the extreme Left. Among the victims of the *Freikorps* were Liebknecht and Rosa Luxemburg (who, ironically enough,

L

had spoken against the *coup* as premature). The two were clubbed unconscious with rifle-butts, then finished off with bullets.

The same month saw the election of a Constituent Assembly to meet at Weimar, the Social Democrats emerging with the largest number of seats, though without an overall majority. A coalition was unavoidable; and, as the U.S.P.D. refused to co-operate with the Social Democrats, the Social Democrats were obliged to look to the bourgeois liberal parties as partners in government. This marked the end of the Social Democrats' opportunity to be a dynamic social reforming party under Weimar. It was, however, questionable in any case whether they would have gone significantly beyond the reforms of the previous November. Ebert was opposed to the nationalisation of German industry, because he feared that this would delay economic recovery, and would also facilitate the Allies' attempts to ear-mark choice industries for reparations. He was likewise opposed to the break-up of the large *Junker* estates in eastern Germany, because he feared that the landowners would retaliate by not sowing next year's harvest; and Germany had enough difficulties without adding a food crisis.

Turning to the second question, parliamentary democracy failed to establish itself in Germany for complex reasons. The Weimar constitution preserved in a somewhat modified fashion the federal character of the pre-war German Empire. Each of the eighteen states that made up the German Republic had its own cabinet and legislature, with both state and national elections based on a system of proportional representation. This gave some representation to all parties, but made it correspondingly more difficult for the largest party to obtain an overall majority. Even Hitler with his landslide of July 1932 obtained little more than a third of the seats. The outcome was that every government had to be a coalition government, the life of the government depending not so much on an effective vigorous policy, but on the readiness of the members of the coalition to agree. Not surprisingly the average life of a cabinet under Weimar was less than eight months.

It was rare, however, for a government to be defeated outright in the Reichstag. In most cases it was reshuffled because the ministers of one of the constituent parties disagreed with the rest and decided to walk out. It was also an unfortunate fact that the party leaders themselves generally preferred not to compromise themselves by accepting office in these coalition cabinets, unless it was the chancellorship itself, or one of the key ministries. Consequently the party representatives who took the bulk of the portfolios in each cabinet were for the most part second-rate men. Had each cabinet change included a complete turnover of personnel, no minister would ever have had a chance to get to know his job. But it was regular practice for the new chancellor to persuade some ministers to stay on, if he wanted them, with the result that chancellors were often tempted to appoint technocrats rather than statesmen.

The working of national politics was well exemplified in June 1920. This is commonly regarded as a turning point in the Republic's history, since it was then that the Social Democrats had to make way for the bourgeois parties of the Centre. The existing Social Democrat government of Hermann Müller consisted of six Social Democrats, four members of the Centre party, and three Democrats. In the elections of June 1920, however, the Social Democrats and Democrats lost a number of seats, while conversely Gustav Stresemann's moderately right-wing People's Party made some gains. The position of the Centre Party remained unchanged. The result was that the Social Democrats resigned, their places in the cabinet being largely taken by the People's Party. The leadership of the cabinet passed in consequence to the Centre Party which was the common denominator in both cabinets. Moreover, five of the eleven members of the new cabinet had been members of the old – and this, it should be emphasised, was the state of affairs in a cabinet which is regarded as marking a decisive break in the Republic's political history.

In subsequent cabinets the differences were even less marked, the leadership remaining largely with the Centre Party. The Centre Party had little preconceived policy, other than its traditional defence of Catholic and federalist interest. Indeed the absence in it of the controversial aims that characterised the left-wing and right-wing parties made it the obvious linchpin of a system where compromise was the supreme political virtue. Although it was nearly always in power, most observers had to conclude that it had little of real value to offer the country.

The political life of the Weimar Republic was therefore characterised by a constant reshuffling of cabinets, but with no real change in policy, and with little chance of a vigorous policy. The prevailing policy was whatever minimum policy all members of a coalition were prepared to accept, with the consequence that the system was unlikely to inspire much interest or loyalty among the German people. The result was that when the system was put to a real test in the Depression, and failed to function adequately, few people were inspired to defend it against its political assailants. Significantly the last typical Weimar cabinet broke up in March 1930 on the failure of its constituent parties to agree. The Social Democrats, who headed the coalition, were forced by the rank and file of their party to abandon the usual policy of compromise and insist on an increase in the funds of the unemployment insurance scheme. But the businessmen's People's Party, which formed the right wing of the cabinet, claimed that the government could not afford to subsidise the unemployed any further. So the cabinet broke up, and the next government, that of Heinrich Brüning, was little more than a tool of President Hindenburg, himself the last relic of the Wilhelmine past.

Turning to the third question, a major factor that helped to bring Hitler to power was his own flair for taking advantage of circumstances. He was forty-three when he became Chancellor, and had fourteen years of extremist right-wing activity behind him. Son of an Austrian customs official, he had unsuccessfully tried to make a living before the war from his mediocre talent as an artist. It was then, when living in very straitened circumstances in Vienna, then Munich, that he was influenced by the antisemitic writings of Jörg Lanz von Liebenfels, which encouraged him to link his contempt for social democracy with a hatred of Jews. The irrationality, indeed the psychopathic character, of his antisemitism is revealed in his later recollections. 'Was there any shady undertaking, any form of foulness, especially in cultural life, in which at least one Jew did not participate? On putting the probing knife carefully to that kind of abscess one immediately discovered, like a maggot in a putrescent body, a little Jew who was often blinded by the sudden light.' And again: 'The Jews were responsible for bringing negroes into the Rhineland with the ultimate idea of bastardising the white race which they hate and thus lowering its cultural and political level so that the Jew might dominate.'

With the outbreak of war, he enlisted with the German army. But when peace came he was once more without the prospect of secure employment. Not only was he living with his own humiliation but he was obsessed with the humiliation of the Central Powers, which he felt personally and very deeply. Joining the *Freikorps* (see p. 321) he was then used as a contact with extremist right-wing political groups. As a result of this work, however, he became himself the leader of the National Socialist German Workers' Party (February 1920), largely composed of ex-soldiers. Since Hitler and his party sought to put the blame for Germany's defeat on the shoulders of the civilians who had negotiated the armistice, it was not surprising that he should attract the attention of soldiers like Ludendorff. Indeed Ludendorff went as far as to co-operate with him in an abortive *putsch* in Munich in November 1923. But Hitler also had admirers among the industrialists, who saw his strong-arm gangs as a useful weapon against socialism. The result was that although Hitler was imprisoned for his part in the Munich *putsch*, his influential military and business connections ensured that his imprisonment was short and relatively comfortable.

Hitler's great gift was his insight into mass-psychology and the use he made of it in his public oratory. 'The receptive powers of the masses are very restricted and their understanding is feeble. On the other hand they quickly forget. Such being the case, all effective propaganda must be confined to a few bare necessities, and then must be expressed in a few stereotyped formulas.' Or again: 'The broad masses of a nation are always more easily corrupted in the deeper strata of their emotional nature than consciously or voluntarily, and thus in the primitive simplicity of their minds they more readily fall victims to the big lie than the small lie. . . . It would never come into their heads to fabricate colossal untruths and they would not believe that others could have the impudence to distort the truth so infamously.' And: 'Only those who are passionate themselves can arouse passion in others.'

Hitler's success in the 1932 and 1933 elections really sprang from the sudden impoverishment of the middle classes. The working classes could always turn to the Communists; and a large number did. The Communists in fact got over a sixth of the seats in the November 1932 elections. This is not to deny that the Nazi Party had always had a strong working-class element among its supporters, especially desperate people who were out of work or who had a grievance. Indeed a large percentage of the Nazi vote in 1932 and 1933 was working class. But what gave Hitler such a massive increase in votes was the fact that an enormous number of middle-class voters, who had usually voted for the People's Party, the Independents and the Democrats, now turned to Hitler in desperation. The Nazi Party had the attraction of being a party that advocated drastic solutions, but which was neither specifically working class nor attacked private property as such. The Nazi Party also had the attraction of pillorying certain human factors as being responsible for Germany's tribulations – the Allies and their demands, the Jews, the Communists and the Left in general, and a succession of incompetent ministries. These were much easier to hate than the impersonal economic forces that were the real cause of Germany's hardship. During the war, a determination to win, or at least stave off defeat, had enabled people to endure a great deal. But the economic problems of the Republic were an enemy that could not easily be personified; and frustrated people looked for someone to blame and someone to hit. Part of Hitler's success was his finding of the necessary scapegoats. Jewish businessmen were as much the victims of the Depression as other Germans, but their racial distinctiveness and their more acute business acumen made them a distinctive target for the dislike and envy of desperate people. Moreover, the fact that the Jews were only one per cent of the nation made them easy to bully. Further support for the Nazis came from those who normally did not bother to vote at all, but who now felt sufficiently desperate to do so. The force of Nazi ideals had appeal for the young voter, who preferred the unintellectual excitement of the Nazis to the rather dreary theorising of the Communists.

At the same time the nationalist character of Nazism made an appeal to all sections of the German public, even to people who sympathised with the Communists. It was the Communists, after all, who had claimed that France and Britain were turning Germany into a colonial tributary.

Given Hitler's parliamentary strength, and given the division of opinion among the traditional right-wing parties, President Hindenburg agreed to Franz von Papen's suggestion that Hitler become Chancellor, with Papen as Vice-Chancellor. Hitler took office on 30 January 1933.

But, of course, he was Chancellor under the Weimar constitution, which scarcely gave him the powers he sought. Much as he wanted to seize more power, he was acutely conscious that he had only a third of the seats in the Reichstag; and therefore felt that it would be unwise to attempt anything drastic until he could first dazzle his critics with an impressive demonstration that the German people had confidence in him. The most desirable solution would be a general election, managed by the Nazis, in which intimidation and propaganda would assure him a majority; this was arranged for 5 March 1933. His principal henchman, Hermann Göring, was now Prussian Minister of the Interior, and could therefore provide the intimidation. Moreover, fortuitous circumstance provided him with a useful piece of propaganda. On 27 February an unbalanced Dutch Communist took the extraordinary step of setting fire to the Reichstag building. This gave the Nazis plenty of scope for alleging a widespread Communist plot; and more immediately it gave Hitler an excuse to exclude the Communist deputies from the newly-elected Reichstag, thereby converting the Nazi simple majority of 44 per cent to an absolute majority. But the most important use that he made of the incident was to demand emergency powers for the next four years. When he put the necessary Enabling Bill to the Reichstag on 23 March, the building was surrounded by his storm-troopers, shouting 'We want the bill – or fire and murder'. It was therefore not surprising that only ninety-four deputies dared to vote against it. With the enacting of the bill, Germany passed from the unhappy democracy of Weimar to the dictatorship of Hitler.

HITLER'S GERMANY

The social outcome

It is probably true to say that until 1939 Hitler's impact on the German people was moral rather than material. The 600,000 Jews and the 50,000 political victims of the regime knew material change at its harshest; but life for most of the rest was materially less hazardous than it had been during the Inflation and the early years of the Depression. It is true that by July 1939 a large proportion of Germany's young men had been conscripted, and had left civilian life for the mixed advantages of being members of what was thought of as a victorious army. But for the great majority of the remainder, earning a living proceeded in its familiar way.

Economists disagree on the movement of real wages in those years, but taking industry as a whole the value of hourly wages probably dropped by about 5 per cent. It would seem that the average German worker was earning little more than two-thirds of what he could have earned in Britain, and for a working day that was becoming longer. The ten-hour day rapidly became the norm in the armaments industry, spreading to the building industry in 1936, though wages in these industries were admittedly more attractive. In other industries, however, workers often worked overtime or went on piece-work to compensate for the slight drop in real wages. Conversely the National Labour Law of January 1934 guaranteed that most workers got twelve to eighteen days' holiday with pay a year, while the humourlessly titled Strength through Joy organisation offered them cheap holiday travel and cheap tickets for sporting and cultural activities.

The great advantage of the period, however, was high employment. By 1938, unemployment was less than 1 per cent, as compared with 11 per cent in Britain. This increased employment was not, of course, primarily of the government's doing. World trade, which had contracted during the Depression, had sunk below consumer demand, so there was now an upswing in the trade cycle which brought back business and employment. But the government was responsible for the big expansion in capital industry which provided new employment, just as it was also responsible for the huge autobahns and other public works that gave jobs to three-quarters of a million men.

Yet freedom to move from one job to another was increasingly restricted. In June 1935 the public employment offices were given a monopoly of placing workers in employment, which meant that the state could virtually direct new labour as it wanted. Every worker, moreover, was issued with a workbook, kept by his employer, without which he could not change his job (February 1935). By the latter part of 1936 it was increasingly common for employers to keep their more valuable workmen by refusing to give up their books; indeed the government in December officially instructed the labour-courts to ignore workers' complaints of this kind. Full employment, however, made these restrictions easier to bear, and it was still fashionable to look back on the freedom of the Weimar period as 'freedom to starve'.

By 1939 only an eighth of the population were directly dependent on agriculture.[1] But perhaps the most important event for the peasantry was the Hereditary Farm Law of September 1933. This stipulated that farms of under 300 acres could not be seized for debt, nor could they be divided among heirs on the death of the owner; they had to be given undivided to a single heir. As a result many of the landless members of the family now went to the towns, a process that was encouraged by the fact that in 1933 agricultural workers were excluded from unemployment insurance. Nevertheless the remainder were stronger for this absence, though they found themselves increasingly subjected to the directives of the Reich Food Estate, which restricted their choice of produce and methods.

It was the middle class, however, who in many ways had provided the decisive impetus to Hitler's coming to power; and there is a case for saying that it was the middle class who paid the greatest price. On the material level the price was comparatively small. Superficially the industrial employer had a lot to be grateful for. Not only was his control over his workers

[1] In a population that increased from about 61·8 million to about 69·8 million in the years 1920 to 1940, excluding annexations.

increased, but in some industries he could demand longer hours of them. At the same time the abolition of trade unions in 1933 deprived the workers of their most effective means of fighting back. There is no doubt that Hitler was anxious to keep on the right side of German big business, since, among other things, rearmament depended on capital industry. He was likewise careful to keep the left wing of the Nazi Party in check, and prevent any talk of nationalisation or social reform that would unduly alienate or alarm big-business circles. But it would be a great mistake to regard the Nazi government as in any way the tool of big business. The fact that Hitler suppressed the trade unions and broke the bargaining power of the manual classes was not the result of pressure from big business; it was Hitler who put it forward. Big business was indeed only too glad to agree, and was lavish in its gifts of money to the Nazi Party. Nevertheless businessmen were afraid of Hitler, so that these monetary gifts need to be seen as protection money rather than bribes. Hitler favoured big business only in so far as it suited his purpose.

The management of consumer industries had much less cause for gratitude, for even in capital industry the owners were finding that Hitler was taking away with one hand what he was giving with the other. Although the management now had more control over their workers, the government had increased its control over the management and was in fact using the management as its means of regulating labour. This was also one of the government's motives for encouraging the concentration of private enterprise in larger units. In July 1933 many enterprises were legally compelled to become members of cartels or *Konzerne*, while twelve months later a minimum size for limited liability companies was legally established. One company in eight was thereby forced either to revert to individual proprietorships and partnerships or to amalgamate with others. Furthermore industrial profits that had hitherto gone to the shareholders and directors were now being compulsorily reinvested in expansion. In March 1934 dividends were legally limited to 6 per cent, while in January 1935 maximum interest rates were pegged at $4\frac{1}{2}$ per cent for long-term loans and 3 per cent for short-term. Moreover a law of January 1937 severely reduced shareholders' rights in limited companies. The share-holders were no longer allowed to elect the directors, while conversely the directors were no longer obliged to answer shareholders' questions. It is true that there was no significant nationalisation of industry, but as Hitler brought in more and more controls, he deliberately kept the industrial owners in a vague state of uneasiness.

Many shopkeepers, businessmen and members of the professions profited in the short run from the elimination of their Jewish competitors. But the government was determined to restrict the demand for consumer goods, so as to favour capital industry and rearmament. Therefore salaries and profits did not rise at the same rate as the upswing in the international trade cycle.

Since the middle class held the bulk of the thinking population, it was here that the moral issues posed by the Nazi regime were most acute. It should be remembered that the worst excesses of Nazism came mainly after 1939 – such atrocities as the extermination of the Jews, 'scientific' experiments on living humans and free licence for large-scale sadistic practices in camps and prisons. Yet in the thirties, the concentration camps were kept constantly full at 20,000 or more, while political prisoners were tortured and beaten up – often just for 'fun'. The full extent of this was probably not known to the general public, but that it did exist they could scarcely doubt. Indeed the persecution of the Jews was specifically enacted by public decree. In 1933 successive decrees excluded Jews and political undesirables from many occupations, including teaching and farming. 1934 saw them excluded from the stock exchanges, while September 1935 deprived them of German citizenship. Not only were they forbidden to marry or have sexual relations with Aryans, but half of them had lost their jobs by 1936. There was in addition the unofficial persecution: the shop-smashing and beatings by the S.A. and other para-military organisations. Many private citizens also joined in the Jew-baiting; shops would refuse to serve them and hotels to accommodate them. In November 1938, moreover, the government imposed a fine of £50 million on the Jewish population and organised a popular wave of terror against them, some 20,000 Jews being imprisoned in the course of these 'disturbances'.

What inclination the public may have had to take a moral stand against Hitler was gradually sapped by the Nazi programme of education and propaganda. In September 1933 his Minister of Public Enlightenment and Propaganda, Josef Goebbels, set up the Reich Chamber of Culture with the intention of dragooning creative art into supporting the regime. Goebbels brought a remarkable blend of imagination and vulgarity to his task, which enabled him to be infinitely more effective than a man of more refinement. The works of Stefan Zweig and Thomas Mann were publicly burnt, together with those of Proust and Zola. Music, however, being less polemical in its possibilities suffered less; it was also Germany's principal cultural export, and, as in the case of big business, Hitler had no intention of killing the goose that laid the golden eggs. (It was also flattering to have Richard Strauss as President of the Reich Music Chamber.) Neglect or over-repetition was the worst that the existing classics suffered. The more popularly known orchestral excerpts from Wagner's operas were virtually made unbearable for many Germans by their constant repetition and incorporation into Nazi ceremonies, while Mendelssohn by contrast was forbidden as Jewish.

It was perhaps inevitable that Hitler as an unsuccessful painter should seek to impose his views on German art. In July 1937 he declared: 'works of art that cannot be understood will no longer openly reach the German nation. The end has come of artistic lunacy and the artistic pollution of our people'. Accordingly the German galleries were stripped of some 6500 modern paintings, including masterpieces by Cézanne, Gauguin, Matisse, Picasso and Van Gogh.

The Press was likewise shackled, the number of daily papers falling by a third in these years. Many foreign newspapers, however, were still allowed to circulate in Germany, while there were few restrictions on foreign travel by Germans, other than financial. In this, as in many other respects, the regime was much less rigorous than that of Soviet Russia.

But the real hope of Nazi indoctrination lay with the young. As Hitler declared in November 1933, 'When an opponent declares "I will not come over to your side", I calmly say, "Your child belongs to us already. You will pass on. Your descendants, however, in a short time will know nothing else but this new community."' The University of Berlin instituted twenty-five courses in racial science, while the director of the Dresden Institute of Physics denounced Einstein's work as 'an instrument of Jewry for the destruction of Nordic science'. Not only were a quarter of Germany's university teachers dismissed as Jews or political undesirables, but the institution of labour and military conscription reduced the number of university students by 60 per cent. For school-children the emphasis on outdoor exercise and para-military training undoubtedly made for healthier bodies, but academic standards fell correspondingly. In 1938 membership of the Hitler Youth became compulsory for boys of fourteen and over, younger boys from six onwards being obliged to spend their leisure time with the preparatory bodies, the *Pimpfe* and *Jungvolk*. At eighteen they were claimed by military and labour service, while girls passed through a similar hierarchy of organisations, ending with the League of German Maidens. At eighteen they worked as land-girls for a year. Like the scouts and guides, these organisations provided a great deal of enjoyment for many children, especially those from poor urban homes, while they also contributed to a certain breaking down of class barriers. Nevertheless this drastic reduction in time available for personal interests produced a person who had lost much in individuality; indeed the effect of persistent indoctrination from six to eighteen gave the stereotype that emerged something of the two-dimensional dullness of a strip-cartoon hero.

The economic factors

The economic development of Nazi Germany was a remarkable reflection of Hitler's overall policy at the time he came to power. In discussions with his subordinates, and in *Mein Kampf* and elsewhere, it is clear that he believed that Germany could get nowhere without rearming. As preconditions of this, however, he believed that Germany must do two things. She had to develop her heavy industry; and she had to build up a strong peasantry which would provide Germany with food and produce soldiers of high morale. With this basis, she then had to develop her armed forces, with particular emphasis on tanks and aircraft.

The emphasis which Hitler put on heavy industry is reflected in the fact that on the eve of the Depression capital industry accounted for just over two-fifths of German industry, whereas by 1937 it accounted for over half. As has been shown (see pp. 328–9), Hitler increased the output of capital goods in two ways. First, he squeezed more work out of the labour force by lengthening the working day and restraining wages – which also restricted the demand for consumer goods. Secondly, he forced industry to plough back a greater proportion of its profits into expansion, instead of passing them on to the shareholders.

The increasing emphasis on capital industry and armaments, however, diverted effort from the production of exportable articles, while increasing imports of raw materials. This threatened to create growing trade deficits, which were only kept in check by the vigorous action of the minister of the economy, Hjalmar Schacht. Schacht's solution in principle was to refuse to pay foreign countries in their own currency. They were paid instead in 'blocked marks', which could only be used for the purchase of certain German goods and services. In practice, however, Britain and several other powers insisted on being paid in gold or convertible currency, with the result that Germany shifted an increasing proportion of her trade towards Latin America and eastern Europe. Nevertheless even in 1938 her best customers were Britain (7 per cent), Italy (6 per cent) and Sweden (5 per cent); and despite the achievement of a favourable balance of trade in 1935–7, exports in 1938 were still only 40 per cent of those of 1929.

On the other hand German industrial production as a whole had increased by a half, compared with the late twenties; and if it is compared with 1932–3, when the Nazis came to power, the increase was nearly double. The main exports continued to be coal, metal products, dyes and chemicals.

Schacht, however, resigned in December 1937, when he found the economy becoming increasingly subject to Hermann

Göring's four-year rearmament plan; and his successor, Walther Funk, abandoned the attempt to resist Göring's encroachments.

The political factors

After the Enabling Bill, the political history of Nazi Germany was little more than a catalogue of eliminations, about as interesting to read as a *Who's Who* entry on a successful business-man. In January 1934 Hitler proceeded to centralise power in Germany by abolishing the sovereign rights of the component federal states. In the previous May he had already transferred the property and functions of the trade unions to a government-controlled Labour Front, while the handling of wage agreements was committed to so-called Labour Trustees, also appointed by the government. Furthermore within the next few weeks the destruction of the unions was followed by that of the various political parties (June–July 1933), the clean sweep soon extending to his own supporters.

Hitler was determined not to let the left-wing Nazis get out of hand (see p. 330). His main difficulty was that the dis-contented have-nots in the Nazi movement were backed by Ernst Röhm's militia of Brown-shirts, the S.A. But Röhm was also an embarrassment on a second score. He coveted the idea of a new overall ministry of defence which would give him control of both the S.A. and the German army. The army, however, had consistently made it clear that it would tolerate Hitler's regime only so long as Hitler left the army alone. Hitler, for his part, had particularly strong reasons at this point for not offending the army, for he wished to unite the presidency and the chancellorship in his own person on President Hindenburg's death – which could only be done with the army's goodwill. Hitler found a characteristic solution in the 'Night of the Long Knives'. During the small hours of 30 June 1934, Röhm and four hundred others were murdered – an act that chilled even the heart of Mussolini. But it brought the desired reward; the army duly responded to this gracious gesture of friendship by supporting the union of presidency and chancellorship (August 1934).

The new alliance, however, was soon shaken by Hitler's excessive demands on the army. In the opinion of his generals, Hitler was not only proceeding too fast with rearmament but, what was more dangerous, he apparently imagined that Germany was ready for a campaign of eastward expansion. Despite the warnings of his generals, Hitler was determined to have his way, even if it meant getting rid of the leaders of military hesitation. In January 1938 he indirectly forced the resignation of the minister of defence, Field-Marshal Werner von Blomberg, by unearthing indecent photographs of Blomberg's new wife in her lighter days. In the same month, he likewise forced the resignation of the commander-in-chief, General Werner von Fritsch, on charges of homosexuality. Having thereby decorously cleared the decks, Hitler then reorganised Blomberg's former responsibilities, taking part of them himself and giving the rest to General Wilhelm Keitel, who could be relied on to be subservient to Hitler's wishes. In this way Hitler had overcome the last bastion of German independence. What he did with this mastery is described in the two final chapters.

CHAPTER TWELVE

Democracy Surviving

France

THE SOCIAL OUTCOME AND ECONOMIC FACTORS

When Alexander Werth was living in Paris in 1920 the cook coming in one day pinned up a picture of the President of the Republic on her kitchen wall. After looking at the picture with evident pride, she tapped the President affectionately on the cheek, and said: 'The dirty old rascal!' This incident exemplifies remarkably well the attitude of many devoted Republicans to those in power. It was a curious mixture of acceptance and distrust. Not a bus passed the Palais Bourbon without someone muttering what ought to be done to 'ces * * * de députés'; and yet if occasion demanded, the same person might well be prepared to fight on the barricades in defence of the regime.

The benign scepticism of the average Republican was sorely tried in the inter-war period. For a people who were technically a victorious power, these years did not offer them the prosperity which they felt they deserved. It was only in 1929 that real wages in many industries rose above their pre-war level; and even in the thirties they remained a quarter below those in Britain.

Life for the unemployed was naturally much harder. Even the charms of France wear thin on an empty stomach, as many a foreign student has discovered. Only one man in twenty had the foresight or money to be insured against unemployment, which meant that the rest had to resort to whatever poor-relief the *bureaux de bienfaisance* could give. It was fortunate for them that work had been plentiful during the reconstruction era of the twenties, but their luck was to be rudely shaken in the mid-thirties when the Depression put nearly a quarter of the industrial population on the streets.[1]

Those with work, however, could profit from the social legislation of the period (see Table 26), especially that of Léon Blum's Popular Front government of 1936. For the first time in France, a substantial number of working-class families had a seaside holiday. The *plages* that had been the preserve of the bronzing bourgeoisie were now littered with red-faced, red-handed, white-bodied people; indeed this was not the least of the social changes that caused the more obtuse type of conservative to say: 'Plutôt Hitler que Blum' – despite the fact that Hitler had brought about a similar phenomenon in Germany (see p. 328).

TABLE 26

	1921	1936
Proportion of population dependent		
on agriculture and fishing	c. 43%	c. 36%
on industry	c. 28%	c. 31%

Social benefits in industry

Eight-hour day	Apr 1919
Sickness benefits and old-age pensions	
increased to the level of 40–60 per cent	Apr 1928
	Aug 1929
	Apr 1930
	(take effect July 1930)
Forty-hour week	
(at a forty-eight-hour wage)	June 1936
Fortnight's holiday with pay and	
cut-rate travel facilities	June 1936

For the peasantry, however, 'the depression' was a much more permanent state of affairs. In common with farmers the world over, their fortunes fell with the slump in post-war prices (see p. 271) but, as always, they had a good friend in parliament with its surfeit of rural politicians. Nevertheless it was Blum's

---

[1] If short-time is included. Even so, France was less hard hit than some of her neighbours (see p. 262, Table 19).

Popular Front government that, through the Wheat Board, doubled the price of wheat, and it was likewise under Blum that overall agricultural prices rose between 40 and 50 per cent. Indeed by the summer of 1939 wheat in France cost three times what it did in Britain. Though the peasantry profited, the urban worker suffered, for it cost him more to buy that traditional hazard of the busy pavement, the hat-squashing, eye-poking, long French loaf. In consequence the increase in wages established by Blum was largely swallowed up by rising food prices.

The warm rays of government favour likewise shone on the wine-growers of the south (June–July 1935) and the beet-growers of the north, in that they could count on their surplus produce being siphoned off by the authorities for conversion into industrial alcohol – though the prices paid were unexciting. At the same time the peasantry also profited from the determination of parliament to keep direct taxation low; in the late twenties the average French taxpayer paid only about two-thirds of the amount of direct tax levied in Britain. Conversely indirect taxes were more numerous, especially on foreign imports; and, as is so often the case with indirect taxes, it was the poor who suffered most from them.

Like the peasantry, the middle classes profited from low direct taxation. But, as in other countries, people who depended on fixed incomes based on savings were hard hit by the inflation that affected France in the post-war period. By 1920 the franc had already fallen to a fifth of its pre-war value, while the prospect of German reparations encouraged the government to print more paper money, so diluting the franc that it fell to a tenth by 1926. However, the stern-eyed Gallic cock, Raymond Poincaré, was called in to mount a rescue operation, and in November 1926 he managed to stabilise the franc at a fifth of its pre-war level.

While it is doubtful whether earlier governments could have avoided some degree of severe inflation, it is nevertheless arguable that they could have solved some of their difficulties by increasing income tax and profits taxes, thereby putting the burden on those who could best support it. But the strength of

the agricultural and industrial interests in parliament prevented
any large-scale increase in taxation; while the government for
its part was understandably anxious to help industry recover by
minimising its financial obligations to the state.

Many industrialists, however, made substantial profits from
reconstruction. The fact that France had been an invaded
country meant that there was much to be done, and indeed the
resultant head of steam and the recovery of Alsace-Lorraine
pushed industrial production beyond the pre-war national level
as early as 1924.[1] The price, of course, was paid by those who had
been the victims of devastation – and by the public exchequer
in so far as it helped them. But although France eventually
received a total sum of about £1600 million from Germany,
her debts to other countries diminished her net gain to about
£600 million, a mere fraction of the overall cost of the war to
France.

The installation of new equipment, however, gave French
factories an acceleration that soon carried them beyond many
of their undamaged competitors. At the same time, the fall of
the franc on the international market (however undesirable in
itself) encouraged foreign buyers to buy French goods. Indeed
by 1928 French exports were two-thirds higher than they had
been in the immediate pre-war period, though once again the
recovery of Alsace-Lorraine was an important factor. Characteristically French industrial interests put sustained pressure on the
government to limit the proportion of manufactures that France
would accept from Germany as reparations, so reducing competition to their own products. Although the Depression broke
this rapid rise in productivity, France did not feel its worst
effects until 1932, because of her reconstruction programme.
She also suffered less than countries that were heavily dependent on industrial exports, such as Germany and Britain, or
those with a poorer internal market, such as Italy (see p. 262).
The effects, however, were to last well into the late thirties,
whereas in most other countries recovery was well under way by
the middle of the decade. In 1935 French industrial production
was a quarter less than in 1929, while exports were down by

---

[1] Since the pre-war totals do not include Alsace-Lorraine, the recovery was not
quite so startling as this comparison may at first suggest.

nearly half, reducing the French share of world exports from 6 per cent to under 4 per cent.

As presented in many histories, the economic differences between France and Germany suggest nothing so much as a cautionary diagram in a child's encyclopedia, comparing John who smokes with Jack who doesn't. The French economy still suffered from its characteristic drawbacks, many of which were beyond French control. Mineral resources still remained relatively poor, although the recovery of Alsace-Lorraine brought some extremely valuable iron deposits; while the development of hydroelectric power helped to compensate for her comparative shortage of coal. Yet while it is true that her water-power was roughly equivalent to her coal resources, together they represented only a quarter of Germany's coal. At the same time the continued prevalence of the small family concern in industry, commerce and agriculture made the introduction of new large-scale techniques very difficult.

The economic scene was dominated by innumerable *patrons* and *chefs de famille*, disdaining the help of shareholders' money, just as parliament was dominated by their political counterparts, the deputies 'with minds of their own'. Nearly half the French agricultural holdings were run by families with no hired labour whatsoever, with the result that agricultural productivity in proportion to manpower was only half of what it was in Britain. In French industry, moreover, mechanical horsepower in proportion to manpower was only a third of that in Britain. Compared to her Anglo-German neighbours', French production graphs were sadly wilting.

As in the pre-war years, France counted on her invisible exports to cover an adverse balance of trade. A dangerously large proportion of these, however, came from the tourist trade – three-quarters in the later twenties; inevitably, when the Depression came, the flow of tourists fell to a trickle, bringing in less than a tenth of the spendings of former years. Similarly German reparations had been an additional source of income that disappeared with the Depression. The thirties saw exports fall to a level of less than three-quarters of the import level; and, deprived of tourists and reparations, France had no alternative counterweight. The result was that the balance of payments changed from a surplus, averaging £44 million between 1926 and 1930 (excluding reparations), to a deficit, averaging £29 million between 1931 and 1937.

Eventually 1938 brought hopeful signs of recovery, especially after the second devaluation of the franc in May. This helped to increase exports, and the overall payments deficit was reduced to £1·5 million. As in the years before 1914, Britain, Belgium and Germany continued to be France's best customers, until war once more broke the network of international trade.

TABLE 27

Population

	1920	1939
	c. 40 m	c. 42 m
Return of Alsace-Lorraine	(+c. 2 m)	
Immigration	(+ at least 3 m)	
Direct military and civilian war losses	(−c. 1·5 m)	
Deficit of births	(−at least 1·5 m)	

French governments spent much time worrying about the population 'deficit' – an obsession that may strike the modern reader, living in an age of population explosion, as about as curious as the legendary Victorian magnate worrying how he was to invest his surplus capital.

Conscious that the German population was increasing twice as fast as their own, the French government tried hard to shorten the lead by offering large family allowances, restricting the sale of contraceptives, and encouraging a substantial influx of foreign labour. The largest group of immigrants were Italians, followed by smaller numbers of Poles, Spaniards and Belgians. Not surprisingly most of them went into industry; but sufficient went into agriculture for there to be complaints that farm wages were being kept low in the south-east of France.

COLLECTIVE ACTION AND POLITICAL FACTORS

The fact that material conditions for the working classes were no better than they were, was to some extent the result of the relative weakness of French as compared with British trade unionism. Collective trade agreements were not made compulsory until June 1936, although they had been legally recognised since March 1919, and union membership was low. The war had weakened French socialism in general by the split that occurred between those who urged international working-class solidarity and an end to the war, and those who supported French war claims. The Russian Bolshevik Revolution both deepened and complicated the split. The Left wing mostly decided to support the Moscow-based Third International, while the rest remained loyal to the defunct Second International. Indeed this rift between Communists and Socialists became decisive at the Socialist Congress of Tours (December 1920), where a majority of the delegates sided with Communism, taking with them most of the Socialists' assets, including their newspaper, *L'Humanité*. This was followed by a corresponding split in the Confédération Générale du Travail, when the Communists formed the C.G.T. Unitaire in July 1922.

The popular belief, however, that the C.G.T.U. took its orders from Moscow made it suspect in the eyes of both employers and a growing section of the working population; and the result was that the C.G.T.U. share of union membership fell from nearly two-thirds in 1921 to a quarter by the early thirties.

Yet even before this split became a material reality, trade unionism had suffered a much more serious blow in the failure of an attempted general strike in May 1920. The episode left bitter memories on more than one score – notably the identity of the principal strike-breaker, Premier Alexandre Millerand. A renegade Socialist was as abhorrent to a French trade unionist as an unfrocked priest to an Irishman, so feelings were all the more savage when this ex-Socialist broke the strike with all the ruthless efficiency that his realistic mind could command. Thereafter many of the larger employers decided to employ only non-union labour. Fathers of families lost their nerve before the prospect of no work, with the result that union membership soon fell from two million to little more than 800,000.

The twenties were the years of wandering in the wilderness for French unionism, though the Depression of the thirties, like

Pharaoh's army, made the workers conscious once more of the need for collective action. Membership rose to 1,350,000, while 1935 brought a marriage of convenience between Socialists and Communists (see p. 349) resulting in a reunited C.G.T. (March 1936). Nevertheless the reconciliation had little hope of permanence.

The most remarkable product of adversity, however, were the following month's elections which brought to office France's first Socialist premier, Léon Blum. A brilliant Jewish intellectual, whose political commitment went back to the *jours héroiques* of the Dreyfus Affair, he was nevertheless a latecomer to professional politics, who was always to retain something of his dandified youth as a successful literary critic and bright young lawyer of the Conseil d'État. Essentially an intellectual, the contrast between him and a Ramsay MacDonald (let alone a Keir Hardie) tells one much about French parliamentary Socialism and its distance from the grimy-handed world of the unions. Yet he had the ability to hold large working-class audiences, and it would be a mistake to regard him as remote from the realities of plebeian life.

To the historically minded, a Socialist premier seemed the long-awaited reward of over a century of socialist effort in France. The net profit was somewhat blurred from the historian's point of view by the fact that just a week before he took office (4 June) there broke out what was to be France's biggest strike. This has given rise to endless argument as to whether Blum's government or the strikers could claim most credit for the concessions which were wrung from the employers in the so-called Matignon agreement of 7 June. It represented the consent of the employers to the various reforms already noted (p. 338), and their agreement to an average increase of 12 per cent in wages. Blum had committed himself to these reforms before the strike, but the strike probably helped to make the employers more co-operative. The fact that collective wage agreements now became compulsory greatly strengthened the C.G.T.'s position, its membership rising to five million within a few weeks. Blum was nevertheless determined to keep the government independent of union pressure, and was careful to institute a compulsory arbitration procedure in the following

December, which would theoretically preserve him from the threat of protracted strikes.

Turning to parliamentary pressures, it is tempting to see in the period the ghostly outlines of a two-party system. Put crudely, there was an alternation in power between two shifting alliances, a broadly based Bloc (then Union) National(e), representing national recovery under right-centre leadership, and a Cartel des Gauches, which was more united in its dislikes than in its positive policies, but which embodied many of the attitudes of the pre-war Radical Party.

Before the war, the possibility of a broad conservative alliance had been prevented by all-too-recent differences over the nature of the regime and the religious question. The war had helped to bury these; and it could now be said that the main issues in French politics were undisguisedly economic and social, with national security an important adjunct. As a result conservative economic interests could group together without embarrassing memories of dynastic or clerical quarrels. The fruits of this situation were gathered in the elections of November 1919, when victory went to the Bloc National, which included the more conservative wing of the Radicals, and most of the groups to their right. Their victory in reality came from the widespread desire among the electorate for sturdy safeguards against future German aggression, and from the widespread fear of Communism and fellow-travellers. They were also aided indirectly by new electoral procedure, which put a premium on that rare combination, flexibility and discipline. Symbolically enough, the Bloc soon got rid of Clemenceau, by snubbing him over the presidential election (January 1920). Indeed, the extent of the snub was to receive subsequent if unforeseen emphasis when the preferred candidate, Paul Deschanel, was to distinguish himself by a series of growing eccentricities which eventually culminated in insanity. These included dismounting from the presidential train in his pyjamas, and on another occasion, embracing a war-veteran with the words: 'Feel my heart beat with pride for you.'

The premiers of the next four years distinguished themselves by a characteristic hard-astern programme of suppressing strikes, sending forces against the Russian Bolsheviks, establishing diplomatic relations with the Vatican and occupying the Ruhr when Germany was lagging behind with reparations.

The Bloc's prestige was nevertheless broken by the material failure of Raymond Poincaré's Ruhr operation of 1923 (see pp. 318 and 382). Many of the right-wing Radicals had already been growing restive under the Bloc's 'reactionary' policies, with the outcome that in the elections of May 1924 most of them either returned to the Radical fold or decided to stand independently. The result was a victory for an alliance of the non-Communist Left. Unfortunately the leadership of this Cartel des Gauches was in the hands of the old standard-bearers of Republican ideals, the Radicals. They had characteristically learnt very little in the last twenty years, their main sally in the domestic field being an attempt to revive anticlericalism. Predictably enough the Cartel was to break up on the old familiar reef of state intervention, when the Radicals refused the Socialists' demand for higher taxation to keep prices in check. In fact, the Cartel's only worthwhile activity in its two years of office was Premier Édouard Herriot's attempts to achieve a détente with Germany (see p. 383), though in this connection the Cartel did at least leave France with a useful legacy in the shape of Aristide Briand at the foreign office (see pp. 383–4).

Like Blum and other political leaders, Herriot owed many of his convictions to the Dreyfus Affair, which was 'to alter my life and impose new duties on me'. There, however, the resemblance ends. Mayor of Lyon for half a century, he was to be called 'the symbol of Radicalism'. Indeed the remarkable force of his personality, combined with the basic nullity of his material achievements, embodied to perfection the party whose pervasive presence remained such an abiding feature of the Third Republic. Like the smell of the Métro, the Radicals had an evocative charm for the foreign observer, but scarcely compelled admiration.

In 1926, as in 1919, the Radicals broke in two, and once more the right-wing Radicals looked to their erstwhile companions of the Bloc National. Indeed a number of prominent Centre Radicals joined them when they decided to call on Raymond Poincaré (July 1926) to get France out of her financial difficulties. One of the remarkable features of Poincaré's stabilisation of the franc was the series of administrative and judicial economies that he carried out by simple government decree. Such measures had to be submitted to the Chamber for ratification within three months, but it seemed to many observers that a promising way had been found of loosening the parliamentary stranglehold that had choked effective government since 1877. The only precedent for this was the licence given during the war to Clemenceau to legislate by decree (February 1918). Significantly a financial crisis was needed to permit its use again; and parliament certainly had no intention of allowing the procedure to become normal constitutional practice.

Poincaré did not allow the task of financial stabilisation to stand in the way of his other main preoccupation, national defence. A third of the 1929 budget was allocated to national defence, while Maginot's concept of an impenetrable wall of defences that would resist the most massive German attack was put under construction. The French general staff had learnt the great lesson of the early years of the First World War that modern weapons gave enormous advantage to the defence. But they had learnt it too well, and failed to take sufficient account of some of the less obvious lessons of the later stages of the war. Foreign writers – followed by Charles de Gaulle – saw that tanks and aircraft, if intelligently used, could restore the war of movement that the French generals believe lay for ever buried in the trenches of the western front.

Ill-health, however, obliged Poincaré to resign in July 1929, and his later successors had neither the ability nor the prestige to preserve the old Union Nationale against the unpopularity that came with the Depression and the cessation of reparations. Consequently the May elections of 1932 resulted in the Cartel des Gauches being given a second innings – but one which proved no more productive than the first. Indeed its two years of rule probably saw the regime at its worst, from the point of view of ineffectiveness and lack of courage. Nothing could better exemplify its character than the way it came to a close.

Its demise arose out of the activities of the right-wing opponents of the regime. The extreme Right in French politics was

small and divided, though the royalists had some good publi-
cists, notably Léon Daudet and Charles Maurras; while the
quasi-fascists for their part had some well-known names, such
as François Coty, the perfume manufacturer. The fact, however,
that a number of their able men achieved office or influence
after the defeat of France in 1940 has tempted some historians
to exaggerate their power and influence in the 1930s.

Trouble began when Charles Maurras's newspaper, *L'Action
française*, suggested that the government was responsible for the
death of Alexander Stavisky, a professional swindler who was
being pursued by the police. Stavisky had taken refuge with his
mistress in a chalet near Chamonix. When the police broke in,
they found him dead – or so they claimed. Stavisky probably
had committed suicide; but Maurras insinuated that it was the
police who had murdered him – on the orders of the government, which allegedly feared that if Stavisky were brought to
book, his trial might reveal that Radical politicians were
involved in his shady financial enterprises.

On 6 February various extreme right-wing groups staged a
demonstration in the Place de la Concorde, ostensibly to protest
against the alleged corruption of the government. Railings were
torn out as pikes, and a bus set on fire. When the crowd surged
towards the Chamber of Deputies, the police decided that
baton-charges were not enough. While the time might be past
when a minister's head could be paraded on a pike (though
many of the police would scarcely have lamented a revival),
they certainly feared trouble for themselves if they allowed the
crowd to reach parliament. The result was that drastic counsels
prevailed and they opened fire, killing eleven and wounding
three hundred others.

There is little evidence to suggest a broad-based plot against
the regime. Certainly the situation by no means required a new
broad-based cabinet to deal with it, though this was in fact what
happened. Édouard Daladier's Radical ministry feebly resigned
in a panic, while Gaston Doumergue was rushed into office like
a fire-engine, with a ministry of all the talents. Admittedly in a
country which was fortunate in being spared much physical
violence in the inter-war years, it was perhaps understandable
that the episode should become something of a legend, both

then and subsequently. Yet in reality it remained an incident of slight consequence; and Doumergue's ministry achieved very little.

The later ramifications of the Stavisky affair, however, provided the Press with much sensational news. One of the investigating magistrates was subsequently found tied to the railway-line near Dijon, his body cut in three by the Paris–Dijon express. The popular speculation surrounding the incident was further confused when it was known that the son of Rasputin's secretary had been travelling to Dijon on the train that killed the magistrate – but on his honeymoon, as it turned out. *Paris-Soir* led the general excitement by announcing that it had commissioned three well-known English detectives to investigate the mystery on the paper's behalf, one of them being 'Sir Thompson [sic], the man of iron'. With its characteristic sense of occasion, *Le Canard Enchaîné* riposted with the news that it had commissioned the great Chinese detective, 'Ki-san-fou, the man of straw'.

Another investigating magistrate in the case was assailed by a colleague who had apparently taken leave of his senses. *Le Temps* reported him as

breaking the windows . . . tried to strip himself naked. . . . Then taking a number of bank-notes from his pockets he proceeded to tear them into small fragments . . . continued to shout 'Vive la France! Debout les morts! Take off your hats! For here is God!' Then he proceeded to sing the *Marseillaise*. In the end he was tied to a stretcher and taken off to an asylum.

As in other countries, any right-wing activity was bound to be associated in the public mind with the spread of fascism in Europe. And indeed fear of European fascism caused the French Communists to look more benignly towards the Socialists. Conversely the Radicals for their part saw an alliance with the Left as the only way of regaining power. By July 1935 the three parties were holding joint rallies, their reward coming in the April–May 1936 elections, when they received an overall majority. It was precisely this policy of mutual co-operation that brought Léon Blum to office with a Socialist–Radical cabinet, and which led to the various reforms that are the Republic's main achievement in the inter-war period (see pp. 338, 344).

It was a belated achievement, however, and one which was vitiated by economic difficulties. Basically Blum's failing was his inability to deal with the fundamental problem of the Depression. This daunting task was admittedly beyond the powers of any minister, as far as a basic cure was concerned; but it can be argued that Blum could have brought about a greater improvement. An immediate devaluation might have increased sales of French goods abroad; but by October, when devaluation took place, the expense of his various social measures had already raised home prices. Nevertheless even Blum's sternest critics had to admit that his task was a heart-breaking one. The darkening international situation obliged him, despite his pacific idealism, to take the agonising step of allocating more money to national defence, this limiting still further the resources that were available for social reform. Indeed the impossibility of further progress had to be publicly stated in February 1937, when Blum was forced to announce a 'pause' in reform – a euphemism which was meant to deceive no one. It is true that in June he obtained the Chamber's authorisation to allow him to follow Poincaré's precedent of tackling the financial problem by decree; but the Senate refused to permit him to use decrees in dealing with the vital matter of the foreign exchange rate. Disappointed, Blum resigned on 21 June; and with him went the last hope of any large-scale reform, for although he made a brief second attempt in March 1938, this likewise was frustrated by the Senate.

It was here that France paid the price of both her economic weakness and her political system. The way the Senate was elected (see p. 141) predisposed it in practice to be out of sympathy with the current social needs of the urban working classes; and, unlike the House of Lords, not even the elapse of a time-limit could invalidate its veto. Nevertheless Blum's brief year in office left France with much that was tangible. Not only were there the measures already described, but he also inaugurated the gradual take-over of war industries and the aviation industry. He likewise brought about a merger of the French railways, with the state holding 51 per cent of the stock.

COLONIALISM

Though the war on balance had added half a million people to Metropolitan France, it had in fact enlarged the French overseas empire by nearly seven million. Turkey lost Syria and the Lebanon, and Germany lost Togo and Cameroon, all four becoming mandated territories under French trusteeship. None of them, however, were of much economic importance; indeed Syrian and Lebanese exports covered only half their imports, while those of Togo and Cameroon covered only about three-quarters to four-fifths.

Not surprisingly the pattern of French trade with her Empire remained broadly similar to the pre-war situation (see pp. 148–9). But as in other countries, the Depression tightened French commercial links with her Empire, the proportion of her exports going there rising from about 16 per cent in 1930 to 27 per cent in 1938. This was also reflected in the fact that the proportion of French goods in the colonies' imports rose from about two-fifths to nearly a half; while conversely France came to be taking slightly more than half of the exports of her colonies, these accounting for more than a quarter of her own imports.

The inter-war period saw what theorists have claimed was a large-scale switch from the idea of assimilation to the idea of association in French colonial practice (see p. 149). The idea of association recognised that it may not be possible or even desirable to achieve identity between colonial subjects and the metropolitan Frenchman. While it recognised that France had a duty to develop the native's judgement and responsibility, it conceded that the road along which the native had to travel to self-fulfilment might be a very different one from that of the Frenchman. The practical outcome was as follows. The native was encouraged to participate in governing himself in his own territory, according to the laws that most suited him. But there was to be no extension of the nineteenth-century system of colonial representation in the French parliament, nor was he necessarily to be subject to the same laws as Frenchmen.

Accordingly the administrative councils of the various African colonies were enlarged in 1920 to include representatives of the native population. The native members were

restricted to about a third of the total membership, while the
native franchise was restricted to those who fulfilled a property
qualification or who had been engaged in public service. French
civil status (see p. 149) was not itself a necessary qualification
for the native voter – illustrating the associationist view that
French citizenship on the one hand and the right to have a
voice in the territory's affairs on the other were not the same
thing. It must, however, be recognised that these African
councils were administrative councils, and that unlike the
British African councils they were not legislative bodies. At the
same time a slightly different process took place in Indo-China
where various councils were enlarged to take in a more significant native element.

Except in the mandated territories of Syria and Lebanon, the
French refused to envisage the question of ultimate independence. Nevertheless the inter-war years did see a significant
growth in native nationalism, which, as in other colonial
empires, was most developed in Asia, and least sophisticated in
Black Africa. In Indo-China the most dynamic elements in
native nationalism were the right-wing Vietnam Nationalist
Party on the one hand and Ho Chi-Minh's much smaller Indo-
chinese Communist Party on the other. Both participated in the
large-scale native revolt in Tonkin (1930) – which was repressed
with many of the brutal features of the Algerian war of the
1950s. In Black Africa, by contrast, the only significant native
political party in the inter-war period was the Senegalese
Federation, which, formed in 1936 as a branch of the French
Socialist Party, was a party laying no initial claim to being
pro-independence. It was in fact essentially the war, and the
division between Vichy and Gaullist France, which enabled the
first significant steps to be taken in the development of political
self-consciousness in French Black Africa.

CHAPTER THIRTEEN

The Collapse of Democracy

Italy and Spain

ITALY

> 'Live long, O King', cried the multitude.
> 'I ruddy well mean to', said the King.
> TRAD.

During the Second World War the *Beano* comic maintained the morale of British youth by publishing a cartoon series, entitled 'Musso, the Wop; he's a big-a-da flop!' This, however, was a verdict that was easier to accept in the 1940s than earlier; and it was not until the mid-thirties that British opinion towards Mussolini became markedly hostile.[1] Although Italy provided Europe with the first prototype of modern dictatorship, the Mussolini regime had aroused interest rather than apprehension among other Europeans. Mussolini today, however, is chiefly remembered for the devastation that Italy suffered during the Second World War, and his domestic record from October 1922 is largely forgotten outside Italy.

THE POLITICAL FACTORS — THE SEIZURE AND CONSOLIDATION OF POWER

The Italy that emerged from the First World War felt treated like a poor player in a victorious football team. The Austro-German breakthrough at Caporetto in November 1917 had

---

[1] Left-wing opinion, however, had consistently opposed him.

M

been a traumatic experience, despite the many redeeming features of the Italian withdrawal. The Italian victory of Vittorio Veneto a year later had been won against retreating troops in a lost cause, and, as such, could only partly efface the humiliation of the previous year. Italy moreover felt snubbed at the peace settlement, where her reward fell short of her expectations (see p. 256). Demoralised in spirit, she was likewise materially impoverished. The lira fell to a sixth of its pre-war value, and people whose money lay in savings were ruined. Government was still bound by the old bad habits and restrictive practices of the pre-war period, and seemed to offer little more than a repetition of the ineffectual antics that had discredited parliamentary democracy in the past. It was in these circumstances that Mussolini came to power in October 1922.

Mussolini was thirty-nine when he became premier. Son of a blacksmith with Bakunist leanings, he had started life as a schoolmaster, soon making a name for himself as an organiser of a socialist strike against the Libyan war of 1911–12. An acquaintance asserted that his 'radicalism and anticlericalism were more the reflection of his early environment and his own rebellious egotism than the product of understanding and conviction ... this hatred of oppression ... sprang from his passion to assert his own ego and from a determination for personal revenge'. As a boy he was expelled from school for sticking his penknife into the posterior of a boy who jogged his arm when writing, while his basic desire to dominate was evident throughout his later life, private as well as public. He was, however, capable of deep affection.

He himself confessed in the pre-war period: 'I require to be somebody. ... I must make a bound forwards to the top' – just as later, when premier, he was to say: 'I have a frenzied ambition which burns, gnaws and consumes me like a physical malady. It is my will to engrave my mark on this age, like a lion with his claw.' It was quite within the logic of his personality that he should gradually become an advocate of authoritarian government, though it was not until 1920 that he had fully become what the world now associates with the word 'fascist' – the advocate of extreme authoritarian government, achieving its aims through intimidation and propaganda. When Mussolini and various of his associates founded the Fascist movement in Milan in March 1919, their programme still included much that was socialist in inspiration. But they denounced the pacifism of the Socialists and claimed that Italy was being cheated in the post-war settlement. This mixed programme of social reform at home and aggressiveness abroad appealed particularly to the type of person who had emerged from the war with less than he hoped: army officers who had had rapid promotion in the war and were now out of a job, and people living on fixed incomes who were hit by the inflation. Fascism had no clear doctrine as such; Mussolini himself proclaiming in 1919, 'we Fascists have no preconceived doctrine. Our doctrine is action.'

Yet for Mussolini to make any headway in the 1921 elections he would need the support of the working class. Since the Socialist Party still held the allegiance of the discontented working elements, he determined to smash it, thereby making Fascism the only alternative to the existing liberal parliamentary regime. In 1920 and 1921 the Fascists embarked on a campaign of burning down Socialist headquarters and beating up Socialist leaders, the savagery of which owed something to Mussolini's bitter memories of his own expulsion from the Socialist Party in November 1914. Since the propertied classes who dominated parliament were afraid of the Socialists, the authorities made little or no attempt to prevent or punish these outrages. In fact, in the two years before Mussolini came to power, it has been estimated that 3000 of his opponents died in clashes with the Fascists, as against 300 Fascist losses. The climax came in August 1922 when the Socialists called a general strike. The Fascists announced that if the government did not put an end to the strike in forty-eight hours, the Fascists would – and they did. They set on fire the strikers' homes, breaking the strike almost immediately. The Italian voter might well ask who ruled Italy, especially when Fascist forces proceeded to take over a number of northern town councils by force.

A march on Rome was rumoured, though Mussolini knew only too well that there was little that his poorly armed blackshirted thugs could do against the forces of order, if the government had the courage to use them. But it was precisely this courage that was lacking. King Victor Emmanuel III and his advisers behaved like the timid owner of a fierce alsatian dog – the type of person who tries to guess what the dog wants to do, and commands it to do just that. Fearing a *coup d'état*, they asked Mussolini to form a government (29 October), despite the fact that the Fascists had only thirty-five deputies in the Chamber. Unshaven and clad in black shirt, bowler hat and spats, Mussolini arrived in Rome to accept office from the King: 'Please excuse my appearance, your majesty, but I come from the battlefield'. With this melodramatic announcement, Italy's sad attempt at liberal democracy came to a semi-farcical conclusion. The only verdict that can be given is that Mussolini had triumphed through the disunity and timidity of his opponents.

Mussolini nevertheless began his rule warily. A new electoral law (November 1923) automatically gave two-thirds of the Chamber to whatever party obtained the most votes, Mussolini's prefects seeing to it that the next elections gave the result he wanted (April 1924). After this success, however, he could behave more boldly, the shape of things to come being foreshadowed in June 1924, when his agents murdered his most outspoken parliamentary critic, the Socialist Giacomo Matteotti. It is possible that his agents exceeded their brief in this instance, but whatever the truth, the parliamentary opposition made the mistake of quitting the Chamber in protest, which enabled Mussolini to exclude them permanently (January 1926). The Chamber was now composed almost wholly of Mussolini's supporters, with the result that he could make what laws he wanted. He obtained the right not only to veto unwelcome debates in the Chamber (December 1925), but also to legislate by orders in council (January 1926). The trade unions moreover were put under government control and the right to strike abolished (April 1926). Predictably enough, the next step was that all parliamentary candidates had to obtain the approval of the Fascist Grand Council before they could stand (May 1928), with the result that only 136,000 votes were cast against the government in the next elections (March 1929).

This gradual but determined advance to a fully-fledged dictatorship was matched by a tightening state control of the economy. In June 1932 the government assumed control of the various consortia of Italian firms that had sprung up in response to the economic difficulties of the time, it being established that when a consortium covered 70 per cent of the firms within a particular industry, the other 30 per cent could be legally constrained to join. The outcome was that the government now had a direct part in the mutual agreements that these firms made in tailoring production to the current demand, and in the allocation of production quotas among the member firms. The control that the government could now exercise over both management and trade unions further encouraged Mussolini to remould the country's legislative system, so that these bodies should be directly represented as such in the 'legislature'. Accordingly in January 1939 the Chamber of Deputies voted its own dissolution, and was replaced two months later by the Chamber of Fasces and Corporations. This high-sounding body consisted of the members of the National Council of Corporations, representing labour and management, but also included representatives of the Grand Council of Fascism and the Fascist Party in general. Indeed the monarchy was the only significant element in government that remained 'untouched'.

Like Hitler, Mussolini was a great orator. A hostile English critic had to admit: 'What struck me was the beauty of this ugly customer's gestures – there *was* something of the artist in him, of the artistry of his people'. And like Hitler, his appeal to the masses was the product of a careful exploitation of his histrionic gifts.

> For me the masses are nothing but a herd of sheep as long as they are unorganised. I am no wise antagonistic to them. All I deny is that they are capable of ruling themselves. But if you would lead them, you must guide them by two reins, enthusiasm and interest.

Indeed for many Italians the press photographs of him playing the violin, horse-jumping, fencing or fondling children seemed to reveal a Universal Man of Renaissance stature, even if now they seem like stills from Chaplin's *The Great Dictator*, with Mussolini substituted for Hitler.

THE SOCIAL OUTCOME AND ECONOMIC FACTORS

It has been argued that Mussolini achieved more for the Italian people than any of his predecessors since 1870. Looking at the debit side he did them a catastrophic disservice by involving them in the Second World War. But it should perhaps be remembered that he did at least wait until he thought that the outcome of the war was no longer in doubt. This may have been ignominious and the war itself immoral, but from the material point of view it had something to commend it. Secondly, there was the repression of free speech and the familiar restrictions on political freedom that dictatorship involved. Political opponents were confined to remote villages or imprisoned; and if persistent, beaten up or murdered. Dosing detainees with castor-oil was another favourite pastime of his strong-arm men. But antisemitism did not become a feature of Italian fascism until the late 1930s, when Mussolini drew closer to Hitler. For one thing Jewish physical features were less noticeable in a brown-eyed dark-skinned nation where Roman noses were a source of pride – though most Italians could distinguish Jews with little difficulty. But in September 1938, four months after Hitler's visit to Rome, Jews were forbidden to teach in state schools or be members of Italian learned bodies. And in the following month they were forbidden to marry gentiles without special authorisation, and prohibited from employing more than a hundred workmen or owning more than 120 acres of land.

As far as the mass of the population was concerned, what mattered most was employment, wages and the cost of living. The aftermath of the First World War and the Depression of the thirties weighed much more heavily on them than did Mussolini, who after all made real efforts to cushion them against the economic malaise of the time, however much the Abyssinian War of 1935–6 and its repercussions may have nullified these attempts later on. Under Mussolini, however, Italy experienced the mixed blessing of her largest increase in population – from thirty-seven to forty-four million, despite the permanent departure of over a million emigrants. This was a tribute to advances in medical care and the new American immigration laws rather than to Mussolini's exhortations that Italy touch sixty million by 1950. One prefect achieved unintentional fame by publicly announcing his resolve to apply himself personally to achieving the target. But the increase threatened to create employment problems when the new generation left school. As it was, Italy, like all European countries, had unemployment problems during the Depression. The percentage of unemployed rose from about 3 per cent in the mid-twenties to well over a quarter of the working population in 1932. It is true that Mussolini could claim some credit for preventing it being worse than it was, for he found work for many in his massive public works undertakings, and after 1927 he obliged employers to keep on more labour than they actually required. This was admittedly an uneconomical way of tackling the problem, but given the government's shortage of capital it would have been difficult for Mussolini to create yet further public works to employ the men involved. Only a steep rise in taxation would have made this possible, a step that Mussolini should perhaps have taken. Given his relations with big business and the large landed proprietors, however, it was a measure which he understandably if reprehensibly avoided.

When Mussolini came to power in 1922, prices were six times what they had been before the war. Mussolini succeeded in stopping the inflation, though when he eventually managed to peg the lira in December 1926, the cost of living still remained at four times what it had been in 1913. Wages managed to keep up with prices, and by 1934 real wages in industry had risen to about a quarter above what they had been before the war. Nevertheless, largely as a result of the expense of the Abyssinian War of 1935–6, they had fallen again to the pre-war level by 1938. And throughout the inter-war period real wages in Italy remained less than half of those in British industry, and were even a fifth lower than those in Spain.

As in most western countries, the eight-hour day in industry was achieved in the immediate post-war period, the state first introducing it in certain of its undertakings in June 1919, and Mussolini then extending it to the private sphere in March 1923. Nevertheless Mussolini was determined to industrialise Italy as quickly as possible. 'An end to the representation of

Italy as a nation of inn-keepers, the goal of every loafer armed
with his odious Baedeker. . . . We are and are resolved to be a
nation of producers.' Accordingly a nine-hour day made its
appearance in 1926, lasting until 1934 when unemployment
permitted the establishment of a forty-hour week. As for social
insurance, the principal landmarks had been established before
Mussolini came to power, unemployment benefit in October
1919 and old-age and invalidity pensions in January 1920, the
Duce extending the latter to include non-industrial workers.
Similarly, if it was often hard to obey the tenth Fascist Com-
mandment – 'Thank God every day that he has made you an
Italian Fascist' – at least Italians were among the first to be
guaranteed a fortnight's holiday with pay (May 1928).

Even the industrial worker, however, was not immune from
political repression. Although he might be tempted to scoff
when the Fascist Decalogue told him that 'Mussolini is always
right' and that 'Days spent in prison are always merited',
nevertheless from January 1935 he could not obtain employment without a work-book, testifying not only to his ability as a
worker but also to his political reliability. The result was that
only convinced supporters of Mussolini dared express their
political views in public. Furthermore as early as March 1928
employers had been obliged to obtain all their labour through
the government employment exchanges, which gave specific
preference to workers who were members of the Fascist Party.

The majority of the Italian people, however, were peasants –
56 per cent in 1922, and 48 per cent even as late as 1941. The
flow to the towns would probably have been greater, if the
peasant's movements had not been dependent on a prefect's
permit (December 1928), which tended, of course, to keep
agricultural wages low. But for the peasant possessing or able
to buy land, Mussolini's rule had much to offer, at least until
the war came. By the summer of 1940, Mussolini was in the
process of reclaiming something like a sixth of the area of Italy,
while at the same time the economic difficulties of the inter-war
years had obliged many owners of middle-sized estates to sell off
part of their land to their landless labourers or smaller neighbours. The result was that by 1933 nearly two-and-a-half

million acres had changed hands, nearly half a million landless peasants obtaining holdings. Together with Mussolini's reclamation activities this meant that by 1940 nearly three-quarters of the Italian peasantry held some land of their own (as compared with little more than two-fifths in 1871). It is nevertheless important to realise that most of these holdings were small and scarcely viable, as was evident when each year an average of 7000 holdings were confiscated for failure to pay the land-tax. And Mussolini refused to take the essential step of breaking up large estates that were badly managed. It could be argued that he was in a stronger position to do this than any of the governments since 1945; though it is still ironically revealing to hear present-day Christian Democrats rebuking him for his failure to do so.

Mussolini's programme of land reclamation was matched by the dissemination of modern farming techniques, which resulted in a 50 per cent increase in the wheat yield in several parts of Italy. The peasant farmer was aided moreover by government subsidies and protected by high tariffs against foreign food imports. This, of course, had its harsh aspect in that life was correspondingly dearer for the townsman, who had to buy grain that was half as expensive again as American wheat; and in the late thirties Italian wheat was priced three or four times higher than the average world price. However, Mussolini had brought about a two-third increase in Italian wheat production – though it must be remembered that part of this increase was obtained by diminishing the acreage given to olives and other crops.

A welcome feature of Mussolini's public works programme was that nearly three-fifths of it was spent on the south, with the exception of railway-construction and housing programmes. A vast improvement on the record of past governments, it probably reflected the fact that once Mussolini was in power and had altered the constitution, he was not reliant on the electoral support of the north in the same way that the liberal governments had been. While he could not afford to ignore the interests of the Lombardy farmers and businessmen, he was not as dependent on their vote as were his predecessors. At the same

*

time, Mussolini did much to reduce illiteracy in the south.
When he came to power, three-fifths of the population of
Calabria were illiterate, whereas by 1940 the proportion had
been reduced to nearly a third.

In accordance with his grand design for a greater Italy,
Italian women found themselves surrounded with various state
inducements to stay at home and bear children. Large families
were heavily subsidised, and bachelors were not only heavily
taxed, but in February 1939 were actually disqualified from
promotion in government service. Women were also excluded
from teaching in state schools, a measure that not only aimed to
keep potential breeding-stock at home, but also reflected the
growing divergence between Mussolini and the Church, whose
influence was strongest among women. No Italian ruler could
ignore the Church, and Mussolini had made a shrewd move in
settling the old Italian dispute with the Vatican that dated back
to 1870 (see pp. 186–9). The Lateran Treaties of February 1929
recognised the Vatican as a sovereign state, declared Catholicism the sole religion of Italy and gave the Vatican a number
of generous financial concessions. But the totalitarian nature of
Fascism was bound to clash with the spiritual claims of the
Church, relations becoming very strained from 1931, when
Mussolini dissolved Catholic lay organisations. This created a
serious clash of loyalties for the many Catholics who were
admirers of Mussolini; and since Catholicism was most firmly
rooted among women, he was determined to keep them out of
the schools.

Until the Abyssinian War, big business and the large landowners had good enough reason to be satisfied with Mussolini.
They felt that they could rely on him to control wage demands
and resist any attempt to break up the large estates. Mussolini
had in fact brought about the disappearance of Micheli's bill
for breaking up large estates – a bill which had actually passed
the Chamber of Deputies in 1922. Other popular measures with
the monied classes were the reduction of death duties by half,
and the dissolution of the commission on wartime profiteering.

Industrial production moreover had almost doubled between
1923 and 1929. But when Mussolini pegged the lira in 1926 he
set an excessively high exchange rate, which dampened the

readiness of foreign buyers to take Italian goods. The Depression moreover brought production down to three-quarters of the 1929 total. 'Recovery', however, was quicker than in many countries, in that Italian industry had only a small share of the foreign market, and there was in consequence less to recover. By 1939 production was a fifth higher than in 1929, and could have been better but for the Abyssinian War. There was no disguising the fact, however, that Italy's share of world manufacturing production was falling. In 1926 it had been 3·3 per cent, but in 1938 only 2·7 per cent. Part of the trouble was that Italian industry remained stubbornly orientated towards the home market, which was not a rich one, the result being that three-fifths of Italian industry produced consumer goods.

Yet whatever cause for gratitude the Italian people may have had, Mussolini's real preoccupations were clearly reflected in the way he spent their money. Even in the Depression years of 1931–2, 22 per cent of the budget was allocated to defence, while only 6 per cent went on education, and as little as 0·2 per cent on public health. In 1938–9, defence was taking 35 per cent, education 5 per cent and public health only 0·1 per cent. This was the material price paid for a policy of exhibitionism. Even if he was realist enough to make war only against the defenceless or the defeated, the façade of military might still had to be paid for. When on returning from Munich in 1938 he was greeted as a peacemaker by enthusiastic Roman crowds, he exploded: 'Who's responsible for this carnival? . . . [The Italian] character must be moulded by fighting.' And later: 'To make a people great it is necessary to send them into battle, even if you have to kick them in the pants'. The kick, however, was a very expensive one.

SPAIN

Although the Spanish like other people were hard hit by the world depression, their history between the wars exemplified the increasing role of political factors in shaping men's lives. Their fortunes are perhaps best understood if discussed within the three broad political divisions of the Monarchy, the Republic

(April 1931) and the Civil War (July 1936). Nevertheless the social reality reflected in Table 28 was largely influenced by certain general factors. The remarkable increase in population despite emigration and the civil war, was mostly the outcome of improved medicine and ignorance of birth control (or moral

TABLE 28

	c. 1920	c. 1940
Population	c. 21 m	c. 26 m

Peace-time emigration	over 1 m
Civil War deaths and émigrés	over 800,000

	1920	1929	1940
Proportion of population in agriculture			over 50%
Proportion of peasantry land-holders		c. 70–80%	
Proportion of land-holders with income of 9d a day or less		c. 80%	
Agricultural wages (8-hr basis)		min. 1s 6d (Andalusia) max. 6s (Basque)	
Industrial real wages as proportion of British equivalent		60% or less	
Proportion of population literate	c. 50%		c. 70–80%

aversion to it), while emigration would undoubtedly have acted as a greater safety valve, had not many Latin American countries enacted immigration restrictions. Families who might otherwise have gone overseas now looked to the towns. Yet although industry was expanding, it could not have absorbed all the rural overspill, and, as Table 28 shows, pressure on land remained great.

THE MONARCHY

From an economic point of view, Spain's neutrality in the First World War paid dividends. It enabled her to make considerable economic progress through supplying the needs of countries whose productive energies were geared to war; so much so that the net profit of these years was to remain unsurpassed in the first half of the century. That the working classes were able to draw some advantage from this prosperity owed something to the activities of the C.N.T. and U.G.T. (see p. 202). Strikes in Barcelona (March 1919) induced the government not only to institute an eight-hour day in industry, but also to bring in a compulsory scheme of old-age insurance, whose cost was largely borne by the employer and the state. Conversely the strikes had shown the difficulty of maintaining working-class solidarity against military intervention. Troops made mass arrests among the strikers, while magistrates dealt out 'exemplary' prison sentences, though, as so often in Spain, most of these draconian punishments were not carried out.

False hope came with a scheme for unemployment insurance, likewise outlined in 1919; but it was never operated in the inter-war years. The sad truth was that the social gains of these relatively prosperous years were a mere break in the clouds rather than the dawn of a bright new day. For one thing not enough of the economic profits was used to improve equipment. And although the world industrial boom of the 1920s encouraged Spanish iron and coal production to rise by a quarter and her steel production to double, foodstuffs still accounted for more than half Spain's exports, and manufactures for only a sixth. In a period of agricultural slump, her exports came nowhere near to matching her imports of foreign goods; so much so that even in 1928 exports only covered three-quarters of imports. At the same time, unlike Britain and other countries with advanced economies, she had few invisible exports to make up the deficit. Foreign tourists were as yet too few to bring in much money from abroad.

The chances moreover of the working classes consolidating their post-war successes were prejudiced by the split nature of their militant spearhead. It has been cogently argued that the strength and individualism of the C.N.T. and U.G.T. was in the long run something of a disadvantage to the working class, in that they prevented the emergence of a strong socialist party. Backed by a unified union movement, such a party might well have succeeded in obtaining greater social concessions.

By 1919 the C.N.T. claimed to have 700,000 members, and was to have double this by the early thirties. Authorities differ, however, on the strength of the U.G.T.; even for 1932, estimates vary from 200,000 to a million. Not only was unionism split, but it was showing a growing penchant for violent action, with questionably productive results.

In part this was a legacy of the abortive general strike of 1917. During the early years of the war, wages had not kept pace with prices, with the result that in August 1917 the unions had launched a general strike. The strikers aimed to go further than obtaining better wages: they intended to overthrow the government. But at this point the army had intervened, breaking the strike completely. This, together with post-war unemployment, encouraged the C.N.T., and to a lesser extent the U.G.T., to turn increasingly to violent methods. Hired assassins were regularly used by employers, the unions and the government as well. The early twenties in fact were increasingly treated to strong doses of the Latin-American type of violence that the New World had inaugurated in the pre-war period; so much so that in the streets of Barcelona alone, 230 people were shot in sixteen months. Gerald Brenan describes how the chief of police in Barcelona gave his gunmen

a list of the syndicalist leaders whom they were to shoot at sight. In the first thirty-six hours twenty-one leading syndicalists were killed. Another method was the so-called *ley de fugas*. The police arrested syndicalists and shot them as they were being conducted to the police station: they were reported as 'shot trying to escape'. A third method was to arrest workmen and then release them; a gang of *pistoleros* would be waiting for them outside the prison and they would be killed before they could reach the comparative safety of the workers' districts.[1]

The syndicalists, for their part, gave as good as they got.

The strike of 1917 had set in train other long-term repercussions of an ominous kind. The intervention of the army had marked its return as a domestic political force, while on the other hand, the strike had indirectly given a fillip to Catalan regionalism. The Catalan political leaders had successfully taken advantage of the government's difficulties to force their way into a new coalition cabinet, this victory encouraging them

[1] *The Spanish Labyrinth* (C.U.P., 1960) p. 73.

to use subsequent crises to press their demands on Madrid. Both the army and regionalism were disruptive forces, the net result of 1917 being to weaken the political system. Indeed there were to be no less than thirteen ministerial crises in the next seven years.

The army was to play a key role in bringing Miguel Primo de Rivera to power (September 1923). This *coup*, like most *coups*, was the product of fear, though it had a fairly solid buttress in the king's own prior intentions. Alfonso XIII, like many monarchs of his vintage, fancied himself as a strategist as well as a statesman – the price that countries have to pay for rearing princes as soldiers and sailors (though history may yet prove that a prince with a degree in political science may be an even greater hazard to his country). The king's enthusiasm had led him into giving direct advice to his operational commander in Morocco – 'do as I tell you and pay no attention to the Minister of War, who is an imbecile' – with the result that a large Spanish column was wiped out by a small force of Abd-el-Krim's rebel tribesmen (July 1921). The Cortes thereupon set on foot a public enquiry which was widely expected to reveal the king's interference. Since Alfonso had counted on the prestige of a military victory in Morocco to enable him to dispense with the Cortes altogether, this was for him a particularly embarrassing turn of affairs. The army's prestige would likewise suffer. So, before this could happen, army leaders encouraged the Captain-General of Catalonia, Primo de Rivera, to take over government by force, dismissing the Cortes.

Primo de Rivera, as Gerald Brenan suggests, was personally one of the less repellent dictators of the inter-war period. He

was a man of immense optimism and felt an unlimited confidence in himself because he was always sure of his own good intentions. ... Though he worked long hours, these hours were very irregular. ... He and a few friends (including women) would shut themselves up in a country home, disconnect the telephone and let themselves go for a couple of days. Then he would return to work with renewed energies. ... The doctor would come and put him on a strict diet, but this was more than he could stand and in the middle of the night, he would get up, steal down to the kitchen and finish the remains of his servants' supper.

The seven years of his quasi-dictatorship brought greater
financial stability to Spain, as well as military victory in
Morocco. The twenties also saw the irrigation of some three-
and-a-half million acres of Spanish soil with a consequent
increase in yield of six to thirty times in the treated areas. But
his dependence on the army prevented him trying to deal
seriously with either the social or the Catalan questions. Despite
the eight-hour law of 1919, nearly a quarter of the industrial
population were still working a basic nine- or ten-hour day,
while low wages made overtime a necessity. Nor could *bonhomie*
counter the Depression. The army and the king began to share
the discontent of the middle classes, who had little love for a
regime that opened their letters and left their problems un-
resolved.

Sensing the opposition all around him, Primo de Rivera
abandoned power in January 1930. But Alfonso XIII for his part
failed as usual to recognise the situation for what it was. Morally
he had fallen with the dictator; but it was not until April 1931
that he finally deciphered the writing on the wall and abdicated.
Most of those who mourned his departure did so for negative
reasons, chiefly for fear of what might come.

THE REPUBLIC

What did come fell between many stools. The new Republic
was dominated by liberal and 'radical' intellectuals with little
political experience or contact with the people. On social issues
they were not sufficiently progressive to appeal to the C.N.T. or
to the left wing of the U.G.T.; but on the other hand they were
too 'radical' to have the trust of the bourgeoisie, except initially
in Catalonia.

Their most representative figure was Manuel Azaña – Premier (October 1931–September 1933; February 1936–May
1936), then President of the Republic (May 1936). Gerald
Brenan describes him as

> A short stumpy man with a green bilious complexion and staring
> expressionless eyes, he reminded people who saw him for the first
> time of a toad or frog. His history had been uneventful . . . he had
> lived alone in his home . . . seeing few people and immersed in his

books. . . . Then he turned to politics . . . and it was his activity in organising a Republican movement [in the Madrid Ateneo, a literary and political club] . . . during the last months of the Monarchy . . . that brought him a post in the cabinet. . . . 'The man with the brilliant future behind him', as the Trotskyist Maurín called him. . . . Until the rise of a revolutionary Socialist movement, he dominated the political scene . . . he showed, more than any other Republican politician, the qualities of a statesman and parliamentarian without ever compromising his honesty. It was mainly due to his drive and persistence that the huge mass of new legislation was piloted through an increasingly recalcitrant Cortes.

The genuine desire of the Republicans to improve living conditions was reflected in the fact that the Republic's first Minister of Labour was Largo Caballero (April 1931–3), President of the U.G.T., an ex-plasterer, with a lifetime's hard work in union and municipal government. Always afraid of losing ground to the more powerful C.N.T., he was much readier than the bulk of his U.G.T. followers to collaborate with the middle-class Republican politicians. But his experience in office was to lend weight to the misgivings of his fellow unionists. He 'found that even the officials in his own ministry refused to obey the directions given them. There was a conspiracy to make nonsense of everything' (Gerald Brenan). Quarrelling with Azaña, he resigned in 1933, while February 1934 found him declaring: 'the only hope of the masses is now in social revolution. It alone can save Spain from Fascism.' As Maurín put it, 'Caballero, the representative of opportunist reformism, became in 1934 the man of the masses'.

The Republicans consciously set out to improve the peasant's lot, as was evident in the spate of agrarian legislation enacted in the summer of 1932. On the face of it, there was something for everyone. Starting at the bottom, the wage-labourer became entitled to an eight-hour day – though when work was hard to find, this was small consolation. On the next rung of the rural ladder, the tenant was given the right to appeal against rent increases and unjust evictions; while conversely his chances of becoming an owner were theoretically improved by the grandiose programme of expropriation that was being rapidly elaborated. Certain classes of noble and ecclesiastical estates were put on the chopping-block, amounting to a third of a million acres. But a much more promising step was the decision to expropriate land that was being neglected by lazy or absentee owners. As always, however, it was one thing to legislate and another to act on it.

The government, with considerable reason, feared that a rapid implementation might result in active resistance by the landlords. Indeed the plots and conspiracies of the next few years showed how volcanic was the real nature of the situation; while the swing to the Right in the elections of November 1933 showed that universal suffrage was by no means a guarantee of progressive government. At the same time those officials who had close connections with the gentry often hamstrung the government's measures by creating imaginary obstacles. Yet the decisive factor was much more simple. Expropriation involved compensating the owners, which in turn meant money – the one commodity that no Republican government ever had in these years. However limited the social intentions of the Republicans, the Depression restricted them still further. There could be little question of social reform when exports in 1935 were only a quarter of what they had been in 1930. The net result was that very little was done before 1936, the year in which the weight of popular frustration started to crack the fences and many peasants took the law into their own hands.

Nevertheless the earlier years did see isolated examples of what the law could mean when vigorously applied. In the Estremadura, 19,000 peasants were given land, while less spectacular distributions were made elsewhere. Indeed this beginning was sufficient to make many landowners suspicious of 'improvement' in general. Even straightforward irrigation schemes, with no repercussions on ownership, were often resisted for fear that they might be the prelude to expropriation.

The landlords found allies in unexpected places. Opposition to land distribution came not only from the owners, but also from the U.G.T. and C.N.T., who believed in collectivisation as their long-term aim and were therefore opposed to further fragmentation, despite their hatred of the big landlords.

Shortage of money hit urban as well as rural reform. It is true that the idea of unemployment insurance was revived by a decree of March 1931, but the scheme remained voluntary, and only a small minority of workers were prepared to make the necessary deduction from their meagre wages. Conversely the initiation of a week's holiday with pay (November 1931) affected the government less than the employers; but, as already noted, work not leisure was what everyone was looking for in the early thirties.

A clash between the Church and the Republic was only to be expected. Yet its violence could have been attenuated with more tact on both sides. Although the attitude of the Republicans to the Church was understandable enough (see pp. 36–7), it could be argued that their anticlerical activities made their task unnecessarily difficult. Half of Spain's secondary schools were run by religious orders, while in Madrid itself this was true of half the primary schools as well. To prohibit the orders from teaching, as the government did in May 1933, was to create a massive breach in the educational system, which the government with its limited resources could not hope to fill. Indeed, had the letter of the law been followed, the government would have destroyed with one hand what it was laboriously building up with the other. Only the desultory application of the law prevented a gigantic setback in the country's battle against illiteracy, yet even so, a third of Madrid's children were now receiving no education whatsoever.

Anticlericalism likewise created a cruel division of loyalties for Catholics who were sympathetic to the Republic, notably a significant section of the clergy, many of whom had voted Republican. Although only a fifth of the population were practising Catholics, others respected the Church for various social reasons – some of them morally questionable – even if their own visits to church were confined to baptism, marriage and burial. The separation of Church and State (December 1931) deprived the clergy of their salary, which had hitherto been regarded as representing the interest on Church property confiscated by the state in the nineteenth century. Much ink has been spilled on whether justice demanded a compensatory lump sum, but whatever the verdict, the refusal of compensation left a sense of grievance.

It has also been argued, often unfairly, that the Republicans could have made more determined efforts to prevent the outbreak of church-burning and priest-killing that occurred in May 1931 and 1936. These excesses were undoubtedly the work of extreme anarcho-syndicalists, with little popular backing, even if a large section of the public was incensed by the unsympathetic attitude of many of the bishops towards the Republicans. It is clear that the government realised that nothing but discredit could come of these outrages; but it was hesitant to take vigorous preventive action, for fear of creating enemies on the Left as well as the Right.

On another front, the search for support in a dangerous world led the Republicans to buy the support of the Catalan bourgeoisie by granting Catalonia a substantial degree of autonomy (September 1932 to December 1934). But this was a short-lived episode in that the divisions of the Radicals and the Left gave the Right an electoral victory in 1933, which enabled them to undo some of their predecessors' work. The Radicals had made the tactical (albeit well-intentioned) mistake of giving women the vote (December 1931), which, as any French Radical could have told them, resulted in the election of an unwelcome number of Catholic deputies of the Right.

As in France, 1936 brought a Popular Front government of Radicals and Socialists, led by Manuel Azaña, who superficially might seem a glaucous forerunner of that other intellectual in politics, Léon Blum. Azaña, however, intended to keep the Socialists in check; so much so that they grew increasingly restive as the months went by. Indeed their leader, Largo Caballero, was being commonly spoken of as 'the Spanish Lenin'; thereby increasing the fears of the bourgeoisie that Azaña might suffer the fate of Kerensky and leave Spain to the mercy of 'the Reds'. The fact that Caballero was an indigenous Socialist, not a Communist, was small consolation to a class in fear for its money. At the same time the orgy of church-burning and priest-killing by extremists (see above) led the 'respectable' elements in society to doubt the government's ability to keep order, an impression that grew still worse when the peasantry started seizing land. The fact that the government started at last to implement the expropriation law merely confirmed their fear that the cabinet was emulating their great fellow country-man, the Duke of Plaza Toro, who 'led his army from behind; he found it less exciting'.

CIVIL WAR

For all classes the thirties had their greatest impact in the consequences of the Civil War. Half a million people died; another 340,000 went into exile; a quarter of a million houses were wrecked; and a third of the country's livestock was lost. The direct cost alone of the war exceeded £3000 million, the equivalent of sixteen years' national revenue, while the indirect cost is incalculable. To instance just one effect, exports in 1937 were only a twelfth of what they had been in 1930. Moreover the victorious Franco regime was to inflict massive reprisals on the defeated Republicans. In the year following the war some 9000 political prisoners were executed, while in the next three years another two million were subjected to varying terms of imprisonment, the final amnesties being granted only in 1966. At the same time countless others lost their jobs or were the victims of discrimination.

Atrocities on both sides left savage memories. The anti-Republican forces, having less appeal for the working classes, frequently resorted to terror as the quickest means of sub-jugating the regions they had overrun. As one farmer reported

In Segovia mass executions take place at night in the cemetery. A searchlight and two machine-guns are used. As a result of this summary procedure it often happens that men and women, who are not yet dead but only wounded, are thrown into the mass grave.

The Republicans, for their part, were guilty of reprisals, especially against prisoners from Legionary and Moroccan regiments, which had the worst record of atrocities. At the same time some 6000 priests and thirteen bishops were killed, thereby giving the Church a lot of emotional capital which it was not slow to exploit.

Such a gigantic disaster as the Civil War would seem to sug-gest deep-rooted causes. As with all wars, however, a distinction must be made between conditions and causes. On one hand there was the undoubted suspicion of the propertied classes against the Popular Front government and their fear that it would not be able to control extremist elements. But on the other hand there existed an organised movement to subvert the regime. Its most remarkable civilian figure was José Calvo Sotelo, who in 1935 had assembled the monarchic Nationalist Bloc, with its own private army and assassins. His sympathisers, however, extended far beyond the ranks of royalism, and included a number of prominent military leaders, notably Generals Emilio Mola, Francisco Franco and José Sanjurjo. Mola and his colleagues represented the greatest danger to the Republic, in that they could reasonably count on the support of a large section of the army, beside which even Sotelo's following would seem very small beer.

Franco was a career soldier who might very well not have become involved in politics, but for two things. First he achieved a great reputation in Spain as a result of his campaigns in Morocco in the 1920s, with the result that the various political factions that were active in Spain in the early 1930s were constantly trying to enlist him on their side. Franco's military prestige moreover resulted in his being given the Ministry of War in a short-lived cabinet in 1932, which brought him, however briefly, into the world of politics. Secondly, running parallel with these consequences of his own career, there was his growing concern, as a Catholic and conservative, with what seemed to him the inability of the Republican governments of the 1930s to keep the wilder elements of the Left in order. At the same time, like all conservatives, he had no desire to see the landowners expropriated and heavy taxation brought in.

It was the advent of the Popular Front that decided the generals to prepare seriously for a take-over of power; and it is possible that the murder of their fellow conspirator, Sotelo, by the 'forces of order' in July 1936 may have helped to convince them that the time had come to strike. On 18 July Franco issued a *pronunciamento* against the government from his post in the Canary Islands; and with Sanjurjo as overall commander, the three generals took control of officers' risings that broke out in the garrisons of Morocco and Spain. Sanjurjo's death in an air crash (20 July), followed by that of Mola (June 1937) soon left Franco as undisputed leader of the rebellion; indeed the Nationalists had declared him Chief of the Spanish State as early as October 1936.

The fact that the Nationalists had the majority of army officers on their side was a sufficient guarantee of ultimate victory, in that it would require remarkable courage and political conviction for an ordinary soldier to disobey the orders given him by his superiors. Most soldiers fought on the side of their officers. Foreign aid might partly have redressed the balance in favour of the Republicans, had not Britain restrained France from helping them (see p. 392). France was the country best situated geographically to influence the outcome, and her inaction was a major factor in the Republican defeat. It is true that the Republicans received considerable aid from Soviet Russia (including 242 aircraft and 731 tanks), but the Nationalists received over three times as much from Italy and Germany (including 763 aircraft and 950 tanks). The amount of foreign aid to each side was therefore roughly proportionate to the initial Spanish strength of each side before the foreign aid arrived. So, ironically enough, all that the foreign aid did was to give the war the same outcome, but at a much greater cost in life and property.

One important effect of foreign aid was to increase the importance on each side of those political groups whose aims were in closest accord with the donor nations. Thus Russian aid gave the Communists a totally disproportionate influence on the Republican side, while Italian and German help obliged Franco to take much more notice of the Falange, a fascist group founded in 1933 by Primo de Rivera's son. Nevertheless Franco remained firmly in control throughout the war, whereas the real power in Largo Caballero's Popular Front was disputed between the C.N.T., the U.G.T. and the Communists, the first two of which each administered large regions of Spain in accordance with their own principles.

The war officially ended on 1 April 1939. Superficially the regime that emerged bore the stamp of the Falange, some of whose ideas Franco had officially adopted in April 1937. But, like Miguel Primo de Rivera, Franco was basically a pragmatist, who had found it politically necessary to adopt certain standpoints. Franco's own Catholicism and his desire to placate his strong conservative supporters encouraged him to give greater concessions to the Church than the Falange would have wished. At the same time he avoided any appearance of fascist-type 'spiritual totalitarianism' that might alienate the Church. Nevertheless the regime was unquestionably a dictatorship. The right to strike had already been abolished by Franco's Labour Charter of March 1938. It is true that a Cortes was eventually established in July 1942, but it merely consisted of representatives of the various organs of state who could be relied on to endorse the government's policy. Similarly the administration was now filled with Nationalist ex-army officers who had been out of a job, and who owed everything to Franco.

CHAPTER FOURTEEN

'Good Intentions and The Road to Ruin'

International relations

CURRENT accounts of inter-war diplomacy tend to adopt a tone of worldly-wise cynicism. Phrases like 'Locarno honeymoon' and 'Stresa front' are delivered with a real or metaphorical curl of the lip that make these innocuous lakeside resorts seem the very essence of make-believe or duplicity. To appreciate the aims and dilemmas of the statesmen of the time, the reader must restrain himself from looking round the corners and seeing what the men of the time could not see. This is not to deny that good-will, gullibility and self-deception were often found hand in hand.

LES HOMMES DE BONNE VOLONTÉ

European diplomacy in the inter-war period presupposed two potential trouble-makers: Germany and Russia. It is true that Germany had been theoretically hobbled by the Versailles settlement, but Russia remained an ominous unknown quantity. The war had shown her current limitations, but she seemed to have a large potential that would presumably one day be harnessed to the government's wishes; and since these wishes ultimately seemed to be directed at the overthrow of other European governments, Russia was a subject for uneasy speculation.[1]

---

[1] See Appendix B, 'The Comintern and Soviet foreign policy'.

The countries that were not regarded as potential trouble-makers experienced mixed emotions between the wars. People who are uncommitted to an ideology tend to rise and fall in their own estimation. For much of the time they congratulate themselves on their independence of judgement and on their refusal to be enslaved by dangerous half-truths. At other times, however, they wonder whether life is not passing them by, and whether history will not view them as passive bystanders who missed their chance of contributing to human progress.

The thinking members of the so-called liberal democracies often found themselves in this predicament. The ideals they stood for were largely negative: 'freedom from this', 'freedom from that', 'freedom to do as one pleases, provided that it hurts no one else'. And all these were less satisfying to propagate than the impelling imperatives of Communism or Fascism, however illusory the benefits of these ideologies might prove to be. The freedom of liberal democracy so often seemed to be freedom for the strong to oppress the weak; and the democratic ideals which Wilson had championed from his Washington pulpit had less appeal against the background of Europe's more limited economic potential. Sceptics could pertinently ask whether the mass of the population would be so much better off under the capitalists of the inter-war republics than under the semi-autocratic monarchs of pre-war Germany and Austria. It was charges of this sort that occasionally drove liberal democrats into passionate bouts of political 'commitment', especially when a big match was clearly about to be played, where mere bystanders would come in for hard knocks from subsequent historians. The Spanish Civil War was to find mild men of the political centre shouting with uncharacteristic raucousness from positions much to the left or right of their accustomed places; and many people said and wrote things that they subsequently questioned or regretted. On the other hand perhaps an even greater number of those who said and wrote nothing during the war subsequently regretted their silence.

Whatever the shortcomings of 'the open society' in social affairs, many laymen felt that it was precisely some of the attributes of 'the open society' that needed to be more in evidence in international relations. It seemed to them self-evident that the open forum was preferable to secret diplomacy, and that a national policy of equal dealing with all nations within a collectivity of all nations was preferable to traditional alignments in rival power blocs. Generally speaking, therefore, it would be true to say that the League of Nations could claim much more loyalty from the general public than from the professional diplomats.

Indeed the statesmen who paid it most respect were precisely those who embodied or tried to embody popular idealism. Ramsay MacDonald was such a man, as Mr Malcolm Muggeridge has indicated in an unkind but evocative passage:

> He was the great exponent of the nations getting together round a conference table, he presiding. . . . 'I feel that looking forward into the future we must be inspired by a new faith of fraternity, with a new courage to follow large and stirring moral aims and supplement all our material achievements by things that belong to the spiritual excellencies of the peoples of the world.'
>
> . . . He introduced, it was felt, a badly needed element of poetry into the dreary wrangles which followed the Treaty of Versailles. When a journalist saw him early one morning, looking rapt, across the Lake of Geneva, and greeted him, he mournfully answered: 'The day is for the worrrld, but the morrrning is for myself.'
>
> The League reached its prime with him, expired with him too. . . . Twinkling lights of Geneva, noisy, smoky cafés of Geneva, Lake of Geneva beside which men walk unfolding newspapers in the wind – newspapers which tell of such a speech, such a resolution, such exchange rates and stock prices; conversation of Geneva, unceasing, ebbing and flowing like the sea's tide but never abating – theirs was a kingdom, once flourishing, now decayed and scarcely existent.[1]

The League of Nations could be no more than the sum of its parts, and was often something less. To hope that its existence would of itself breed restraint and good sense, where these did not already exist, was to attribute magical powers to institutions. Mixing vinegar and gas does not make champagne. But this was not to say the League did not have its uses. Irascible people, with a choice line in coarse phrases, sometimes find it helpful to count ten before opening their mouths when someone spills coffee down their trousers. Similarly the existence of

[1] *The Thirties: 1930–1940 in Great Britain* (Hamish Hamilton, 1940) pp. 62–3.

formal machinery to which states felt it advisable to show outward respect, could act as a delaying factor in an explosive situation. Tempers had time to cool off. But the readiness of states to respect this machinery depended entirely on their respect for the members of the League; and nothing in the machinery itself could restrain a nation that decided to ignore it. Collective sanctions depended entirely on the will of the member states to apply them; and collective action did not require a League to be effective.

Apologists for the League, however, pointed out that its membership was so vast that collective action would be like divine wrath: the mere threat would be an effective deterrent. Indeed it might well be the case that no one would need to do more than look fierce when occasion demanded. With no League, however, it would only be 'interested' nations that would band together to restrain a transgressor; and their smaller numbers would be less of a deterrent. But the fact had to be faced that there would always be some transgressors who doubted the existence of divine wrath; and perhaps with reason. Even with the League, the difficulty still remained that the less 'interested' members might not be prepared to do their share of collective action, if growling and teeth-gnashing was not enough to deter the wrong-doer. Although the expense and danger for each might be small, most of the members without a personal interest in the dispute preferred no expense to slight expense, whatever the long-term benefits. And so the short history of the League was characterised by the attempts of its members to evade their responsibilities.

Yet the League's apologists might still object that if the League did not do much good, then at least it did not do much harm; and that on balance the good outweighed the harm. This is a plausible argument in that, apart from anything else, the League had a number of ancillary bodies clustered around its Genevan headquarters, such as the International Labour Office, which performed useful work in collecting information and promoting international co-operation. To quote Mr Muggeridge again, 'White-slave and drug-traffickers had to suffer the humiliation of having their activities discussed by international bodies in the very town they had chosen for their headquarters'. While these bodies did not require the League for their existence, the League did at least give them a certain standing which they might have found more difficult to acquire by their own efforts. Turning, however, to the peace-keeping functions of the League, it could be argued that the danger was that the quasi-fiction of collective League action would tempt countries to throw away the old traditional life-belts of mutual agreements between 'interested' nations. The result might be that faced with a wrong-doer, the less 'interested' members would default, leaving the 'interested' members unprepared to act on their own.

In fact few members had illusions about the League. Most nations continued to maintain their traditional methods, side by side with their League membership; and it is probably true to say that the existence of the League made very little difference to the course of events in the inter-war period.

It has, however, been pointed out in the League's defence that it dealt successfully with thirty-five of the sixty-six disputes that were submitted to it in the course of its brief life, and that it only failed to resolve eleven. Yet only four of the thirty-five settled disputes had involved any fighting, and it could be argued that their solution by international action would probably have taken a similar shape, League or no League, just as it would have done with the other thirty-one. Inevitably, however, it is the eleven failures that are the most interesting, and it was precisely these that involved the real elements of danger for peace. The League's apologists often lament that all would have been well had the League been stronger; but to lament the League's weakness is to lament the problem of international conflict itself. If the League's powers had been stronger, and had it been able to enforce membership on all nations and to enforce collective action, the problem of international conflict would already have been solved, and the League would already have achieved its object. This would in fact have been the ideal solution, but like many ideal solutions, it was beyond the grasp of reality.

The early post-war years were marked by a whittling away of the League's limited powers on one hand, and by the

construction of traditional alliances on the other. Undoubtedly
the refusal of the American Senate to ratify Wilson's work was a
crippling blow to the League. Wilson disappeared from Europe
like some strange forerunner of Sunny Jim, the emblem of a
popular breakfast cereal whom visually he closely resembled.

> High o'er the fence leaps Sunny Jim.
> Force is the food that raises him.

Wilson had leapt over the traditions and susceptibilities of the
old European diplomacy with all the force of his lean-shanked
idealism. But if America's disappearance was a crippling blow
to the League, it was, more significantly, a disastrous blow to the
general chances of international stability in Europe. Soviet
Russia was now diplomatically an unknown quantity and had
to be counted out of any peace-keeping power structure that
might be planned for the immediate future; and indeed she
might prove to be a threat to it. Furthermore America had
disowned the guarantee that she had given to France in March
1919 to protect her against German aggression. Britain, likewise
a party to this guarantee, now became alarmed that she might
be called on to help France on her own; and rather than face
such a prospect, she let her responsibility lapse with that of
America. France realised that she was once more facing Germany alone. Germany would obviously try secretly to rearm,
as indeed happened throughout the Weimar period; and France
therefore tried to compensate for this desertion in the west by
constructing a poor man's substitute for the old pre-war
Franco-Russian alliance. The outcome was a series of treaties
with Germany's eastern neighbours, Poland (February 1921)
and eventually Czechoslovakia (October 1925), Romania (June
1926) and Yugoslavia (November 1927). Since Czechoslovakia,
Yugoslavia and Romania were already linked by a network of
alliances (August 1920–June 1921), it could be argued that
France now had a sizeable ally of sorts in this 'Little Entente';
though it was clearly no substitute for the help of Russia,
America or Britain. Even so, it was France's sense of isolation
that led her to take the initiative in occupying the Ruhr in 1923
(see p. 318); and indeed much of the stridency of the French

tone over reparations sprang from her sense of isolation, though her material need for reparations was real enough.

Certainly all powers, not only France, were resorting with increasing regularity to procedures outside the League machinery. Although Britain had initially accepted the Covenant's provisions with fewer reservations than most countries, America's withdrawal had made Britain suddenly conscious of her dangerous obligations as the foremost naval power within the League. This was reflected in her growing preference for traditional methods rather than League channels, despite MacDonald's brief bid to draw her on to the side of the angels. Stanley ('You can trust me') Baldwin was to express the secret feelings of many statesmen when he said: 'I do not myself know what the word "Internationalism" means. All I know is that when I hear it employed it is a bad thing for this country.'

The mid-twenties nevertheless saw a relaxation of tension between France and Germany, after the ex-Socialist Aristide Briand became French foreign minister in April 1925. People in the anxious years of the late thirties were to think back with nostalgic affection on the genially *louche* figure of Briand, a cigarette dangling from the corner of his mouth. He was then to seem like some indulgent bachelor uncle, a benign vision from a lost carefree childhood. Briand listened sympathetically to British suggestions for reducing tension; and the difficulties of the situation were eased by the presence of Gustav Stresemann at the German foreign ministry. Looking like every film-goer's idea of a typical German businessman, Stresemann had made a favourable impression on the French through his attempts to soften the German reaction to the occupation of the Ruhr; and the eventual outcome was that Germany became a member of the League (September 1926).

The real rehabilitation of Germany, however, had been made on the autumn-tinted shores of Lake Maggiore, where Briand and Stresemann, like a middle-aged Romeo and Juliet, brought the houses of Montague and Capulet together. The Locarno Conference (October 1925) found France, Germany and Belgium mutually guaranteeing the Franco-German and Franco-Belgian frontiers. But, unlike most honeymoons, the lawyers and insurance-brokers were already in attendance. Briand was careful to take out policies with Poland and Czechoslovakia, the signatories promising mutual assistance against the possibility of German aggression. Britain's Austen Chamberlain, while a witness to the marriage, was not prepared to be advance witness to a divorce. While signing the western frontier agreements, he would take no part in the eastern treaties; and Briand noted the fact with apprehension. Even so, Locarno inaugurated a feeling of optimism among statesmen, which received further encouragement when America joined with France in submitting to the League a plan for the renunciation of wars of aggression (August–September 1928). The limitations of this Kellogg–Briand Pact were obvious, and the fact that all the major powers, including Russia, had signed it by 1930 made little difference to the prospects of peace. But any American initiative in peace-keeping was welcome; and hope is generally more productive than despair.

The prospects of a lasting peace, however, were more accurately reflected in the vicissitudes of the disarmament campaign. The restrictions on German armaments in the Versailles settlement had been made in the context of a vague undertaking that there would be a general reduction in armaments on all sides, an undertaking which Ramsay MacDonald tried to make a reality in his couple of spells in office. But it was not until May 1926 that a preparatory commission met to explore the possibilities; and it was only in December 1930 that it produced a document for the eventual Disarmament Conference to discuss. Even then the document enshrined the failure of the commission to agree. France not only rejected any increase in German armaments, but refused to make corresponding reductions in her own armaments to achieve parity; and neither Germany nor Russia was prepared to sign. When the Disarmament Conference eventually met in 1932, it foundered on French insistence that disarmament be preceded by the establishment of an international peace-keeping force. When it next met in 1933, Hitler was in power.

In the meantime the League had received a shattering blow to its prestige when it failed to deal with the Japanese occupation of Manchuria, an integral part of China, in the winter of

1932–3. A commission of the League tried to compromise by suggesting that Manchuria be left in Japanese hands, but under nominal Chinese suzerainty. Although most League members welcomed this shabby face-saver with unconcealed relief (February 1933), Japan herself was not prepared to accept it, and withdrew from the League (March). This was undoubtedly the turning-point in the League's declining reputation.

THE GAMBLER

Hitler's arrival on the international scene brought a new voice to diplomacy. The inter-war years were the heyday of the domestic utterance for foreign consumption; and since so many of Hitler's home sayings took the form of harangues to mass rallies, the ears of foreign statesmen had to accustom themselves to an entirely different level of sound. Even the Russians had merely replaced the understatements of the old order with a doctrinal jargon that was equally muffling in its effect. Not so with Hitler.

In such a brief account of the speed and success of his diplomacy in the 1930s, it is impossible to give much indication of the extraordinary histrionic display that accompanied it. Just as Hitler's mass oratory was a strange mixture of careful calculation and emotional outburst – with calculation directing the outburst to maximum effect – so his handling of foreign statesmen would vary from quiet attentiveness to screaming rage, followed by periods of remarkable charm. At times his switching from tirade to charm showed something akin to the psychological awareness of the modern 'interrogator', who may achieve what he wants from a tortured prisoner by suddenly handing him a cigarette. At other times Hitler's attempts to impress visitors struck them as childish or vulgar. Alan Bullock well describes such as occasion, in September 1940, in a scene that is strongly reminiscent of Chaplin's *The Great Dictator*.

After he [Franco's emissary] had passed through the portico of the massive new Reich Chancellery, with its row of Doric columns, and crossed the vast marble gallery which stretched into the distance, he was ushered into the Führer's presence. Hitler had assumed the
N

role of the 'world-historical' genius for the occasion, exhibiting
the calm confidence of the master of Europe and leaning over
maps to demonstrate with assured gestures the ease with which he
could take Gibraltar. He greeted Suñer with the famous magnetic
stare, and walked across the room with carefully controlled, cat-
like steps. His glance took in whole continents, and he spoke of
organising Europe and Africa as a single bloc for which he would
proclaim a new Monroe Doctrine.[1]

If Hitler, like Chaplin, had had an inflatable globe, he would
surely have danced with it.

Hitler's coming to power gave the German republic new
objectives in the international field. From his public and private
utterances it is fairly clear that Hitler in 1933 had three principal aims in foreign policy. First he wanted Germany to expand
her frontiers to include all those Germans who lay outside them,
and this had dangerous implications for the Sudetenland,
Danzig and the German-speaking parts of Poland. Secondly
Hitler had emphasised Germany's need of strategic frontiers,
which meant that he was prepared to envisage the annexation
of areas that were not necessarily German. Lastly, and most
ominously, he maintained that Germany should acquire new
food-producing areas – a term clearly envisaging much larger
non-German areas. In February 1933, for instance, he told the
High Command that the only effective solution to Germany's
economic problems was the 'conquest of new *Lebensraum* in the
East and its ruthless Germanisation'. And from various other
statements, it is clear that these ambitions stretched as far east
as the Ukraine.

These aims, however, differed sharply from those of the army
leaders and the traditional conservative circles in Germany. The
generals and conservatives believed in the restoration of the old
Bismarckian frontiers and the undoing of the Versailles settlement. But Hitler was not interested in this as such. He looked
to the future, not the past, and saw no advantage in recreating
Wilhelmine Germany for its own sake. Like his Weimar predecessors, he believed that Germany could get nowhere without rearming; and as already shown (see pp. 333–4) he tried to create
the preconditions of rearmament by developing German heavy

[1] *Hitler. A study in tyranny* (Penguin, 1962) p. 603.

industry and building up a strong contented peasantry, which would both supply food and produce soldiers of high morale.

When Hitler came to power, Germany was already committed to attending the Geneva disarmament conference. Britain and Italy moreover were prepared to grant Germany equality in armaments. It was proposed that the victors of 1918 should strip themselves of arms to an agreed level, to which Germany would be allowed to rise. This was clearly a generous offer which Hitler could have refused only with bad grace. But Daladier's government feared that Germany would supplement her official allowance with secretly manufactured armaments and might thereby achieve a superiority. The French therefore proposed that the scheme should only come into operation after a four-year period during which Germany should remain officially disarmed.

This was Hitler's opportunity; and he took it with characteristic speed and resolution. He abandoned the conference (14 October) and withdrew Germany from the League. As yet, this was no more than a gesture; but a gesture from Germany, like smoke from a volcano, was seen as something ominous. The reality within was ominous enough in that the process of rearmament entered a new phase. Admittedly it was not until the inauguration of the Four-Year Rearmament Plan in September 1936 that the proportion of German revenue spent on armaments became appreciably larger than that of other countries; but taking the period March 1933 to March 1939 as a whole, Germany was to spend about half as much again on armaments as Britain and France put together. By 1938 in fact German arms expenditure represented 15 per cent of the gross national product (as compared with about 7 per cent in Britain). As against this, however, Germany in 1933 had a much greater leeway to make up; and despite her secret rearming under Weimar, she was still a long way behind France and Britain.

Hitler's foreign policy in the 1930s can be regarded as a series of gambles, in which he hoped each time that he could either rush or intimidate the other powers into acquiescence. Until August 1939 his hopes seemed largely justified. But this did not mean, as is sometimes suggested, the he had not envisaged what

he would do if any of the gambles failed to come off, or if Britain
and France decided to take armed action against him. There is,
moreover, strong evidence to suggest that by the end of 1936
Hitler regarded German rearmament as enabling Germany to
take the initiative against the west, if it should become too
obstructive; and that it was only the western powers' policy of
appeasement that made him think that a German initiative
might not be necessary.

These gambles might be listed as follows. First, the walk-out
from the disarmament conference and the League of Nations in
October 1933. Second, the institution of conscription in March
1935. Third, the military occupation of the Rhineland in March
1936. Fourth, the annexation of Austria in March 1938. Fifth,
the occupation of the Sudetenland in October 1938. Sixth, the
occupation of Bohemia and Moravia in March 1939. And lastly
the invasion of Poland in September 1939.

Until 1935 Hitler was prepared to move fairly gently. His
withdrawal from the League and the disarmament conference
in October 1933 had been a relatively modest gamble in that
Germany was not the first country to leave the League. Brazil,
and notably Japan, had already left, and the gesture was
becoming a commonplace. The disarmament conference, moreover, had been a purely voluntary venture, from which Germany was fully entitled to withdraw. It would nevertheless
raise serious doubts in the minds of other countries as to
Germany's future intentions. Among other things it automatically put paid to Mussolini's scheme of March 1933 for a Four-
Power Pact.

The scheme probably resulted from Mussolini's fear that
should Hitler occupy Austria he might revive Austria's claim
to the South Tyrol, where some 300,000 Germans were living
under the Italian flag. Mussolini had proposed that Italy,
France, Great Britain and Germany should become guardians
of the European peace and set about adjusting the Versailles
settlement where points of friction were apparent. Hitler had
in fact signed the pact in July 1933, but France was still hesitant,
and it still remained unratified when October's events killed it.

Hitler was nevertheless extremely careful to avoid making

any belligerent move towards his eventual objectives. Apart
from the limited extent of his rearmament, he probably had an
eye to the Saar plebiscite that was due to take place in January
1935. If he misbehaved in the meantime, it was possible that
France might be tempted to occupy the Saar with its valuable
mineral deposits; and France was already alarmed by the
Non-Aggression Pact which he had concluded with Poland, one
of France's allies (January 1934). Poland understandably
regarded Russia as her main potential enemy, since the million
Germans within her frontiers were as nothing compared with
the six million Ukrainians who might invite a Russian liberation.

Russia, however, had even more cause for alarm than France,
since Poland was Hitler's high road to the coveted black soil
regions of the Ukraine. Russia thereupon began to look to the
west, especially France, with a friendlier eye; so much so that
in September 1934 she became a member of the League of
Nations, rather like the village reprobate turning up at church
to pray for rain. Hitler could likewise expect little sympathy
from Mussolini. Indeed, when the Austrian Nazis murdered the
Austrian Chancellor, Dollfuss, on 25 July 1934, Mussolini sent
troops to the Austrian frontier to deter any attempt at a German
take-over.

After the Saar plebiscite, however, which gave the region to
Germany by a nine to one vote, Hitler could afford to be more
adventurous. Germany received the Saar in March; on 16
March Hitler announced universal military conscription,
thereby openly repudiating the disarmament clauses of the
Versailles treaty. This was a much more open gamble than the
withdrawal from the League two years earlier, and provoked
alarmed reactions in the east and west. Meeting at Stresa in
the following month, Britain, France and Italy agreed to resist
any attempt to change the Versailles territorial settlement by
force, while in May Russia and France made a rather nebulous
alliance. French foreign affairs were now in the hands of Pierre
Laval, who in spirit and appearance suggested a reincarnation
of Aristide Briand as the Devil might have wished him. Since
Laval secretly hoped for an eventual understanding both with
Hitler and Mussolini, 'the Stresa front' and the Russian alliance

meant little to him. Russia, by contrast, wanted to make the alliance a military reality, and it was symptomatic that she consolidated the alliance with a pact of mutual assistance with Czechoslovakia.

Once Hitler had publicly repudiated the disarmament clauses of the Versailles settlement, he had every reason to exaggerate rather than minimise the extent of German rearmament. It was clear to him that the western powers were not prepared to go to war to preserve the Versailles settlement as such. But it was far from clear what they would do if Germany actually started to annex territory. It seemed to Hitler that the bigger his forces appeared to be to the outside world, the greater would be the reluctance of the western powers to go to war against him. He accordingly told Sir John Simon that the German air-force was already as big as the R.A.F. (March 1935) – a piece of 'news' that so shook the British government that it brushed aside the principle of solidarity and set about bargaining with Hitler man to man. The result was the Anglo-German naval agreement of June 1935, which restricted the size of Germany's projected navy to a third of that of Britain, thereby putting Britain's *imprimatur* on Germany's unilateral breach of Versailles.

Under these circumstances the Stresa front was little more than a plywood façade from its inception. What split it, however, was the Abyssinian crisis. Mussolini was far and away the oldest established figure in European diplomacy. He bullied, patronised or smiled at his smaller neighbours with the arrogance of an oversize first-former kept down for a second year. From 1934 he had been intent on conquering Abyssinia. Apart from liquidating the memory of Adowa (see pp. 198–9) and bolstering his prestige, it is possible that Mussolini feared that the presence there of American speculators might involve Italy in another Tunis-type humiliation (see p. 198). The fact, however, that Abyssinia was a member of the League of Nations meant that the other European powers could not ignore the issue, as they would probably have liked. Accordingly, when Italian troops crossed the frontier in October 1935, the League declared economic sanctions against Italy. Only Italy's satellites, Albania, Austria and Hungary, voted against the declaration.

Indeed it is a measure of how times change that fifty years earlier Mussolini's action would have provoked little reaction except among those countries with adjacent interests; and now, thirty years afterwards, people are amazed that Europe did not operate sanctions more effectively.

The difficulty was that neither Britain nor France wanted to drive Mussolini into the arms of Hitler. The trade boycott was at best only partial, and failed to include oil, the one commodity on which the Italian air-force and motorised army was entirely dependent. There was similarly no attempt to close the Suez Canal to Italian ships, despite the permissive clauses in the International Statute of the canal. The sell-out came, however, in December 1935. Pierre Laval and the English foreign minister, Sir Samuel Hoare, secretly agreed to a plan by which Abyssinia was to be persuaded to abandon half her territory to Mussolini in return for an end to the war. But the plan reached the newspapers, and its flagrant betrayal of previous Anglo-French statements of principle was more than the British public would stand. The Cabinet disowned the plan, and Hoare resigned, George V jovially commenting: 'No more coals to Newcastle, no more Hoares to Paris.' Nevertheless by May 1936 the whole of Abyssinia was in Mussolini's hands, while elsewhere the example of the Hoare–Laval pact decided most countries to slacken sanctions, until in July 1936 they were officially lifted.

The collapse of the flimsy Stresa front, and the isolation of Mussolini, was a propitious time for Hitler to make his next move. After conscription and rearmament, the next logical step was the remilitarisation of the Rhineland. The Rhine was Germany's strategic frontier in the west, and militarily and emotively its full occupation meant much to her; but this would be a specific breach of the Locarno pact of 1925 in which Germany had undertaken to keep the Rhineland demilitarised, a pledge which Britain and Italy had underwritten. There could be no doubt that Britain and France fully realised Hitler's intentions. Yet Britain decided, after consultation with her service chiefs, that the Rhineland was not a 'vital British interest' and that its remilitarisation would not justify her going to war. Predictably enough, the Radical French government felt unable to act without British support; and like all French Radicals it was almost exclusively preoccupied with the forth-coming general election. The result was that Hitler sent troops into the Rhineland on 7 March 1936, and no action was taken against him. Yet, as Hitler later confessed:

> The forty-eight hours after the march into the Rhineland were the most nerve-racking in my life. If the French had then marched into the Rhineland we would have had to withdraw with our tails between our legs, for the military resources at our disposal would have been wholly inadequate for even a moderate resistance.

The reprieve from positive action that this unedifying episode seemed to represent for the western powers, was an uncertain one. The outbreak of the Spanish Civil War threatened to provide a cockpit for the rival ideologies of Left and Right, which might worsen relations between the European nations. Britain, anxious to prevent this possibility, encouraged the French government to ignore the public clamour that France should help the Republican Front. Accordingly in August 1936 France announced that she would refrain from intervening in Spain, if the other powers followed suit. Twenty-seven other nations, including Russia, Germany and Italy, agreed to follow this policy of non-intervention; but in varying degrees few remained strictly loyal to the agreement. Britain perhaps tried hardest to preserve this attitude, but there was a tendency in Britain for official circles to regard France as more likely to achieve the stability that Spain needed, and which the peace of Europe demanded. At the same time British business interests felt that Franco was less likely than the Republicans to be tempted to confiscate British assets in Spain. The British government was moreover anxious to come to terms with Mussolini on how the waves were to be ruled in the Mediterranean, and Italy was deeply if privately committed to supporting Franco.

In November 1936 Mussolini undertook to give substantial aid to Franco in return for co-operation in the western Mediterranean, and for 'benevolent neutrality' in the event of a general European war. In March 1937 Hitler was to come to a similar agreement in which German aid was made conditional on the promise of Germano-Spanish consultations in the event of a European war. Characteristically both agreements gave Italy and Germany economic concessions in Spain; and predictably enough the Spanish Civil War rapidly brought Mussolini and Hitler much closer together. Both to some extent had already isolated themselves from the other European powers, and their co-operation in Spain made Mussolini increasingly reliant on his partner. Indeed at the end of October 1936 Hitler and Mussolini had made a pact, establishing the Rome–Berlin Axis in which they agreed to follow a common policy in Spain and south-eastern Europe, and in which Germany also recognised Italian pre-eminence in the Mediterranean. Significantly enough, however, neither was as yet obliged to support the other in the event of a European war.

The Spanish Republicans for their part were now receiving considerable supplies from Stalin. Since the purges, the west saw in Stalin Caligula as well as Machiavelli; but it was Machiavelli they feared most. Despite Stalin's abstention from any attempt to subvert the Republican regime, his intervention increased the suspicion of the other European powers. This suspicion, if understandable, was unfortunate in that part of Russia's purpose was to strengthen the international 'Popular Front' against Fascism, and to discourage any tendency to appease the dictators.

Appeasement acquired an important evangelist when Neville Chamberlain became British premier (May 1937). Chamberlain looked deceptively like an angry bird, and Britain's youthful addicts of 'Toytown' might have thought that Mr Growser had stepped into their midst, umbrella and all. Chamberlain's voice, however, was more like that of a bishop's anxious secretary, and was to prove the truer harbinger of his policy towards Europe.

As far as the east was concerned, Hitler regarded both Austria and Czechoslovakia as areas for eventual German expansion. And here Hitler was helped by Czechoslovakia's domestic difficulties. In October 1937, members of the Sudeten German Party in Czechoslovakia complained that they had been attacked by the Czech police; and there were increased

*

demands from the Sudeten Germans either for autonomy or, preferably, for direct annexation to Germany. There is evidence to suggest that on 5 November 1937 Hitler told his principal advisers that he was in favour of occupying Czechoslovakia and Austria in the fairly near future, perhaps as early as 1938 or 1939. Allegedly he might then expel two million Czechs and a million of the less co-operative and less desirable Austrians, and then settle people from Germany on the land made vacant. This would also give him strategic frontiers and a much larger population from which to conscript soldiers. Hitler's generals, however, were strongly against such an early attack, since they did not feel that the army would be sufficiently strong to deal with the possibility of intervention by the western powers. Their views were nevertheless rejected (see p. 336), and in December 1937 German military plans were modified to give priority to the occupation of Czechoslovakia and Austria.

The question of Austria blew up sooner than Hitler probably wished. In January 1938 the Austrian police raided the headquarters of the Austrian Nazi Party, and found evidence that the Austrian Nazis were actively counting on a German annexation of Austria. Accordingly the Austrian Chancellor, Kurt von Schuschnigg, decided to confront Hitler by putting the issue of independence or annexation to a plebiscite. He expected that a large majority would vote for independence. So did Hitler, for the Führer thereupon intervened in Austria to secure Schuschnigg's resignation and the cancellation of the plebiscite. Moreover, having shown his hand, Hitler decided on the final step, and invaded Austria on 12 March. Predictably enough, he met with the usual shamefaced acquiescence from the other powers. The most likely objector had been Mussolini, but Hitler's new friend felt too isolated in Europe to risk losing German amity, and consequently had agreed to the *Anschluss* beforehand.

Hitler celebrated the *Anschluss* with characteristic rhetoric. On 9 April he told a Viennese audience:

> I believe that it was God's will to send a youth from here into the Reich, to let him grow up, to raise him to be the leader of the nation so as to enable him to lead back his homeland into the Reich. . . .

In three days the Lord has smitten them. . . . And to me the grace was given on the day of the betrayal to be able to unite my homeland with the Reich. . . . I would now give thanks to Him who let me return to my homeland in order that I might now lead it into my German Reich. Tomorrow, may every German recognise the hour, and measure its import and bow in humility before the Almighty who in a few weeks has wrought a miracle upon us.[1]

The blatancy of this move focused attention on Czechoslovakia, which was regarded as Hitler's next most likely field of activity. The French government reaffirmed its readiness to stand by the Franco-Czech treaty of 1925, Russia doing likewise in respect of the Czech–Soviet Pact of 1935. Chamberlain, however, was much more circumspect. He stuck to Britain's traditional refusal to guarantee the frontiers of Germany's eastern neighbours (see p. 384). All that he undertook was that if Germany attacked France as a result of an east European crisis, Britain would support France. Even so, Britain told Germany in May 1938 that she would do her best to persuade Czechoslovakia ' to show the utmost measure of accommodation to the Sudeten Germans'. And three weeks later she also warned France that she should not take British armed assistance too much for granted – which of course, took most of the resolution out of the French pledge to Czechoslovakia.

In the meantime the Sudeten German party had published demands at Karlsbad (April 1938) in which they insisted on full autonomy for the German regions, and a friendlier attitude on the part of Prague towards Germany. Hitler urged them to greater insistence and greater intransigence, and it seems highly probable that Hitler's purpose in exploiting the issue was not merely to annex the Sudetenland but to provoke a war with Czechoslovakia, in which the whole of the republic could be seized. Hitler not only wanted *Lebensraum* and a passage farther eastward, but if he was at any point opposed by Britain and France, it was essential that there should be no danger of a Czech stab in the back. Indeed on 28 May 1938 he spoke to his generals and close subordinates of the future possibility of a German extension of her North Sea coastline to include Holland and Belgium, and pointed out that such an operation would

[1] Bullock, p. 435.

require complete security from an attack from the rear. Though it is true that this operation was still largely a daydream, there was no reverie about the directive that he issued two days later. Plans were to be made for an invasion of Czechoslovakia to take place by 1 October at the latest – and he added: 'Events inside Czechoslovakia and elsewhere which create a favourable opportunity might lead me to take early action'.

Such events were to be provided by the Sudeten riots that started on 12 September. The Prague government had given way to Anglo-French entreaties to be conciliatory; and on 7 September President Beneš had announced his readiness to accept the Karlsbad points in their virtual entirety. Symptomatically the Sudeten German leader, Konrad Henlein, was embarrassed by the offer since, like Hitler, he really wanted German annexation, not mere autonomy. But he got out of the difficulty by alleging that a Sudeten-German deputy had been struck by a Czech police officer, and used the occasion to incite German rioting. This was Hitler's opportunity, and when the Czech government tried to suppress the riots he decided that this was the time to demand that the Sudetenland be given to Germany (15 September).

Hitler almost certainly counted on a Czech refusal and a war in which he would annex the whole of Czechoslovakia. But to his fury (one may assume), Chamberlain and Daladier succeeded in persuading Beneš of the necessity of surrendering all territory where more than half the inhabitants were German. If Hitler wanted war with Czechoslovakia, he certainly did not want it as yet with Britain and France. He was now faced with the problem of provoking Czechoslovakia once again, without provoking Britain and France. He therefore told Chamberlain at Godesberg (23 September) that Germany must be allowed to occupy the areas in question immediately, without waiting for a proper transfer under international auspices. Hitler was right in assuming that Beneš would not accept this – but he was unpleasantly surprised to find that neither would Chamberlain nor Daladier.

France ordered partial mobilisation on 24 September, while Britain mobilised her navy. Three days later Hitler was categorically told that if France was drawn into war Britain would support her. Nevertheless Chamberlain's whole attitude to the situation was quite apparent in his broadcast speech to the British people on 27 September: 'How horrible, fantastic, incredible, it is that we should be digging trenches and trying on gasmasks here because of a quarrel in a faraway country between people of whom we know nothing'.

At the same time, however, there was strong evidence to suggest that Russia was ready to intervene. Both Hitler's generals and Mussolini urged him to hold his hand, and it was in this mood of surprise and frustration that he agreed to discussions at Munich with Chamberlain, Daladier and Mussolini. The result was a face-saving compromise by which Hitler was to be allowed to occupy the German areas, but under the brief auspices of an international commission. He undertook at the same time to respect what was left of Czechoslovakia. Chamberlain told the cheering crowds at London airport that it was 'peace in our time'; but Daladier's reaction to the cheering crowds in Paris was more realistic: 'Ah, les * * * * !'

Given the state of allied rearmament, it is not difficult to understand why Chamberlain was prepared to push Czechoslovakia into making such extensive concessions, especially as he believed that Hitler's claim to the Sudetenland had quite a lot to recommend it. It must furthermore be admitted that Britain and France had clearly demonstrated that they were prepared to resist Hitler's subsequent Godesberg demands with force – though if they were uncertain as to the adequacy of their armaments, it is hard to know whether they regarded their ultimatum to Hitler as a gamble or a calculated risk. Russia seemed an uncertain quantity in that the western powers felt that they could not be sure of her participation, and if she did participate, the quality of her armed forces could only be guessed at. The fact that so many of her senior officers had been liquidated in Stalin's great purges suggested that the west could place little faith in Russia's strength as an effective fighting power.

Yet if the western attitude over the Sudeten crisis was understandable, their attitude to Hitler's occupation of Czechoslovakia in March 1939 presents the sympathiser with greater difficulties. Hitler felt cheated after Munich, and on Hitler's instructions

General Keitel set about drawing up plans for an all-out attack on France and Britain, tentative outlines being ready by 26 November 1938. Hitler was likewise prepared to entice Poland and Hungary with the prospect of territorial gains in the eventual dismemberment of Czechoslovakia; though Poland made it clear that she was not prepared to take Hitler's gifts at the price of Danzig or any of the German-speaking parts of Poland.

The dismemberment of Czechoslovakia came on 15 March 1939. Hitler crudely, but wisely, tried to make it seem the outcome of existing divisions in Czechoslovakia. It was true that Slovakia and the Carpatho-Ukraine were regions which resented the control of Prague. Nevertheless the Czech government discovered at the beginning of March that Germany was actively encouraging them to declare their independence. Although it acted quickly and removed the offending ministers from office, Hitler was now presented with a situation similar to that in Austria the previous year: if he was to act at all, he must act at once, before the Czech government could consolidate the fruits of its energetic action. He thereupon brought to Berlin the Slovak ex-premier, the barrel-like Mgr Joseph Tiso, and bullied him into raising the standard of Slovak independence. Tiso once admitted: 'When I get worked up, I eat half a pound of ham, and that soothes my nerves'. A whole pig, however, would scarcely have calmed him after the interview with Hitler. At the same time Hitler gave Hungary the go-ahead to occupy the Carpatho-Ukraine. Czechoslovakia was visibly breaking up – and this was Hitler's moment to strike. Using the crisis as a pretext, he declared the rest of Czechoslovakia 'under the protection of the German reich' (15 March); and two hours later the protector's troops swept over the frontier. Hitler's exuberance knew no bounds. Rushing into his secretaries' room, he kissed them, exclaiming: 'Children, this is the greatest day of my life. I shall go down in history as the greatest German'.

He had taken Europe by surprise. The speed of his action and the fact of Czechoslovakia's internal dissentions were gratefully seized on by France and Britain as justifications for inaction. Sir John Simon pointed out that no country could be expected to guarantee a nation which had ceased to exist, while the

French foreign minister, Georges Bonnet, commented: 'the renewed rift between Czechs and Slovaks only shows that we nearly went to war last autumn, to bolster up a State that was not viable'. Yet the enormity of what Hitler had done was much greater than what Britain and France had jibbed at in the previous September – and greater than what was eventually to send them to war in the following September (unless one assumes that they knew that most of Poland – and not just the German-speaking parts – were at stake in September 1939). Moreover the public outcry was proportionately greater; so much so that Chamberlain was convinced that the morale of the western powers could not withstand another blow of this sort.

Accordingly Chamberlain drew up a declaration of collective security which he presented to France, Russia and Poland. France and Poland were quick to agree, but Stalin made his acceptance conditional on France and Poland signing first; he did not intend to be left guarding eastern Europe on his own. Poland, however, was anxious to continue her former policy of steering a delicate course between Germany and Russia, and was therefore prepared to sign a declaration with Britain – but not with Russia. The outcome was that the only system of mutual security that existed in east Europe was the resultant Anglo-Polish pact of 6 April, and the old Franco-Soviet pact of 1935, which Georges Bonnet had foolishly if truthfully told Ribbentrop no longer had any effective significance (7 December 1938).

In the meantime a seasick Hitler, aboard the pocket-battleship *Deutschland*, threatened to bombard the Lithuanian coast unless Memel was ceded to him (23 March). Subtler methods were tried with Poland over Danzig; but when Poland refused to emulate Lithuania's compliance, Hitler ordered the drawing up of an invasion plan (3 April), with 1 September as the last suitable date for attack, so that the campaign should be over before the onset of the Polish winter. He told General von Brauchitsch that he intended to annex the whole of the north-western half of Poland.

Such an invasion, if it took place, would be the biggest gamble that Hitler had yet undertaken, since Britain was in the

process of giving to Poland a specific guarantee of help which
Chamberlain was later to reaffirm in parliament (10 July).
Nevertheless the existing Anglo-French record of help to eastern
Europe considerably reinforced Hitler's hope that his luck
might hold once more.

It seemed furthermore that Hitler might be able to count on
powerful support. In Russia the westward looking Maxim
Litvinov had been replaced by Vyacheslav Molotov as foreign
minister (3 May), and Hitler knew that Molotov had long been
the principal advocate of an understanding with Germany.
Stalin himself in fact had seriously entertained the idea of such
an understanding since 1935, but Germany's relatively friendly
relations with Poland had suggested that positive Russian
approaches would meet with rebuff. The changed situation in
1939 meant that it was now Germany's turn to seek the understanding, and on 20 May Molotov indicated that a specific
German proposal might be favourably received.

Hitler was nevertheless anxious not to spoil things by too
rapid an approach, and it was not until August that he dis-
played real eagerness. By that time he was determined on war
with Poland, and though he told Mussolini (12 August) that he
was confident that the western powers would not intervene, this
statement was probably intended to encourage Mussolini to
commit himself militarily. Mussolini, however, repeated earlier
pleas of unpreparedness, thereby making Hitler increasingly
reliant on Russian friendship. He sent Ribbentrop to Moscow,
and on 21 August Stalin agreed to a pact, signed two days later,
based on the mutual partition of Poland. Hitler also hoped that
the Russian alliance would convince Mussolini that if he joined
Hitler, there would be no danger of a Romanian or Turkish
attack against him – Russia would see to that. Mussolini, however, refused to be drawn, and after a four-day postponement of
the attack, due to the Duce's refusal, German troops crossed the
frontier on 1 September.

Even in August Hitler still had hopes that Britain and France
would not intervene. He attached quite a lot of importance to
the fact that even at the end of the month the French were not
evacuating the civilian population of the frontier provinces of
France, which to him seemed to indicate that they were not

contemplating war in the immediate future. But however real these hopes may have been, Hitler was clearly quite ready to take the risk of war with the west; and he knew that the risk was a very serious one. He believed, however, that if there was war with the western powers it would begin in a fairly anodyne way. He knew that Britain and France had told Belgium and Luxemburg that the Allies would respect their neutrality and that they would not set foot in Belgium and Luxemburg, unless invited. This meant that an Anglo-French attack on Germany would have to come from Lorraine and Alsace, and would come up against the heavy fortifications of the West Wall. In this way Hitler was confident that the western attack could be kept in check until Poland was defeated, when he could thereupon transfer all his forces to the western front. He would then by-pass the deadlock in eastern France by violating the neutrality of Luxemburg and Belgium, and invade France from the north-east.

CHAPTER FIFTEEN

Visions of Uniformity

War and reconstruction

I T is hard to think dispassionately about the Second World War. It cost the lives of over thirty million people, leaving the world with nearly forty million wounded to care for. Even for many of those who were physically unscarred, it brought great suffering; for as early as 1943 there were already thirty million homeless refugees in Europe alone. When peace came the industrial production of the Continental belligerents was less than two-fifths of what it had been before the war, and their agricultural production little more than a half. The overall financial cost to the world was something over £200,000 million, while a large part of eastern Europe lost its economic and political independence.

It was understandable that Europeans should regard Germany with extreme bitterness. It was much easier to identify the suffering of the war years with the activities of the Germans than had been the case in 1914–18. While the victors of 1918 were in no doubt as to where war guilt lay, it was nevertheless the nature of the war itself – the impasse, the mud, the lice and the frustration – that was chiefly remembered. In the Second World War, however, the enormities that first spring to mind are the extermination of six million Jews; the concentration camps; the deportation to Germany of 7·5 million foreign civilians as slave-labour; and the sadistic experiments on living captives. Even among military prisoners of war, two million Russians died in captivity and another million were never accounted for. The statements that stick in the memory are of the type that Himmler made in October 1943:

What the nations can offer in the way of good blood of our type, we will take, if necessary by kidnapping their children and raising them here with us. Whether nations live in prosperity or starve to death like cattle interests me only in so far as we need them as slaves for our *Kultur*; otherwise it is of no interest to me. Whether 10,000 Russian females fall down from exhaustion while digging an antitank ditch interests me only in so far as the antitank ditch for Germany is finished.

As early as November 1941 Göring had commented: 'In the camps for Russian prisoners they have begun to eat each other. This year between twenty and thirty million persons will die of hunger in Russia. Perhaps it is as well that it should be so, for certain nations must be decimated.'

Yet barbarity and indifference were not confined to the Germans. As early as 1939 the Russians massacred several thousand captive Polish officers. And in February 1942 the British air ministry stated that Bomber Command's attention 'should now be focused on the morale of the enemy civil population, and, in particular of the industrial workers'. On 30 May 1942 the first thousand-bomber raid on Cologne took place, until by the end of the war Allied air-raids had killed half a million German civilians and wounded 780,000 more. The attitude of the belligerents to killing civilians is well indicated in the communiqué from the Supreme Allied H.Q., describing the raid on Dresden in February 1945, in which some 25,000 people were killed. 'The Dresden raid was designed to cripple communications. The fact that the city was crowded with refugees at the time of the attack was coincidental *and took the form of a bonus*.'[1]

Although the sum total of cold-blooded barbarism was greater in the Second than the First World War, as always the greatest suffering was inflicted by military or economic 'necessity'. This was true not only of the vast majority of the killed and wounded, but also of the displaced. And although European military casualties were fewer than in the 1914–18 war, civilian casualties were much higher.

As in all wars, there were moments of relief and glimmers of positive achievement. Military necessity encouraged new discoveries and new techniques in technology and medicine, while

[1] Author's italics.

economic necessity did something to blur class divisions. The living conditions of German and British troops when not actually fighting were better than in previous wars; indeed the officer with a working-class background often found himself in comfort that he was later to remember with some wistfulness.

TABLE 29

	Peak strength	Battle deaths
Belgium	650,000	7,760
Denmark	25,000	3,006
France	5,000,000	210,671
Greece	414,000	73,700
Netherlands	410,000	6,238
Norway	45,000	1,000
Poland	1,000,000	320,000
U.S.S.R.	12,500,000	7,500,000
United Kingdom	5,120,000	244,723
United States	12,300,000	292,131
Yugoslavia	500,000	410,000
Bulgaria	450,000	10,000
Finland	250,000	82,000
Germany	10,200,000	3,500,000
Hungary	350,000	140,000
Italy	3,750,000	77,494
Romania	600,000	300,000

(Esposito, *Concise History of World War II*)

Post-war reminiscing likewise tended to preserve the happier or more amusing moments of wartime experience at the expense of the unpleasant. N.C.O.s were often later remembered less for their bullying than for their verbal gems: 'I want you to dismantle them guns, clean all the parts, and mantle 'em up again'. Many soldiers made acquaintance with countries and whole areas of life that had been completely unknown to them. But this of course cut both ways – and mostly the other way. People saw cruelty and degradation that they had thought beyond the bounds of human possibility.

THE ECONOMIC FACTORS

Unlike 1914, 1939 found the domestic economies of the belligerents partially prepared for war. Not only was there no

repetition of the 1914 run on the banks, but in several countries
the legal restrictions on the working day had already been
waived in the munitions factories; indeed 1940 brought a
seventy-two-hour week in certain key German industries.
Characteristically both Germany and Italy outlawed strikes,
other countries either providing compulsory arbitration or
obtaining gentlemen's agreements to avoid strikes. At the same
time co-ordinating bodies were set up to gear the whole national
economy to the war effort, while food and clothes rationing and
direction of labour (including women) were introduced with
increasing comprehensiveness. As a result the gross national
product of Germany increased by a fifth in the first two years
of war – despite the fact that two-fifths of her peacetime labour
force were now in uniform, but a large proportion of this
increase was destined to be scrap-metal on the battlefields of
Europe. In 1944 Germany was producing an average of two
thousand fighter planes a month, while Russia was producing
nearly twice that number, with the outcome that the standard
of living in Germany dropped by a quarter between 1939 and
1944, even though Germany was still living at the expense of the
occupied countries. It has been estimated that Germany obtained a tenth of her total wartime income from the occupied
countries; indeed in the case of France, Germany took half the
national revenue, and nearly a third of her food production.
Moreover, one in three of the German labour force was an
imported foreigner. This, however, could not prevent German
public expenditure increasing three and a half times in the war;
and although income tax doubled, it still covered only a
quarter of the expense.

TRIUMPH IN THE WEST

The German attack on Poland was a typical example of the
German *Blitzkrieg*: a rapid war of movement with massed tanks
supported by aircraft. The Germans, on the most conservative
reckoning, had 1640 aircraft against Poland's 935, only about
400 of which were modern. Indeed the pathetic state of Poland's
defences may be gauged from the fact that in the initial fighting
only one of the twelve Polish cavalry brigades was armoured,

the rest being horse-cavalry, armed with swords and lances. It was scarcely surprising that the effective campaign should be over in three weeks – for the Poles were also being pressed from the rear by the Russians.

Characteristically Stalin felt that advantage should be taken of the success of the campaign to occupy the remaining trunk of Poland that the Soviet-German pact had left intact. And so a Soviet-German treaty (28 September) gave Germany the remaining provinces of Lublin and Warszawa, while Lithuania was to be regarded as in the Russian sphere of influence. Russia's westward expansion, however, was not without its problems for Stalin. As Sir Ronald Storrs related:

> The [Russian] soldiers were greatly impressed by the variety of the goods displayed in the shops of Wilno, the poorest of the large provincial towns of Poland. . . . Gramophones, watches and pen-knives fascinated the Red soldiers more than anything else. Within two days the entire stock of cheap watches and penknives in the shops was sold out. . . . But the unhappy soldiers were not allowed to enjoy their purchases for long. As soon as these happenings reached the ears of the authorities, all the watches and penknives were taken away and strict orders were given that none of these . . . objects was to be taken into Russia, as they might demoralise the population.[1]

It was in Poland that Hitler was to inaugurate 'the Final Solution' for the Jews, little more than a year later. Eighty thousand were to be gassed in extermination camps in the first half of 1941, the process soon being accompanied by mass executions of Russian Jews after the start of Hitler's Russian campaign in June 1941. Thereafter the numbers grew geometrically, and it was in Polish camps that over a million were gassed in 1944 – 300,000 people in six weeks at Auschwitz alone. The horror of this record is further heightened by the self-congratulation with which it was perpetrated. Addressing S.S. generals in October 1943, Himmler was to say of the extermination of the Jews: 'To have stuck it out, and at the same time – apart from exceptions caused by human weakness – to have remained decent fellows, that is what has made us hard. This

---

[1] *A Record of the War, The First Quarter* (Hutchinson, 1940) pp. 349–50.

is a page of glory in our history which has never been written and is never to be written.'

Following the defeat of Poland, Hitler then offered peace to the western powers (6 October) – though it is hard to tell whether this was a genuine offer or merely a public gesture of 'being reasonable'.

The offer was in any case refused; and now that Poland no longer existed, the refusal logically committed the Allies to the aim of defeating Germany and demanding restitution of what she had taken. Britain had only four divisions in France, alongside some seventy-two French. And, apart from cautious patrolling of frontier territory, virtually nothing was happening on the western front; so the war there proceeded much as Hitler had anticipated.

In the meantime Russia tried to bully Finland into making an extensive treaty of mutual assistance, which Finland was unwilling to grant. Following what was probably a rigged 'incident', Russia invaded Finland on 30 November. Since Finland had only 175,000 men to hold back a million Russians, equipped with a thousand tanks and 800 aircraft, there could be no doubt as to the outcome.

The Finns nevertheless took advantage of the thick snow-filled forests to employ highly skilled encircling tactics in which large Russian contingents were captured or wiped out by much smaller Finnish units exploiting the restricted visibility. Some 200,000 Russians probably lost their lives, as against 24,000 Finns; but the overall odds were overwhelmingly against Finland, and she finally sued for peace. The settlement (March 1940) gave Russia the Karelian peninsula, Finland thereby losing her narrow defensible doorway.

The relentless character of Hitler's purpose was demonstrated four weeks later, when he invaded Denmark and Norway. He had a double purpose. Over two-thirds of Germany's iron-ore came from Sweden, and during the winter months when the Gulf of Bothnia was frozen, the ore was sent to Narvik and shipped via the west coast of Norway. This sea-route, however, was particularly vulnerable to British attack. With the

Norwegian and Danish ports in his hands, not only could Hitler protect it, but he would now have a string of naval and air bases from which to raid both Britain and her Atlantic shipping.

A curious by-product of this occupation was the replacement in Britain of Chamberlain by Churchill (10 May). Churchill, as First Lord of the Admiralty, had been responsible for the sorry British efforts to help Norway. But there was so much dissatisfaction in Britain with Chamberlain's pale over-gentlemanly conduct of the war that the public was ready to saddle Chamberlain with the responsibility. Churchill had the drive and personality of a war-leader – just as Chamberlain had the constructive vision and conscientiousness of a great domestic reformer. But Churchill's political judgement was shaky, and as long ago as 1916 Lloyd George had remarked that 'his steering gear is too weak for his horse-power'. Yet his defects loomed less important in wartime, when the objectives seemed clear, and energy the prime requisite. No one could doubt that he had been the most outspoken critic of the policy of appeasement, so much so that in 1940 he was popularly thought of as one of the few who had seen international issues for what they were in the late thirties. Whatever else he lacked, he had confidence in himself and the power of inspiring it in others. 'I felt as if I were walking with destiny and that all my past life had been a preparation for this hour and this trial. . . . I was sure I should not fail.'

On the same day as Churchill's appointment, Hitler launched his attack on France. When Hitler instructed the high command of the armed forces (O.K.W.) to prepare for an invasion of France, its plans were based on a Schlieffen-like right hook, in which 37 divisions were to cross the Low Countries, while a straight left of 27 divisions would smash through the Ardennes. But with the First World War in mind, this type of attack was what the Allies anticipated; they accordingly stationed the bulk of their forces along the Belgian frontier, ready to cross when Germany violated Belgian and Dutch neutrality. General von Manstein, however, had won Hitler over to the idea of making the main thrust from the centre through the forested hills of the Ardennes, where the Allies would not expect it. It would then be pushed forward to the Channel coast, thereby cutting the Allied forces in two – one part in Belgium and the other in the crook of the Maginot Line.

This and the rest of the western campaign was to be a triumph for German planning and execution. For the whole campaign the Germans had no more than 136 divisions, against the Allies' 135, while their tanks, which were to play such a decisive role, were numerically inferior to the Allies' (2439 to 2689). Only in aircraft and anti-tank weapons were the Germans better provided (3200 aircraft to the Allies' 1800). Once more, as in Poland, the *Blitzkrieg* method of massed armoured thrusts, closely supported by aircraft, was hard to combat except in kind, the French making the fatal mistake of scattering their tanks among infantry divisions as local tactical support. At the same time the British bombers had virtually no training in the tactical support of armies, for they had been regarded essentially as an independent strategic weapon, to be used on its own against enemy installations and industry.

As Cyril Falls points out, the lesson of the Polish campaign had been that

In a country of good roads, such as France or Belgium, it would be even easier to maintain the impetus of the armoured divisions than it had been in Poland, especially if supplies of fuel could be captured along the routes. A few voices and a few pens [had] called attention to the deductions to be made from the Polish campaign, but in general they were not understood.[1]

The plan might have had virtually a one hundred per cent success had not Hitler been worried lest his advanced detachments in the north be cut off from the rest. He therefore held back for a fateful two days, with the result that the British were able to evacuate 338,000 men from Dunkirk (27 May–4 June). He nevertheless assumed that once France had capitulated, Britain would come to terms. And by 14 June the Germans were in Paris.

In the south meanwhile, Mussolini had felt the issue to be

[1] *The Second World War, a short history* (Methuen, 1948) p. 19.

sufficiently settled for him to be able to slide off the fence and declare war on the Allies (10 June). The French Commander-in-Chief, General Weygand, was convinced that an armistice was essential; and on 16 June the premier Paul Reynaud resigned his office to Marshal Philippe Pétain, who was firmly resolved on making peace.

For many of the more simple-minded in France, especially on the Right, Pétain, the 83-year-old veteran of Verdun, was a symbol of all that was great and good in the French tradition. After the armistice of 22 June he was rapidly to become a kind of father-figure, presiding over a France which looked back to her 'glorious past' – the old France that was monarchic, agricultural and Catholic. Right-wing poets were to extol him in odes, of which the following is not untypical:

> Our father who stands before us, thy name be glorified, thy kingdom come, thy will be done on earth so that we may live. Give us our daily bread, though we give nothing in return. Give once more life unto France. Lead us not into false hope nor into deceit, but deliver us from evil, O Marshal.

This was yet to come, however, and in the meantime there was much soul-searching among Frenchmen as to what personal course of action should be theirs. One man who was in no doubt was the former Under-Secretary of State for War, General Charles de Gaulle, who left secretly for London on the following day where he broadcast an appeal to true patriots to join him in England. 'France has not lost a war, only a battle.'

The vast majority, however, saw no real alternative to staying behind and enduring the humiliations to come. Pétain lost no time in obtaining an armistice. Hitler insisted that the railway-carriage in which the 1918 armistice had been signed should be brought out from the transport museum in the château of Compiègne, and set up in the forest clearing where Germany had admitted defeat in 1918. The armistice which Hitler signed there (22 June) divided France into two parts: an occupied zone including all the northern half of France plus the Atlantic coast, and an unoccupied zone consisting of the south-eastern third of France. The French government (which took up new headquarters at Vichy) was to govern both parts; but its rule in the occupied zone could be directly subordinate to the wishes of Germany.

Britain and her empire were now Hitler's only opponents. His triumph was that of Napoleon after Tilsit; indeed he went to Paris to gaze on the tomb of that other gambler who had become master of Europe. Looking down on the red porphyry, he later described it as 'the greatest and finest moment of my life'. Like Napoleon he would have been content to have a *modus vivendi* with Britain, as was demonstrated on 19 July, when he publicly offered her peace. The terms he had in mind would in fact have deprived Britain of few of her possessions, notably her mandate over Iraq and her control over Egypt. But Churchill made it clear (3 August) that Britain would not consider peace unless Germany first restored freedom to Czechoslovakia and all the nations she had occupied thereafter.

Hitler was therefore obliged to examine the possibilities for forcing peace on Britain, rapidly coming to the conclusion that his success would depend on how completely the *Luftwaffe* could establish air supremacy over Britain. The German navy was no match for the British navy, and the hazards of a Channel crossing, if one were unavoidable, could only be overcome if German air supremacy was overwhelming, or if the British were intimidated into making no attempt to defend themselves. For this reason 'Operation Eagle' took priority – the elimination of the R.A.F., especially its fighters. So on 13 August the *Luftwaffe* attacks were transferred from shipping and docks to airfields and aircraft factories.

As the Germans anticipated, the strength of the British defence lay in the Spitfire, which outclassed the Messerschmitt in movement and firepower. The R.A.F. had about 720 Spitfires and Hurricanes in operation, while the Germans had about 2500 bombers and fighters at constant readiness in France, the Low Countries and Norway, with another thousand in a state of near-readiness. The greatest danger for Britain was that she would lose too many of her pilots; for while under Lord Beaverbrook's unorthodox drive the aircraft factories were keeping up their fighter strength, a trained fighter-pilot took months to replace. The R.A.F., however, had the best early-warning system in the world, thanks to the British discovery and development of radar and the establishment of a network of swift communication by which radar reports were digested at head-quarters and passed on to the pilots. The Luftwaffe, on the other hand, were badly informed, over-estimating the degree to which their bombing had crippled Fighter Command.

For this and for other reasons the Germans decided to transfer the bombing to London, which had the triple attraction of being the seat of government, the largest port and the largest centre of population. Fewer British fighters, however, were needed to ward off concentrated attacks on London (7–15 September) than would have been required to ward off multiple attacks on scattered airfields, the result being that Fighter Command had the opportunity of resting some of its over-worked pilots and of reconditioning their aircraft. Indeed the outcome was that a massive German attack on London on 15 September was repulsed with heavy losses, and from then onwards the Germans acknowledged British air supremacy over south-east England.

THE GREATEST GAMBLE

The alternative to an armed subjugation of Britain was economic strangulation. Britain's dependence on sea-borne trade meant that there was a strong case both for building up Germany's stock of U-boats and for striking at Britain's control of the Suez Canal. Hitler's mind, however, was fixed on an invasion of Russia, and he was not prepared to take either of these measures with much seriousness – at least not until later.

His obsession with *Lebensraum* in eastern Europe and the attraction of the Caspian oil-fields were powerful stimulants to his Russian schemes. He may also have felt that a Communist power with the strength of Russia might turn on Germany when he was less well prepared to meet it. But there was little indication of this. Stalin had told the British ambassador, Stafford Cripps, that although he feared that Hitler might attack Russia in 1941, Russia had no desire to provoke him. Hitler, however, was irritated by various examples of what he regarded as Soviet non-co-operation. Russia had not only annexed Latvia, Lithuania and Estonia without consulting Hitler (June–August 1940), but had also taken Bessarabia and Northern Bukovina from Romania (June 1940). Furthermore in November Russia informed Hitler that she intended annexing Finland. This and other difficulties convinced Hitler that there was no point in dclaying the attack on Russia, the outcome being that on 18 December 1940 he signed the outline plan of 'Operation Barbarossa'. It was initially proposed that it should be launched on 15 May 1941, so that it should be completed before the Russian winter set in. But the attack was delayed a month, as a result of unwelcome developments in the Balkans.

To Hitler's annoyance, Mussolini had launched an invasion of Greece (28 October 1940); and as Hitler feared, it was not long before Mussolini required help. Mussolini's humiliation was the greater for having acted against Hitler's known wishes. Just before the invasion, Mussolini had told his son-in-law, Galeazzo Ciano: 'Hitler always faces me with a *fait accompli*. This time I am going to pay him back in his own coin. He will find out from the newspapers that I have occupied Greece.' Churchill sent part of Britain's small Egyptian force to Greece (5 March), with the result that Hitler felt obliged to send German troops to clear them out (6–30 April). This in fact held up 'Operation Barbarossa' for a month, as did a further distraction in Yugoslavia. It should be understood that Hitler had bolstered the Axis position in the Balkans by securing the adherence of Bulgaria (1 March 1941) and Yugoslavia (25 March) to the Axis. But a number of young Yugoslav officers rebelled against being tied to Germany, their defiance taking the form of a provisional government in Belgrade, which nevertheless proclaimed its loyalty to King Peter. Understandably, though mistakenly, Hitler decided on immediate action to crush this challenge to Axis power in the Balkans. Sending in troops on 8 April, he smashed the revolt within ten days; but the time and energy had been spent at the expense of the Russian campaign.

The character of the German attack on Russia was foreshadowed in Hitler's address to his military leaders. 'This struggle is one of ideologies and racial differences and will have to be conducted with unprecedented mercilessness and unrelenting harshness.' And later: 'There's only duty: to Germanise this country by the immigration of Germans and to look upon the natives as redskins.'

The campaign started on 22 June, without any preliminary declaration of war. Hitler committed just over 3 million men, together with half a million Finns, and a quarter of a million Romanians. Initially he had 3350 tanks, and 2500 aircraft, while against him the Russians probably had about 2,300,000 men in the west, and possibly as many as 10,000 tanks and 7000 aircraft, most of them superseded types. As a result, moreover, of Stalin's purges, the Russians were severely handicapped through having inexperienced senior officers, who made the familiar mistake of distributing their resources equally over the whole front, without any concentration that could be swung against the spearhead of the German *Blitzkrieg*. This was especially disastrous in view of the fact that German armour was now massed in panzer groups (equivalent to an army), with even greater hitting power than before.

The German army high command were anxious for an all-out drive on Moscow which they thought would finish the war. Hitler, however, wished to give priority to the north and south flanks, and instructed the central army group to halt and send reinforcements to the southern army group. 'The most important objective to attain before the onset of winter is not the capture of Moscow but the taking of the Crimea, the industrial and coal-mining areas of the Donets basin and the cutting off of Russian oil supplies from the Caucasus. In the north it is the locking up of Leningrad and the prevention of union with the Finns.' 'My generals know nothing about the economic aspects of war.'

Yet by 6 September, having second thoughts, he decided to compromise with the recommendation of his generals and launch an attack on Moscow that would comprise other objectives as well, including Leningrad. The northern and southern groups were now required to send reinforcements to the centre, which after six weeks' enforced idleness was able to move into action. As the vast columns surged forwards, the first snow began to fall. By the middle of November, in the words of General Guderian,

ice was causing a lot of trouble since the calks for the tank tracks had not yet arrived. The cold made the telescopic sights useless. In order to start the engines of the tanks, fires had to be lit beneath them. Fuel was freezing on occasions and the oil became viscous. . . . Each regiment had already lost some 500 men from frostbite. As a result of the cold the machine guns were no longer able to fire.[1]

By almost superhuman effort the Germans managed to drag themselves within sight of Moscow. But the delay of the previous months proved fatal. The Germans were not equipped for the winter, having assumed that the campaign would be over beforehand. The cartoon-figure 'Winter Fritz' was born, 'wrapped up in women's shawls and feather boas stolen from the local population'. Furthermore the Russians had been following a scorched-earth policy, destroying everything they left behind, while Stalin had had time to rush up reinforcements to meet the German attack. As increasing quantities of tanks and vehicles broke down with frozen engines, the commanders claimed that the offensive would have to be postponed.

It was at this point that General Zhukov launched a Russian counter-attack (6 December). Although the Russians had already suffered huge casualties, they still maintained over 280 divisions on the western front, with reinforcements coming up in even greater strength. This was a time of agonising decision for Hitler. Hitherto his armies had known nothing but victory; retreat would be a tremendous blow to their prestige. But prestige now meant less to the divisions floundering in the desolate reality of the snow, with the prospect of a mounting hail of blows from a growing enemy. Hitler finally agreed to a large-scale withdrawal (15 January), but insisted on a dogged defence of the new German positions, with the result that the Russian advance was brought to a halt (7 May). The effect of this winter campaign on Germany was somewhat ambivalent. On the one hand, Hitler's decision to stand and fight was later recognised as the right decision, whereas the generals' demand for a general withdrawal would have probably led to a rout with

---

[1] *Panzer Leader* (Michael Joseph, 1952) pp. 189–90.

enormous losses of equipment. But on the other hand Walther
von Brauchitsch had resigned as commander-in-chief of the
army (19 December); and Hitler, more convinced than ever of
his own superiority of judgement, assumed the post himself.
Thereafter it became almost impossible for his military advisers
to influence his decisions – which was to prove fatal in the later
western campaigns of 1944–5.

THE SECOND MISTAKE

In many ways December 1941 was the turning point of the war.
Not only did Hitler encounter his first military reverse, but he
was rash enough to declare war on the world's leading power,
the United States. The situation arose out of the activities of the
Japanese, whose skill at beating the west at its own game led
them to challenge American supremacy in the Pacific.

In November 1936 the Germans had struck up a vague
understanding with their Asiatic counterparts, which led them
to hope subsequently that the Japanese could be prevailed upon
to attack the British base at Singapore. Hitler certainly had no
desire to be involved in war with America; indeed Pearl
Harbor came as even more of a bombshell than the Italian
invasion of Greece. As in the case of Greece, however, Hitler
was himself partly to blame for the Japanese secrecy about their
intentions in the Pacific, for the German attack on Russia had
come as an unwelcome surprise to them. Having concluded a
neutrality treaty with Russia (April 1941), the last thing they
wanted was to be drawn into a Russo-German contest. And
indeed they managed to avoid entanglement until August 1945,
an example which Hitler would have been well advised to try
to follow in respect of America.

As it was, however, he thought that he was making the best
of a bad job by declaring war (11 December). Later events were
to show that this was a mistake that ranks only with the Russian
campaign as an explanation for Germany's eventual downfall.

Admittedly America and Britain had been drawing closer
together during the past year. Yet the meetings between
Churchill and President Roosevelt, begun in August 1941, had
not succeeded in committing America to armed intervention

against Hitler. British readers had looked hopefully at the succession of photographs that showed the two leaders enjoying a succession of private jokes, Churchill, like a ferry-man, in an assortment of service caps, and Roosevelt, elegantly cloaked, like an advertisement for a rather expensive brandy. It is true that America had been supplying Britain with goods on long credit terms ('lend-lease') since March 1941; and it is probable that the increase of American shipments to Britain in American and neutral ships had served to increase Hitler's doubts concerning the effectiveness of U-boat warfare. But such aid was infinitesimal as compared with the dangers to Germany that armed American intervention might entail. One compensating advantage was that after war had been declared on America, U-boats could now make indiscriminate attacks on shipping heading for Britain; and this, plus U-boat successes in 1941, may have helped to convert Hitler to an all-out U-boat construction campaign in 1942.

Within a month of America's involvement in hostilities, the various nations that were at war with the Axis agreed to fight together and make no separate peace (1 January 1942). These 'United Nations', to the surprise of many, now numbered twenty-six, though most were third-class powers, making relatively little contribution to the overthrow of the Axis. Their names to the European were mainly suggestive of postage-stamps and flags of convenience, though the British radio-listener was now treated to all their national anthems before he went to bed. They also subscribed to the 'Atlantic Charter', a rather vague declaration of democratic ideals, which Roosevelt and Churchill had drawn up in August 1941. The relevance of these ideals to the political reality that existed in some of these states was about as close as the Thirty-Nine Articles to the beliefs of many of the men listed as 'C of E' in the British army.

Of more immediate importance, however, were the Anglo-American discussions on the future conduct of the war. America persuaded Britain to accept the institution of a Combined Chiefs of Staff which would co-ordinate campaigns on an international basis. But from Britain's point of view the most encouraging

o

outcome of the talks was the fact that America was still prepared to regard Germany as the dominant member of the Axis,
to be eliminated first, despite the more direct relevance of
Japanese aggression to America's immediate interests. It was
also agreed that Britain's main commitment, apart from the
Far East and the sea, was to be in North Africa and the strategic
bombing of German-occupied Europe.

Russia in the meantime was demanding a Second Front
(May 1942). Roosevelt was amenable to these demands, personally favouring an attack on northern France; but Churchill
believed in the 'backdoor to Europe' approach as he had in
1915. While recognising that an invasion of northern France
was an ultimate ideal, he believed that this would only be
effective after Germany had been greatly weakened in subsidiary campaigns. Indeed, with the vast resources of the United
States at the Allies' disposal, the 'wearing-down' type of war
had its attractions for the powers which did not own these
resources. Those who did, however, tended to prefer swifter and
less expensive methods, especially since the final struggle with
Japan would follow afterwards. Yet, given the fact that a French
campaign would not be feasible before 1943, and given
Roosevelt's wish to engage American troops against Hitler
before then, Churchill was able to persuade the Americans to
agree to an Anglo-American attack on north-west Africa for the
autumn of 1942.

Set against the slaughter and cold of the war in eastern
Europe, the Anglo-American discussions must often have
seemed to the Russians strangely academic. It is impossible to
convey the misery and suffering on both sides that accompanied
the repulse of the German attempt to occupy the Caucasian
oil-fields in 1942. Even when shorn of the legend and propaganda that surrounds it, the Stalingrad campaign (November
1942–January 1943) remains an appalling monument to the
heroism and fatuity of human action.

There was no doubt that the Soviet army had gained enormously in technique and confidence. Although still preferring
broad front advances of shallow depth, they were nevertheless
prepared to experiment with the German armoured punch, as
at Belgorod (August 1943), which opened the way to the

Dnieper. The Germans moreover were now in the difficult situation of falling back on land devastated by the Russians during their withdrawal of 1941, while Hitler's determination to yield as little ground as possible prevented them retiring to more easily supplied positions. Indeed Hitler's obstinacy entailed enormous losses of men – 900,000 from July to October 1943 alone, and after the Allied invasions of Italy, then France, the reinforcements that Germany could send to Russia were severely limited. By as early as December 1943 the Germans had only three million troops in Russia to face 5·7 million Russians enjoying complete superiority in tanks and artillery. The Germans likewise noted that the wider tracked Russian tanks were able to make headway where their own were hopelessly bogged in mud, the same being true of the American-built lorries which were being sent to Russia in large quantities. Consequently by July 1944 the Russian advance in the centre had reached the outskirts of Warsaw; while farther south, Romania changed sides and declared war on Germany (August), with Bulgaria following suit a fortnight later.

The German presence in Russia had not only brought the death and destruction of a merciless war, but it had also seen the systematic extermination of Jews and Communist officials. Although the total was under a million, and small compared with the victims of the gas-chambers of Central Europe, eyewitness accounts testify to both the brutality and the indifference with which the work was done.

The people who had got off the trucks – men, women and children of all ages – had to undress. . . . An old woman with snow-white hair was holding a one-year-old child in her arms and singing to it and tickling it. The child was cooing with delight. . . . The father was holding the hand of a boy about ten years old and . . . pointed to the sky, stroked his head and seemed to explain something to him. . . .

I walked around the mound and found myself confronted by a tremendous grave. . . . The pit was already two-thirds full. I estimated that it contained about a thousand people. I looked for the man who did the shooting. He was an S.S. man, who sat at the edge . . . his feet dangling into the pit. He had a sub-machine-gun on his knees and was smoking a cigarette.

O 2

The people, completely naked, went down some steps and clambered over the heads of the people lying there to the place to which the S.S. man directed them. . . . Then I heard a series of shots. . . . The next batch . . . went down into the pit.[1]

Compared to this, the North African desert campaign might seem to be gentility itself, for the comparative absence of a civilian population reduced it to a straightforward contest between opponents, with little or no emotional attachment to the areas fought over. At the same time it also saw the confrontation of two of the most able commanders that the war produced – Erwin Rommel and Bernard Montgomery. Nevertheless there was no lack of human suffering.

The Anglo-American commitment to a North African campaign resulted in General Montgomery being sent to Egypt with increased supplies. In October 1942 he launched a gigantic offensive at El Alamein, which was followed by Anglo-American landings along the Moroccan and Algerian coasts a fortnight later. Very rapidly Montgomery drove Rommel's forces back through Libya, until in April 1943 contact was made in Tunisia with the Anglo-American forces. Within a month the Axis forces surrendered with the loss of 240,000 prisoners, bringing their total casualties during the North African campaign to 950,000, a number greatly in excess of Allied losses.

North-west Africa had also been the scene of the Casablanca Conference (January 1943) between Roosevelt and Churchill, at which the Allies agreed to 'unconditional surrender' as their peace terms. From a practical point of view, the most important decision of the conference was to give a partial endorsement to Churchill's plan for an invasion of Italy. True to his Dardanelles past, Churchill had what was probably a misguided predilection for 'the back-door to Europe', and spoke rather speciously of 'the soft under-belly of the Axis' – which in fact was heavily protected by the Apennines and the Alps. Fortunately for the future of the war, Churchill soon accepted that this invasion should be followed by a much more substantial invasion of northern France, provisionally fixed for May 1944.

[1] Reproduced in William Shirer, *The Rise and Fall of the Third Reich* (Pan Books, 1964) pp. 1143–4.

Landings were made in Sicily in July 1943 – the immediate effect being a change of regime. In Churchill's words:

> Mussolini now had to bear the brunt of the military disasters into which he had, after so many years of rule, led his country. He had exercised almost absolute control and could not cast the burden on the Monarchy, Parliamentary institutions, the Fascist Party, or the General Staff. All fell on him. . . . So durable however was the impression of his authority and the fear of his personal action in extremity that there was prolonged hesitation throughout all the forces of Italian society about how to oust him. Who would 'bell the cat'? Thus the spring had passed with invasion by a mighty foe, possessing superior power by land, sea, and air, drawing ever nearer.
>
> During July the climax came. Since February the taciturn, cautious-minded, constitutional king had been in contact with Marshal Badoglio, who had been dismissed after the Greek disasters in 1940. He found in him at length a figure to whom he might entrust the conduct of the State. A definite plan was made. It was resolved that Mussolini should be arrested on July 26, and General Ambrosio agreed to find the agents and create the situation for this stroke. The General was aided unwittingly by elements in the Fascist Old Guard, who sought a new revival of the party, by which, in many cases, they would not be the losers. They saw in the summoning of the highest party organ, the Fascist Grand Council, which had not met since 1939, the means of confronting the Duce with an ultimatum. On July 13 they called on Mussolini and induced him to convene a formal session of the Council on July 24.[1]

As a result of this meeting, Mussolini was duly dismissed and imprisoned (25 July), Marshal Badoglio forming a new government. Heavy bombing moreover induced Badoglio to ask the Allies for peace (2 September), with the result that Italy changed sides within six weeks and declared war on Germany, by which time the Allies had occupied a third of the peninsula. After this speedy beginning, however, the campaign became a slow grind over difficult mountainous country against stubborn German resistance. Indeed the pace of the advance may be measured by the fact that it was still incomplete when the war in Europe ceased in May 1945.

[1] W. S. Churchill, *The Second World War*, v (Cassell, 1952) pp. 40–1.

NEMESIS

'Operation Overlord', the gigantic Second Front in France that the Russians had been demanding for so long, was at last launched on 6 June 1944 against the Caen–Cotentin coastline. The success of Anglo-American action against U-boats in 1943 had enabled America to build up her manpower in Britain to 1,300,000 by May 1944, thereby making Britain the springboard for the main attack. The Germans had only 58 divisions in France, of which a mere 24 were fully comparable to what the Allies were launching against them. Furthermore the Germans were slow to arrive in the battle area in strength, partly because Hitler insisted that all moves be referred to him, and partly because the Germans, still fearing an attack in the Pas-de-Calais, did not wish to commit too much of their strength to western France.

Hitler's fanaticism, however, and his suspicion of his military subordinates had been daily gnawing at his powers of effective leadership. His distrust and contempt for expert advice had been greatly increased by the unsuccessful attempt on his life by a group of army officers on 20 July. Convinced that Hitler was leading Germany to destruction, these officers arranged for one of their number, Count von Stauffenberg, to place a briefcase containing a time-bomb near to Hitler at a military conference.

[Stauffenberg] then left the room unobtrusively on the excuse of a telephone call to Berlin. He had been gone only a minute or two when, at 12.42 p.m., a loud explosion shattered the room, blowing out the walls and the roof, and setting fire to the debris which crashed down on those inside.

In the smoke and confusion, with guards rushing up and the injured men inside crying for help, Hitler staggered out of the door on Keitel's arm. One of his trouser legs had been blown off; he was covered in dust, and he had sustained a number of injuries. His hair was scorched, his right arm hung stiff and useless, one of his legs had been burned, a falling beam had bruised his back, and both ear-drums were found to be damaged by the explosion. But he was alive. Those who had been at the end of the table where Stauffenberg placed the briefcase were either dead or badly wounded. Hitler had been protected, partly by the table-top over which he was leaning at the time, and partly by the heavy wooden support on which the table rested and against which Stauffenberg's briefcase had been pushed before the bomb exploded.[1]

Henceforth no one could claim his confidence. Indeed it was partly as a result of his over personal control of the campaign that Paris fell to the Allies on 25 August. Three weeks later American forces had reached the German border.

Hitler's position was desperate. The capitals of his eastern empire were rapidly cut off: Warsaw (2 October), Belgrade (20 October) and Budapest (27 December). And two days later Hungary went the way of Romania and Bulgaria, declaring war on Germany; indeed Hungary, like Poland and Yugoslavia, was now in the hands of a Soviet-sponsored Communist government. Hitler's position was very much like that of a Shakespearian king, assailed on all sides by breathless messengers bringing bad tidings. Yet his frenzied belief that all could yet be recovered made him refuse to consolidate his resources.

On 7 March 1945 the first American troops crossed the Rhine; and once across, the Allies had 85 divisions against Germany's 26. The Russians had meanwhile crossed the Oder, and were breaking through the German defences masking Berlin.

It was in Berlin, in an underground bunker in the garden of the Chancellery, that Hitler still continued to direct the war. His hopeless belief in ultimate success had given way to a terrifying nihilism, as was evident on 19 March when he ordered the destruction of everything that lay before the enemy.

If the war is to be lost, the nation will also perish. This fate is inevitable. There is no need to consider the basis even of a most primitive existence any longer. On the contrary, it is better to destroy even that, and to destroy it ourselves. The nation has proved itself weak, and the future belongs solely to the stronger eastern nation. Besides, those who remain after the battle are of little value; for the good have fallen.[2]

On 29 April when Russian troops were already fighting in the suburbs of Berlin, he dictated his political testament:

After six years of war, which in spite of all set-backs will go down one day in history as the most glorious and valiant demonstration

[1] Alan Bullock, *Hitler*, pp. 743–4.   [2] Reproduced in Bullock, pp. 774–5.

of a nation's life-purpose . . . I have decided . . . to choose death at
the moment when I believe the position of Führer and Chancellor
can no longer be held. . . . From the sacrifice of our soldiers and
from my own unity with them unto death will spring up in the
history of Germany the seed of a radiant renaissance of the
National Socialist movement and thus of the realisation of a true
community of nations.

Significantly it ended:

The efforts and sacrifice of the German people in this war have
been so great that I cannot believe they have been in vain. The
aim must still be to win territory in the east for the German
people.[1]

On the following day he committed suicide – two days after
Mussolini had been killed by Italian partisans. Hitler's body
and that of his newly married wife, who had taken poison, were
carried into the Chancellery garden, where, in Mr Alan
Bullock's words:

the bodies were laid in a shallow depression of sandy soil close to
the porch. Picking up the five cans of petrol, one after another,
Hitler's S.S. adjutant poured the contents over the two corpses
and set fire to them with a lighted rag. A sheet of flame leapt up,
and the watchers withdrew to the shelter of the porch. A heavy
Russian bombardment was in progress and shells continually
burst on the Chancellery. Silently they stood to attention, and for
the last time gave the Hitler salute; then turned and disappeared
into the shelter.[2]

On 7 May, Hitler's successor, Admiral Doenitz, accepted the
Allied demand for unconditional surrender.

THE POLITICAL OUTCOME

The phoenix that arose from the ashes of Hitler's Europe has
been described as a two-headed eagle, bent on self-destruction.
That, at least, was how the pessimists of the late forties viewed
it. The present-day division of Europe into a Communist and
non-Communist bloc was essentially the result of how the war
was waged. State Communism in Europe might have remained

---

[1] Reproduced in Bullock, pp. 794 and 798.   [2] Ibid., pp. 799–800.

EUROPE 1945-1948

- ---- 1937 Frontiers
- Allied Control Zones of Germany & Austria
- Ceded to Russia by Britain & America
- Cities divided into 4 Occupation Zones
- Annexed by Russia in 1945
- States which became Communist between 1945 & 1948
- Yugoslav gains from Italy 1945
- The 'Iron Curtain' from 1948
- Germany since 1945

FINLAND

Viborg   °Leningrad

ESTONIA   °Pskov

°Riga   LATVIA

Baltic Sea

Memel   LITHUANIA
Danzig   Königsberg
EAST PRUSSIA   °Vilna   °Minsk
annexed by Russia

Szczecin   RUSSIA
(Stettin)

American

Bremen   Poznan   Warsaw   Pinsk°

HOLLAND   Berlin   POLAND
British   Russian
Wroclaw
Erfurt   (Breslau)

American   Prague°   °Cracow   °Lvov

Nuremberg°   CZECHOSLOVAKIA   Czernowitz
Trials
1945-46
French   Vienna°   Uzhgorod   Kishinev
Russian
SWITZERLAND   USA   Budapest°
French   AUST   British
HUNGARY   ROMANIA
Monarchy abolished 1947

Trieste   YUGOSLAVIA   Belgrade°   Bucharest°
BRITISH & US
OCCUPATION
1945-1955
°Pola   Monarchy
abolished   BULGARIA
ITALY   *Adriatic Sea*   Sofia°
Monarchy   Monarchy abolished
abolished   1948
after
June   Communist activity
1946 Plebiscite   ALBANIA   1946 1949
Monarchy abolished   GREECE   Monarchy restored after
1946   September
1946
Plebiscite   *Aegean*
Miles   TURKEY
0   100

confined to Russia had the Western Allies been able to launch a successful Second Front a year earlier. They might then have reached Berlin in June 1944, while the Russians were still on the borders of Poland and Romania. Ironically enough, it was the failure of Churchill and Roosevelt to give Stalin the Second Front that he wanted that made Stalin the master of eastern Europe. Churchill believed in the back-door to Europe, and a triumphal march through France only when the issue was decided; while Roosevelt wanted to floor Germany with a massive blow through France which would both leave him free to deal with Japan, and would make Stalin easier to deal with in the eventual settlement of Europe. Yet Roosevelt was not so much thinking in *realpolitik* terms of what was later called 'the race to Berlin'; he was more concerned with obliging Russia with speedy military relief, so that a grateful Stalin would not make impossible demands at the peace settlement.

Churchill, on the other hand, felt that Stalin would be much more reasonable in his territorial demands if the issues were settled while he was still dependent on western aid. Broadly speaking, however, Churchill capitulated to Roosevelt's wishes in this respect, though not without a tussle. When Churchill went to Moscow in October 1944 to make clear what he felt the west would accept in the way of an east European settlement, Washington told him that America was in no way bound by his view of what was acceptable; and the consequent wavering in western policy towards Russia made Stalin even more suspicious of the west's intentions. The matter was further complicated by the death of Roosevelt in April 1945 and the replacing of Churchill by Attlee in July. Neither President Truman nor Attlee could make appeal to Stalin as comrades-in-arms, while Stalin for his part was tempted to exploit his superior experience.

It must be realised that in December 1941 Stalin had made it clear to Anthony Eden that he wanted to retain all the gains that he had made in collaboration with Hitler, together with whatever extra he could get – which would directly affect Poland, Finland and Romania. By the autumn of 1944, however, Stalin was prepared to compromise by accepting the Curzon Line in the case of Poland, though he insisted on retaining the parts of Finland and Romania that he had obtained in 1940 (see pp. 407, 413). This was ethnically fair to Poland, however much she wanted more; and on Stalin's insistence, she was more than compensated by being given *de facto* extension of her western frontier to the Oder–Neisse line (July–August 1945). This in fact gave her land that had not only supported seven million Germans, but which contained the great industrial and mineral wealth of Silesia. The truth was that five million of these Germans had fled westwards into central Germany to escape the advancing Red Army while the Poles were to evict all but three thousand of the rest in the following years. Indeed there can be no question that the Oder–Neisse concession was a gross violation of ethnic criteria in determining frontiers, so much so that the Anglo-American leaders insisted that it was not to be regarded as a definitive arrangement until the terms of a German peace treaty could be worked out.

From Stalin's point of view, however, it had the supreme advantage of making Poland dependent on Russia for protection against German irredentism. Stalin had already paved the way to making Poland a satellite by favouring the Communist self-styled provisional government; for while the Russian armies were pushing the German armies eastward, Stalin had handed over each liberated area of Poland to the Communists. Even the Anglo-American leaders eventually recognised them (July 1945), when it became clear that the Communists were the only Polish government who would accept the Curzon Line (see map). Not surprisingly their rivals, the 'legitimate' government of London exiles, had insisted on the pre-war frontier, thereby alienating their former protectors. At the same time Stalin had similarly prepared the ground for Russian dominance in Romania by forcing King Michael to accept a largely Communist government in March 1945. He was less successful, however, in Finland, where there was no German irredentism to act as a lever; and in any case he did not regard Finland as an essential bulwark to Russian security requiring especial efforts on his part. He was in fact obliged to content himself with making Finland an economic satellite by a careful delineation of reparations terms.

The biggest question facing 'the Big Three' was: what was to happen to Germany? Stalin had initially demanded the dismemberment of Germany, but by 1945 he was prepared to accept a system of joint occupation. Indeed the Yalta agreement of February consigned the eastern third of Germany to Russian occupation, while Britain for her part was to occupy north-western Germany; France, the south-west; and the United States, the south. This occupation would be co-ordinated by an Allied Control Council in Berlin; and although Berlin was situated in the Soviet zone, the city would itself be divided into four zones. The length of the occupation would depend on the success and speed of the proposed process of 'de-Nazifying' and 'demilitarising' Germany, the amount of reparations remaining initially unsettled – though the Allies in the meantime took what they wanted from their respective zones. Russia in fact took nearly two-thirds of the industrial potential of the eastern zone, as well as obtaining additional material from the western zones. The subsequent fortunes of Germany, however, are part of the Cold War story, and lie outside the scope of this book. Suffice to say that 1949 gave birth to both the liberal democratic regime in West Germany and the Communist regime in East Germany.

Territorially Germany was deprived of Austria and Czechoslovakia, which were restored to independence. Like Germany, Austria was put under Allied occupation, the eventual peace treaty of May 1955 following the Versailles precedent of prohibiting future union with Germany. Government in the interim, however, was carried on by a coalition of the People's Party and the Socialists, working under the old democratic constitution.

In the meantime, across the border in Czechoslovakia, the new government was a coalition of the main pre-war parties; but the Communists had characteristically insisted on having the Ministry of the Interior, with its control of the forces of order and the conduct of elections. Russia had been careful to be first on the scene in the liberation of Czechoslovakia, and it was this that helped to give the Czech Communists their strength. Indeed it was precisely the Communists' control of the forces of order that gave them such an advantage in the *coup d'état* of 1948. They were also greatly aided by the fact that Soviet training of the Czech army had made it a Trojan horse of Communism.

The Communists exploited a similar situation in Bulgaria, where they obtained the Ministries of the Interior and Justice in the Fatherland Front coalition government. The Fatherland Front, containing the main wartime resistance elements, had seized control from the pro-German regime in September 1944. But the Communists used this ministerial power to eliminate many of their opponents on charges of collaboration with Germany, while further arrests and intimidation were to assure the Communists of an impressive majority in the elections of October 1946. This in fact had the direct result of enabling George Dimitrov to institute a totalitarian Communist regime, which was soon second only to Russia for its dictatorial thoroughness.

In Hungary, however, it was not until 1948 that the Communists were in secure possession of power. The Red Army had replaced the pro-German regime with a left-wing coalition; but since the autumn elections of 1945 gave the Communists and Socialists only a sixth of the vote, it took three years of political wrangling to bring Hungary into line with the other Soviet satellites. In Albania, by contrast, the elections of December 1945 gave 93 per cent of the votes to the Communist-dominated coalition that emerged from the anti-Axis resistance. It must be recognised, however, that the political apathy of so many of the Albanian peasantry left an open field for the group with the best organisation.

Yugoslavia lay outside the exclusively Russian sphere of influence, yet was perhaps the only country outside Russia where Communism was a strong indigenous growth. This was largely due to the effectiveness of Marshal Tito's Communist partisans against the Germans and the ambiguous attitude towards the Axis of the other principal resistance leader, which decided the Big Three to back Tito. Much of Tito's political success, however, lay in his all-out pursuit of his opponents on alleged charges of collaboration with the Axis. As a protest, the opposition made the mistake of boycotting the November 1945 elections, which enabled the Communists to obtain a 96 per cent victory – whereupon Tito abolished the monarchy. Nevertheless the strong indigenous roots of Yugoslav Communism enabled Tito to pursue a strong independent line of policy which did not depend on Moscow, and which was later to come into sharp conflict with the Soviet government.

TABLE 30

European recovery in production
(U.S.S.R. excluded)

	Industry 1938=100				Agriculture 1934–8=100				
	1947	*1948*	*1949*	*1950*	*1946*	*1947*	*1948*	*1949*	*1950*
Austria	56	89	120	142	70	71	75	81	98
Belgium	106	114	116	120	84	86	92	112	111
Czechoslovakia	93	110	127	147	84	66	76	81	—
France	92	108	118	121	82	77	96	96	108
Germany									
Western Zones	33	50	75	96	69	64	77	84	104
Berlin	31	28	19	28	—	—	—	—	—
Soviet Zones	47	60	72	91	67	58	74	71	—
Italy	86	91	96	109	85	89	97	102	109
Netherlands	95	113	127	139	87	88	104	117	123
Poland	104	143	175	213	—	62	65	71	—
United Kingdom	115	128	137	150	117	108	124	121	130
U.S.S.R.				173					

(Clough and Cole, *Economic History of Europe*.)

N.B. These figures are not internationally comparative, since the pre-war base-line of 100 is different in each country.

The case of Italy had to await the peace treaty of February 1947, by which time a republic had been declared. Italy lost her acquisitions on the eastern shores of the Adriatic, even Trieste being temporarily designated as a free territory. She moreover not only had to recognise the independence of Ethiopia, but also lost sovereignty over her older colonies. It is an interesting fact that like West Germany, her post-war politics were to be dominated by a largely Catholic Christian Democrat party. But whereas the Catholic success in West Germany was based on the loss of the Protestant territories of East Germany, Catholic success in Italy largely stemmed from the enfranchisement of women.

The political fortunes of the other western countries did not undergo radical change, most of them reverting to the type of regime that they had experienced in the inter-war years, with their attendant virtues and vices. It was above all in the economic field that times had changed; and it was from this that most of the other changes sprang. Nevertheless, as the accompanying table shows, Europe was not slow in regaining the production levels of the 1930s, once factories were redirected from wartime to peacetime production. Even so, it must be remembered that the 1930s were years of depression, and that the post-war recovery needs to be seen in a longer and less flattering context.

VISIONS OF UNIFORMITY

The war had brought uniformity at its most depressing: millions of drab uniforms, mile upon mile of rubble and row upon row of war graves. If August 1945 saw the end of the war in the Far East, it also saw the dropping of two atomic bombs on Japan. In future all thinking men would be united in a latent uniformity of unease, for by the late fifties no place lay outside the orbit of possible destruction. And this in turn caused many to wonder whether civilisation itself would not end in the ultimate uniformity of nuclear devastation.

Post-war reconstruction, however, brought uniformity into the realm of the living as well as the dead. American armies of occupation, American money and American technological aid greatly extended the New World influences that had appeared before the war. The needs of reconstruction also gave rise to a proliferation of international advisory bodies whose work in the devastated and underdeveloped regions encouraged a cosmopolitan style of building that owed little or nothing to the cultural identity of the country concerned. There is no doubt that the rebuilt cities of Europe contained much that was vastly superior to the old; but from Brittany to the Urals the rising rectangles of concrete and glass suggested a Europe that had only one thing to offer.

The 1950s moreover brought television and foreign holidays within the reach of many working-class families, it now being possible for the mass of the population to see how foreigners lived, even if only on a television screen in the local café. On the one hand this encouraged a certain jackdaw-like kleptomania in the styles that were given to the inexpensive items of life, thereby making for considerable variety in dress and interior decoration. On the other hand it encouraged a universal demand for 'the best' as far as the expensive or lasting necessities of life were concerned; and houses, cars and machinery began to look the same all over Europe.

Nevertheless, if current trends suggested that the European way of life would gradually become the same from one end of the continent to the other (despite ideological barriers), it was a way of life that allowed for a remarkable degree of individual self-expression. The creative artist, even in Soviet Russia, had a wider choice of styles that were acceptable to the official 'public' than any of his predecessors; and the range of clothes and furniture available to the mass of the population had never been so great as in the late fifties and sixties. Yet a traveller would have to admit that, compared with the diversity of nineteenth-century Europe, the rising cosmopolitan way of life had uniformity rather than variety as its key-note.

For the majority of people, however, who seldom left their home country, the new way of life offered far more variety than the national culture that their great-grandparents knew. Its variety moreover was buttressed with a material security that past generations would have thought beyond human attainment. Indeed the dreams of nineteenth-century Utopians seem very small beer beside the reality of the welfare state, even if their hopes for moral transformation seem as Utopian now as then. It could nevertheless be further argued that more people today can afford the luxury of honesty and peaceable living than was the case when sheer necessity drove people to crime. Like 'gourmet's liver', nostalgia for 'the good old days' is an affliction that mainly strikes those with long-standing material means.

Not everything has changed for the better, but on balance the changes of the last hundred years have been beneficial rather than otherwise – as a backward glance at Chapter 1 may suggest. Provided that nuclear war can be avoided, it would be hard to deny that the opportunities for self-fulfilment among the mass of the population are greater today than they have ever been.

But whether 'the satisfied man' of the future will be a Socrates or John Stuart Mill's pig still remains to be seen.

The Franco-Prussian War
A closer look[1]

ORIGINS

Bismarck had always kept in view the possibility of French intervention to prevent German union; indeed his military advisers had been urging him since 1866 to strike France before she was ready to intervene. On the other hand, French reactions would depend on prevailing circumstances; and Bismarck was prepared to wait on events. In effect, justification seemed to come his way in May 1869, when the French general elections greatly strengthened the political opposition to Napoleon III's government. It was arguable that, given these domestic difficulties, Napoleon would be anxious not to commit himself to foreign entanglements in the immediate future. It is likewise arguable that Bismarck may have felt in consequence that unification could be brought about peacefully, without the expense and hazards of a war with France.

To understand what followed, one must temporarily turn one's eyes from the broad view and look closely at the narrow sequence of diplomatic events that led to war. In a book of this size on post-1870 Europe, the enigmatic Napoleon III must remain enigmatic; and so must much else that provided the background to war.[2] Conversely the chain of events that led to it and decided its outcome has to be examined link by link, if one is to grasp the significance of the war to subsequent generations of statesmen and generals.

Although Napoleon's domestic difficulties did not guarantee Germany a clear field, Bismarck seems to have felt sufficiently sure of the situation to try for a diplomatic victory at French expense. Queen Isabella II of Spain had recently been deposed (1868), the

---

[1] See first the brief synopsis on pp. 42–7.
[2] Bismarck, however, is extensively treated in Chapters 3 and 7 by virtue of his later activities. For his personality, see pp. 112–13.

upshot being that Bismarck was secretly pressing the Spanish interim government to offer the throne to a relative of the Prussian king, Prince Leopold of Hohenzollern-Sigmaringen. Unquestionably a Prussian success here would be humiliating to France, since she would find herself between two Hohenzollern rulers. But if Leopold was invited by the Spanish parliament, Napoleon III could not formally object without seeming to deny the right of choice to the Spanish people. Bismarck could therefore probably count on French acceptance, however reluctant. Certainly the main attraction of the scheme was the effect it would have of increasing Prussian prestige in the eyes of the south German states lying outside the Confederation. It would demonstrate Prussia's ability to snap her fingers at France, so encouraging the southern states to throw in their lot with Prussia.

The chances of French acquiescence, however, were diminished, though certainly not destroyed, by a new turn in Napoleon's domestic fortunes. A plebiscite held in May 1870, on his latest constitutional reforms, approved them by an overwhelming majority. From Bismarck's point of view this could be construed as a demonstration of confidence in Napoleon's rule, which might encourage Napoleon to feel that affairs at home were sufficiently secure for him to be able to take a stronger line once more in international affairs. Certainly Bismarck could not overlook the fact that Napoleon now proceeded to appoint the anti-Prussian Duc de Gramont as his foreign minister.

Whatever his views on what France might do, Bismarck continued with his scheme undeterred. He persuaded Leopold's father and the Prussian king to accept the Spanish offer; and indeed it only needed the ratification of the Cortes to make it an accomplished fact. There then occurred, however, one of those relatively minor accidents that nevertheless have enormous repercussions. Owing to a misunderstanding, the Cortes was adjourned for the summer before the matter was put to them. It would have been miraculous if a secret involving so many people had survived the summer undisclosed. As was only to be expected, the news of the candidature leaked out months before a vote of the Cortes could choke hostile criticism.

The outcry, led by France, was deafening – so much so that King Wilhelm lost his nerve and urged Leopold's father to withdraw the candidature, which he did (12 July). This was unquestionably the greatest blow that Bismarck's ambitions had yet received, or indeed were ever to receive. Not only had Prussia renounced an important opportunity of gaining prestige in the eyes of the southern states, but she had now suffered a diplomatic defeat at the hands of France.

This was scarcely likely to encourage the southern states to join Prussia.[1]

So abject was the defeat that no one could have predicted a reversal, let alone a reversal within forty-eight hours that was virtually a gift from France. Hard though it was to spoil the French advantage, this was exactly what Gramont succeeded in doing. The suddenness of the Prussian withdrawal had taken him by surprise, leaving him still conscious of the need for something that would prove to the public the government's determination. Existing evidence, however, suggests that the general feeling in France was mainly one of relief; for although right-wing groups in parliament and in Paris demanded 'satisfaction of Prussia', their clamour was almost certainly a minority opinion, and one for which Gramont was ultimately responsible. Indeed acceptance of the Prussian withdrawal was the clear policy of commonsense. But Gramont, anxious to show a bold front, instructed the French ambassador to seek a guarantee from the Prussian king, then staying at Ems, that the candidature should not be renewed.

Wilhelm understandably rejected this request as unnecessary (13 July), informing Bismarck by telegram of his reply. It was precisely this *faux pas* of Gramont that gave Bismarck the chance of retrieving what had been lost; for he thereupon released the news to the Press in such a way as to make France appear snubbed. Bismarck's paraphrase of the telegram gave the king's treatment of the French ambassador a much sharper character than had been the case, though in substance Bismarck's version still remained true to the basic facts. There can be no doubt, however, that Bismarck's intentions were provocative, since he reinforced his action by circulating the telegram among the other European powers. Bismarck was in fact giving France the choice of humiliation or war. As explained earlier (see p. 45), either would suit his purpose. For Bismarck a victory over France would completely outweigh Prussia's recent loss of prestige, thereby convincing the southern states that the only sane policy was union with Prussia. On the other hand, in the unlikely event of France choosing humiliation, Bismarck would have won a diplomatic victory which would likewise efface Prussia's earlier capitulation.

Although the southern states had already signed treaties with Prussia to help her in the event of war, these treaties in no way altered their uncommitted attitude to the question of unification; indeed there was no guarantee that they would honour their treaty obligations when war occurred. However, Bismarck's gamble was to

[1] On Baden's application to join the North German Confederation, see p. 44, note 1.

come off. On 15 July the French parliament voted credits for war, the formal declaration coming four days later. Fortunately for Prussia the southern states mobilised to help her, the result being that within eighteen days a total of 1,183,000 German soldiers were mobilised, with 462,000 of them already transported to the French frontier.

THE GERMAN VICTORY

The French conscription system was the worst example of France's failure to utilise her resources (see pp. 45-6), and as such requires close consideration. In the North German Confederation a healthy man reaching twenty was liable for three years' service in the regular army, followed by four in the reserve and twelve in the Landwehr. The French, however, preferred a national lottery. On reaching twenty, the Frenchman drew a number. If it was 'a good number' he was exempt. But if it was 'bad' there were three possibilities. He might either be among the half of the annual contingent who were detailed to serve with the regular army; or he might be among the half to serve with the reserve. In peacetime, the nine years' reserve service involved no actual training, only liability for call-up in the event of war. If, however, he was drafted instead into the regular army, he did five years there, followed by four in the reserve. The third possibility was that he might pay a substitute to do his service for him.

The obvious danger of the system as a whole was that a majority of Frenchmen had no training whatsoever in the regular army, this proving a serious disadvantage in the later stages of the war. As shown earlier (pp. 45-6), it was here that Napoleon III reaped the results of the hybrid regime he had established in France.

The inadequacies of the French mobilisation have already been indicated (see p. 46). The practical outcome was that when France managed to rush 170,000 troops to Lorraine to meet the expected German attack from Mainz, the subsequent reinforcements arrived only slowly. Had the French army advanced at once on Mainz, it might well have had a series of early victories, since the flow of Prussian troops into Mainz was initially subject to delay. The French decided, however, to wait until their expected full force of 385,000 was ready. This was a particularly unfortunate decision, since it gave the Prussian transport system time to overcome its initial difficulties, and start pouring troops into Mainz at a much higher rate than the French could emulate. The result was that France not only lost her initial advantage of numbers, but allowed Germany to take from her the offensive role.

The first two major battles of the war, Spicheren and Worth (6 August), both consisted of a German attack on the leading corps of the French army in Lorraine and Alsace. Both moreover were lost by France through the failure of French reinforcements to arrive in time – the result, admittedly, of bad generalship, rather than shortage of troops in the theatre of war. Yet time was on the side of Germany in that she could now rely on a steady supply of trained troops; while France would shortly feel her lack of a well-ordered system. If France lost battles now, she had much less hope of success in the future.

Another factor in the German success in these opening battles was their intelligent use of artillery, which they kept well forward from the beginning of an engagement, whereas the French tended to maintain the Napoleonic practice of keeping the artillery in reserve until a final breakthrough was planned.

Even so, the situation was still far from lost, and a swift French counter-offensive might conceivably have moved the war on to German territory. Napoleon, however, ordered a general retreat, and, as explained earlier (see p. 47) it was this that decided the subsequent character of the war.

APPENDIX B

The Comintern and Soviet Foreign Policy

RUSSIA was in the unusual position of having a potential 'fifth column' in most European countries – or so it seemed to nervous foreign observers. But from Russia's point of view her problem was that the Communists of other countries were numerically weak (see p. 286), while their loyalty to Russia was open to question. After all, Communism as a political ideal was much older than Soviet Russia, and there was no overwhelming reason why foreign Communists should accept the Kremlin as their Vatican. Russia nevertheless tried to achieve this situation by her manipulation of the Third Communist International (or Comintern) which Lenin had established in Moscow as a rival to the remnants of the old Second International (March 1919). The intention was that the Comintern should comprise representatives of all the national Communist parties in the world, and that there should be annual congresses which would determine the policy that international Communism should follow in the coming year. Between these congresses a permanent Executive Committee (which was provisionally situated in Moscow) should take the day-to-day decisions that would arise.

Pending revolution in western Europe, however, this Executive Committee was to consist not of delegates sent by each country, but rather of those foreign Communists who happened to be living in exile in Russia. This meant, of course, that the Executive Committee rapidly became a mere tool of the Soviet government. It is true that the annual congress of the Comintern still continued to be democratic in that it contained representatives from the various countries where there were significant Communist parties; and it was still democratic in that the four main national groups, Russia, Germany, the United States and France were each allowed the same number of votes. But in fact the annual congress ceased to be annual after the fourth congress in 1922. The fifth and sixth did not meet until 1925 and '28, while seven years were to elapse before the seventh and last

Congress in 1935. In the meantime the Presidium or inner ring of the Executive Committee of the Comintern took all the decisions. After 1928 moreover Stalin decided that the Presidium should no longer have a chairman, which in effect reduced the Executive to being little more than a faithful echo of the Kremlin.

The Comintern classified the countries of Europe into two main types. There were first the 'advanced capitalist societies' such as Germany, France and Great Britain, where it was felt that the most appropriate form of revolution was a straightforward 'proletarian-socialist' revolution of the type that Marx had predicted for Germany. In second place there were the countries of so-called medium capitalist development – Spain, Portugal, Poland, Hungary and the Balkans – where the appropriate revolution was thought to be a 'bourgeois-democratic' revolution of the Kerensky type, which would then 'grow over' into a proper socialist revolution. Such a revolution might well be expected to follow the Russian pattern, in which a period of so-called state capitalism would be followed by genuine socialism. Indeed in the case of Poland, Hungary and Bulgaria, it was considered that their state of development and proximity to Russia might even permit them to plunge straight into a 'proletarian-socialist' revolution.

To western observers, the Comintern's policy in the inter-war years seemed to oscillate between single-minded extremes with the intensity and inconstancy of women's fashions. Perhaps more so, in that there were at least six distinct changes of hem-line in the course of the period. First there was the period from March 1919 until the end of 1921, when both Russian and western Communists hoped that there would be revolution in Germany and elsewhere, and that Europe would rapidly become one vast proletarian state. During these years the various national Communist parties were urged to take matters completely into their own hands and not to make tactical alliances with the other left-wing parties, such as the Social Democrats. Western intervention in the Russian Civil War naturally intensified this policy.

This, however, was followed by the second phase of Comintern strategy, which lasted from the end of 1921 until the spring of 1928. This period was marked by the Comintern's realisation that Europe was not going to be plunged into revolution, and that the Communists could not afford to ignore other left-wing parties. The effective cause of this realisation was the failure of the Russian armies to bring about revolution in Poland in 1920; and also the failure of the Communists in Germany. This second phase of Comintern strategy is normally and somewhat ironically called the United Front policy, since basically it urged the Communists to steal the membership of the other left-wing parties by seeming to co-operate with them. The plan was to seduce the rank and file of these parties, while at the same time attempting to undermine the authority of their leaders. It was in fact to be a 'united' front from below not from above. From the point of view of the various western national Communist parties, this was a somewhat embarrassing change, for they had spent the period until 1921 abusing the Social Democrats and other left-wing groups, as Moscow had told them to. They were now expected to be friendly with them – explaining away their earlier uncomplimentary remarks as best they could. This, however, was to be only the first of many such changes of strategy. It is perhaps worth noting that this Communist United Front policy in the west coincided with Lenin's New Economic Policy in Russia, the so-called period of state capitalism, when government policies were relatively moderate and non-aggressive.

In 1928 there came the important change to what is called 'the Third Period', a return in fact to the attitude of intransigence – or what the other parties were later to call 'Bolshy bloodymindedness'. The outcome of the British General Strike of 1926 had at last convinced the Comintern that even the rank and file of the Labour movement in Britain had little sympathy for Communist aims. At the same time, at the other end of the world, the attempt by the Chinese Communists to give tactical support to the nationalist forces of Chiang Kai-shek had ended in disaster when Chiang Kai-shek had finally turned on the Communist leaders and imprisoned them. These unfortunate experiences gave rise in 1928 to a change of policy which was to last until 1934. This third period was one of disillusioned reaction, in which the western Communist Parties were advised to give up tactical friendships with other parties and concentrate entirely on building up their own following among the proletariat. The Comintern now declared in fact that there was no intrinsic difference between a bourgeois democratic government like that of Britain on one hand, and a fascist dictatorship like that of Italy on the other. Each was as bad as the other. For this reason the Comintern also declared that should fascists attempt to take over power in the west, there was no point in Communists wasting their energies in the defence of existing bourgeois democratic institutions. The only real alternative to fascism was Communism, and Communists should save their energies for the Communist take-over. Perhaps significantly this policy coincided with Stalin's First Five-Year Plan, which marked a change from the more easy-going New Economic Policy of Lenin to the all-out establishment of 'socialism in one country'.

In view of Communist intransigence, it was perhaps not surprising that Russian pleas for international disarmament were heard with some scepticism. Mr Malcolm Muggeridge, describing the Disarmament Conference in 1932, relates:

> Mr Litvinov [proposed] the total abolition of all weapons, whether technically offensive or defensive. This proposal led Señor Madariaga, the Spanish delegate, to tell an instructive parable. Birds and animals, he said, came together for a disarmament conference. The lion suggested to the eagle that it should dispense with its talons, the eagle appealed to the bull to give up its horns, the bull appealed to the tiger to abandon its claws. Finally, the bear suggested that all should disarm and join him in a universal embrace.

The Comintern, however, could not ignore the activities of the European Right. The old clothes had to be bundled away, and new ones brought out. By 1934 Moscow was becoming genuinely worried by Hitler and Mussolini, with the result that Stalin was prepared to consider negotiating a defensive agreement with France. It was now once more recognised that capitalist democracy was preferable to fascism, western Communists being urged to join with other left-wing parties in the west to protect their liberal institutions against fascism. There was now in fact to be a United Front from above as well as below, while the western Communists were advised against undermining the authority of the other left-wing leaders. This meant, of course, that the ultimate goal of a Communist revolution was pushed back further in time, and that the immediate aim of Communism was now declared to be the purging of the undesirable elements in capitalism, rather than its destruction. It was this policy which gave rise to the co-operation of French Communists in the early stages of the *Front Populaire* in 1936, and in Spain to the relatively co-operative attitude that the Communists adopted towards other Republican groups during the Civil War.

This fourth phase, however, lasted only until 1939, when it was brutally shattered by the German-Soviet pact of August 1939, in which Stalin came to terms with Hitler. This perhaps was the most embarrassing change of all for the western Communists. After this even the Comintern could neither think up convincing ideological reasons to justify the change, nor suggest a positive policy for the western Communists. Clearly the Communists could not go on denouncing Hitler and fascism, now that Hitler and Stalin were allies; yet it would be ludicrous for the Communists to pretend to like Hitler. All that the Comintern could now recommend was that the western Communists should stop their verbal attacks on Hitler and fascism, and that they should break with the other left-wing parties. It was now back to the old policy of abusing the Socialists and other left-wing groups.

In France and Britain moreover this embarrassing situation obliged the Communists to oppose the Allied war against Germany – an awkward situation that was to last until 1941, when Hitler's invasion of Russia enabled a return to the earlier policy of abusing fascism and being friends with the Left. On the whole this was a much more congenial role for the western Communists, and one which they adopted with considerable relief.

Nevertheless foreign governments often wondered whether they were dealing with a snake or a chameleon.

APPENDIX C

Some of the smaller nations
between the wars

THE nations neglected in the body of this book contained a third of the European population, but given exigencies of space, only a selection of them can be looked at here. Although the choice may seem an arbitrary one, an attempt has been made to select those that had particular interest for the rest of Europe. It should perhaps be stressed that this appendix is intended for reference rather than reading, and it is hoped that no reader will push enthusiasm to the point of attempting to dispose of them all consecutively.

SWEDEN

With a population that was still only 6·3 million in 1939, Sweden made a greater impression on the European imagination than any other small power. From Greta Garbo to the treatment of labour problems, Sweden seemed to offer much, especially in the sphere of domestic comfort, where Swedish houses and furniture set new standards for the rest of Europe. Foreign critics spoke of a Godless society, exemplified by 'sexual licence'; they pointed to the high suicide rate (which, like Denmark's, was twice that of most European countries), and they hinted at that most elusive of phenomena, 'nude bathing' – which after all had been a pastime of the early Victorians. But often what they were attacking were either the activities of a very small minority or were features already present in other countries.

Perhaps the most remarkable feature of the Swedish standard of living was its relative buoyancy during the Depression. The Depression made comparatively little difference to the continual European demand for pulp and wood-products, commodities which made up two-fifths of Sweden's exports. This enabled Sweden to survive the Depression without resorting to heavy protective tariffs, except against foreign agricultural produce. Moreover the absence of high tariffs helped to keep down the cost of living (except food prices) and it also allowed Sweden to pursue a general economic policy of expansion, when other countries rightly or wrongly were committed to recession. At the same time the relatively adventurous attitude of Swedish industry to new techniques, as compared with the older-established industries of Britain, enabled Swedish manufactures to continue to compete in foreign markets, despite foreign tariffs.

Apart from periodic demonstrations, organised labour in Sweden did little to hamper the progressive development of industry. Legislation of 1928 made collective agreements between trade unions and employers' organisations legally binding, while strong union organisation enabled the workers to demand high wages in these agreements. The employers moreover were often prepared to grant their demands, since they knew that they were legally protected against unofficial strikes. The result was that real wages in industry were seldom less than 90 per cent of what they were in Britain, though it should be noted that they were nevertheless still consistently lower than those in Denmark. Denmark likewise demanded smaller insurance contributions for benefits that were comparable to Sweden's.

Inter-war politics were dominated by the Social Democrats who tended to favour a pragmatic rather than a doctrinaire approach to problems. In partnership with the Liberals, they established universal male suffrage at the end of 1918; while in the 1930s they conducted an effective defensive campaign to protect Sweden's high standard of living against the threat of the Depression.

PORTUGAL

Portugal ranked with Albania and Greece as having the lowest standard of living in Europe. Real wages in industry were only a third of those in Britain, and even as late as 1940 over half the population was illiterate.

Portugal's basic problem was a lack of material resources. She regularly imported two to three times the amount she produced, though some of this was re-exported at a profit. The world depression moreover reduced the demand for Portuguese exports, especially port wine; and the only new export-product, wolfram, still represented only 1 per cent of total outgoings in the late thirties. Even in 1930 industry continued to employ less than a fifth of the population, as compared with well over half in agriculture. It is true that an impressive effort at reclamation in three years resulted in nearly a fifth of her area being added to the land in productive use;

but the increase in population from 5·6 million to 7·2 million partially offset this rising agricultural productivity.

Most Europeans identify inter-war Portugal with the quasi-dictatorship of Antonio de Oliveira Salazar, and saddle him with the blame for Portuguese backwardness. It is easy to forget that Salazar could only work within the framework of Portugal's material resources, and as a specialist in finance he could not avoid being preoccupied with the size of the government's debts. But his rule did see some attempt to improve working-class conditions. He instituted a semi-comprehensive system of sickness and old-age insurance (January 1931; September 1933) and also inaugurated an extensive public works programme for the unemployed (September 1932–November 1933). And the programme of land-reclamation likewise owed much to his impetus; indeed Portugal became almost self-sufficient in wheat. This, however, cannot disguise the fact that greater taxes on wealth would have enabled further progress; and higher minimum wages could have been made compulsory, even within the limitations of Portugal's overall capacity. His dictatorship moreover destroyed political freedom, leaving the thinking man with overwhelming doubts as to whether the little that the economy had to offer was being fairly apportioned.

There could, however, be no doubt that Portugal's experience of democratic government between 1910 and 1926 had been a far from happy one. Attempted *coups* averaged one a year, four months being the average life of a government; in fact some five hundred people held cabinet office at one time or other in these sixteen years. The Democrats had proved unable to deal with the financial consequences of the war, with the result that by 1922 the escudo had fallen from 4s to 2½d. Wages moreover did not keep pace with rising prices, and by 1920 their proportion to prices had dropped to a third. Clearly a drastic 'solution' could not be far away. In fact, the end came in May 1926, when a military junta under General Gomes da Costa overthrew the government; and as an indirect result of this event, the country's finances were eventually put into the hands of Salazar, at that time (April 1928) a professor of economics.

As finance minister, Salazar succeeded in balancing the budget, but at the cost of dictatorial government and an ultra-cautious attitude to social reform. After he became premier, however, in July 1932, Salazar legalised the regime by introducing a constitution (February 1933) which gave power to a prime minister nominated by a popularly elected president. The vote was restricted to men who were either literate or taxpayers, but was extended to women with a secondary school qualification. Yet it was plain to all that parliament was in no sense representative in that the candidates for the lower house consisted entirely of a block list presented by the government; all that the elector could do was to cross out names he found objectionable, but without the right of substituting others. Parliament moreover could initiate no legislation that would involve an increase in expenditure, while the government could always by-pass parliament by legislating by decree. Strikes (and lock-outs) were characteristically declared illegal. Having thus effectively locked away the instruments of opposition, the constitution, with delicate if unconscious irony, enclosed its provisions with a firm appeal to the social teaching of the Church, as contained in recent papal encyclicals.

POLAND

It is easy to forget that the domestic life of Poland was a personal matter for no less than 27 million people – 35 million by 1939. Of these moreover nearly a third were not Poles: 15 per cent were Ukrainians, 8 per cent were Jews, 4 per cent White Russians and 4 per cent Germans. If the war gave the Poles national independence, it nevertheless destroyed a fifth of their capital wealth, leaving them in no state to face the agricultural slump of the twenties and the industrial slump of the thirties. Reconstruction was a life-giving occupation as long as there was capital to finance it – but foreigners in the post-war period were reluctant to lend to a country with such little apparent potential as Poland.

In the 1920s two-thirds of the population lived by agriculture, and only a seventh by industry and mining. The old Polish custom of dividing land among heirs, together with the consequences of the Tsarist agrarian reforms (see pp. 153–5), had reduced the bulk of peasant holdings to under twelve acres; and although the land reforms of July 1920 and December 1925 resulted in a tenth of the cultivable area of Poland being redistributed among 153,000 of the smaller farmers, this still left the rural population with insufficient employment and with no immediate prospect of being absorbed by the nation's slowly growing industries. In any case real wages in industry were less than a half of those in Britain.

Yet Poland's record in social legislation was respectable for a relatively poor country. All workers were entitled to 60 per cent of their normal pay during sickness (May 1920) while unemployment benefit for urban workers was about a third of normal pay (July 1924). Urban workers moreover were also brought into a compulsory old-age insurance scheme (March 1933), and given a fortnight's holiday with pay (May 1922).

The position of the minorities, however, was an anxious one.

Although the international Minorities-Treaty gave them a certain minimum protection, a law of July 1924 and Stanislaw Grabski's educational policy of 1925 set about replacing the minority schools with bilingual schools of a markedly Polish character. In opposition to this and other measures, the Ukrainian Nationalists subsequently launched a guerrilla war (July 1930) which itself led to the Polish government embarking on a savage 'pacification', dragonnade-style. The culmination came in September 1934, when the government renounced the Minorities Treaty. Antisemitism was likewise growing in Poland; and it was not surprising that the minority groups figured highly in the 100,000 emigrants that left Poland annually in the inter-war period.

Poland adopted a constitution on the French model with all its attendant risks (March 1921). Government rested on fragile coalitions of small parties, and as in France the average life of a cabinet was only seven months. The most influential figure in Poland, however, was Joseph Pilsudski, chief of the general staff, who had been the foremost Polish opponent of the Tsarist regime. Tiring of the inability of the regime to deal with Poland's economic and financial problems, he forcibly took over government in May 1926. Using the Ministry of War as a personal base, he strengthened the executive's constitutional power, but relied principally on his personal prestige to carry on government. Indeed Poland's survival of the financial crisis of 1926–7 owed something to him, in that foreign financiers saw him as an element of stability, and were prepared to help.

His death transferred power to a junta of his former comrades-in-arms in May 1935. The new government learnt a lot through observing the methods of its more sophisticated neighbour states, and it broke its political opponents by using the strong-arm tactics that were becoming such a familiar and depressing feature of the Europe of the 1930s. Nevertheless tough methods were no substitute for tough numbers when it came to a confrontation with Germany in 1939; but the outcome of this hopeless struggle is described elsewhere (see pp. 405–6).

CZECHOSLOVAKIA

The Bohemians of the old order had become the Czechs of the post-war world – and in the popular imagination of western Europe had somehow or other slipped eastwards. There used to seem nothing extraordinary about the fact that Mozart had felt more at home in eighteenth-century Prague than in Vienna; but after 1918 Prague seemed to become 'Slav' in an alien sense. The illusion was to become intensified after 1945, when the Czechs exchanged the orbit of Vienna for that of Moscow.

Czechoslovakia nevertheless came nearest to being the heir to the Austro-Hungarian Empire. It had something of the Empire's multi-nationalism, and even a slight element of dualism. The Czechs, who were the largest group (7·3 million in 1930) were less than half the total population (14·7 million), while the other group in the duality, the Slovaks (2 million), were in fact less numerous than the largest 'foreign' minority, the Germans (3·25 million). Nevertheless the disadvantages which afflicted the non-Czech peoples were largely the result of economic circumstance and the legacy of the past, rather than government discrimination.

Bohemia was economically much more advanced than Slovakia, and Austrian rule there had been more enlightened than that of Hungary over Slovakia. Whereas all but 3 per cent of the Bohemian population were literate, well over a quarter of the Slovaks were not. Bohemia moreover now possessed most of the Sudetenland which held the kernel of Habsburg industry. About two-fifths in fact of the Czechoslovak population were engaged in manufactures, and most of these were Czech or German, whereas Slovakia was almost entirely agricultural. The Sudeten industry nevertheless suffered from the loss of the Austro-Hungarian internal market. It now had to traverse the tariff walls of the successor states, with the result that real wages in Czech industry were only about half of what they were in British industry. Furthermore although textiles were still her main export, her increasing specialisation in luxury goods, such as glassware, meant that her exports were among the first to be hit by the Depression, unemployment reaching 700,000 in the early 1930s. The workers then had to fall back on unemployment relief of up to 2s a day, paid by the trade unions with the government paying half the cost (1918 and July 1921).

During sickness both industrial and agricultural workers received two-thirds of their pay and upwards of a third during retirement (October 1924), the total premium ranging up to a tenth of their wages. The eight-hour day moreover had been established in 1918, and a week's holiday with pay was guaranteed (April 1925).

Nevertheless for the two-fifths of the population in agriculture, land reform was what mattered most. Legislation of April 1919 and 1920 expropriated arable estate land over 370 acres, the owners being compensated at the average pre-war price. Nearly a tenth of Czechoslovakian farming land was redistributed in this way for the benefit of over 600,000 peasants, thereby increasing the number of land-holding families to three-quarters of the agricultural population.

German and Magyar landowners were inevitably prominent among those expropriated; and since the redistribution policy gave priority to peasants who had furthered Czechoslovak independence, it was often claimed that the Czech and Slovak gains had been made at the expense of the minorities. The result, however, really stemmed from the pre-1918 geographical pattern of land-tenure.

Proportional representation in a country of such regional and racial divisions meant that every government was bound to be a coalition. Initially the Socialists and the Agrarian Party were the most powerful of the five leading parties. But the 1925 elections weakened the Socialists, and permitted the Agrarian prime minister, Antonin Svehla (October 1922–February 1929) to form a purely bourgeois administration in 1926. Svehla granted Slovakia some autonomy, including an elected Assembly with its own budget, thus helping to calm some of the Slovakian discontent which Father Andrew Hlinka's autonomist party had hitherto embodied.

Eventually the premiership passed to a Slovak, Milan Hodza (November 1935), who inherited a difficult situation *vis-à-vis* Konrad Henlein's Sudeten German Party – a group vociferously demanding annexation to Nazi Germany. The rest of what was to be a very unhappy story is related in Chapter 14 (pp. 395–8).

HUNGARY

'A kingdom without a King, in which the Regent was an Admiral without a navy' (A. J. P. Taylor), Hungary was one of the great losers of the war, in that she was left with only a third of her pre-war population – 7·5 million instead of 21. Nor was it just a question of non-Magyars achieving independence: 3·25 million Magyars had been allotted to neighbouring states, nearly 400,000 of these making their way to Hungary as refugees, thereby putting further pressure on the diminished resources of the country. Nevertheless the material hardship of the Hungarian peasantry was more the outcome of the selfish interests of the Magyar magnates, than of the limitations imposed by the peace settlement.

Just over half the population was directly engaged in agriculture, two-thirds of these holding land, the rest being landless labourers. Altogether two-thirds of the peasantry lived at subsistence level, occupying only a tenth of the land, while agricultural wages in the 1930s were less than what they had been before the war. At the other end of the scale 2,431 landowners held a third of the land.

For most of the period Hungary was a conservative republic

disguised as a kingless monarchy. The country's foremost politician, Mihaly Karolyi, had resigned the presidency (March 1919) rather than accept the loss of Transylvania; and in the confusion that followed, Lenin's chief agent, Béla Kun, set up a Communist dictatorship on the Bolshevik model. But instead of the redistribution of land, which Karolyi had promised, Béla Kun alienated the peasantry by proposing nationalisation; and in August 1919 Romanian intervention brought his regime to an end. Conservative, agrarian and military interests then established Admiral Horthy as 'Regent' (March 1920), and proceeded to govern Hungary to their own advantage. Land redistribution (August 1920) was restricted to about a fifteenth of the total, the oligarchy assuring its continuance in power by carefully manipulating elections. The Depression, however, unseated them, and the Regent felt obliged to call on the quasi-fascist Right Radicals (October 1932) who, remaining in power for the rest of the period, were responsible for introducing a growing body of antisemitic legislation.

AUSTRIA

With the spread of the gramophone and the development of electrical recording, the average cultured European became aware at first hand of what Vienna had to offer; and a remarkable number of the Vienna recordings of the 1930s remain unsurpassed as performances. But if Vienna's musical empire was growing, her political empire had been drastically reduced – to 6·5 million. Indeed, the majority of those who were politically articulate in the twenties were thought to favour the complete disappearance of Austria as a sovereign state. The Hitler regime, however, aroused second thoughts in all but the right-wing parties; and when it came in March 1938 the *Anschluss* was the wish of only a minority of the Austrian population – despite a subsequent favourable vote.

Nearly a third of the population lived in Vienna, and although agriculture occupied another third of the Austrian people, its produce was not sufficient to feed the country. Manufactures by contrast represented nearly three-quarters of her exports, though Viennese industry now had to surmount the high tariff walls which the Habsburg successor states had put up against their former supplier. The result was that overall exports covered less than two-thirds of Austrian imports. Fortunately she still possessed important sources of invisible exports, the tourist trade being but one of them.

In the twenties real wages in industry were less than half of what they were in Britain; and unemployment in the immediate post-war period was well over a tenth of the working population. But these years did at least bring unemployment insurance (March 1920), the eight-hour day (December 1918) and a fortnight's holiday with pay (July 1919). The twenties moreover brought the remarkable housing programme of the socialist city council of Vienna with its scheme of subsidised rents. Nevertheless the Depression of the 1930s found nearly a sixth of the working population on public assistance; while the Dollfus regime added to their difficulties by gradually reducing social insurance benefits.

The constitution of October 1920 was ultra-democratic in so far as it gave complete power to an elected parliament, based on the proportional representation of both sexes. But the ruling Christian Socialist party set dangerous precedents for the future by using the *Heiwmehr* (an Austrian equivalent of the German *Freikorps*) as a counter-force to the labour organisations. The growing boldness of the Hitlerite elements in the *Heimwehr* eventually decided Engelbert Dollfuss, premier and a former Christian Socialist, to institute a non-parliamentary regime (May 1934) which proved successful in suppressing hostile elements on both Right and Left. The Nazis replied, however, with an attempted *coup*, killing Dollfuss (July 1934). Nevertheless his work of clerically-inspired dictatorship was carried on by Kurt von Schuschnigg – and all that it lacked was a Habsburg restoration. Before the Schuschnigg regime could strike lasting roots, however, Hitler intervened, resolving the situation in characteristic fashion (see pp. 394–5).

THE BALKANS

The western reader at breakfast tended to assume that news from the Balkans was bad news. Compared with pre-war years, however, the newspapers had little to say about them. Yet all was far from well there.

The various Balkan peoples suffered from the same basic problems, in that their economy failed to keep pace with the increase in population. The Balkans were at last experiencing the drop in infant mortality that medicine had brought to western Europe a century earlier; but they had not as yet absorbed western methods of birth control. The result was that the increase in children reaching manhood led to the small peasant holdings being subdivided to provide for them, since the industry of the towns was far too small to accommodate the surplus population, while American restrictions on immigration closed what had been an important safety-valve.

Similarly the relative infertility of the soil and the difficulty of introducing modern farming techniques to tiny holdings kept production low. Whereas each west European cultivator produced on average enough food for four people, the Balkan peasant produced enough for only one and a half. Credit facilities moreover were very poor; and even if a peasant's holding was large enough to make modern techniques viable, the village usurer might charge him 200 per cent or more for the money he needed to buy new equipment.

The peasant's lot was further worsened by the reliance of Balkan governments on indirect rather than direct taxation, which meant that clothing, fertilisers and tools cost more because of purchase and import taxes. The root of the problem was that these governments were desperately if understandably anxious to promote industry, and were even prepared to put heavy export duties on their own agricultural produce to obtain revenue to finance it. And so if the Balkan farmer was to compete in the world market, he had to content himself with a smaller percentage of the total market price. The outcome was that the cost of the preferential treatment that industry enjoyed was borne by the peasantry, the class least able to bear it. At the same time the poverty of the countryside encouraged doctors to set up practice in the towns rather than in rural areas, with the result that the proportion of doctors to peasants was little different from that in India. In fact nearly one baby in five died in its first year, as compared with one in fifteen in Britain. Balkan poverty likewise resulted in many qualified professional men being unable to find work, so that the frustrated intellectual was as much a feature of Balkan towns as he was in the Middle East.

Although governments favoured industry, manufacturers too struggled under difficulties. Foreign credit was expensive and siphoned off too much of their profits. At the same time the growing subordination of the Balkan economy to Germany tended to encourage production of the agricultural goods that Germany needed, and not the industrial goods that were the object of government policy. Germany was admittedly prepared to pay high prices for Balkan cereals and tobacco, but only in 'blocked marks' (see p. 334) which had to be spent on German goods. Moreover, when Germany occupied Austria and Czechoslovakia, her hold over the Balkan economy was immeasurably strengthened.

Brief Lives

In a short book that lays emphasis on the population as a whole, there is always a danger that many of the outstanding individuals of the period are overlooked and that the product emerges as a landscape without figures. This is particularly true of the thinkers and creative artists, whose impact on humanity may be more enduring than that of many of the 'active' leaders of social progress, but whose influence is much more difficult to assess. A few of these men, whose work affected or reflected their time, are singled out in this appendix, with the intention of supplementing the information on them given in earlier pages. The page references indicate where they are mentioned in the main part of the book.

Mikhail Bakunin (1814–76), pp. 85, 87, 162 and 202

Lurching from one trouble-spot to another, Bakunin was to tour Europe like a gigantic performing bear. Eldest son of a retired diplomat, he resigned an army commission in order to study philosophy (1834). Under the influence of Arnold Ruge, however, he became a revolutionary agitator (1841); and it was as a result of his participation in the Dresden insurrection of 1849 that the next twelve years of his life were spent in prison and Siberian exile. Shortly after his return to Europe, the example of the Polish rising of 1863 shattered his belief in national movements as an instrument of social revolution, making him thereafter a campaigner for universal anarchy. Denouncing Marxism as 'the vilest and most formidable lie which our century has engendered', he struggled with Marx for ascendancy over the International Working-men's Association, until he was finally expelled in 1872. The nature of the man and his beliefs can best be sampled in his pamphlet, *The Knouto-German Empire and International Socialism* (1871).

E. H. Carr, *Michael Bakunin* (Knopf, 1961).

Claude Debussy (*1862–1918*), pp. 59–60

While his technical innovations have earned him the title of 'the father of modern music', his compositions are in essence 'largely parallel expressions of the aesthetics of Marcel Proust, consist[ing] of finely drawn musical images that arouse innumerable sensations and half-forgotten memories' (Edward Lockspeiser). Son of a former marine, he was intended for a naval career until his musical gifts were discerned by Antoinette Mauté (one-time pupil of Chopin, and the mother-in-law of the Symbolist poet, Paul Verlaine). Strongly influenced by Impressionist painting and Symbolist literature, his finest works include the opera, *Pelléas et Mélisande* (1902), and the three symphonic sketches, *La Mer* (1905), which remain unsurpassed as an artist's evocation of the forces of nature. 'Whereas in most works of art inspired by the sea, . . . we are given the sea as a highly picturesque background to human endeavour and human emotion, . . . *La Mer* is . . . a picture of the sea itself, . . . a seascape without ships' (Constant Lambert).

Edward Lockspeiser, *Debussy: his life and mind*, 2 vols (Cassell, 1962–5).

Fëdor Dostoevski (*1821–81*)

Epileptic and a compulsive gambler, Dostoevski's life from the outset was one of high drama. When he was eighteen, his father, a doctor and a tyrannical landlord, was murdered by his serfs; and five years later Dostoevski resigned an army commission to devote himself to novel-writing and revolutionary propaganda, principally directed against serfdom and censorship. Sentenced to death but reprieved on the execution ground (1849), he was sent to Siberia, where he made what was to be a disastrous first marriage (1857). Following his return to St Petersburg (1859) he wrote his greatest works, *Crime and Punishment* (1866), *The Idiot* (1868–9), *The Devils* (1871–2) and *The Brothers Karamazov* (1879–80). Towards the end of his life he came to believe that humanity could find salvation only in traditional Russian values. The reconciliation of good and evil was possible only in a patient peasant society, guided by an autocratic Tsar and the Orthodox Church. For, in his own words, 'evil is buried more deeply in humanity than the cure-all socialists think'. His contempt for the revolutionary tradition of his time is best expressed in *The Devils*, a masterpiece of pathos and ironic humour, with a plot based on an incident of 1869, when a young disciple of Bakunin, Sergei Nechayev, murdered a fellow revolutionary.

David Magarshak, *Dostoevsky. A Life* (Secker & Warburg, 1962).

Sergei Eisenstein (1898–1948), p. 268

Son of a wealthy Russian shipbuilder, Eisenstein sided with the Bolsheviks in the Civil War and, after a brilliant debut as director of the Proletcult theatre, turned to films. His finest achievements include *Strike* (1924), *The Battleship Potemkin* (1925), *October*, (1928), *The General Line* (1929), *Alexander Nevsky* (1938) and *Ivan the Terrible* (1944–6) – the last incurring the disapproval of the Soviet authorities. The opening of the great battle-scene in *Alexander Nevsky* is arguably the most exciting sequence in cinema-history.

Marie Seton, *Sergei M. Eisenstein* (Bodley Head, 1952).

Sigmund Freud (1856–1939), pp. 57–8

Although his father was a Moravian Jew, most of Freud's life was spent in Vienna, until the *Anschluss* drove him to London in 1938. Starting his professional career as a neurologist (1886), he was later inspired by the physician Josef Breuer to attempt to cure hysteria by inducing the patient to recall past events and their attendant emotions, while under hypnosis. By the mid-1890s, however, he had replaced hypnosis with the method of free association, thereby laying the basis of modern psychoanalytical technique. Of his written work, *The Interpretation of Dreams* (1900) remains the best-known among laymen.

Ernest Jones, *The Life and Work of Sigmund Freud* (Penguin, 1964).

Franz Kafka (1883–1924), pp. 174 and 267–8

'His tragic vision of life is presented with the vividness of a profoundly disturbing nightmare in which painful, grotesque and fantastic details all assume a terrifying reality. . . . These deal with the predicament of man in an incomprehensible and apparently hostile universe, hopelessly and helplessly attempting to come to terms with a remote and absolute power whose manifestations remain ambiguous throughout. Kafka's technique [is] a strange and intimate fusion between symbolism and realism, shot through with irony' (Eliza Butler). Extremely sensitive, his life was overshadowed by conflicts with an unsympathetic father, a self-made Jewish merchant of Prague, and by the vicissitudes of two broken love affairs. After earning a monotonous living in insurance, he moved to Berlin to devote himself fully to writing. Unable to face the responsibilities of marriage, he broke off his first engagement, while the second was to end when it was discovered that he had tuberculosis. Supremely diffident about his literary work, he instructed his friend, Max Brod, to destroy his manuscripts at his death – a destiny which Brod happily reversed by publishing them.

Max Brod, *The Biography of Franz Kafka* (Secker and Warburg, 1948).

Thomas Mann (*1875–1955*), pp. 97, 106–7 and 332

The product of a patrician merchant family of Lübeck Mann, started life in an insurance office. His first novel, *Buddenbrooks* (1901), deals with one of his favourite themes, the conflict between art and life. His masterpiece, however, was *The Magic Mountain* (1924). Set in a Davos sanatorium in the years before the First World War, it is 'a study in microcosm of the forces which disrupted European society'. Hitler's rise to power, however, decided Mann to leave Germany (1933) and ultimately to become an American citizen (1944).

Georges Fourrier, *Thomas Mann; le message d'un artiste bourgeois, 1896–1924* (Belles Lettres, 1960).

R. H. Thomas, *Thomas Mann. The mediation of art* (Clarendon, 1963).

Karl Marx (*1818–83*), pp. 38 and 85–8 (see also index, 'Marxism')

Marx was an uneasy partnership of three men – an economist, a practical revolutionary and a Hebrew prophet. Son of a Jewish lawyer turned Protestant, he was strongly influenced as a student by the dialectical view of history propounded by Georg Hegel. As editor of the *Rheinische Zeitung* his strong liberal views led to the paper's suppression and his departure to Paris (1843), where he made contact with leading French socialists and with his future collaborator, Friedrich Engels, the son of a textile-manufacturer. Engels's observations in Manchester helped to accelerate Marx's evolution towards socialism; and in 1847, in *The Poverty of Philosophy*, Marx attacked the Utopian socialists for their preoccupation with 'the morally desirable' rather than 'the historically inevitable'. The following year saw *The Communist Manifesto*, which gave the Marx–Engels partnership its definitive character. The failure of the revolutions in Germany, however, decided them to move to London, where they devoted themselves to writing and to the eventual organisation of the International Working-men's Association (1864). Apart from wrangling with Bakunin, Marx's main activity in these years was the composition of his great economic treatise, *Capital* (1867–94).

Isaiah Berlin, *Karl Marx* (O.U.P., 1963).

Friedrich Nietzsche (1844–1900), p. 57

Like so many influential German writers, Nietzsche was the son of a Lutheran minister. While professor of classical philology in the University of Basle, he developed a significant friendship with Richard Wagner, until his independence of mind antagonised the older man. Resigning his post in 1879 he devoted himself to writing, producing a book a year, *Thus spake Zarathustra* being the best known. He suffered acutely from ill-health and solitude, his scheming sister destroying the only deep relationship he enjoyed in these years. This was his friendship with Lou Salomé, who later became Rilke's confidant and a friend of Sigmund Freud. When at last his reputation took wing and swept Europe in the 1890s, it came too late to give him satisfaction, for insanity overtook him in 1889. Richard Strauss's tone-poem, *Also sprach Zarathustra* (1896), and Thomas Mann's novel, *Dr. Faustus* (1947), represent two extremes of the impact of his life and work on the European imagination.

Walter Kauffmann, *Nietzsche: philosopher, psychologist, anti-Christ* (Princeton U.P., 1950).

Pablo Picasso (1881–), pp. 267 and 332

An ape-like figure, most often clad only in a pair of shorts, Picasso now seems to tower over the cultural scene with an acknowledged pre-eminence that no individual writer or composer has enjoyed since the nineteenth century. This may reflect the quality of his competitors, but his unique position remains a fact. After early training by his father (an art-teacher in Barcelona), Picasso moved to Paris in 1904, where with Georges Braque he initiated Cubism (1906–10). His best-known work, however, belongs to the style that he developed after 1925, notably *Guernica* (1937), a terrifying memorial to a town destroyed in a German air-raid during the Spanish Civil War. From his early rather sentimental circus portraits (1904–6) to his present style, he has inspired successive generations of artists, and has long been recognised as the outstanding influence in twentieth-century painting.

Frank Elgar and Robert Maillard, *Picasso* (Thames and Hudson, 1956).

Marcel Proust (1871–1922), pp. 59–60, 70 n., 128, 267 and 332

Two years before Proust's birth, his father had been travelling on horseback through Persia, Russia and Turkey, laying the foundations of the *cordon sanitaire* against cholera. His elder son, by contrast, rapidly became a *dévoté* of the salon life of Paris, so much so that his literary friends despaired of his ever being more than a dilettante, a writer of percipient pastiches and a sympathetic translator of Ruskin. The steady deterioration in his health after 1902 seemed to confirm these fears. But it was in the solitude of his cork-lined room, surrounded by all the apparatus of hypochondria and genuine ill-health, that he wrote his huge flowing masterpiece, *À la recherche du temps perdu* (1914–27). Using the form of an extended novel, he subtly recreates the sensations and aesthetic experiences of his past life, from early childhood to middle age in wartime Paris. The crux of the book is the narrator's discovery of the pleasure that comes through the sudden and unexpected recapture of past sensations. The book also provides an unsurpassed fresco of leisured society during the *Belle Époque*, an achievement that is especially remarkable for its acute psychological observation.

George Painter, *Marcel Proust. A Biography*, 2 vols (Chatto and Windus, 1959–65).

Richard Strauss (*1864–1949*), pp. 59, 101, 332 and 457

Strauss and Debussy were as different as beer and oysters. Indeed, on his mother's side, Strauss was descended from a notable dynasty of brewers, a fact that was often recalled by critics of the flatulent swagger of his music. His father was a celebrated horn-player in the Munich court orchestra, and his son's early promise was encouraged by Hans von Bülow and Alexander Ritter. Rapidly ascending the hierarchy of German opera-houses, his career as a conductor still left him time to establish a reputation as a young composer of extraordinary imagination. The series of tone-poems that began with *Don Juan* (1889) and ended with *Ein Heldenleben* (1899) were remarkable both for their technical innovation and for their prolongation of the old Romantic tradition. The prodigality with orchestral sources that characterised the work of the last German Romantics reached its apotheosis in his *Sinfonia Domestica* (1904), where the home life of a bourgeois family of three is portrayed by a vast orchestra, part of whose gigantic energies go into depicting a yelling child disturbing its parents' sleep. The immediate pre-war period brought him not only the directorship of the Berlin Opera but also his remarkable partnership with Hugo von Hofmannsthal, which resulted in his finest operas, *Elektra* (1909) and *Der Rosenkavalier* (1911). The inter-war years, however, saw a certain simplification of his style and a distinct flagging in his inventiveness. When Hofmannsthal died (1929), it seemed that Stefan Zweig might step into his shoes. But what might have been a fruitful collaboration was destroyed when the advent of Hitler drove the Jewish Zweig into exile. Despite the honours Strauss received from the Nazis, his relations with the government became progressively less cordial, his growing pessimism reaching its depths in his last significant work, *Metamorphosen* (1945).

The Correspondence between Richard Strauss and Hugo von Hofmannsthal (Collins, 1961).

Leo Tolstoy (1828–1910)

Tolstoy was 'not one man but ten or twenty, all sworn enemies of one another: an aristocrat jealous of his prerogatives and a friend of the people who dressed as a peasant, an ardent Slavophile and a Westernising pacifist, a denouncer of private property and a landowner enlarging his domains, a keen shot and a protector of animals, a hearty trencherman and a vegetarian, an Orthodox believer of the *moujik* type and an enraged assailant upon the Church, an artist and a despiser of art, a sensualist and an ascetic. This multitude of psychological impulses enabled him to put himself into the skin of a great many characters and thus to become a matchless novelist' (Henri Troyat). Member of a long-established land-owning family, Tolstoy was brought up by French tutors in the cultural tradition of eighteenth-century France. Resigning a commission in the army (1857), he undertook various philanthropic works on his estates, while following up his early successes as a writer. It is arguable that *War and Peace* (1869) and *Anna Karenina* (1875–7) represent the high point of the nineteenth-century Realist novel, the second giving a remarkable picture of the Russian society of its time. But 1876 found Tolstoy increasingly looking for a religious justification for his life, and by 1884 his evolving beliefs had assumed the status of a sect. Rejecting both the idea of a personal God and the immortality of the soul, he saw salvation in love of mankind and the avoidance of violence, including the authorised violence of 'the forces of order'. The growing eccentricity of his last years put an increasing strain on his adoring family, so much so that he secretly left home in October 1910, only to fall ill and die at a small railway-station several days later.

Henri Troyat, *Tolstoy* (W. H. Allen, 1968).

A Short Bibliography

THE date given is that of the most recent edition. Where two editions are available, the less expensive is listed. For fuller lists of books on the period, the reader should look at W. N. Medlicott, *Modern European History 1789-1945. A Select Bibliography* (Historical Association, 1960), and Alan Bullock and A. J. P. Taylor, *A Select List of Books on European History 1815-1914* (O.U.P., 1957). There is a particularly well-annotated bibliography in David Thomson, *Europe since Napoleon* (Penguin, 1966), listed below.

BOOKS RELEVANT TO THE PERIOD AS A WHOLE

David Thomson, *Europe since Napoleon* (Penguin, 1966) – the best introductory survey.

S. B. Clough and C. W. Cole, *Economic History of Europe* (Heath, 1952) – sound but non-technical, integrates economic changes with the social and political developments.

F. H. Hinsley, *Power and the Pursuit of Peace* (C.U.P., 1967) – penetrating essays on international relations, covering the period chronologically.

Martin Gilbert, *Recent History Atlas, 1870 to the present day* (Weidenfeld and Nicolson, 1967) – diagrammatic maps containing much information, clearly presented.

COMPILATIONS AND REFERENCE BOOKS FOR THE PERIOD

The New Cambridge Modern History, vol. XI, *Material Progress and World-Wide Problems 1870-98* (C.U.P., 1962); vol. XII, *The Shifting Balance of World Forces 1898-1945* (C.U.P., 1968).

Pierre Renouvin, *La crise européenne et la première guerre mondiale (1904-1918)* (P.U.F., 1962).

Maurice Baumont, *La faillité de la paix (1918-1939)* (P.U.F., 1960) – these two works are useful supplements to vol. XII of the N.C.M.H., which is thin on national history.

The Cambridge Economic History of Europe, vol. VI, *The Industrial Revolutions and After* (C.U.P., 1965).

The Cambridge Modern History, vol. XII, *The Latest Age* (C.U.P., 1910) – still useful, especially for the political history of the smaller countries.

William L. Langer, *An Encyclopedia of World History* (Harrap, n.d.) – a useful manual for checking chronology.

The Statesman's Year-Book (Macmillan) – an invaluable source of information on all countries, especially useful for its statistics of trade, literacy, population, etc. An issue for every year since 1863.

Michael G. Mulhall, *Mulhall's Dictionary of Statistics* (Routledge, 1884) – a jackdaw's nest of curious information arranged alphabetically, ranging from records of 'obesity' to extremely useful comparative wage-tables.

Edward Young, *Labor in Europe and America* (Philadelphia, George, 1875 and subsq. edn) – a unique compilation of facts on wages and working conditions.

CHAPTERS 1 AND 2

N.C.M.H., vol. XI, chapters 1–9, and 21–3, – chapter 1 is an excellent résumé of the main developments of the period.

David S. Landes, *The Unbound Prometheus. Technological Change and Development in Western Europe from 1750 to the Present* (C.U.P., 1969) – a lively explanation of what can be a daunting subject.

Charles Ambrosi and M. Tacel, *Histoire Economique des grandes puissances à l'époque contemporaine (1850–1958)* Delagrave, 1963) – contains a clear analysis of trading and monetary problems.

E. H. Carr, *Studies in Revolution* (Cass, 1962) – a readable short introduction to the leading socialist thinkers.

G. D. H. Cole, *A History of Socialist Thought*, vol. II, *Marxism and Anarchism 1850–1890*, vol. III, *The Second International* (Macmillan, 1954–6) – a systematic survey of socialism country by country.

James Joll, *The Second International 1889–1914* (Weidenfeld and Nicolson, 1968) – a shorter but more readable account than Cole's.

James Laver, *The Age of Optimism 1848–1914* (Weidenfeld and Nicolson, 1966) – despite its emphasis on England, an informative and entertaining survey of social life, sumptuously illustrated.

R. L. Schoenwald, *Nineteenth Century Thought: the discovery of change* (Prentice-Hall, 1966) – selections from Marx, Darwin and Spencer.

D. G. Charlton, *Secular Religions in France 1815–1870* (O.U.P., 1963) – gives insights into some of the consequences of the loss of Christian belief.

*

D. K. Fieldhouse, '"Imperialism": an historiographical revision', *Economic History Review*, 2nd series, xiv (1961–2) 187–209 – examines recent changes in interpretation.

Michael Howard, *The Franco-Prussian War* (Fontana, 1967) – the opening chapters are particularly valuable.

CHAPTER 3

A. J. P. Taylor, *Bismarck* (New English Library, 1968) – always stimulating. Controversial on the events of 1870.

Erich Eyck, *Bismarck and the German Empire* (Allen & Unwin, 1968) – a sound introduction, if less entertaining than Taylor.

W. H. Dawson, *The German Empire, 1867–1914*, 2 vols (Allen & Unwin, 1966) – a reprint of an old survey that is still useful.

Gordon Craig, *The Politics of the Prussian Army, 1640–1945* (O.U.P., 1964) – contains some lively reflections on the nature of German government under the Empire.

Pierre Renouvin, *L'Empire allemand sous Guillaume II* (Tournier, n.d.) – a useful supplement to Dawson.

J. Alden Nichols, *Germany after Bismarck: the Caprivi era, 1890–1894* (Harvard U.P., 1958) – provides a close-up of a short section of the Wilhelmine period.

Pierre Bertaux, *La vie quotidienne en Allemagne au temps de Guillaume II* (Hachette, 1962) – entertaining and informative.

Charles Ambrosi, as for Chapters 1 and 2.

Agatha Ramm, *Germany 1789–1919. A political history* (Methuen, 1967) – the most recent sizeable study of nineteenth century Germany. More detailed than its predecessors.

CHAPTER 4

Jacques Néré, 'The French Republic', chapter 11 of *N.C.M.H.*, vol. xi – an excellent short résumé.

Emmanuel Berl, *Cent ans d'histoire de France* (Arthaud, 1962) – an absorbing collection of photographs, illustrative of most aspects of French life.

Sir Denis Brogan, *The Development of Modern France* (Hamish Hamilton, 1967) – remains by far the liveliest account of the political history of the Third Republic.

David Thomson, *Democracy in France since 1870* (O.U.P., 1964) – a percipient analysis of the peculiarities of French political life.

S. B. Clough, *France, a History of National Economics, 1789–1939* (Octagon, 1964) – a brief exposition of the main developments.

Robert Burnand, *La vie quotidienne en France de 1870 à 1900* (Hachette, 1947) – an affectionate description of social life.

Roger Shattuck, *The Banquet Years: the arts in France, 1885–1918* (Cape, 1969) – essays on Alfred Jarry, Henri Rousseau, Eric Satie and Guillaume Apollinaire.

René Rémond, *The Right Wing in France from 1815 to de Gaulle* (O.U.P., 1966) – a clearly planned survey.

Cornelia Skinner, *Elegant Wits and Grand Horizontals. Paris – La Belle Époque* (Joseph, 1963) – essays on Tristan Bernard, Jeanne Detourbey and others.

Henri Brunschwig, *French Colonialism 1871–1914* (Pall Mall, 1966) – examines the economic myths and realities of the subject.

Charles P. Kindleberger, *Economic Growth in France and Britain 1851–1950* (O.U.P., 1964) – a stimulating critique of traditional assumptions.

CHAPTER 5

Nicholas Riasonovsky, *A History of Russia* (O.U.P., 1963) – a short sound up-to-date introduction.

Lionel Kochan, *The Making of Modern Russia* (Penguin, 1963).

C. E. Black, *The Transformation of Russian Society: aspects of social change since 1861* (Harvard U.P., 1967) – an invaluable collection of essays, comparing conditions under Tsarist and Soviet rule.

Hugh Seton-Watson, *The Russian Empire 1801–1917* (O.U.P., 1967) – the best detailed survey.

Henri Troyat, *Daily Life in Russia under the Last Tsar* (Allen & Unwin, 1961).

A. J. P. Taylor, *The Habsburg Monarchy, 1809–1918* (Penguin, 1964) – a fast-moving account of political developments.

A. J. May, *The Habsburg Monarchy, 1867–1914* (O.U.P., 1951) – more informative than Taylor on economic and social problems.

C. A. Macartney, *The Habsburg Empire 1790–1918* (Weidenfeld and Nicolson, 1968) – the most recent general account.

J. Stavrianos, *The Balkans since 1453* (Holt Rinehart, 1958) – a lucid up-to-date history, well planned.

CHAPTER 6

Denis Mack Smith, *Italy. A modern history* (Michigan U.P., 1959) – a brilliant survey, particularly good on political issues.

S. B. Clough, *Italy, an Economic History* (Scribner, 1963).

Raymond Carr, *Spain, 1808–1939* (O.U.P., 1966).

CHAPTER 7

A. J. P. Taylor, 'International relations', chapter 20 of *N.C.M.H.*, vol. XI – a useful brief introduction.

A. J. P. Taylor, *The Struggle for Mastery in Europe, 1848–1918* (O.U.P., 1954) – the most readable of the fairly detailed surveys.

F. H. Hinsley, as for general reading.

Pierre Renouvin, *Histoire des Relations internationales*, vol. VI, *Le XIXe siècle 2e partie* (Hachette, 1955) – a lucid and well-balanced account.

Fritz Fischer, *Germany's Aims in the First World War* (Chatto and Windus, 1967) – the opening chapters are particularly useful.

R. Robinson and J. Gallagher, *Africa and the Victorians. The official mind of imperialism* (Macmillan, 1967) – contains many insights into the attitudes of statesmen towards the Eastern Question. Primarily concerned with the influence of Indian defence on expansion in Africa.

CHAPTER 8

A. J. P. Taylor, *The First World War* (Penguin, 1966) – a lively well-illustrated introduction.

Cyril Falls, *The First World War* (Longmans, 1960) – readable, if over weighted on the western front.

C. R. M. F. Cruttwell, *A History of the Great War* (O.U.P., 1936) – the most comprehensive of the short histories.

Vincent J. Esposito, *A Concise History of World War I* (Praeger, 1964) – useful for its diagrams and maps.

Robert Graves, *Good-bye to All That* (Penguin, 1960) – the western front at first hand.

Rohan Butler, 'The Peace Settlement of Versailles, 1918–33', chapter 8 of *N.C.M.H.*, vol. XII.

Harold Nicolson, *Peacemaking, 1919* (Methuen, 1964) – a participant recalls the atmosphere and personalities of the conference.

CHAPTER 9

Ingvar Svennilson, *Growth and Stagnation in the European Economy* (United Nations, 1954) – useful for its introductory chapters and tables of statistics.

David S. Landes, as for Chapters 1 and 2.

W. Arthur Lewis, *Economic Survey 1919–1939* (Allen & Unwin, 1966) – a concise explanation of complex issues.

G. D. H. Cole, *A History of Socialist Thought*, vol. IV, *Communism and Social Democracy*; vol. V, *Socialism and Fascism 1931–1939* (Macmillan, 1958–60).

Zevedei Barbu, *Democracy and Dictatorship* (Routledge & Kegan Paul, 1956) – an interesting exploration in social psychology.

CHAPTER 10

Riasonovsky, Kochan and Black, as for Chapter 5.

Isaac Deutscher, *Stalin* (Penguin, 1966).

E. H. Carr, *A History of Soviet Russia*.

——*The Bolshevik Revolution 1917–1923*, 3 vols (Penguin, 1966).

——*The Interregnum, 1923–1924* (Macmillan, 1954).

——*Socialism in One Country, 1924–1926*, 3 vols (Macmillan, 1958–64) – the best detailed history of the subject.

R. N. Carew Hunt, *The Theory and Practice of Communism* (Penguin, 1963) – a useful introduction to Communist theory.

W. H. Chamberlin, *Russia's Iron Age* (Duckworth, 1935) – the objective observations of a western correspondent.

CHAPTER 11

A. J. Ryder, *The German Revolution, 1918–1919* (Historical Association pamphlet, G.40).

Godfrey Scheele, *The Weimar Republic: Overture to the Third Reich* (Faber, 1946).

Erich Eyck, *A History of the Weimar Republic*, 2 vols (Harvard U.P., 1962–4) – a detailed political history.

Alan Bullock, *Hitler. A study in tyranny* (Penguin, 1962) – the most readable book on Nazi Germany.

William Shirer, *The Rise and Fall of the Third Reich* (Pan Books, 1964) – at its best on life in the Third Reich (e.g. chapter 8) but less satisfactory on foreign affairs.

Erwin Leiser, *A Pictorial History of Nazi Germany* (Penguin, 1962) – an annotated collection of photographs.

Jacques Rueff (ed.), *The Third Reich* (Weidenfeld & Nicolson, 1955) – a useful compilation of essays on different aspects.

Arthur Schweitzer, *Big Business in the Third Reich* (Eyre & Spottiswoode, 1964) – has a wider scope than its title suggests.

CHAPTER 12

Brogan and Thomson, as for Chapter 4.
Alexander Werth, *The Twilight of France, 1933–1940* (Fertig, 1966)
– first-hand observations by a resident journalist of left-wing
sympathies.
Elliot Paul, *A Narrow Street* (Penguin, 1947) – an evocative and entertaining portrayal of life in Paris in the inter-war years.

CHAPTER 13

Mack Smith and Clough, as for Chapter 6.
Sir Ivone Kirkpatrick, *Mussolini* (Odhams, 1964).
Maurice Neufeld, *Italy: school for awakening countries* (Cornell U.P.,
1961) – particularly informative on social and economic issues.
Christopher Hibbert, *Benito Mussolini* (Penguin, 1965).
Raymond Carr, as for Chapter 6.
Gerald Brenan, *The Spanish Labyrinth* (C.U.P., 1960) – a lucid
analysis of Spanish problems before the Civil War.
Hugh Thomas, *The Spanish Civil War* (Penguin, 1965) – the best
detailed account.

CHAPTER 14

F. H. Hinsley, as for general reading.
J. L. Brierly, 'The League of Nations', chapter 9 of *N.C.M.H.*, vol.
XII.
W. N. Medlicott, *The Coming of War in 1939* (Historical Association,
1963) – useful preliminary reading.
E. M. Robertson, *Hitler's Prewar Policy and Military Plans* (Longmans,
1963) – a well-informed well-balanced interpretation.
Pierre Renouvin, *Histoire des Relations internationales*, vols VII and
VIII, *Les crises du XX⁰ siècle* (Hachette, 1957–8) lucid and well-
balanced, like its predecessors in the series.
Malcolm Muggeridge, *The Thirties: 1930–1940 in Great Britain*
(Collins, 1967) – contains some pungent sketches of the statesmen
of the time. Entertaining if not always fair.

CHAPTER 15

Alan Bullock, as for Chapter 11.
Chester Wilmot, *The Struggle for Europe* (Fontana, 1967) – an exciting
examination of the long-term issues.

Cyril Falls, *The Second World War, a short history* (Methuen, 1948) – a readable chronological survey.

J. F. C. Fuller, *The Second World War, 1939–45* (Eyre & Spottiswoode, 1954) – a factual account of the blow-by-blow variety.

Vincent J. Esposito, *A Concise History of World War II* (Praeger, 1964) – useful for its maps.

W. S. Churchill, *The Second World War*, 6 volumes (Cassell, 1948–54) – history in the grand manner, by a leading participant.

A. J. P. Taylor, *English History, 1914–1945* (Oxford, 1965), chapters 13–16.

Alexander Werth, *Russia at War, 1941–1945* (Pan Books, 1966); *France 1940–1955* (Hale, 1956) – lively and informative comment by a first-hand observer.

Hugh Seton Watson, *The East European Revolution* (Methuen, 1956).

Index

Subjects have been grouped alphabetically under their respective countries, with the exception of persons and ships, and places mentioned in a diplomatic or military context. Where a subject is discussed both in general and national terms, the general discussion is listed as a separate item in its own right, while national aspects are listed under the general heading of the country concerned. (Thus the general issue of industrial wages is to be found under 'Wages, industrial', but French industrial wages are listed under 'France: wages, industrial'.) International agreements have been grouped alphabetically under 'Treaties, international agreements, etc.'.

482 INDEX